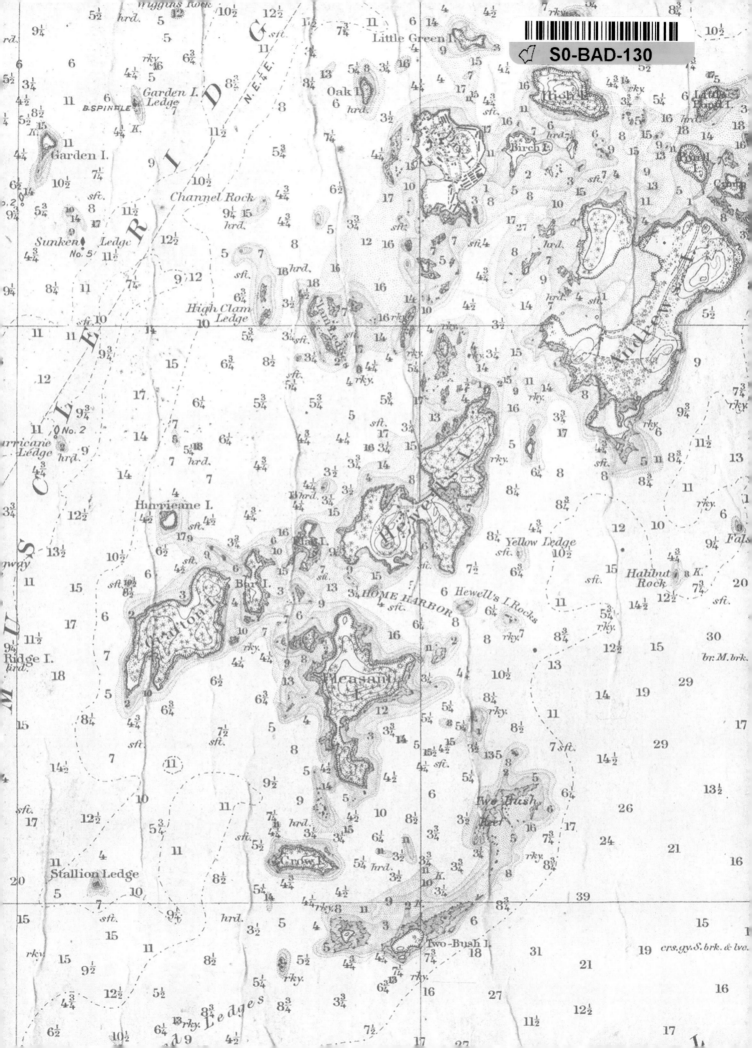

ISLANDS IN TIME

November 18, 1999

To Al and Judy —

    With deep appreciation for your long and loyal interest in the Institute's work among the islands and waters of the Gulf of Maine.

with warm regards,

Philip

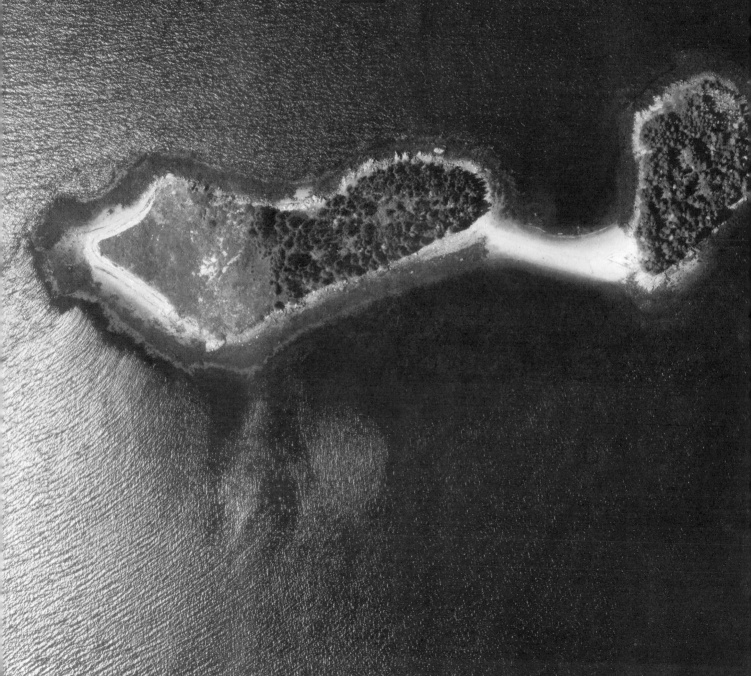

ISLANDS

Philip W. Conkling

IN TIME

A Natural
and Cultural History
of the Islands of
the Gulf of Maine

Island Institute, Rockland, Maine • Down East Books, Camden, Maine

2   4   5   3   1

Down East Books / Camden, Maine

LIBRARY OF CONGRESS CATALOGING-IN-PUBLICATION DATA

Conkling, Philip W.
    Islands in Time: a natural and cultural history of the islands in the Gulf
of Maine / Philip W. Conkling. — 2nd ed.
        p.   cm.
    Rev ed. of: Islands in Time : a natural and human history of the islands
of Maine.
    Includes bibliographical references and index.
    ISBN 0-89272-406-4 (hc.)
    ISBN 0-89272-478-1 (pb.)
    1. Island ecology—Maine.   2. Islands—Maine—history.
3. Maine—History.   I. Title.
QH105.M2C66   1999
508.741—dc21   98-23981
                                                       CIP

Frontispiece: Barred Island and tombolo beach, northern Penobscot Bay.
COURTESY MAINE DEPARTMENT OF INLAND FISHERIES AND WILDLIFE

Jacket/Cover: Fox Islands Thorofare.
PETER RALSTON

Contents

Acknowledgments
7

Introduction to the First Edition
10

Introduction to the Second Edition
14

1. Cold Coast: Island Communities
16

2. Downwind Histories and Ecologies
44

3. Island Vegetation: Yew, Hazel, "Aspe," and Spruce
86

4. Landforms: Island Cliffs, Caves, Cobbles, and Domes
114

5. Birds of the Islands: Mews, Medricks, Hawks, and Hernshaws
130

6. Mammals Great and Small: Whales, Sea Hogs, Stags, and Coney
158

7. Submerged Islands: Clams, Scallops, Lobsters, and Urchins
184

8. Four Centuries of Island Fisheries: Herring, Mackerel, Tuna, and Cod
210

9. The Gulf of Maine: The System in the Sea
242

10. Islands at the Ends of the Gulf
272

Epilogue
292

Sources and Resources
296

Index
307

Acknowledgments

There are not many things in life you get to do over again, but this book is one of them. The idea of updating and revising *Islands in Time* originated with Kathy Brandes, who some two decades ago edited the first edition. Tom Fernald and Karin Womer at Down East Books were interested in the project, and worked long and hard to guide this effort along; then Neale Sweet led this story into a safe harbor.

Because this revision contains much new material from the annals of the Island Institute, I want to acknowledge the two people who helped get the Institute started, Tom Cabot and Betsy Wyeth. Tom was passionate about the Maine islands and had spent forty years exploring them with his family, buying and conserving more of them for future generations than anyone else. He was the original inspiration for an organization dedicated to teaching others about the biology of the archipelago, and was the institute's first supporter. I first met Betsy Wyeth on Allen Island, where we hammered out many of the fundamental ideas for the Island Institute on the anvils of its headlands and coves. Without Betsy and Andrew Wyeth's early and steady support two decades ago, it's doubtful we'd still be traveling this archipelago today.

I also met Peter Ralston during those early years on Allen Island, and have been privileged to have worked with him ever since. Peter is the archipelago's preeminent photographer, and graciously lent many of the images to this new edition. David Platt's skill as the institute's Director of Publications has always been to make complex things look easy, and for his steady good cheer during this complicated project, I could not be more grateful. Charlie Oldham's design, layout, and production skills have never been more elegantly apparent, and Anne Leslie tirelessly verified facts and extracted errors from various drafts; any that remain are mine alone. Deborah DuBrule took the index in hand in its final stages.

The narrative has been shaped by scores of people who have willingly shared their stories with me, including Ernest Maloney of Benner Island; Dorothy Simpson and Elisabeth Ogilvie of Criehaven; Steve Kress of Hog Island; Bill Drury of Green's Island; John Beckman, Jason Day, and Bert Dyer of Vinalhaven; Chellie Pingree of North Haven; Ted Ames of Stonington; Doug Boynton, Mary Beth Dolan, and Lexi Krause of Monhegan; Sonny Sprague of Swan's Island; David Lunt of Frenchboro; Donna Damon of Chebeague; Willie Spear of Cousins Island; Junior Bachman of Beal's Island; and Jim Salisbury of Steuben. My friend and colleague David Conover of Compass Light Productions helped assemble and transcribe several of the interviews.

Finally, I received unending help from home, including general forgiveness for late dinners and dispensations for absences from the family hearth, amid the taut lines of everyday life. Finally, and not least, I am grateful for the help I got at the end of the epic from Tim Conkling, who collaborated in the essential and difficult task of assembling the index.

— **Philip W. Conkling**

Dedication
For Jamien, 1951–1999

That first winter on Vinalhaven, I heard about a woman who lived there but had taught school for some time on North Haven, across the Fox Island Thorofare. She kept a skiff, I was told, at the public landing on the north end of Vinalhaven and rowed across the Thorofare each morning to teach. When the weather got too bad for rowing, she would go across in the J.O. Brown boat with the crew who worked the North Haven ferry. But mostly she rowed.

It was like other stories I heard that winter of the kind of quiet, willful determination that islanders routinely call upon in their daily lives. "You oughta meet her," I was told, and, through great good luck, I did. Her name was Jamien Morehouse, and we were married a year later.

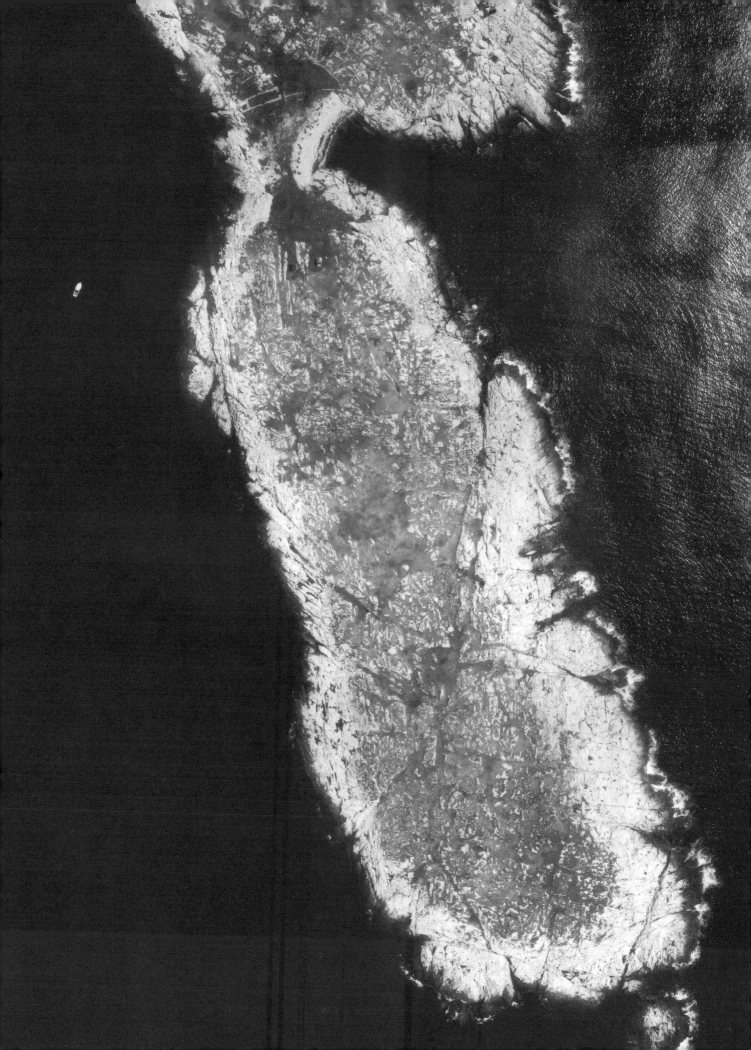

Introduction to the First Edition *(1981)*

APART AND BETWEEN

Out there, between the point where you can take your last dry step and the faint horizon of your mind's eye, lies another world, apart. It is a world of islands—part sea, part rock; part wild, part subdued; part fish, part man; with winged birds between. From the tip of Cape Elizabeth or Cape Wash, from Cape Small or Cape Split, from the ends of Schoodic Point or Pemaquid Point, from Newbury Neck or Linekin Neck, from Owls Head or Schooner Head, you can see them out there like sequins—small and shining objects in the water. Islands. Not just a few islands, but countless multitudes of great and little wave-washed rocks. A lifetime's worth of islands, apart and between.

How many islands are out there? Maybe we should know, but we don't. Can't even count them. The number changes too often with storms, history, and the tides—but mostly with the tides—to make the effort seem worthwhile. If you count the islands at high water, for instance, you end up with a lot that are actually attached to the mainland or to other islands at low tide; if you count them at low water, you count hundreds that disappear ten to twenty feet under at high tide. In most places in this world you might be able to accept Webster's definition of an island as a piece of land smaller than a continent surrounded by water. Not in Maine. These islands are, like their inhabitants, hard to pin down.

From time to time, various earnest landsmen have tried counting Maine islands. In 1913, for example, one Moses Greenleaf, Esq., was hired to count the islands for the state, but he was only one man (an esquire at that), and he didn't have a boat, which meant that his transportation was—how should we put it?—at the mercy of fishermen. Oh, he got most of the big islands—including Louds, a Muscongus Bay island with a year-round population that had simply been left off previous maps—but either Greenleaf did not consider the little islands important, or his informants considered them too important to let the state know about them.

More recently, someone in Augusta remembered that the state owned all unclaimed islands as a result of the same legislative mandate that had sent Mr. Greenleaf out to count them some sixty years earlier. With U.S. Geological Survey maps, the state set about counting the number of islands between the Piscataqua and St. Croix rivers to the head of tidewater, in order to determine just how many remained in the public domain. The fact that these landsmen counted as islands a few bathymetric circles on the geological survey maps and did not count those islands with more than four houses on them (where the political heat was likely to be intense in the event that their titles were not secure) means that one still can't say how many islands are out there. It's one of their essential characteristics.

Opposite: Wooden Ball Island, with its scoured landscape and stone corral, is at the edge of the Gulf of Maine, where a productive lobster fishing privilege has been maintained for a century and a half.
COURTESY MAINE DEPARTMENT OF INLAND FISHERIES AND WILDLIFE

Out there, apart and between, there are, to be exact, a lot of islands.

More than three thousand, anyway; more than on the rest of the East Coast if you stopped to figure it. The Greeks would simply call them an archipelago, a wonderful word that means "a group of islands in the sea." If the Greeks were writing their myths here in the Maine archipelago, no doubt the stories would resemble those from the Aegean. Zeus would hurl huge stones at the Titans to create new islands from time to time, Bacchus would be having a good time celebrating the power and fertility of nature, and serious Apollo would be much given over to introspection on wave-lapped promontories.

ISLANDNESS

In an age when all of us have seen that our entire world can look like a tiny island in and from space, islands have once again become powerful metaphors. Anyone who has set foot on an uninhabited island cannot fail to appreciate the feelings of security, simplicity, and proprietorship that isolated islands are able to convey. To have spent a few days closed in by a thick-o'-fog and missed an appointment on the mainland, or to have waited in the spruce woods and listened to the play of wood warblers, or to have sat on a shore watching the silver moon flecks refracted on the black water makes concerns and cares Back There seem momentarily small and distant.

On quite a separate level, islands present us with a unique opportunity to do something we cannot do on the mainland. Because of their watery isolation from contiguous ecosystems, they become experimental natural laboratories that record the passage of time *here,* on this exact piece of ground. On the mainland, effects of the hands of the past are frustratingly masked by the influences of neighboring pieces of land; it's very hard to sort out. But on islands, each with a unique history, the centuries of human and natural history are carefully indexed in the landscape, and the reading is curious, diverting, and pleasurable.

Another characteristic of islands that scratches at this historical and vaguely scientific itch that most of us feel is that islands are, quite simply, fun to describe and explore. There are very few landscapes in the United States that have been visited so often by such disparate sorts of people who felt compelled to put their impressions in writing. Generations of mariners, naturalists, navigators, explorers, merchants, yachtsmen, and vacationing rusticators have been describing islands since the first sail rose off the southern rim of the Gulf of Maine prior to 1600. Before then, fishermen and Indians described the profits and pitfalls of the islands to one another—though the former left few records, as is their habit, and the latter left only hints of their lives in archaeological deposits and place names incompletely deciphered.

Finally, because islands are so separate, insular, and entire, ecological differences among them are striking. You don't have to be carefully trained in ecological theory to be struck by the differences between an island that is composed of greenstone and one composed of granite, an island that supports a colony of herons and another that supports a colony of gulls, or an island that once supported a colony of stonecutters and one that supported a colony of woodcutters. Each is presently the domain of a unique combination of plants that limit the appetites and numbers of animals, and of animals that utilize and alter the collection of plants in patterns that depend on their diverse pasts. Plants over animals, animals over plants—the kind of reciprocal, temporal interdependencies in which nature seems to delight.

ISLANDS AND THE URGE FOR WILDERNESS

When it comes to tossing around impressions of the islands out there, it's tempting to think of them as pieces of wilderness. After all, they are largely uninhabited, except by various species of

From Southern Island shores, the approaches to the expanse of Penobscot Bay and the other world of outer islands comes in and out of view.
PETER RALSTON

birds and an occasional deer or mink. Perhaps one in ten has a small summer cabin or fishing camp on it, but there is mile after mile of uninhabited coastline for every foot of developed shorefront. Most of the islands are forested by pointed spruces, which obscure dark, mysterious interiors. Protected coves are altogether absent on some islands, and it is impossible to land on jagged, wave-pounded shores. Perhaps no one has been there before, at least not often enough to have altered the island's ecology. Perhaps this is the forest primeval whispering. Ah, wilderness.

Like many other outwardly satisfying ideas, there is a notion that here in Maine, at relatively short distances from the mainland, are inaccessible pieces of New England landscape that have remained untouched, untrammeled, and unchanged since the white man arrived. Unfortunately, this does not hold up to close scrutiny. The appearance of most of the islands reflects nearly four centuries of human occupation and alteration. In fact, the islands are some of the oldest continuously utilized pieces of landscape in eastern North America. More than fifteen generations of European boat-borne people—not to mention the four to five thousand years of previous Indian use—have altered island ecologies, in some cases subtly, in other cases dramatically.

The present uninhabited look of Maine islands is a result of a little more than half a century of passive neglect following a decline of island populations that was gradual after 1870 and rapid after 1910. The reasons for the exodus are varied and will be traced in the chapters ahead, but all are rooted in the depletion of resources upon which islanders depended or in the disappearance of markets for those resources. For perhaps fifty of the past four hundred years, islands have been left in their natural state.

Even if it is illusory to think of Maine islands as pieces of intact wilderness, many of them are indisputably special in both the ecological and the spiritual sense. Islands of all sizes and descriptions lend themselves to introspective reflections on the relationship between ourselves and the natural world as we circumspectly survey the way things look from an island, apart and between. The mainland looks smaller; the soaring spirits of birds seem larger. A few of these islands are so simple and majestic that even the most callous of human natures is silenced within their sanctuaries where experience of the world is direct and elemental.

In ecological terms, these islands support species of plants and animals made rare on the mainland by too much contact with our own kind. Many of the islands support populations that are at the northern or southern ends of their breeding ranges and therefore serve as refuges where genetic diversity is maintained. For many people, the concept of genetic diversity is a bit abstract, but it is easier to grasp the idea that small populations of puffins or eagles or seals or bird's-eye primrose might have an importance beyond their numbers.

Some islands, whether or not they are naturally covered by forests or grasses, are undoubtedly poorer in species composition after years of wasteful, negligent, and destructive human uses. But if we use diversity of species on islands as a measure of ecosystem vitality and vigor, many other islands are richer after generations of human alteration. When we succumb to simple strategies of protection, we are often preserving nothing so certainly as the alteration that we caused in the first place. Maine islands are as various as their individual pasts, and it makes sense to ask where our human sleight-of-hand has affected them. On such islands it is important to let things take their course as a way to measure the natural processions and progressions of intact insular ecosystems. But on many more islands, to simply "let nature take her course" begs the question: Which, among the thousands of courses available, do we "let" her take?

Aside from the complicated issue of the effects of human hands, there is the matter of the dynamic changes that a tempestuous nature introduces. Islands are subject to the violent moods of the wind, waves, and waters. Everything changes all the time. The infinitely articulated, infinitely modulated biofeedback loops of intact ecosystems are quite capable of going temporarily out of whack on islands without any help from us. Occasionally systems naturally oscillate away from the purposes that benefit us—the beasts who walk upright—to favor species such as mice, snails, or fungi, whose purposes are no more or less grand than our own. When such events take place, there is an urge within most of us to try to deflect those oscillations back to purposes that more nearly benefit us. Whether such activities are reasonable and wholly desirable depends on the unique circumstances at hand. Only one thing is certain—simple and inflexible rules and policies are in no one's best interest.

The tasks at hand on Maine islands are not to re-create the past, or to freeze the present, but to consider the future based upon an understanding of the present and past. It is our ability to do so that defines us as a species. A place can be wild without being a wilderness. A place can impress us deeply with its power and mystery, even when generations of our own kind have come and gone before us and left behind unmistakable signs of their occupation—their successes and failures in little pieces of the past cast in stone and wood. In each beat of the sea there is a pulse of a world not human, but there is also wildness enough in a manmade meadow system, as long as we are able to cast aside our ideas about the meadow and to see it as it is.

Introduction to the Second Edition

Islands resist change, whereas the sea, which wholly defines islands, is characterized by relentless change. I have spent twenty years trying to understand this essential paradox, yet the islands of the tempestuous Gulf of Maine still grip my imagination. They are microcosms of life encompassing elemental tensions between rock and water, between fish and fishermen, and between "from here" and "from away."

This second edition of *Islands in Time* started innocently enough, and shortly became unruly. Natural history is about patterns, and on inhabited islands the lines between natural history and human history weave constantly back and forth into one another. Because understanding even a single island is impossible without absorbing a lot of history, this edition covers more personal histories than appeared in the first edition. There is, of course, an inexhaustible supply of histories for each Maine island in the stories of the islanders themselves (who are also some of the world's finest storytellers). In addition, Charles McLane has added substantially to this tradition by publishing four volumes of island histories covering a huge expanse of island geography between Little River Island off Cutler to Seguin Island off Cape Small.

I have been lucky enough to work for the largest island organization in the Gulf of Maine, the Island Institute, which is dedicated to understanding and celebrating island life. This edition contains journal entries culled from logbooks, notebooks, and sketches I have kept while under way and outward bound along the archipelago during my last fifteen years of work with the institute. I hope these voices hint at the textures and qualities of these places—places you go to when the weather opens up a crack and you remember the field naturalist's simple credo: Never say "no" to an island, an expedition, a visit, a meeting, a rendezvous. What I have tried to add comes from the region where science ends and something else takes over and begins looking for words. I hope that these various voices will enable readers to think about islands on several levels.

The introduction to the first edition of *Islands in Time* began with an essay on how many people have tried (and failed) to count the islands of Maine accurately. So let me take up where I left off. People like myself used to say that there were "about 3,000 islands" off the Maine coast. I hadn't set out to visit every Maine island, but after I had been to about one thousand, I stopped counting carefully; I knew I wouldn't get to the end of them in my lifetime. New computer techniques reveal that there are actually 4,617 coastal Maine islands—a figure at least half again as large as the previous best guess.

Furthermore, Maine's islands are scattered along a coastline that is not "about 2,500 miles long," as people used to say, but is in fact 7,039 miles long—including 2,471 miles of sinuous island shores curling around craggy coves and massive, bony headlands—almost exactly the 1980 best estimate of the length of the entire mainland coastline of Maine.

How could we have been so wrong, missed so much? In an era when so many others of the world's great natural treasures seem to be shrinking, how did Maine's magnificent endowment of island coastline grow so much larger?

The answer to this paradox is, of course, that the number of islands and the length of the coast hasn't changed at all; it is our understanding of their intricate geography that has expanded and, I hope, deepened. We are just beginning to understand the complex linkages between island ecosystems and the rich upwelling currents of the Gulf of Maine. And in our deepened understanding of the region's biological complexity and richness—which ecologists refer to as "biodiversity"—lies a clearer sense of the real opportunities that Maine's islands have to offer a world in which natural resources are becoming increasingly impoverished, and where the resources we find off these shores are increasingly valued and valuable.

— Philip W. Conkling, March 1999

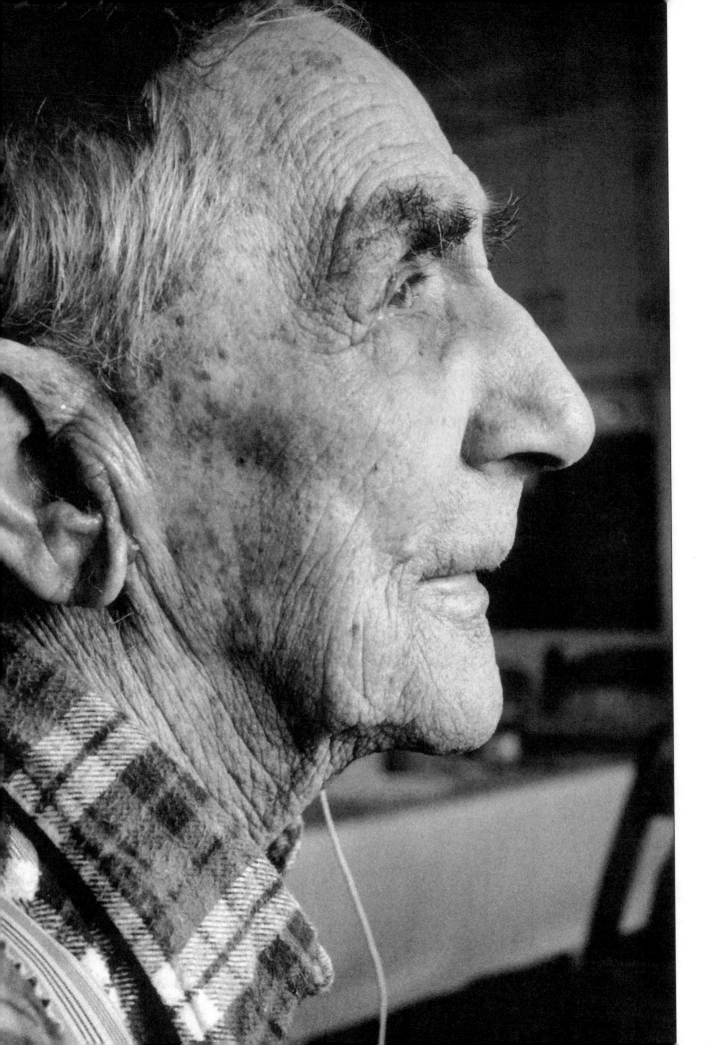

1

Cold Coast: Island Communities

A community narrows down and grows dreadful ignorant when it is shut up to its own affairs and gets no knowledge of the outside world . . . In the old days, a good part of the best men here knew a hundred ports and something of the way people lived in them . . . Shipping's a terrible loss to this part of New England from a social point of view, ma'am.
—Sarah Orne Jewett, *The Country of the Pointed Firs*

ISLANDERS AND ISLANDNESS

Perhaps no other human landscape on the globe produces people more fully possessed of a sense of place than the fifteen surviving year-round island communities of Maine. Those who occupy these bounded places do so fully. They do not easily share the distinction and pride that result from continuous, successful occupation of difficult, dangerous, and bountiful coves and covers—places that have been sanctified by the lives of extended family and weathered with close friends. Those who do not appreciate this distinction sometimes feel alienated from island community life and may never receive its full measure of enjoyment. Those who do not require acceptance are sometimes taken to the edge of the innermost being of islandness.

I am not an islander but a privileged visitor who has been lucky enough to have traveled to the antechambers of the heart of some of these island communities. There I have often been extended a degree of warmth and hospitality that I have not encountered elsewhere. As an outsider I am content to be relegated to the islands' communal periphery. For those attempting to become year-round islanders, the struggle is different; it takes more than your lifetime to become an islander because other islanders must have time to forget when you and your people first came. On the mainland this process takes three generations, more or less; on islands it takes longer.

What I have witnessed of the difficulties constantly faced by Maine's island communities puts me in awe of the kinds of human effort and endurance needed to create and maintain the human family. A Maine island community is like a lifeboat; occupying it requires effort by all who cling there: those in your family and those of your kin; those of your neighbor and those of your neighbor's kin; those who visit; and those who have been cast ashore and taken in—successfully transplanted, you might say—ever so carefully so as to maintain the delicate balance required by occupants of a small craft. An island birthright is, therefore, a hard-won inheritance, a celebration, a bright and shiny brag, and, in quite a few island communities, a significant economic asset of increasing value.

Opposite: Ernest Maloney, 92, Benner Island lobsterman, winter of 1983.   PETER RALSTON

Lane Island, May 27, 1986

From the edge of the harbor you get to see the subtle rhythms of life on the water. Time and the experience of time are different on islands. Waiting and watching for the tide to rise or for the weather to let go is a kind of meditation that is punctuated by short bursts of activity when "everything comes right."

It is said that when you take a periwinkle out of the intertidal zone and put it in an aquarium, the little snail for the first few days will move up and down the sides of the aquarium corresponding to the rise and fall of the tides outside, having completely internalized the rhythms of the lunar cycle.

Most islanders also have to live on a kind of lunar clock, which is strange and inexplicable to those who have never experienced what it means to have the tide going with you, or worse to have lost the tide, and the day's work, and maybe weeks of waiting till it all comes right again.

Island fishermen have a well-deserved reputation for being supremely inventive; they simply have to make do with the materials at hand. Clarence Howard, of Eagle Island in northern Penobscot Bay, was the first to use a brass rudderpost and packing box in his lobster boat in place of the iron pipe through the hull, which often leaked badly when the boat was loaded. He was the first to use an automobile steering box rather than rely on slack tiller ropes, which could break on a hard turn. He was the first to use a jury-rigged Ford rear axle for a lobster-pot hauler. When he turned his attention to the herring fishery, he was the first to set seine nets off a stern roller and the first in the area to use a depth recorder as a fish finder.

Talents such as these are rare anywhere, and are uniquely handy on islands, where new situations are always presenting themselves. It is useful to recall that the entire crew of the America's Cup race was recruited from the fishing port of Deer Isle (when the town was still an island) for the first two years that the challenge took place.

INDIAN ISLANDS

The islands of the Gulf of Maine were inhabited for millennia before the Europeans arrived. Indian artifacts found in campsites now covered by sixty feet of water suggest that humans have occupied this archipelago ever since the landscape emerged from the receding seas. The excavation of the complex Indian site at the Turner Farm on North Haven shows that a large year-round community was established on the island between five thousand and six thousand years ago. Although various aboriginal cultures waxed and waned during the intervening time, and although the earliest occupations have been obscured by inexorably rising seas, it is no surprise that the Indians utilized the islands' rich resources.

Arthur Spiess, an archaeologist at the Maine Historic Preservation Commission, has reconstructed the changes in the animal life of Maine's islands and their effects on Indian habitation of the archipelago over five millennia. For a long time the islands were colonized by a culturally distinct group whose elaborate burial rituals earned them the name Red Paint People. They relied in part on swordfish taken with bone harpoons from warm inshore waters.

At the time of the Red Paint People, the ecology of the Maine coast and islands was dominated by what we imagine was a meandering loop of the Gulf Stream. About thirty-eight hundred years ago, inshore coastal ecology changed as cool upwelling waters replaced the warm waters inshore, especially along the central and western Maine coast. The change in the kinds of bones found in shell deposits suggests that the change in the climate was rapid. Swordfish hunting and the Red Paint People disappeared. Beginning about two thousand years ago, the ancestors of the Etchemin,

Georges Island fishing village, circa 1910. This was one of hundreds of island communities that vanished during this century. Allen Island shore is on the right, and Benner Island is on the left.   EDWARD COFFIN

the Indians that the first Europeans encountered, based their hunting and gathering on the high inshore biological productivity maintained by strong tides and cool surface waters. According to Spiess, sturgeon, flounder, sculpin, and juvenile cod became the most important food fish, probably taken in shallow water with the aid of tidal nets, weirs, and fish spears. The proportion of shorebirds, ducks, and geese in the food supply increased, which probably reflected larger bird populations. The number of seals in the food supply also increased continuously until European contact, another indicator of increasing inshore productivity.

These ecological changes are also evident in coastal terrestrial ecology. Over the last few thousand years, the coastal spruce forest strip appears to have widened and extended westward to its present western limit in Casco Bay. Moose and caribou were favored by such forest cover, whereas whitetailed deer were reduced by the decrease of hardwood-dominated forests. According to the work done by Arthur Spiess and his colleague, Bruce Bourque, the four thousand-plus-year sequence of occupations at the Turner Farm shell midden on North Haven shows a tenfold increase in the number of moose killed for each hundred deer killed at this spot beginning forty-two hundred years ago and ending with the last sample about eight hundred years ago.

THREE HUNDRED ISLAND COMMUNITIES

Various European settlements were attracted to the islands of the Gulf of Maine from the first years of exploration of the New World, not only for the islands' proximity to fishing grounds but because their location had defensive advantages in an insecure and a potentially hostile new country. During the seventeenth and eighteenth centuries, the Isles of Shoals and Richmond, Damariscove, Monhegan, and Matinicus islands developed into important fishing stations and trading centers. Before the turn of the twentieth century, some three hundred Maine islands developed into year-round communities. They consisted of a continuum from multigenerational extended families to sophisticated multilingual communities whose mariners navigated the oceans of the globe. During the days of merchant sail, islanders benefited economically from coastwise trading routes that went literally right by their front doors. All kinds of island products—from woolens to cordwood, from smoked fish to salt cod, from potatoes to cheese—could be put up and then traded in the fall to supply islanders with their winter needs. Islandness was deeply interwoven into the economic way of life on the Maine coast during the age of sail.

Charles McLane, the archipelago's peripatetic historian, has spent the better part of two decades unraveling the changing users and owners of Maine's islands during the eighteenth and nineteenth centuries through painstaking deed research. Reading through the four volumes of his work, covering the coastal islands of Maine from the Kennebec eastward to the Canadian border, gives us remnants of thousands of stories lived out in small but intricate communities. The vast majority of islands, abandoned as places to live year-round, have become summer colonies, conservation islands, or private kingdoms: Fisherman, MacMahan, and Damariscove off Boothbay; Louds, Bremen Long, Hungry, Cranberry, Friendship Long, Morse, Seavey, Hupper, McGee, Benner, and Allen in Muscongus Bay; Metinic, Clark, Criehaven, Hurricane, Dix, and Crotch around Penobscot Bay; Marshall, Gott, Long, Bartlett, Sutton, Ironbound, Stave, and Jordan around the periphery of Mount Desert; Bois Bubert, Foster, and Dyer off Milbridge; Mistake, Great Wass, Head Harbor, Roque, and Cross farther down east. Year-round communities on all of these islands are gone, and with them stories of island life that have been handed down as faint echoes of oral histories, if at all.

> ### Allen Island's Mysterious Button, October 18, 1982
> *Dougie moved about Allen Island like a restless gull between the shore cottage, where he and Alice stayed, to the wharf on north point, tossing rocks out of the way, shoring up a fence post, or cleaning a drainage ditch. His pockets and windowsills were always full of little bits of things he had found along the way—clay pipes, pieces of hand-forged machinery, a fisherman's marlin-spike. One day Dougie spotted a roundish object in the mud and pulled out a thin metal button embossed with gold. It was a beautiful and haunting object. Was it from Captain John Allen's Revolutionary War uniform? Could it possibly have been on the coat of one of Waymouth's crew? Was it something the Indians had brought to the island as a trading item? No one ever knew.*

To Charles McLane's partial list of half-forgotten communities must be added the abandoned island communities to the westward: the Isles of Shoals, all by itself with towns on both Appledore and Star; Stratton and Richmond in Saco Bay; Cushing, Little Chebeague, and Bustins, to mention only the biggest in Casco Bay. Also to be considered are another several hundred family islands, too numerous to list here, that were extinguished as its members "removed," as the culture's expression goes for the depopulation of Maine's islands. The histories of a few of the best known—Butter Island, farmed for most of a century by the Witherspoons, and Eagle Island, populated by the Quinns—are partly recorded. Less remains of the stories of the Eatons of Wreck; the Robbinses of Opechee; or the Teels, Leadbetters, Stimpsons, and Merchants of their named islands. On and on they go, mostly now gone.

To this enduring legacy should also be added seventy-five island lighthouse stations, including precarious perches on the outermost islands where families maintained a tenacious watch. They were true sentinels expressing the most enduring sentiments of a magnificent but frightening coast. On

Matinicus Rock, Abby Burgess, a lighthouse keeper's daughter, became a folk legend for keeping the light burning for four weeks of unrelenting winter gales that struck while her father was on the mainland and could not return for the fury of the seas. From scores of other island lighthouses come similar records of endurance, where duty and care were weathered deep into the family character: the Corbetts of Little River (Cutler), the Wasses of Libby Island, the Gilleys of Great Duck and Baker, the Nortons of Whitehead, and the Pottles of Franklin, to mention just a few. These stories, too, faded as the island lights were gradually automated and lighthouse families "removed."

Why did they leave? The reasons are as varied as the stories of the people who occupied these stony places; but all the stories are rooted in the simple truth that island living, especially in winter, is a hard, hard life.

Benner Island, November 6, 1982

I looked up Ernest Maloney, a fisherman who had wintered out at Benner Island, one of the two islands that shelter Pentecost Harbor, to ask how a barge loaded with pulpwood would ride while waiting for the right tide and weather to haul the load ashore.

Ernest sat at his kitchen window with his daughter, Enid, Port Clyde's postmistress, who had dropped by to check on her father. Ernest has turned ninety-one, but except for slightly stooped shoulders, his long, gaunt frame looks like that of a man still used to being on the water. His eyes are alert like those of a fish hawk, and they look down a long, beaked nose. He started out by telling me the story of a young fellow who had knocked on his door earlier in the week selling magazine subscriptions to help put himself through college. "Sonny, at my age I don't buy green bananas," Ernest said.

"I don't know for sure," Ernest related, "but I think it must have been 1910 when I went down to Benner to lobster fish. I stayed out there six or eight years straight, until Enid got old enough to go to school. When I first started out, I had a little Friendship sloop. Wilbur Morse built her. I gave eighty-five dollars for her. You hauled by hand when you went in the sloop; when you went in the dory, you rowed and hauled by hand. I'd like to have today the lobsters I sold for twelve cents; I'm going to tell you, you didn't have much of a job to count your money.

"It was tougher 'n hell, and you didn't live like a king. In the summer there'd be forty fishermen down there, but in the winter, only six or eight of us. But we had a nice harbor down there. One of the best. Outside the mouth of the harbor, it'd be rougher than hell, but then the tide would run down through and it was just like putting a board through a planer. It would plane those seas right off smooth. You'd never even see them small boats dip their bowsprits.

"Gil Martin had the store out to Benner. He did all right for himself. One winter his pork was so strong I couldn't eat it, so I came into Port Clyde for food. It was bitter cold; you could just see the tops of the island through the vapor once in a while. I ate like a king ashore and stayed aboard the boat that night. The next morning my bedclothes was frozen right to the bunk and the bulkhead. That wasn't very pleasant.

"I fished outside most of the time—out to Monhegan in the winter. You'd come in from hauling and have to get a fire up in the stove to thaw out your oilskins so's the buttons would come apart. We used alewives for

bait, but sometimes we'd have to cook them for supper if we had nothing else. They were bony. We used to say you'd have a hard time taking off your sweater after eating them, they were so bony.

"No, you didn't live very high."

HANGING ON:
YEAR-ROUND ISLAND COMMUNITIES IN THE TWENTIETH CENTURY

All along this archipelago are communities that have been shaped by a deeply ingrained sense of impermanence. Yet in the midst of ceaseless change are those fifteen persistent island communities that have survived, even triumphed. They have put to lie the assumption that all isolated communities pass away, as others have before them, receding into spruce or extinguished by bad luck, human failing, generational change, and the grinding economic realities of island life.

On these islands is an underlying tautness that characterizes much of this lonely coast. It is the tension between rootedness and impermanence, between bounty and failure, between ungiving rock and shifting sand. This cold coast is silent witness to the enduring truth that human enterprise may come and go, may rise and recede like the tide, and that sea and granite alone endure.

Riches Head, Frenchboro, July 30, 1979

Because the wind was moderate and the day fair, we ran down outside of Marshall Island, headed for Frenchboro, one of the outermost inhabited islands of Maine. Passing by the entrance of Lunt Harbor, where all of the human activity on the island is concentrated, we made for Riches Cove, a calm-weather anchorage on the island's wild eastern shore.

Riches Cove makes up between the main island and Long Island Head, with the two parts connected by a huge, steep boulder beach topped with a massive pile of storm-tossed flotsam. We rounded up in the cove, dropped a stern anchor, and rowed ashore. We were speechless at the sight of this towering thousand-foot-long beach made not of sand but of perfectly rounded and smoothed boulders up to two feet in diameter. Exposed to northeasterly seas with a hundred-mile fetch from east of Schoodic, the beach must take unimaginably brutal waves rolling through here in a storm. Even on a calm day, the surge and swash of the tide creates a dull rumbling of the beach's granite spheres, an echo of the fury that must regularly visit this place.

Beyond the beach, up on Long Island's outer head, are piles of field-stones, stone walls, a corral, and cellar holes. What people inhabited this terrifyingly beautiful headland? The miniature community had seemingly melted back into the landscape, leaving behind a few signs like Dorset ruins on a stark, half-wild hillside.

Back across the beach on the main part of the island, I found a trail that headed toward Lunt Harbor and the town of Frenchboro, the name of Long Island's tiny lobstering community. The captain elected to stay at this dodgy anchorage while I followed the trail through the spruce woodland. Two miles across this unbroken forest, I came out of the deep spruce shadows to find two dozen or so fishermen's cottages clustered around a small, steep-sided, protected harbor where a dozen or so lobster boats lay at their moorings. I was startled to see several deer grazing in the backyard of one of the cottages. They seemed unconcerned by my passing. I wandered down the road and found the Frenchboro Post Office, actually the ell of the postmistress's small cottage.

The postmistress, hesitant with information, did tell me that no one had lived out on Riches Head since the turn of the century, when the Riches, who had settled there, moved into Lunt Harbor. Evidently, they chose to abandon their homes to be nearer the island store, church, and school, although I learned that the Riches had maintained their own school out on the head for several generations before they returned to the dubious comforts of town.

At the head of Lunt Harbor was Frenchboro's one-room schoolhouse, next to the church, which was graced atop its steeple with a wind vane in the shape of a large cod. In cod we trusted?

One building used to be a store, another a sail loft and boat shed; all gave silent testimony to a community that seemed to be parting its mooring, slipping away literally before my eyes.

Perhaps because so many island communities have passed away, the experience of change in those that survive is firmly resisted. Old ways hang on longer and are more important than in most of our culture. Sometimes from an island it is possible to look back at the brash and swift pace of change on the mainland and appreciate a little more of what's important; what's lasting. It's as if island time gets telescoped, so you learn to experience things differently.

Here at this edge, any observer with an instinct for local history comes face to face with eternity.

VINALHAVEN

The largest island community off the coast of Maine, Vinalhaven currently has a year-round population of thirteen hundred. It supported at least four times as many inhabitants during the last half of the nineteenth century, when granite quarrying vied with fishing as the island's primary industry.

Vinalhaven is underlain by a huge dome of granite, and much of the original forest was once cleared for pasture, but the island was never self-sufficient on the basis of its land resources alone. With its spectacularly situated and protected harbors facing outward into the Gulf of Maine, Vinalhaven has always depended on the sea. For generations, sons of Vinalhaven fishermen have sailed offshore to hand-line, net, and trap the seemingly limitless supply of cold-water creatures that the Gulf of Maine offers up from fishing grounds as close as a stone's throw or as distant as Georges Bank, while their families waited ashore to learn whether the sea would give back their sons and brothers and fathers, day after endless day.

"God's Sip:" Fish-House Gossip

When I came to Roberts Harbor on Vinalhaven's wild eastern shore to write the first edition of *Islands in Time*, I was two miles from the town of Carvers Harbor, inside the protection of Carvers Reach and situated around the edge of a large, encircling harbor with an easily dammed tidal pond at its head. In short, Carvers was the outermost large, protected harbor at the edge of the most productive and valuable fishing grounds (especially for lobster) in the entire North Atlantic.

I rented the back ell of a farmhouse on the shore of Roberts Harbor, facing across the raging east bay and into the winter sun. No one much else lived out that way, so there were not many distractions while I was writing up the notes from my summer fieldwork. Besides, a huge stretch of this back shore had emptied of summer people and was available for long afternoon walks.

As the days grew shorter and the weather patterns began to be dominated by easterly gales inevitably followed by towering northwesterly fronts screeching for days at a time, I was taken round to some of the fish houses clustered communally around the harbor on Clam Alley, Sands Cove, and Frog Hollow. Some of the younger lobstermen were contemporaries of my landlord, George Putz, who was respected for his knowledge and writing on maritime subjects. I was glad to

Beulah Quinn, with a picture of her father, who kept the Eagle Island Light in Penobscot Bay, after keeping the Avery Rock Light in Machias Bay and Boon Island Light off York.   PETER RALSTON

be sitting near the little woodstoves bespattered with buoy paint hearing the weather rage outside while listening to the gossip.

The quality of fish-house conversation is inversely proportional to the weather. These spells of conversation are, as far as I can see, the only intense time that fishermen have to spend ashore socializing with one another. Impromptu gossip sessions with fishermen who are better known for their nicknames—Tink, Gweeka, Hummer, and Fireball—were wonderfully funny. These were hardworking and inventive young fishermen who, with about a score of their contemporaries, had begun sharing the harbor privileges with older fishermen.

Some of the fish-house conversation was murderously slanderous. I knew it couldn't all be true; people simply couldn't have done all the things that were routinely ascribed to them. When I asked George about the gossip sessions, he explained a fundamental lesson. The word "gossip," he said, derives from the ancient Anglo-Saxon "God's sip," or God's family. If you are embraced in the arms of the community, you'll be gossiped about as a sign of belonging. Veracity isn't the issue. What's important is to know what is being said about you and by whom and how to use the social intercourse of gossip as a currency to reply to your friends and enemies. The worst thing in an island community, George said, is to not know what's being said about you; if you're outside the gossip, you are outside of God's family.

Carvers Harbor, Vinalhaven, September 7, 1985
Shortly after sunset I walked down to one of the town beaches at the outer edge of the harbor. At the far end of the curving gravel fringe, a gull

was hunched with its legs folded under itself; it was midway between the dry brown jetsam of the high-water mark and the slow lap of the harbor waves.

Even from afar I knew there was something wrong with the gull. As I walked slowly in its direction, the bird did not move; its attitude was of intense watchfulness. It watched me watching it. Finally it tried to move. It kicked one limpid pink foot out from under its heavy body and flapped one wing haplessly along the beach; the other was folded uselessly over its black back. I looked at the line of rising tide fifteen feet away and tried to calculate the time it would take for the sea to float this broken creature off the beach of small boys and running dogs. I turned and walked quickly away as the gull, now turned three-quarters to the water, returned to its morbid watch. In the next day or two or maybe a week, its slow dance of death would be enacted. Alone.

It takes time to appreciate the intricate balances that Vinalhaven's fishermen maintain between the fierce competition of the lobster chase and the cooperation regularly displayed when someone is in trouble. No matter how cold or tired at the end of a day of hauling, the men would wait around on the wharves or at the co-op or in their fish houses until the last boat came in. Without discussion, each of them watched the fleet in. And while waiting, there would be time for politics, philosophy, fixing gear, and getting ready for the next day's hauling. Invisible threads knit together a group of outwardly truculent and independent individuals much more closely than one might think possible.

George Putz, a careful observer and my guide to local knowledge, described the inordinate influence that a few primary personalities can exert on island life:

Many islands have been under the domination of certain individuals for as long as half a century. Their emergence and demise radically alter and direct the course of island history —the personal, economic, and political lives of islanders—although the principals are seldom the obvious ones. Selectmen, town managers, ministers, and the like are generally irrelevant to the real power domain of islands. But when minor fluctuations occur in an island economy, ostensible island leaders are generally powerless, and marginal islanders are forced to leave the community, as people must "take care of their own." It's a tragedy for them and a sadness for island life.

Through islanders' eyes I began to understand how the rising tide of newcomers has caused deep conflicts among native-born Maine people. They watch as newcomers purchase second homes from the ancestral holdings of old families who have fallen, perhaps temporarily, on hard times. They feel dismay when visitors appropriate or reduce access to the shores of island places where nets once held fish, clams were dug, and secret trysts were arranged.

Vinalhaven, March 2, 1979
The sea has frozen. Ice eighteen inches thick covers not just Carvers Harbor but Rockland out to the breakwater. In the harbor, lobstermen have been able to walk out to their boats for several weeks. A few lobstermen tried to chop their way out of the harbor and look for a mooring in faster water that is still ice-free, but most of the moorings were frozen like Scott's ship in the thickening harbor ice. The ferry made increasingly futile attempts to keep the harbor open, but it too finally gave up. Those who live on nearby small islands like Green's, across the reach, can, if they're crazy enough, walk over to Vinalhaven to get supplies. Everything is getting strained.

> *At the farmhouse on Roberts Harbor, the pipe from the well froze solid, even though the taps had been left running all night. For the last six weeks we have been hauling water from a spring across the island. One of the island's elderly matriarchs died and was placed in a surface crypt until spring because pickax and crowbar couldn't penetrate the ground.*
>
> *Cut off in the back room of the farmhouse, I feel the winter dark begin to envelop the place; it wraps me in a close grip and won't let go. It's like nothing I've ever experienced; it's like being in a spacecraft that must pass behind the dark side of a huge moon before coming back around to solar light and warmth again. It's profoundly unnerving.*

NORTH HAVEN

North Haven, together with its neighbor Vinalhaven, make up the Fox Islands, a name derived from what might have been a species of fox distinct from those found on the mainland. The fox were reported by seventeenth-century explorers to have inhabited these islands but have long since disappeared. The Fox Islands are the largest inhabited islands off the Maine coast; two of the fifteen islands that still support year-round communities.

Although separated by less than a quarter mile of water from Vinalhaven, North Haven could not be more different if the two islands were located in different oceans.

The early editions of famed *Atlantic Neptune* charts of the Maine coast, commissioned in 1764 by the British Admiralty, show no harbor at the present location of Pulpit Harbor, along the north shore of North Haven. Many students of history have speculated that the Admiralty and her captains knew perfectly well where the most protected harbors of Maine were; the harbors were simply too valuable militarily to locate on charts, lest they fall into the wrong hands. By 1776, however, the *Atlantic Neptune* showed Pulpit Harbor, along with six to eight habitations on the "North Island," overlooking the superbly protected entrance to "Northern Harbor."

PULPIT HARBOR

The original settlers were blessed with not only a favorable and forgiving harbor but also an abundant supply of water from Fresh Pond and a deep millstream that connected the pond and the harbor. Within a few years of the turn of the nineteenth century, boatbuilding sheds, sawmills, and even a gristmill were located along the banks of the harbor and millstream. According to local historian Seward Beacom, throughout the remainder of the nineteenth century, "Pulpit Harbor Village was the population, commercial, and industrial center of the island. Around the Harbor there have been five stores, two fish processing plants, at least six wharves, three boat shops, a cooper shop, four mills, a church, a school, Union Hall, two post offices, and a cemetery." The value that mariners placed on Pulpit Harbor is evident in this 1858 account of a sloop following a schooner into the narrow harbor entrance:

> It was a harbor not marked on the charts and unknown to our seamen, but they said that if a schooner had got in we could of course follow. The Pilot . . . now steered for the entrance, which was very narrow, with a huge black rock rising out of the middle. As the sloop was surging into the entrance the skipper discovered a sunken reef right ahead of the vessel . . . but the sloop glided past the reef which she cleared with a slight touch without damage and we sailed into the harbor and were presently in still water.

This harbor is called Pulpit Harbor from the great, high, isolated rock at the entrance, which the church-going New Englanders have likened to a pulpit . . . It is one of the finest

Fifield's General Store, Vinalhaven. For half a century, proprietors Kim Smith and Bruce Grindle supplied free candy to any island child who happened by "downstreet."

havens I ever saw, if not the very finest. Except for the narrow entrance it was landlocked and calm and sheltered as an inland pond. Its diameter seemed to be about half a mile, and it was surrounded by low hills sloping gently to the water's edge. The summits of the hills were covered with woods but on their cleared and grassy slopes cattle and sheep were pasturing. A few fishermen's houses were in sight, and beside the schooner we had followed in, there were a half dozen fishing vessels at anchor in front of the hamlet.

Nothing could exceed the exquisite freshness of the hillsides . . . Seaward, we looked as through some mighty portal over the black and jagged rocks of the entrance, and thence across ten miles of ocean to the mainland, where the picturesque Camden Mountains reared their summits in full view.

After the Civil War, the fishermen of Pulpit Harbor, unlike their neighbors at Carvers Harbor, began to build a specialized fleet of fishing boats. These elegant mackerel schooners excelled in speed, which was required to supply fresh fish to Boston's Irish and New York's Italian immigrant communities, particularly on Fridays and on saints' days. For a short time in the 1870s, North Haven had a larger and more valuable fishing fleet than did Vinalhaven, a fact that has escaped serious notice.

But in the blink of an eye, everything changed. The harbor community that supported a population estimated at two hundred is virtually gone today. What happened? The mackerel fishery mysteriously collapsed almost overnight in 1888 and 1889 after a huge increase in fishing five to six years earlier. Perhaps the fishermen's resulting financial stress and discouragement caused them to sell their land. It was bought by some of the region's first "rusticators," city folks seeking rural vacation homes. During the last decades of the nineteenth century and the first decade and a half of the twentieth century, the rusticators began transforming the harbor into a pastoral landscape by removing its working waterfront.

The history books record merely the following on the subject: "The Beverage store, storehouse, ice house and wharf no longer exist . . . The William Piper fishhouse and store which stood on Frye Point . . . were demolished and burned between 1900 and 1906 . . . The store on the bank above the Harbor which had been run by Roscoe C. Babbidge since 1891 was taken down in 1906 and transported to Vinalhaven. The Edward Witherspoon house was demolished in 1918 . . . The old schoolhouse, built in 1867 on the curve in the old Pulpit Harbor Road, was also torn down in 1918. The Josiah Parsons house on the road up the hill was torn down in 1918 . . . The fish shacks and storage sheds which stood along the north side of the Harbor also disappeared around 1918." The year 1918 culminated three decades of bad years for the North islanders, leaving a bitter legacy that reaches down to the present on the island.

With the passing of the Pulpit Harbor community, North Haven re-created itself on the south side of the island, where the deep waters of the Fox Island Thorofare divide North and South Island. The J.O. Brown and Son boatbuilding works, which in 1988 celebrated its hundredth anniversary in the same family ownership, began business with the construction of an elegant yacht for the Weld-Pingree family, which settled at Iron Point.

Although rusticators became an important force in all of Maine's remaining island communities, I am aware of no other island where so much cultural history was removed—burned, demolished, and taken away—to re-create in its place a pastoral vision of a preindustrial coast. The legacy of this deconstruction perhaps lives on today in the hearts of many islanders whose kin, now removed, once maintained the Pulpit Harbor Privilege.

Hundredth anniversary of J.O. Brown and Son, Inc. on North Haven, 1888 – 1988.   Peter Ralston

The Privilege, Vinalhaven, September 18, 1989

There is a place on the eastern shore of Vinalhaven tucked up inside the legendary all-weather anchorage of Winter Harbor behind the sheer granite face of Starboard Rock where a small tidal estuary fingers its unhurried way into the spruce and granite shore. Although unmarked on charts, this cove is called "the Privilege," a reverential name for a place that provided generations of fishermen an important part of their livelihood and boatbuilders rare access to "inland" pine and oak stands for building boats that carried stone and fish along the East Coast. Recently sold by one of the island's most productive fishermen, who thereby earned a richly deserved retirement, the land around the Privilege is being subdivided.

Soon there will be summer houses set seventy-five feet or so from the high-water mark, full of the lively sounds of their deserving new owners, who will graciously pay small bounties in taxes to support services of the town and school they will use little, if at all. And like an increasing number of other islanders, they will line up to jockey for a spot on the inevitably crowded ferry. Such is the new economy of the Privilege and of the islands.

What is gained and lost here? The clam flats, with a new spat set, will not see diggers coming overland on foot with their forks and hods to work a tide for grocery money. Mussel boats, though they can still come in and out of the cove at high water, will earn the understandable opposition of those new riparian owners who have a fondness for their own fresh mussels steamed in wine and garlic. The upland stands of pine, oak, and timber spruce will not be felled again to build boats or pay island woodsmen's wages; their value as recreational amenities will be their prime currency and use. Most certainly, the granite monoliths still scattered about will not be hauled again from these shores, for the dust and noise of such industry interrupts the peace and quiet of the Privilege's new economy. The possibility of four kinds of jobs that once helped support the patchwork island economy will be eclipsed here.

The development of the shores of the Privilege will send only small ripples around the island, but they will be noticeable nearly forever. Because the place is not known to many, in a sense its destiny does not matter much. But viewed in the scale of the thousands of subdivisions on the tens of thousands of acres of equally subtle and significant shorelines along the coast, the issue is immeasurably greater. Many ways of life are at stake here. The outcome of hundreds of isolated, individual local decisions in the coming decades concerning island privileges will determine the look and feel and texture of island life for the next century. In the politics of island place that fuel the most intense debates, it doesn't matter where you're from or even especially what you stand to gain or lose individually, privileged or not. What matters is what you care about.

FORMING THE ISLAND INSTITUTE

In 1983, four transplants to Maine pooled their efforts and backgrounds as writer, photographer, forester, and ecologist to start the Island Institute. George Putz, who had lived on Vinalhaven and earned his living as a maritime enthnographer, was the first to convince me that islanders are one of the region's most endangered species. We were joined by Peter Ralston, a widely published profes-

Dorothy Simpson.   PETER RALSTON

sional photographer, and Ray Leonard, a forester with the U.S. Forest Service Research Station and a great single-handed sailor. Two other people provided crucial support: Tom Cabot, an industrialist, yachtsman, and conservationist, and Betsy Wyeth, the wife of artist Andrew Wyeth and the owner of Allen Island, a large uninhabited island off Port Clyde that had once been a thriving community. The Island Institute would serve as a clearinghouse of information about Maine's islands and islanders and provide a forum for the varied, disparate, and sometimes remote voices along the archipelago.

As we began to get to know some of the region's islanders, we were struck by their simultaneous qualities of strength and fragility. The story of the end of Criehaven as a year-round community, related to us by Dorothy Simpson and Elisabeth Ogilvie, was both moving and cautionary. The end of this community in outermost Penobscot Bay, out beyond Matinicus, came all at once. Many factors were involved, but the blow from which the islanders never recovered was the closing of the island schoolhouse during World War II for lack of a teacher. In 1984, Dorothy Simpson wrote: "After the children moved ashore, their mothers followed. With fewer people on Criehaven, the storekeeper couldn't afford to keep the store open except a few hours a day. Without the women and children and store, nobody would take over the mailboat business—the lifeline to the island community. Finally, even the men came ashore."

When the Island Institute was launched, we believed we had some ideas about how Maine's islands might be used for fishing and aquaculture and how various other resources could be marshaled to support year-round communities. As newcomers, we fervently believed that the islands and their surrounding waters could be utilized in ways that respected island history and culture and did not despoil the abundant scenic and wildlife resources.

CONFRONTING THE DEVELOPMENT JUGGERNAUT, 1985–92

Within a year of its founding, the Island Institute was swept into a controversy over a proposed island development in Casco Bay. Less than three miles from Portland's busy Commercial Street, where navy ships are repaired in a huge Bath Iron Works dry dock, one can walk the dirt roads of Great Diamond Island and be reminded of the quiet lanes of a nineteenth-century rural town. Surrounded on two sides by deep channels and with high headlands that overlook the seaward approaches to Portland Harbor, Great Diamond Island was recognized for its strategic value as early as the 1890s. Accordingly, the military appropriated 198 acres of the north end of the island to build Fort McKinley, named after the nation's new president. Meanwhile the association of Portland businessmen that had acquired Great Diamond continued to build cottages for their new summer colony at the south end of the island.

The big naval battlements of Fort McKinley had the range to cover the deep ship channel that runs between Cushing Island and Cape Elizabeth, as well as Portland's "back door" entrance through the deep waters of Hussey Sound. Great Diamond was thus strategically located to protect northern New England's largest and most important commercial port.

Though never attacked, the fort was expanded and refortified during World War II because of its deepwater anchorages and its strategic location close to North Atlantic shipping lanes. Thousands of sailors and soldiers poured through Portland Harbor, and many of the Casco Bay islands were appropriated for military use. Long Island, next door to Great Diamond, became a depot where the entire North Atlantic fleet was able to refuel in less than forty-eight hours.

When the war ended the military left. The U.S. government offered the fort property to the City of Portland for one dollar, but in the 1950s no one wanted the responsibility of maintaining the infrastructure. It languished as the state's largest white elephant until the coastal real estate boom of the 1980s. A local developer acquired the property in 1985 and proposed to turn the fort buildings into three hundred and fifty luxury condominiums and build new summer homes on the site. The Portland City Council voted to approve the development essentially as it had been presented by the developers, as did state regulators in Augusta.

There was (and is), of course, much to be said for renovating the historic structures of the fort; the question was really how much of the rest of the island might have to be sacrificed in the process. For one thing the development would require a new sewage treatment plant. State regulators had approved an overboard discharge license even though the outfall would flow over a large bed of intertidal clam flats. Because these clam flats were already closed to digging as a result of "background" pollution in Casco Bay, the regulators didn't treat this issue as any big deal. "You can't pollute pollution" seemed to be their philosophy.

> ### Great Diamond Island, July 27, 1989
> *Peter Ralston and I tied* Fish Hawk, *the Island Institute's boat, to a guest mooring near the Casco Bay Lines wharf off Great Diamond Island. A short time later we were walking down the island's quiet country roads just beyond the loom of Portland's waterfront condos. After a potluck supper at the Great Diamond Island Association's grand old building, we headed up the hill to the porch of a cottage where a score of islanders had gathered. They were there to discuss the merits of appealing the forty-thousand-gallon-per-day discharge permit granted to developers on the other end of the island by the Maine Department of Environmental Protection.*
>
> *For the past three years, since Great Diamond Island's proposed development was first unveiled, many tenacious islanders throughout Casco Bay had firmly maintained that even the "scaled down" 238-unit development was too big to be environmentally reasonable. It would mean a large, privately operated sewage treatment plant emptying into inner Casco Bay's badly polluted waters, the destruction of a stand of 125-year-old pine and hemlock, and the addition of hundreds of cars to downtown Portland's daily parking gridlock. As the moon rose over the earnest discussion on the porch, it was clear that these sincere and frustrated islanders would do whatever it took to press the issues at the federal level.*

The islanders and the institute seized on the proposed development as an example of terrible public policy. We appealed to the federal government, which overruled state regulators and required the sewage treatment plant (and ultimately the entire development) to be redesigned and further scaled down. By the time the final approvals were in place six years later, not only was the developer bankrupt, so was the local bank that had lent $20 million to this project (not to mention other equally over-reaching real estate investments).

The outcry over Great Diamond's outfall pipe focused public attention on the bigger issue of Casco Bay's water quality. A lawsuit filed by the Conservation Law Foundation and the Island Institute over the Portland Water District's failure to abide by its discharge license ultimately resulted in the upgrading of not just Portland's sewage treatment plant but others around the entire rim of Casco Bay. The lawsuit also catalyzed the formation of Friends of Casco Bay, which has carefully watched over the waters ever since.

In retrospect, it is alarming to realize the scale of the financial feeding frenzy that pumped hundreds of millions of inflated, unrecoverable real estate dollars through the coast. Ultimately in Casco Bay, the real winners were the islanders and their mainland friends who learned how to play hardball with unresponsive state and city decision-makers.

THE LITTLE ISLAND THAT GOT AWAY

From Portland's Munjoy Hill and the Western Prom, the panorama of islands in Casco Bay is one of the most compelling seascapes in Maine. Ridge upon rolling ridge of dark islands are separated from one another by silver slices of the bay—the deepwater channels that form wide boulevards between Portland's island communities.

Peaks Island, twenty minutes from Portland by ferry, was colonized after World War II by a number of the city's welfare cases—housing was cheaper on the island than anywhere else in the city —and then by the artists and craftspeople who helped propel the Old Port revival in the 1970s. Little and Great Diamond islands and Cushing Island, the summer gems of Casco Bay, lie just beyond Peaks. From the top of the Portland Observatory on Munjoy Hill, one can see all the way to the outermost populated island, Cliff, where fifty year-rounders struggle to keep their community afloat. In between are Chebeague and Long islands, two fishing communities that occupy the rich lobster grounds of the midbay. The vagaries of history have separated these latter two islands politically: Chebeague is the only island jurisdiction in the town of Cumberland; Long and its year-round neighbors—Cliff, the Diamonds, and Peaks—have been part of Portland as long as anyone can remember.

Talk of secession began to spread like a fever among Casco Bay islanders in the late 1980s. Maybe it was sparked by the Great Diamond Island controversy and its attendant zoning battles. Maybe it was the intense debate over the proper lot size required to protect the islands' finite groundwater resources. Or maybe it was just accumulated frustration over the chronic lack of basic city services. The talk became a drumbeat when the City of Portland revalued the islands in the city jurisdiction in 1991 and in effect doubled the tax bills of hundreds of islanders.

The city's initial reaction was to shrug off the islanders' discontent as a periodic inconvenience that would wear itself out, as it had in the past. Peaks Island was badly divided over the issue, with passionate advocates for and against independence from Portland. Tiny Cliff Island was not convinced that it had enough human resources to sustain independence. But in 1992 Long Island approached the Maine Legislature and won the right to hold an islandwide referendum on secession from Portland to form its own island town. The political questions began to cascade: What would independence cost? Who would run the school? What would the town budget be? Who would be registered to vote? Would taxes go up or down? Would the new town owe Portland for a part of the city's debts? The institute helped a determined group of Long islanders contact other island towns along the archipelago to address each question as it arose.

The referendum was held in November 1993, and the results were overwhelming: By a four-to-one majority, Long Island voters elected to form their own town—Maine's 455th—and chose July 4, 1994, as the day of their official independence.

> ### *Long Island Town Offices, July 4, 1994*
> *The crowd is assembled outside the little white building that serves as the new town office overlooking the harbor where the entire North Atlantic fleet could refuel in forty-eight hours when Hitler's menace made every minute, every gallon of fuel, precious. The day is as gaudy a display of the island's naturally green, blue, and white colors as could ever be hoped—a stunning, cloudless early summer morning where more than five hundred islanders and their friends have shown up for a real day of independence. There is more red, white, and blue bunting than there are surfaces to display it. It is pure festivity.*
>
> *Everything is in order, although the officials are nervous. Nevertheless, the ceremony begins at the stroke of noon with the raising of the American flag at the entrance to the State of Maine's newest town accompanied by the band playing the "Star Spangled Banner." Just as the flag crests the pole with every eye in the audience staring upward, the air is cracked by the deafening explosion of four jets that appear out of absolutely nowhere and then disappear. The split-second timing leaves few dry eyes as we think about all the wild blue yonders that have paid for the privileges of independence.*

The Long Island vote electrified Portland's other island communities. Peaks, Great Diamond, and Cushing immediately appealed to the legislature for permission to hold similar referendums. Portland City Hall was in a huge pickle. It was plain to anyone who cared to look that the islands were a highly desirable and valuable part of Portland's tax base. Yet throughout the Long Island struggle, the city had steadfastly maintained that the services to islands exceeded the tax revenues generated; it had conveyed the impression that it considered the islanders to be perennially ungrateful for anything the city tried to do. Even islanders who had no desire to secede from the city were alienated by this attitude. Although Portland couldn't publicly suggest that the islands were a cash cow, it also couldn't continue to suggest that the islands were a drag on city service coffers. So it developed a new line—quietly and, as these things are often done, behind the scenes. The city suggested to the legislative leadership that if the remaining islands were lost to the city, Portland would need additional appropriations from the legislature to maintain basic human services to a diminished tax base. A lot of money, know what I mean? The tactic was highly effective.

Partially because the other islands were not as united as Long, the permission to hold any other referendums on independence was unceremoniously buried silently and deeply in Augusta, leaving Long as the little island that got away.

SWAN'S ISLAND

For most of the twentieth century, Swan's Island, like Vinalhaven, has supported families almost exclusively dependent on their ability to catch lobsters. But Swan's is farther east than Vinalhaven, and the waters are cooler in summer, so lobsters and lobstermen are not as numerous here.

On Swan's, as on the islands to the west, the same pressures of increasing second-home devel-

Lining up at Mackerel Cove, Swan's Island, for the first trip of the WILLIAM SILSBY, *first state ferry to connnect the island to the mainland, March 4, 1960.*   COURTESY SWAN'S ISLAND EDUCATIONAL SOCIETY

opment exist, along with an escalating demand for new services. This effect is locally known as Markey's Law, after Mark Stanley, a young lobsterman who asked, "Why is it that when people from away move to Maine, they immediately start changing things around to look just like the places they moved here to get away from?"

In 1989, a large salmon farm was established on Swan's Island by an entrepreneur with international investments who had recently settled in Connecticut. Soon two hundred thousand Atlantic salmon and steelhead trout were swimming in eighteen ocean pens in Toothacher Cove and across the way at Frenchboro. The fish pens were put into place after the fishermen's co-op agreed that the structures would not interfere with lobster fishing. But management mistakes, and losses from an exceptionally cold winter followed by Hurricane Bob, put the company into receivership after four years of operation.

Myron "Sonny" Sprague, a lobsterman who had also been a selectman on Swan's for a quarter of a century, was distressed that a company that employed more than twenty-five islanders and put a payroll of $300,000 through the island coffers was about to be auctioned off by the bank. In a heartening turnaround, Sprague and the Island Institute found backers among state finance officials and others. Sprague's new company acquired the assets of the bankrupt salmon farm and began the long, slow road back to profitability.

MONHEGAN AGONISTES

Monhegan lies twelve miles offshore from Port Clyde at an outermost edge of the archipelago. Only the community on Matinicus Island is farther offshore, but because Matinicus shares its isolation with Criehaven—at least for nine months of the year when Criehaven fishermen are in residence—Monhegan is by this measure more removed.

Monhegan draws its identity from its aloneness. The island's high, dark cliffs and austere seascapes have been an inspiration to artists since Rockwell Kent and other New York painters began coming here in 1903. Fishermen, artists, and poets have shaped Monhegan's essential culture. The strength of the Monhegan character might be said to be born of isolation and loneliness; it is in uncrowded places where ideas visit the mind. When life is too cluttered by entertainment, there is no time to entertain the ideas that become art or pursue the visions that make fishermen go over the horizon to seek a lonely living from the sea.

> *Monhegan, July 3, 1992, Blessing of the Fleet*
>
> *The parade to celebrate Monhegan's 150th anniversary takes place among the rocky outcrops of the island's downtown and is pure antic theater. All seven vehicles on the island have been pressed into service as floats, which lurch through a throng of humanity. At the start, it's hard to tell who is parade and who is audience, but soon there is no distinction; it's all parade. The motley crowd of island residents, tourists, day-trippers, and personalities is briefly thrown into pandemonium when, somewhere between Fish Beach and the Spa, salvos of water balloons are fired at the parade judges from the astonishing sea goddess float. After a cease-fire has been hastily arranged, hundreds gather in the heat of the day to honor the island elders and the twin spirits of dogged individualism and vigilant mutualism that have artfully infused Monhegan's polity since anyone can remember.*
>
> *Then comes the blessing of the fleet: the island's twelve fishing boats; the LAURA B mailboat, which serves as a lifeline to the mainland; and the few summer boats that enjoy mooring privileges in the small, exposed harbor between Monhegan and Manana's grave cliffs. Even the Island Institute's FISH HAWK lines up to pass by the wharf and be sprinkled with holy water from a local holy man. It is an altogether fitting and somber closing note for 150 years out at sea.*

However sweet Monhegan's summer pleasures, it takes winter to create the barren soul of the place. It's worth noting that Monhegan's two most accomplished artists, whose work has sustained itself over impressive spans of time, are the two who spent winters there—Rockwell Kent and Jamie Wyeth. They share more than the house that Kent built on the most exposed southwestern jaw of Monhegan. Kent's images of Monhegan, painted on his subsequent summer visits in the 1950s, reveal the flatness of his visions minus his island winters.

Monhegan's twelve lobster fishermen, who live on an ultimate edge of the Gulf of Maine, collectively help define the soul of winter. The carriers of the torch, they were, historically, the only fleet of lobstermen along the entire archipelago who had imposed a sanction on themselves within the fragile two-mile territory of their waters. They fish the harshest season of the year, from January's Trap Day to June's end, when lobster prices are at their interannual peak. Afterward, gear is hauled back ashore to serve as backdrops for summer artists and crowds of tourists.

Who gets to fish these bountiful waters and who does not as the seasons come and go are solemn matters. There is little margin here, and a stern New England rectitude prevails.

Monhegan Lobsterman, December 6, 1983

I saw Dougie when he was grounded out at the fisherman's co-op in Port Clyde painting Gryphon's *bottom. He was stagy and catlike, maneuvering for room around the wharf, eyes darting about, half wild. He said he was being denied fish-house privileges on Monhegan by the other eleven fishermen, a serious situation. Without being able to store gear and bait at the fish house, he would have to stage his solo fishing from the mainland, which involved incalculably greater risks and expense. No one had ever survived on Monhegan when access to the fish house had been withdrawn. He said there had been trouble; he didn't say what kind. But he said he would fight hard to get his berth back, and I didn't doubt him. Whatever his crime, the punishment had been terrible, swift, and merciless.*

Monhegan, January 4, 1985, Trap Day

No one goes until everyone goes. That's the way Trap Day has always worked on Monhegan. Sometimes the weather won't let you go for days after January 1. Very occasionally it's because someone, usually an older fisherman, has been sick and doesn't have his gear ready. But on the first good day after New Year's when everyone's ready, Monhegan's six-month winter lobster season begins in the waters immediately surrounding the island, just as the mainland season used to wind down. It's a festive time of year on the island; the holidays are over, and the gear has been piled all along the rocky roadsides, lining the hill, and down the sides of the wharf. Today the roadsides, meadows, and gear are dusted with white, and the sea is streaky where the spume has blown. Lobster prices have climbed right steadily through the holiday, and everyone knows that there can be monster hauls in January when lobsters can bring five dollars a pound.

Ever since losing his fish-house privilege over a year ago, Dougie has continued fishing in Monhegan's waters. But he's done so at a severe disadvantage. He's had to stage his bait off Port Clyde, a time-consuming and costly location from which to be supplied with this critical lobstering necessity. Alice, his wife, has been sick with a rare degenerative blood disease that attacks her hip and cripples her. It's been a tough, brutal year for them. "There's one thing that islanders are really good at," says Dougie ruefully. "It's when we get together to exclude someone."

This December, though, under the long afternoon shadows, Dougie piles his gear alongside the other eleven lobstermen's traps, warps, and buoys. No one says a word to him; there's just the baleful silences of another austere winter day. Everyone is waiting, edgy anyway. It's always like this before Trap Day: waiting for the wind to stop shrieking so the gear can be set, waiting so the men can go fishing again, waiting so island families can ease their cash flow hemorrhage. Some years it's taken ten days for the wind to let go or the sea surge in the harbor to steady.

But now, four days into the waiting, the season finally begins early this morning. Everyone is down at the harbor with steaming coffee in thermoses.

Criehaven town landing, around 1900, from a glass negative.

The day promises to be bright blue with a steadily freshening northwesterly blowing at twenty knots. Even the schoolteacher, Mary Beth Dolan, who has a lobster license, is going to set a dozen traps in the harbor. Classes in the one-room schoolhouse up the hill have been called off so everyone can help load gear when the boats jockey alongside the wharf for their turn to load. The younger or impatient fishermen, including Dougie, don't want to wait for the wharf, so they load a dozen or more traps in their skiffs at Fish Beach and scull back and forth to load their boats.

It's like that, edgy energy all around, when Mary Beth Dolan in her skiff rows out from the wharf where her own gear is piled and along the shore to Fish Beach. She hauls up, grapples three big wire lobster traps from Dougie's pile—one, two, three—and lugs them to her skiff. As everyone ashore takes a deep inner breath, she rows quietly out to Dougie's boat and hands him the traps in the stern.

Redemption does not come easily on an island, but maybe the islanders' tough vigilance makes such turning points seem sweeter.

Monhegan's fishermen, even in the best of times during the past quarter century, have been under pressure from a different threat. During the winter of 1997, fishermen from the town of Friendship—in a reenactment of the ancient law of the sea that only fishermen really understand—laid claim to neutral territory seaward of Monhegan's two-mile limit. Drawn knives (to cut warps) glinted in the dreary light of dawn while boats circled one another warily. The lobster fishery, on which the majority of Maine's island winter kingdoms depend, was under pressure from within and without. Migrating female broodstock was being targeted in the western Gulf of Maine by Massachusetts draggermen who could no longer find trips of cod. Urchin boats dragged the cobble

Vivian Lunt and the Frenchboro church, 1993   PETER RALSTON

bottom where juvenile lobsters are known to seek shelter in significant densities. Territorial adjustments were being negotiated by steely-edged men beyond the ken of law.

In a tense set of meetings and hearings, the then-commissioner of the Maine Department of Marine Resources, Robin Alden, embattled on all sides, negotiated a truce in the boundary war where emotions ran high while Monhegan successfully petitioned the legislature for a three-mile zone around its southern territorial periphery.

FRENCHBORO

In 1981, the island Town of Frenchboro, six miles south of Mount Desert, was balanced precariously on the edge of survival. Unless island residents were able to stem the slow tide of families "removing" to the mainland, the island school would close for lack of students, and Frenchboro would join the ranks of hundreds of other islands that once supported flourishing, small, year-round communities where now only seasonal residences remained. In a remarkable show of unanimity, town residents put together a complicated community development proposal that involved island businesses, summer residents, and state and federal agencies investing in the structures that make island living possible: namely, a school, a ferry landing, a fire station, wharves, and housing.

The islanders succeeded in building seven new houses, including a house for the teacher; replacing the existing ferry ramp with a new thirty-six-ton ramp; installing indoor plumbing at the schoolhouse; building a fire station; and creating an area for a helicopter landing pad for emergency medical evacuations. To help make this happen, the town's largest private landowner, a nonresident, agreed to donate a fifty-five-acre parcel of land then worth more than $100,000 on which to build the new homes. And the year-round residents pledged to invest their own money toward refurbishing fifteen existing homes. Finally, the Town of Frenchboro loaned the project funds, and the Lunt and Lunt Lobster Company invested in new wharf facilities. As a result, the town successfully attracted six new settlers and a new schoolteacher. The Island Institute was asked to serve on the board of the development corporation overseeing this complex community resettlement project.

Skeptics had asked who would move into the new community housing if islanders themselves were not able or willing to stay on Frenchboro year-round. Of course, not everyone is suited to island life, but Frenchboro is blessed with an abundance of good year-round fishing bottom, which the community was slowly losing to fishermen from other harbors. In addition, opportunities for new fishing berths like those on Frenchboro did not appear every day. Those willing to work hard and commit to year-round living ensured the future of this island.

Frenchboro, December 4, 1992

Although it's reassuring to know that all seven of the new Frenchboro houses are full—six families and the schoolteacher in the seventh—everyone also knows it's been a struggle. A year and a half ago, four of the original six homesteaders had abandoned their effort to live year-round on remote Frenchboro, victims of weather, isolation, and a downward spiraling economy. One family left after their lobster boat nearly sank in heavy freezing spray. "He kinda lost his courage after that," other fishermen said, knowing how that can happen. Then the salmon farm closed down and two other families left. The youngest couple had just had enough and "removed" to Massachusetts, where for them a lot more was going on. But the two remaining families were survivors and were ready to buy their homes if the final details of the financing could be worked out.

The new families that took the others' places hardly have stars in their eyes. One of them, headed by April Lunt, certainly knows what she's getting into. Another family originally hailed from Swan's Island and moved to Frenchboro from Rockland where the husband worked for the O'Hara fish-processing plant until the groundfish gave out. Maybe not all of the current crop of residents will stay, but there will be more survivors, and slowly, slowly the project will take its final shape. Out here, you tend to take the long view.

A decade ago, when I first visited Frenchboro, except for the Lunt and Lunt Lobster Company wharf at the harbor entrance, the waterfront had deteriorated into a picturesque but sorry state of disrepair. Most of the houses lacked insulation, foundations, and furnaces; a few had only outhouses. Now, the inner harbor has been dredged, which opened up a more secure winter anchorage; tens of thousands of dollars have been invested in a half-dozen wharves; and the small fleet looks, if not exactly prosperous, at least to be holding its own.

Lunt Harbor, August 6, 1996

We are in Lunt Harbor for another celebration—the annual lobster fund-raising dinner to benefit the church, where a cod graces the weather-vane. We arrive early and wander up to the head of Lunt Harbor hard by the Frenchboro school and church, up on the hill whose pastiche of colorful flowers can be seen from the anchorage. The ferry has brought in three hundred and fifty guests, we hear, while others depart from the decks of yachts hailing from disparate ports along the coast. Into the midst of this scene, diesels begin landing people; the SANDI *and the* NATHANIEL ZACHARY *from*

Eagle Island schoolhouse, as it was left following the last day of school, 1941.   Peter Ralston

Frenchboro and the Lunnette Christina from neighboring Swan's fill the harbor for a time with an insistent basso rumble beneath the high cry of gulls and children's laughter. This is a day off from work along the archipelago. At the end of the day, seven hundred lobsters will have been served on the hillside overlooking the harbor.

SEARS ISLAND: CONFLICTING VISIONS OF THE FUTURE

The longest-running environmental battle in Maine history was fought over the future of Sears Island, a nine-hundred-acre island in upper Penobscot Bay. Four governors and every congressional leader since 1978, including environmental luminaries such as senators George Mitchell and Olympia Snowe, lined up to support the proposal for a large, modern cargo port terminal on the western shore of the island, where a deepwater channel exists, to complete Maine's "three port strategy." For a decade the Sierra Club waged a lonely battle objecting to the magnitude of the environmental impacts on the island. Finally the federal Environmental Protection Agency (EPA) weighed in against the state's proposed design, forcing additional costs and delays. With passions running wild and with so much at stake on both sides, and with the outcome hanging in the balance, we decided to mount an expedition to Sears Island from the seaward side.

Penobscot Bay, October 18, 1995, 5:30 a.m.

Low in the east, Venus, the morning star, is the only bright light in the sky as the faint glow of rosy-fingered dawn begins to stroke the sleeping breast of the bay. The flickering eye of Browns Head Light is far off the starboard bow as we come abeam of the Rockland Breakwater Light and then head into the red-rimmed dawn, watching while autumn's slanting easterly rays slowly pull a shade up on the crimson flanks of the Camden Hills. Just a blackbird shy of "Morning Has Broken."

The bay begins to narrow noticeably at Northport, where ancient metamorphic rocks tumble from the land's massive shoulders to the edge of the water. Saturday Cove is the smallest dent in the armament of the bay, but a few hopeful vessels still cling to their moorings in the deeply shadowed light. Belfast is off to port as we head for the shores of Sears Island to see up close the existing cargo port at Mack Point and the site for a new port proposed for the western shore of this uninhabited nine-hundred-acre island.

It's 7 a.m. when we round up into Long Cove; Mack Point is off the bow, and the white clapboards and steeples of Searsport are off our port quarter. We steam by the oak- and spruce-lined shores of Sears Island, passing over the dredged ship channel that terminates at Mack Point. We poke slowly up into Long Cove; with the tide still running out, we can't go too far in, but there's not much evidence of activity here. In fact it would be unusual to see a flock of shorebirds wheel by on the wing, or watch a great blue heron stalk shadows on these sixty acres of tidal flats, or see a seal's surprise surface; this is, after all, an industrial site. Not even a herring gull stirs here, a lasting legacy of a five-thousand-gallon fuel spill back in the 1970s that has never been cleaned up. Although no one knows for sure (because it seems no one has bothered to ask), it appears that the effects of this spill continue to exert a chronic, low-level, toxic stress, which would be expected to hit particularly hard on creatures at the bottom of the marine food chain. There's so little life in the cove because it's sick and there's no food.

There's also a dearth of activity at the long finger pier of the Bangor and Aroostook Railroad, which has a dilapidated, faded, and outdated look to it. This pier is in fact part of the raison d'être for construction on Sears Island, because it so obviously needs to be replaced, but planners have long maintained that Mack Point lacks the space, orientation, and compatibility with existing operations to rebuild here. Only a new port will do. At the next pier over, one man is up in the steel superstructure, and we exchange waves. He looks as though he's waiting for his ship—any ship—to come in, seemingly in limbo until a decision is reached on whether to invest another $65 to $80 million out of the public pocket to build a modern, efficient cargo port a mere stone's throw away on the wild shores of Sears Island.

Although we have not spent any time exploring here, a few things seem obvious. First, Mack Point is hardly the kind of cargo port that instills confidence that it can safely handle the coal and oil that come in to the head of Penobscot Bay—Sears Island or no Sears Island. Second, the lack of a strategy to monitor the effects of the existing source of pollution in Long Cove strains the credibility of those who say that all the environmental issues in the lengthy Sears Island debate have already been addressed. Third, although using two hundred of Sears Island's nine hundred acres for a new cargo port won't be an ecological catastrophe in and of itself, this is an old-style development model: Take a chunk of virgin territory for a new facility and turn a blind eye to the decaying infrastructure staring you in the face.

For almost two decades Sears Island was ground zero for competing visions of the future of Maine: link the industrial northern third of the state to international markets vs. protect rare and pristine areas in perpetuity. What many of us could not understand was why you couldn't accomplish both things by redeveloping Mack Point as the state's third cargo port. Finally, late in 1996, Maine's popular governor, Angus King, angrily threw in the towel and blamed the EPA. But fairly quietly the next year, King used surplus funds to acquire title to the nine-hundred-acre island, even as developers on Mack Point announced plans to build the new cargo port there. Mirabile dictu.

ISLANDED AT THE END OF THE TWENTIETH CENTURY

Islanders are isolated, dispersed, and suspicious of representative government beyond the town office. Maine islanders—five thousand year-round residents scattered across a dozen different legisla-

Sears Island, proposed as an oil refinery, coal-fired power plant and supercargo port site by every major Maine politician for more than two decades.   CHRISTOPHER AYRES

tive districts—constitute, in the best of circumstances, the smallest of footnotes in the political calculus of who wins and who loses when decisions come down.

But there is a more unfortunate side to this kind of political under-representation. It's not just the sense that islands and islanders don't really count; it's a feeling that they don't have any right to count. The undercurrent of this rarely spoken thought goes like this: Maine's islands are home to two kinds of people. First are the quaint but hopelessly unrealistic types who choose to ignore greater economic opportunities on the mainland and then expect public transportation, housing, and education subsidies to help maintain an uneconomic way of life. The second group is a rich elite made up of out-of-state summer people who maintain private estates who have conspired to exclude average Maine people from island life. A pox on both their houses, mutter the mainlanders; the islanders deserve any fate they receive.

Into this kind of vacuum move all kinds of opportunists who know what they want for the islands. All you have to do is look to windward—to places such as Martha's Vineyard and Nantucket—to see what lies in store for Maine's treasure of island communities. In the absence of local and state leadership committed to a future that values working waterfronts, productive waters and mudflats, uncongested islands, and the spiritual resources of wild shorelines, the islands will become like the places from which people long to escape.

Maine's island communities present all kinds of dilemmas. On the one hand, islanders should be able to control their own fate; but when their fate slips out of their hands, as is surely happening, then what? It means that the islanders must be able to draw on sympathetic help from Augusta, from the mainland, or wherever, as the going gets tough and the choices hard. Like all the rest of us, islanders need a lot more friends.

2

Downwind Histories and Ecologies

Though I had lived by the shore all my life, I seemed never to have been near the sea till then. The smell of tar and salt was something new. I saw the most wonderful figure-heads, that had all been far over the ocean. I saw, besides, many old sailors, with rings in their ears . . . and if I had seen as many kings or archbishops I could not have been more delighted. And I was going to sea myself; to sea in a schooner . . . bound for an unknown island, and to seek for buried treasures!

—Robert Louis Stevenson, *Treasure Island*

THE ECOLOGICAL SETTING: CLIMATE AS AN ECOLOGICAL FACTOR

Part of the reason that Maine's islands do not have more inhabitants frequenting their shores is that the seas around them and the air over them can be unpredictable. The islands are like wild animals made into pets, seeming sleek and tame at one moment, only to turn wild, ungrateful, even brutal the next moment. Islanders talk a lot about the weather because on islands the weather determines much of what you will and will not do; it reduces you to a little part of a much bigger world. From all but the most stupid or arrogant (and out there the two are almost interchangeable), the weather commands respect.

The climate of the islands is dominated by the influence of the Nova Scotia Current. This off-shoot of the Labrador Current is a cold, Arctic-born tongue of water that curls around the western end of Nova Scotia, slips southwest along the irregular Maine coast, and is deflected east and then east-northeast by the great arm of Cape Cod and its counterpart current, the Atlantic Gulf Stream. Where the Scotian Current and the Gulf Stream run side by side—miles offshore—the humid tropical air condenses over the brisker waters to produce fog: not little-cats'-feet fog but impenetrable walls of fog. With a light southerly or southeasterly flow of air, the fog rolls in, locking up first the outer islands and then the tips of peninsulas. Those who live "down peninsula" can often drive inland and find a warm, sunny day; the heat of the land has dissipated the fog. But on islands there is no escape.

The fog often approaches with the stealth of an Indian. If you are out on the water, your world view changes in a moment from one of passing interest at the interplay of green water, white shores, and blue sky to one of quiet, intense concentration, forcing you to mentally chart the ledges that lie between you and your home harbor.

Opposite: Whitehead Cliffs on Cushing Island, shore of Peaks Island in background.   RICK PERRY

Lairey Narrows, July 7, 1992
    Sailors used to say that there are two ways to navigate in the fog: fac-
ing forward with a Bible in hand, or facing aft with a bottle of rum. Anyone
who has spent time in the eerie opaqueness of an island fog cannot fail to
appreciate the humor and wisdom of this adage. These days, you are left
simply gripping the wheel, trusting the essential accuracy of your instru-
ments and trying to make sense of all those eerie green targets that sear the
retina. There is, alas, still plenty of room for error, as one of the captains of
the Vinalhaven ferry learned, not once but twice this past summer during
groundings of the GOVERNOR CURTIS *in Lairey Narrows, the tight, rock-*
strewn passage between two islands in west Penobscot Bay that the ferry
from Rockland must twist and turn through. After the second grounding, an
anonymous wit tacked up a large plywood sign on the north end of Lairey
Island, complete with an arrow, that read, "Keep Left."

THE PRECESSION OF THE EQUINOXES

Maine is in the zone of prevailing westerlies, a simple-enough fact that doesn't distinguish our climate from that of most of the rest of the East Coast. The systems that cause Maine's weather orig- inate to the west and move eastward. Either they come down the Saint Lawrence River Valley, thus creating southeast blows of maritime air drawn into the low-pressure trough, or they head out to sea, often near Cape Cod, to generate northeast gales. Northeasters, related to the shift in location of the jet stream, are most frequent during spring and fall, although they are not confined to these seasons. They are a trial to be endured anywhere, but more so on islands. Northeasters bring in the worst of all worlds: so-called maritime polar air. Winds both wet and cold are drawn in from the waters surrounding Newfoundland, Labrador, and even Baffin Island. You cannot weather a north- east gale in spring or fall on an island without recalling the title of a collection of poems by Ruth Moore (who was born and brought up on an island), entitled *Cold as a Dog and the Wind Northeast.* No matter how tight your house may be or how many layers of clothing you try to put between yourself and the cold-fingering rain, you feel a wet and raw easterly in your bones.

Because of the way winds clock around the low-pressure cells that produce gales, the trailing edge of a system is composed of a cold front that ushers in clearing air from the northwest—often cold enough to make you wonder if the gale itself isn't the lesser of two evils. Snapping-clear high pressure from the dry polar continental interior cascades in behind a gale. In summer it drives off the encircling fog within a matter of moments to reveal the long view, the large day; in winter it whistles day after day, churning up white combing seas that freeze on the hulls and in the rigging of boats.

Most islanders cannot help but have something to do with waterborne occupations for at least part of the year, so gales have a special meaning for them. Few island harbors are protected from both the east and the west. (Protection from the south is not as important because very few storm winds come from that direction. The really destructive blows originate in two-thirds of the compass rose, from west-northwest all the way to east-southeast.) You just pay your money and take your chances. But when the winds howl, part of you is listening to the chafe of your mooring pendant or feeling the relentless beating of the sea on wharf pilings and fish-house footings.

Allen Island, April 27, 1983
    This March, there have been light airs mixing over the cold gulf. We feel
little tendrils of southerly winds that have followed cracks in the solid wall
of Canadian Arctic highs. We lean into the wind for the feel of spring. Even

after a cold front roars through, within two to three days the sun, which is now noticeably higher in the sky, has warmed enough of the sharp frontal air to remind us that this too will pass.

Northern spring is so painfully slow to unfold, so attenuated in its promise, so delicately pasteled that if you're not watching carefully you can miss it altogether. Gray seas of leafless trees begin pulling ground sap up their limbs, up into slowly swollen buds until one day you notice that the tops of red maple trees are beginning to give the faintest rosy hue to slopes, where cold air doesn't get trapped. Poplars follow after a few weeks with shades of pale green and yellow against the tarnished pewter of their smooth and slender trunks. Against Allen's stony hillsides, the damningly faint praise of spring is sung.

On the shores of Pentecost Harbor, crowded in by dark spruces, the antics of the gulls are a better harbinger of the turning season. Their drab gray and white winter plumage takes on a brilliant sheen, and a small spot on the tip of their bills begins to deepen to a rosy red, which serves to signal the onset of their breeding ritual. With a flood of hormones coursing through their systems, they are suddenly oblivious to fishermen with whom they share a shore; they behave like foolish teenagers with jerky head bobs, wing extensions, and peals of raucous, throaty keening that issue from beaks arched skyward, as if they had just seen Persephone herself returning from the gates of the underworld.

SUMMER ISLANDS

If for substantial parts of the year the cold and wind bite deeper on islands, why do people still persist in hunkering down out there, waiting for the teeth to be removed from the bite of the dog? Part of it is habit, tradition, inheritance, and plain stubborn Yankee independence in folks too proud to say "uncle." But the better part of it is participating in the drama, the Titan-like interplay of capricious elements that serve to give all who stand and watch a primitive belief in the "will of the gods," luck, fate—call it what you will. The sea is possessed by its own mood and spirits, and men and women are almost nothing to it.

Then, too, there is the matter of summer, which many enthusiastic temporary residents of islands have discovered. Not only are there few landscapes that can match the interplay of colors on "broken islands in the sea" on a high, blue sunny day, but the Gulf of Maine is like a giant thermal sink, absorbing the warmth of the sun throughout the hot months and slowly giving it back to islands through the long months of autumn.

Lane Island, August 3, 1987

The tenor of island life vibrates at a high pitch in August. The thousands of events that change winter to late spring and short spring to a sweet summer are small and quiet. But in August all discretion seems to break loose. The young of the year are out and about. Schools of juvenile fish and tinker mackerel appear inshore, attracting bigger fish and seabirds that feed in frenzies. Lobsters in new shells start to crawl and be caught, and every boat on the Maine coast and half those on the East Coast show up in previously deserted coves and guts. It's a time of manic activity, when all things seem possible.

A fifty-foot wave breaks over the tops of trees on the south end of Hurricane Island, January 4, 1978. N. ELAM

FALL'S FAILINGS

Meted out by the sea, summer heat lingers well into October, when island flowers are still in bloom and gardens are producing long after those on the mainland have turned brown. There may be no other place where the meaning of Indian summer is so real. But then the grand precession of the equinoxes reminds us that the foliage will turn to browns and grays and finally yield to the incredible whiteness of being.

> ### Hurricane Island, October 1, 1983
>
> *A little low-pressure cell that hung around all day has just been shoved off the coast by a cold front, which leaves the autumn night sky flecked both with stars and the shining, metallic moon. It's a melancholy night, with the unmistakable hint of fall falling down, with its leaves ground into the earth mulch. It's the end of the frantic double-time of short summer nights and long, long days. A few lightly turned poplar leaves, scattered on Hurricane's bare granite, dip and spin in little wind eddies. The wind has a little heat in it, a hint of upper-prairie life and high wheat country it picked up some- time yesterday before it blew into Maine.*
>
> *I thought of the sadness to come and the bite of the wind and the sting of the hard frost in the ground. But for tonight, at Hurricane's big stone wharf, I listened to huge, black tidal water surge and lap around the oak pilings, and watched the edges of the standing waves silhouetted in moonlight out in the anchorage where eddies swirl, deep and silent.*

One day in December, winter becomes brutally quick about its business. A cold front roars through the thin fabric of the coast on towering haunches and picks your bones clean. The sea is alight with tongues of sea smoke as it gives up the last of the warmth it has harbored for half a year, and we watch and wait. On the islands, it's called "sitting on a rock."

Vinalhaven, December 18, 1995

Following All Hallows Eve, when gray November prunes the day length, and the air grows more raw and unruly with each passing week, it's pure boneheadedness not to think through the differing conditions that any day can bring. As December's aperture closes down around the fleeting edges of daylight, darkness defines the field of view. But December's days also create an eerie depth of field in which island horizons loom larger; they rise up off the water to greet you, to invite you to the heart and hearth of island winter.

NATURAL CATASTROPHES: WIND, SALT, AND ICE

The Maine coast and islands are such rough, raw, rocky, cold, and tempestuous places to live that their ecosystems must be adapted to survive periodic natural catastrophes, ranging from the yearly spate of gales that batter the coast to an occasional bona fide hurricane. Over the last three and a half centuries, three storms have been so ferocious that they make it onto anyone's hurricane scale, Beaufort or otherwise. That's an average of a hurricane a century.

The storm of August 15, 1635, was apparently the most destructive ever known on the Maine coast. It began early in the morning, when the winds picked up from the northeast and blew "with great fury" for five to six hours, driving up a huge tide twenty feet higher than normal that flooded islands and the mainland coast. Edward Trelawney, of Richmond Island in Saco Bay, wrote back to England that the storm "blew down many thousands of trees, turning the stronger up by the roots and breaking the high pine trees in their midst." The hurricanes of 1815 and 1938, though they caused great damage throughout New England, did not affect the Maine coast quite so drastically, but the damage nonetheless ran into millions of wind-thrown trees.

Aside from the obvious damage to trees, storms whose winds exceed sixty knots exact a more subtle toll on coastal vegetation. They kick up prodigious quantities of salt from the sea, which is lifted into clouds and driven overland. This spindrift dries out and kills the leaves and needles on plants. The composition of the vegetation on low-lying islands is completely dominated by those few species—such as bayberry, creeping juniper, and seaside rose—whose tough, waxy leaves and bristly stems can tolerate the constant dessicating effect of the salt-strand environment.

Storms that coincide with a high tide can work changes that defy the imagination. The storm of January 4, 1978, not only peaked with the high tide, it came on a spring high tide at that. Ten feet higher than normal, the tide caused such havoc that many coastal property owners couldn't recognize their land or find their homes afterward. As the storm raged for six hours, the rising tide was accompanied by an equalization of the barometric pressure over land and water. Just as the tide began to ebb, a cold front moved in, hard on the trailing edge of the storm; now driven by a sixty-knot northerly flow of high pressure, the abnormally high tide began draining out of the bays. For those on shore, worrying over their boats, the effect was frightening. In north/south–trending bays, the water simply disappeared, as though someone had pulled the plug in a bathtub. Boats that had held on during the morning swung around violently, and a few disappeared with the cascading tide. A dinghy that fifteen minutes before had been tied to a pier was hanging taut from its painter. It was called a "hundred-year storm," though it was not a hurricane.

Wives of fishermen also suffer through these periodic gales while their husbands, sons, brothers, and uncles are offshore, perhaps in mortal danger, perhaps not. The endless waiting and not knowing may be more damaging than any storm's lash. The histories of Vinalhaven, Islesboro, Deer Isle, Swan's Island, the Cranberries, and Beals Island—histories that contain genealogies of the original settlers—are full of the names of men lost at sea. It's a wonder that island women continued to participate in the institution of marriage. When a southeast gale struck a fishing fleet at anchor off the Nova Scotia Banks, Cape Sable became a dangerous lee shore for any schooner whose anchor line had parted. The list of the vessels that have been driven up on those shores is long enough to have earned that small island its reputation as the "Graveyard of the Atlantic."

Unusually long or severe winters also can dramatically affect island ecosystems. They reduce species diversity by reducing the availability of food for resident species such as deer, moose, otter, and ground-foraging birds such as grouse. The decade between 1810 and 1820 was Maine's coldest ten-year period since data collection began. In 1816, Maine had no summer. A late frost hit in July and the first snow fell in August. The only vegetables that grew were a few potatoes. Frozen corn was cut for fodder as islanders prepared for a bleak winter. The winter of 1816 was the first one in thirty-five years in which Penobscot Bay froze over completely to the Fox Islands and Isle au Haut; the ice was thick enough to allow passage by sleigh to the mainland to buy hay for famished livestock. In Muscongus Bay, pack ice jammed the waters out to Monhegan, which made the islands completely inaccessible to humans and other large mammals. Twenty years later, all but a few harbors east of Cape Cod were again closed by ice. Although these winters worked extreme hardships on everything alive, they also built ice bridges to the islands for smaller creatures. Fox, rabbit, hare, mice, and other furred animals not accustomed to making the marathon swim found a new route to a new world.

THE PHYSICAL AND CULTURAL SETTING: THE BAYS OF MAINE

The state's mainland has an immensely long tidal coastline. We used to say that 2,500 miles of shore collapsed accordion-like into 250 miles as the crow measures it from Kittery to Eastport. But Maine's entire saltwater interface—including the shorelines of all the islands—has actually been found to be 7,039 miles long. This measurement, taken from aerial photography that has been scanned into a computer, was commissioned by the Maine Department of Environmental protec-

D.W. SHERIDAN, *wrecked on Black Head, Monhegan, 1951.*   GEORGE PUTZ

tion, which is responsible for monitoring every discharge emptying into marine waters along Maine's immense and intricate shoreline.

The islands within this intricate immensity number 4,617 and include every piece of land and ledge that is completely surrounded by water at high tide. The island shorelines increase the overall Maine shoreline by almost a third. This long, sinuous interface is certainly good for fish, which depend on the nutrients washed off this coastal acreage, and for fishermen, who set their gear from the thousands of protected coves and bights.

The Maine archipelago is best seen from a boat. Maine's islands have always been occupied by people who know how to handle small boats: birch-bark canoes, dories, sloops, schooners, and the many variations of the Maine lobster boat. Except for a short period when steamship companies churned the waters carrying tourists between Boston and various island ports, "you couldn't get there from here" unless you owned a boat or knew someone who did. It's still almost like that. Oh, state and private ferries connect a dozen of the big islands with mainland ports, and mail boats reach a handful more. But out of forty-six thousand-odd islands . . . well, you do the arithmetic.

You simply have to have a reliable boat. And you must be able to memorize tricky channels—or, better yet, learn to navigate through the rock-strewn waters—and then put up with being wet and cold even in the warmest months of summer. Because possessing these skills and coping with these inconveniences require a lot of time and patience, island life is not an attractive proposition to most people.

Maybe it should be different, and maybe someday it will be, but for most of the twentieth century, the islands have been shared by a few fishermen, yachtsmen, and nesting birds. Before that, they were shared by a few Indians, fishermen-farmers, and nesting birds.

Getting to know Maine's islands takes a lot of time—a lifetime—and you cannot be in a hurry. Because most of the people who visit Maine come from more populous places to windward, the most logical course to follow in these pages is to proceed from west to east, downwind. And because the present look of each island is dependent on its past, this account includes a lot of history.

Isles of Shoals: From the Pen of the "Lord of the Isles"

If you are crossing the Gulf of Maine from the west and standing in to shore near the border with New Hampshire, you might see a little cluster of islands lying off your larboard side. They don't look like much until you are a mile or so off, but the Isles of Shoals quickly reveal themselves to be one of the densest clusters of islands in the larger Maine archipelago.

Named for the shoals of cod that once caused the nearby waters to ripple with their passage, the Isles of Shoals have lured voyagers for almost four centuries. Sighted by Bartholomew Gosnold in 1602 and fellow English explorer Martin Pring the following year, the islands immediately began to attract settlement interest. Captain John Smith was so taken by them during his expedition of 1614 that he referred to them as "the remarkablest isles" and named them after himself. The Smith Isles faded even as a footnote in history, undoubtedly because the first islanders were more interested in fish than in building an empire, but the islanders dignified Smith's interest by naming a cove for him—Smith Cove, on Appledore Island—permanently commemorating his visit and affection for the place.

Appledore, the largest island in the group of seven, was originally settled by fishermen from the village of Appledore on the Devonshire coast before there was even a house in Portsmouth—or Plymouth, for that matter. Although Appledore had berths for only six small ships, it prospered quickly as an island community. William Woods, the self-styled "Lord of the Isles," acted as the settlers' eloquent spokesman, and he left a vivid written account of the natural resources and society of this little archipelago. And no wonder; they were at the center of an exceptionally sweet spot in the western Gulf of Maine, from where dried fish was shipped to Spain.

Boon Island Light Station, east of Isles of Shoals.   COURTESY U.S. COAST GUARD

Across the way from Appledore, another fishing community grew up at Gosport on Hog Island (renamed Star Island two centuries later). There were soon said to be upward of a thousand fishermen and their families between the two islands at the height of the fishing season, which began in late February and lasted until "half June."

When the original grantees of this part of the New World—Sir Ferdinando Gorges and George Mason—divided their holdings, the line they agreed upon ran from the mouth of the Piscataqua River on the mainland and out through the middle of the Isles of Shoals between Appledore and Hog. It eventually became the line between the state territorial waters of Maine and New Hampshire.

By the early nineteenth century, only a few fishing families remained on the Isles of Shoals. The population stood at eighty-six in 1819 and fell to sixty-nine by 1824. For the remainder of the nineteenth century, the Isles of Shoals reinvented themselves as the premier summer island community of northern New England. The Laighton family, including their daughter, Celia Thaxter, lured the literary lights of the day—including Nathaniel Hawthorne, John Greenleaf Whittier, and James Russell Lowell—to the fabulous family hotel that dominated the landscape on these islands for three-quarters of a century.

Saco Bay: Nut Trees and Vineyards

Unlike all the other Maine bays to the east, Saco Bay has a short and broad topographical configuration, the kind you expect to find when the mainland's massive ridges of rock run parallel to the trend of the shore. Bounded by Biddeford Pool and Cape Elizabeth, Saco Bay is really more closely related biogeographically to Massachusetts than to the rest of the Maine coast. Like the stretch of the coast running southward to Cape Cod, Saco Bay's shoreline is smooth and unencumbered by caves, headlands, or multitudes of islands.

Historically, the two most important islands in this broad bay are Stratton and Richmond. Richmond Island was settled a few years before Stratton, around 1627 or 1628, perhaps by men who had accompanied the Englishman Christopher Levett in his exploration of Casco Bay four years earlier. Within a few years of its occupation, Richmond Island officially passed into the hands of an influential Bristol merchant named Robert Trelawney, who established one of Maine's early fishing and trading posts. Some of the most interesting pictures of island life, as well as the larger picture of early colonial Maine, are contained in the Trelawney Papers, the correspondence between Trelawney and his agent, Jonathan Winter. Between 1630 and 1645, several vessels were built and launched from Richmond Island, carrying cargoes of fish oil, pine clapboards, and oak staves, all of which were harvested from the islands and nearby waters. At the height of the island's prosperity, sixty men worked in its fisheries.

Two decades before Trelawney's men began working the winter cod-fishing grounds that were

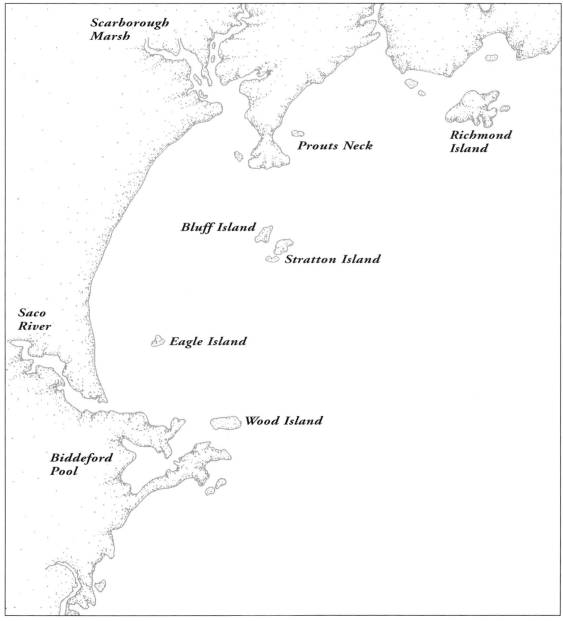

Saco Bay

handy to the island, Richmond had been visited and described by French explorer Samuel de Champlain. Looking for a more suitable location for his country's Acadian headquarters after a disastrous first winter spent on an island in the mouth of the Saint Croix River, Champlain was deeply impressed by what he found on Richmond. The island had "fine oaks and nut trees, the soil cleared up, and many vineyards bearing beautiful grapes in their season." Champlain named the island Isle de Bacchus, and he might have been well advised to try to establish a French settlement there. For some reason the French decided on the gloomier climate of the Bay of Fundy shores. They never were able to establish permanent settlements on the Maine coast.

Whatever else might be said of the early relations between the English and the Indians, trade between the two groups grew in importance. The Indians were at the mercy of the whites for supplies of powder and shot. According to John Josselyn, whose brother owned one of the earliest plantations in Saco, "It was a poor Indian that did not have two guns."

Islands were favorite spots for independent traders to set up business with the Indians, because the traders could conduct their affairs without adhering to the officially sanctioned rates of the fort trading houses. Trade monopolies in fish and fur were granted to merchants in return for their promise to set up permanent settlements. But until the late 1600s, trade monopolies were not very effective against the independents, who knew the coast and the local Indians much better.

Stratton Island was settled in 1630 by an obscure Englishman, John Stratton, who cleared the land and established a small farm. He traded a few goods with the Indians for furs, which were sent back to England to generate a small income. The history of Stratton Island after its first settlement is somewhat hard to follow. It doesn't appear as if Stratton himself stayed very long, but during the remainder of the seventeenth century, the island intermittently was a trading station.

Today, Champlain's oak and nut trees on Richmond and the small farm and trading station on Stratton have all but disappeared. Richmond is largely covered by spruce, and Stratton has recently become a multispecied heronry.

Casco Bay: "All Broken Islands in the Sea"

The Casco Bay islands used to be called the Calendar Isles because supposedly there was one island for every day of the year. Then someone counted islands and found there were 222, including all the islands that are now connected to the mainland by bridges, such as Bailey, Orrs, Sebascodegan, Cousins, Littlejohn, and Mackworth. Of all the Maine bays, Casco has lost the greatest number of islands to bridges. (One of those structures is the ingenious, one-of-a-kind Bailey-to-Orrs granite cobwork bridge, which has withstood not only coastal storms that chewed up much of the rest of the Maine coast but also a daily tidal rip that surges through the cobwork at a speed of four knots.)

Casco Bay is often described in terms of its parallel ranges of islands—an inner, middle, and outer string. Besides these three, the bay boasts another handful of islands east of Harpswell Neck. Each of these ranges represents the weathered roots of erosion-resistant ridges that have been isolated recently from the mainland as the long arms of the sea filled the intervening parallel valleys.

The first European description of Casco Bay comes from Christopher Levett's account of his voyage of 1623. He described the landscape as "all broken islands in the sea which makes many excellent good harbors where a thousand sail of ship may ride in safety." The word Casco, however, apparently derived from an Abnaki term meaning "muddy bay." Their different perceptions may be due to the fact that the Englishman Levett explored the offshore waters in a small ship looking for deep water and secure anchorages, whereas the Indians often utilized canoe routes closer to shorelines and handy to mudflats where they could dig clams. Clam digging occurred mostly in late winter, when food supplies got lean. Clams weren't harvested much in summer.

Although Levett built a fortified house on one of the inner Casco Bay islands in 1624, before

Casco Bay

he returned to England to raise money for a more ambitious plantation, the first permanent settlement within the present limits of Portland was not established until 1632, on Mackworth Island. Like Richmond Island, around the corner of Cape Elizabeth, Mackworth was ideally suited to settlement. Being an island, it was easy to defend, yet it was connected to the mainland by a low-tide bar and was therefore accessible to other settlements along the shores of the mainland.

A few of the remaining Casco Bay islands were settled during the next half century: Sebascodegan in 1639, Orrs and Bailey a few years later, Lower Goose in 1658, and Moshier in 1660. Several others were cleared to pasture livestock; the trees were cut up as cordwood and shipped to Boston. The primary settlements of the region, however, were along the Presumpscot, Fore, and Royal rivers, where deep, rich soils, adequate water, and waterpower for saw- and grist-mills were available.

The larger Casco Bay islands of Peaks, Great Diamond, Long, and Chebeague were important Indian encampments during the summer months, and in some cases year round. It seems that for the first one hundred and fifty years of English presence in Casco Bay, the settlers had neither the numbers nor the nerve to challenge the Indians for these valuable island fastnesses to which the tribes repaired to fish, collect berries, and dry shellfish.

"Chebeague" is an Indian word that translates as "island of many springs." No doubt the settlers were envious of this piece of Indian domain; lack of adequate water was one of the factors that limited settlement of these otherwise highly desirable islands. Until the end of the last French and Indian War in 1760, the whites settled only the islands that the Indians did not use. With few exceptions, they used islands at the mercy or sufferance of the Indians, who commanded the islands by virtue of their superior numbers and mobility in canoes. In 1689, for example, three to four hundred Indians gathered on Peaks Island in preparation for their successful attack on Portland. For most of the seventeenth century, the Indians simply had a more impressive navy than did the settlers. Around the turn of the twentieth century, long after natives had been forced inland, several of the larger Casco Bay islands were bought by associations of Portlanders, who turned them into other sorts of summer encampments. Forts and military installations were constructed on several of these resort islands, ostensibly to protect Portland, one of the East Coast's most important deepwater ports.

Chebeague Island, June 17, 1990

On the way across Casco Bay, we come up through Broad Sound and are hailed by Ernie Burgess, one of Chebeague's fisherman-philosophers, who fills us in on the latest news of Stockman Island. This low, brushy, thirty-acre island had been an important seabird habitat in Casco Bay for decades, until recent years when people suspected that raccoons were mysteriously introduced to make the island more marketable. In any case, the raccoons did in fact appear and clean out the gull and eider nests. To add insult to injury, Stockman's designation as a Resource Protection Area was inadvertently left off Cumberland's recent zoning map, so there is no legal way to prevent the construction of the residence that is now proposed for the island. Gunwale to gunwale in the midmorning swells, lobstermen and environmentalists ponder a strategy to keep Stockman what it ought to be: a seabird nesting habitat in an increasingly busy and built-up Casco Bay.

Merrymeeting Bay

The history of Merrymeeting Bay—the place where the Kennebec and Androscoggin rivers meet—is closely linked to the activities that have centered around its adjacent and tributary rivers. From thousand-acre Swan Island at its northern end (named for the Indian word for eagle, swanagon) to Lines Island below Chopps Point, Merrymeeting Bay is an inland sea containing an archipelago. There is no place else like it on the coast of North America.

Kennebec, the Indian word for "long, quiet water," refers to the long stretch of river below Augusta without rapids or falls. This river was the first waterway to lead explorers into the North Maine Woods. Trappers navigated the river to its head at Moosehead Lake; with a short portage (called Northeast Carry), they were able to enter the west branch of the Penobscot River and travel throughout additional thousands of square miles of wilderness in northern Maine.

The Indians planted wild rice, introduced from the Midwest, in the shallow waters of Merrymeeting Bay, hunted waterfowl, and fished for salmon and sturgeon that were migrating upstream to spawn. Two of the secondary rivers that empty into Merrymeeting Bay, the Eastern and the Abagadasset, are the only waterways in the eastern United States where the endangered short-nosed sturgeon still spawn. Merrymeeting Bay continues to be the most productive waterfowl hunting area in Maine, largely due to the abundance of forage from the wild rice that still grows a millennium after it was first introduced to the bay's tidal flats.

Between 1860 and 1900, the Merrymeeting Bay and Kennebec River area experienced another boom—exporting "white gold" (ice) from the river to as far south as the West Indies. By the end of the century, some three million tons were cut and shipped south annually; then the introduction of artificial refrigeration sent this local industry into decline.

Sheepscot Bay, Johns Bay, and Boothbay: The First Permanent Settlements in Maine

Like Casco Bay to the west and Muscongus Bay to the east, Sheepscot Bay, Johns Bay, and Booth Bay (shortened, at some point in history, from Booth Bay) are part of the all-but-weathered-away rootstocks of the ancient fold of mountains that once were foothills of the Appalachians. Except for Boothbay, the head of which is now called Boothbay Harbor, these waters are not the well-protected embayments for which Maine is most well known. They have, nevertheless, figured centrally in Maine's maritime history—particularly if we include Damariscove and Fisherman islands

Merrymeeting Bay

offshore, and Southport Island, which since 1869 has been connected intermittently to the mainland by a bridge.

Coastal and inland-based Indians—who were good seamen—regularly visited all of Maine's islands, even those ten to twenty miles offshore. Their birch-bark canoes were, according to one account, "strengthened with ribs and hoops of wood . . . with such excellent ingenious art as they are able to bear seven or eight persons, far exceeding any in the Indies." Christopher Levett wrote that the canoes "can take an incredible great sea," and Captain John Smith related that the Indians "would row their canoes faster with five paddles than our own men would our boats with eight oars."

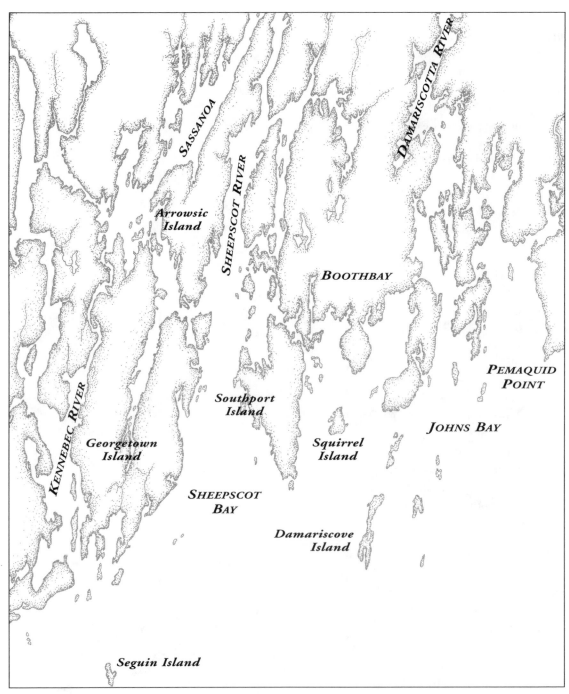

Sheepscot Bay

The Indians encountered by the Europeans used the islands as headquarters for summer hunting and fishing. From their canoes they hunted for food and used whale oil for heat, seal fur for winter clothing, and porpoise skins to make snowshoes. In early summer the men collected eggs and young birds from nesting islands at various times of the year; women and younger children dried fish, collected berries, and dug clams, which they shucked and dried by hanging them on spruce roots stretched between trees, out of reach of the dogs.

So many of the islands show signs of encampments that the Indians must have lived primarily in small family groups or clans spread throughout the bays that the various tribes controlled. There may have been a few larger encampments on the big islands. The chiefs, or sagamores, returned to the same island year after year: Cocowesco to Mackworth, Samoset to Louds Island in Muscongus Bay, and Asticou to a small cove of Somes Sound on Mount Desert Island.

Damariscove Island was probably named after Humphrey Damarill, an independent fish trader who set up headquarters on the island's southern cove before 1614. Because the hapless Popham Colony had already failed by this time, Damariscove Island has the distinction of being the site of the first permanent settlement in Maine (The Popham colonists returned to England in 1608, following the deaths of its leaders). Like Richmond Island off Cape Elizabeth, Damarill's Cove (or Damariscove) was ideally situated near the important winter cod spawning ground located a few miles off the mouth of the Sheepscot River. Along with Monhegan and Matinicus, Damariscove quickly became one of the most important fishing stations in the midcoast region. When the District of Maine petitioned the Massachusetts Bay Colony to provide some sort of government for the area in 1687, Damariscove and Monhegan were the two colonies assessed with the largest tax, a reflection of their greater populations.

The Indians who inhabited the region were of a different tribe from those who confined their summer encampments to the Casco Bay islands. We do not know very much about most of Maine's original Indians, but it appears that each river valley was the home of a separate tribe. Although different authors apply a bewildering variety of names to the various tribes, Europeans ascribed Anglicized geographic names to them, based on the river along which they lived.

The Sheepscot Indians appear to have been friendly with the English during the early years of European settlement, but whether this relationship would have lasted long we do not know, because the Sheepscots were nearly wiped out in the plague that swept through the coastal tribes during the winter of 1618–19. Archaeologists who have studied this tragedy estimate that 75 percent of these coastal Indians died during a three- to four-month period.

The Kennebec, Androscoggin, and Saco Indians—all closely related to one another—were collectively known as Abnakis, or "People of the Dawn." The other large group of Indians, whose primary contact was with French missionaries, was known as the Etchemins. They consisted of at least three tribes: the Penobscots, the most powerful tribe in colonial Maine after the plague; the Passamaquoddies; and the Maliseets, or Micmacs. John Smith estimated the total population of Abnakis in Maine at five thousand and of Etchemins at six thousand. After the plague, the total number of both groups was estimated at three thousand.

The fishermen who were headquartered on islands such as Damariscove appear to have gotten along well enough with the native inhabitants, perhaps because their ideas of property rights were similar to those of the Indians. Boundaries were loose and shifting and were enforced by controlling the resource rather than the ground itself. Relations began breaking down only after farming along the river valleys limited the Indians' access to the tidal flats.

Throughout most of the nineteenth century, the harbors of Southport Island made it one of the premier fishing centers on the East Coast. The harbors sheltered a large fleet of schooners that fished the offshore cod grounds. Southport Island was also the home port of several of the Maine coast's most successful mackerel seining vessels. When the menhaden, or pogy, fishery boomed, Southport fishermen supplied the oil and fertilizer plants in Boothbay. At one time, so the story goes, Southport Island fishermen had the highest per capita income of those in any port in Maine.

In recent years, the Boothbay region has become a necessary stop for auto-borne tourists looking for an authentic coastal fishing village; yet the waterfront is now almost entirely taken up by

Seguin Island Light Station, commissioned by George Washington in 1793 and completed in 1795, off the Kennebec River. PETER RALSTON

restaurants and other tourist establishments, and there are few fishermen left in the harbor. A tour boat runs between Boothbay Harbor and Monhegan. Several of the islands in the bay have been purchased by associations and developed as private summer colonies in a manner similar to those of Casco Bay. Some islands are private nature preserves, including Outer Heron, which has been a thriving heronry for great blues for at least the past four centuries.

Outer Heron Island, June 18, 1980

Probably every region of the world has its legends of buried treasure, and the coast of Maine is no exception. Islands are favorite places for treasures to be buried, and there is a corking good story about Outer Heron. It seems the British nobility were continually squabbling about rightful heirs, ascendancy, and other such matters. Depending on who was monarch and who had the monarch's ear, either the Drakes or the Cavendishes were recognized as the rightful Dukes of Devonshire. Elizabeth took the dukedom away from the Cavendishes and gave it to the Drakes after Sir Francis Drake returned from his circumnavigation of the globe. But James I gave it back to the Cavendishes, and so it went back and forth for centuries. The Drakes always insisted that they were the rightful heirs and eventually pressed their claim in court in the nineteenth century. The judge ruled that if the Drakes could present visible proof of their claim, the dukedom, valued at about $22 million, was theirs.

Checking through the family history, the Drakes discovered that Elizabeth had placed the signet ring of the House of Drake on Sir Francis to establish him as the Duke of Devonshire. This ring had been handed down through several generations until it had come to the Maine coast on the finger of Drake's great grandson, who sailed to Falmouth (Portland) in 1680 to deliver a load of goods. Unfortunately, while passing off the coast of Monhegan, Captain Drake had a heart attack and died. Because a Christian burial was necessary for all noblemen, his crew rowed the body ashore to Outer Heron Island and buried him, supposedly with the signet ring still on his finger.

When this bit of history was discovered by later generations of Drakes, they dispatched an expedition to Outer Heron to find the ring and claim their dukedom. Several fishermen from the area spoke of knowing the location of the grave, but when the party arrived in the spring of 1850, they could find no trace of the grave, and after some months of digging they returned to England.

Periodically it gets in someone's head to go and look for the ring again, which is still recognized by the English courts as proof of rightful ownership. Someday along the tide line of Outer Heron some beachcomber may be just lucky enough to catch sight of a piece of gold that washed down to the shore over the centuries and perhaps be able to claim the dukedom.

Muscongus Bay: "The Fishing Place"

The substantial rivers that empty into Muscongus Bay—the Saint George and the Medomak—and the bay's several smaller rivers create a lobster heaven. The rivers are warmer than the Gulf of Maine, and because the bay is shallow, the water gets warmer the farther up the bay you go. The rivers also carry a load of suspended nutrients, which, in combination with the moderate water temperatures, create ideal lobstering grounds. In fact, "muscongus" is an Abenaki word for "fishing place"—probably referring to smelt rather than lobster, according to Fannie Hardy Eckstorm, whose indefatigable efforts to unravel Indian place names give us one of the best pictures of Indian uses of the coastal islands. Anyone who has tried to navigate Muscongus Bay between June and November can confirm that it has an extraordinary number of lobster-pot buoys. It is not unheard of for the most industrious lobstermen, so-called highliners or crushers, to fish 1,200 traps.

Muscongus Bay is steeped in history; depending on whom you believe, it may have supported the first settlement in Maine. At the eastern edge of Muscongus, Allen Island hosted George Waymouth and his crew for two months in 1605 and was the site of the first religious service held in New England. But after this early flurry of activity, serious island settlement was slow to develop on any Muscongus Bay island, no doubt because colonists preferred to huddle close to the mainland fort at Pemaquid during the long, tragic Indian Wars.

Warfare between the settlers and the Indians may have been inevitable, given their nearly antithetical concepts of property rights, but the Englishmen's history of occasionally kidnapping local Indians to show to the folks back home certainly did nothing to increase the Indians' trust of whites. In 1605, Waymouth and his crew, after being shown around the islands and the mainland by the local Sheepscots for nearly two months, "suddenly laid hands upon [five] Savages, two canoes with all their bows and arrows." According to seventeenth-century naturalist James Rosier, who accompanied Waymouth aboard the ARCHANGEL, another Indian, "being too superstitiously fearful of his own good, withdrew himself into the wood" and escaped. (Two of these kidnapped Indians later returned to Maine when Sir John Popham attempted to found a settlement on Georgetown Island.) Captain Edward Harlow kidnapped three more Indians from Monhegan in 1611, and Thomas Hunt, part of John Smith's expedition of 1614, kidnapped twenty-four more Indians and sold them as slaves in Spain "for a little private gain."

Because the Indian code of law made a whole tribe (or settlement) responsible for the acts of one of its members, the activities of Waymouth, Hunt, and Harlow, among others, set the stage for later terrorist attacks by the Indians on innocent English settlements. In addition, there were indications that some Englishmen intended to make the kidnapping and selling of Indians a regular busi-

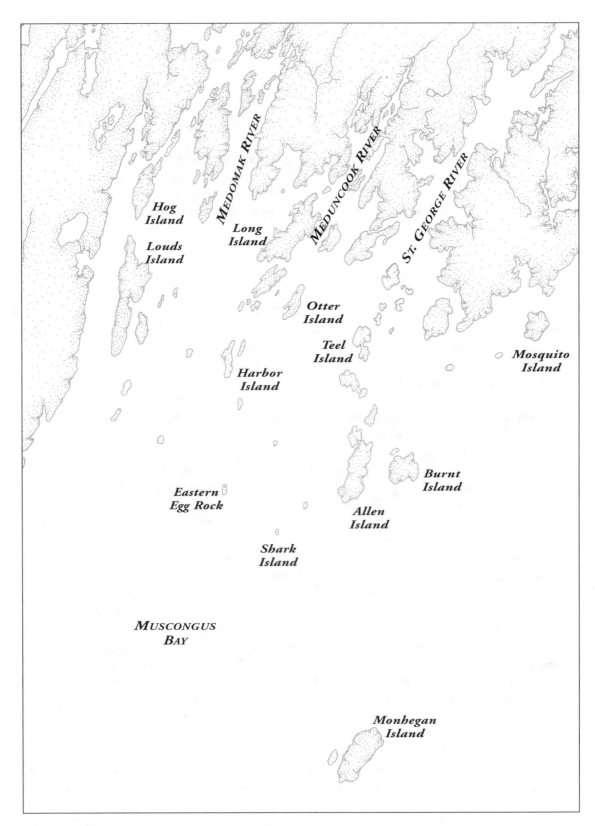

Muscongus Bay

ness. In 1675, after nearly three-quarters of a century of increasing hostility between the farmers and the Indians, the first Indian War broke out.

After a wave of Indian attacks on isolated farms in 1675, the settlers from Arrowsic and Southport islands evacuated to Damariscove and then to Monhegan. For a short time in 1676, Monhegan sheltered virtually the entire white population of the District of Maine. During the various Indian Wars, islands, including Monhegan, and Jewell and Cushing in Casco Bay, served as temporary refuges where the settlers retreated to defend themselves.

The end of the first Indian War in 1676 was a distinct victory for the Indians. Every farmhouse between Falmouth and Pemaquid had been burned to the ground; every settler had been killed, captured, or driven away. With peace reestablished, the English settlers could reoccupy their lands, but each planter had to pay the Indians a tribute of a peck of corn. The settlers also promised not to inhabit land above the tidal waters of the rivers where many Indians were now headquartered during the major part of each year. In exchange, the Indians agreed not to go out to "ye fishing islands," presumably Monhegan, Damariscove, and Matinicus.

The first peace soon degenerated into a second war with the Indians, this time with the French actively participating on the Indian side. As the conflict developed, the fighting grew into a war for control of the new continent, which had been claimed by both France and England. Pemaquid marked the easternmost stronghold of the English; Mount Desert was the westernmost part of French Acadia. For the next eighty years, everything in between, including the islands, was a wartorn no-man's-land. During the second Indian War, which raged from 1688 to 1697, nearly every farmhouse east of Wells was destroyed. Even Monhegan was attacked by a French frigate carrying a force of several hundred Indians.

During the third war, which lasted from 1703 to 1713, Maine lost between a fourth and a third of all her white settlers, but the Indians suffered more. At the end of the declared hostilities, there were no more than perhaps three hundred Indian fighting men remaining east of the Kennebec River, and several of the smaller tribes simply ceased to exist.

By 1713, Maine's white population reached its lowest ebb since the 1660s. The Town of Biddeford in southern Maine was incorporated in 1718, and only two other towns were established in the following forty years. With the exception of fishermen and fur traders, whites were nowhere to be seen in much of the territory. In 1720, for example, there was only one house standing between Georgetown and the Saint Croix River, and it was located on Damariscove Island.

A fourth war broke out between 1722 and 1725, and about a third of the remaining Indians were killed or died of starvation. At some point during the long and bitter century of wars, the conflict of terror and blood boiled over into what can only be described as genocide. The Indians, their tribes reduced to a few old men, women, and children, were hunted down like animals. Cut off from the coastal clam flats, they had only their cornfields to avoid starvation, and these were systematically destroyed. Although the last French and Indian War would not be concluded until Montreal fell to the British in 1760, Maine's Indian tribes had largely been exterminated by 1725.

Today Muscongus Bay islands are dominated by spruce forests. Many of the islands were used to pasture livestock after the Revolutionary War, when the bay region began to be settled rapidly, but there are fewer records of island farms here than in Penobscot and Blue Hill bays, to the east. It appears that the settlers of this area preferred to farm in the river valleys, where access to saltwater shipping routes was just as good and the soils were decidedly more productive.

Hockamock Narrows, July 1, 1982

Up in the inner edge, where the Medomak River spills into a corner of the bay, lies the hull of an enormous old schooner—the CORA CRESSY.

Designed to carry huge loads of up to four thousand tons, this 278-foot five-masted schooner was obsolete before she was launched in 1902, because steam-powered ships could haul larger cargoes faster. She was used primarily to carry coal from Virginia to Maine and was said to be "cranky" and hard to handle when light. Several steam donkeys and a crew of eleven men were required to hoist the gaff-rigged sails. She had such a rake forward that a bow pilot was required to guide the ship inshore.

She rode out several ferocious gales, including the March gale of 1924, in which the famous six-masted WYOMING *disappeared. The* CORA CRESSY *weighed anchor before the gale and rode out the storm offshore, whereas the strain on the* WYOMING's *anchors probably pulled the bow out of her. Nevertheless, the* CORA CRESSY *was sold that year for $3,610. After serving as a floating nightclub in Gloucester, Boston, and Providence, she was towed to her present location, where she was scuttled to be used for a lobster pound. This scheme didn't work out either. Now, supporting a small grove of birch trees on her bow, she serves as a breakwater for the two lobster pounds just to the north of her.*

Penobscot Bay: "Beautiful Ports and Channels"

It is not just an irrational regional preference to suggest that Penobscot Bay is Maine's grandest stretch of water, and its largest, measuring twenty miles across from Whitehead Island to Isle au Haut and trending thirty miles north to the mouth of its equally superlative namesake river. Encompassing almost a thousand miles of shoreline and encircling 624 islands and ledges, Penobscot Bay is also the second largest embayment on the east coast of the United States, after Chesapeake Bay.

Penobscot Bay's rich and productive waters lap against a constellation of white-rimmed, mostly granite islands. Here the cobalt blue of the sky plays against blue-green waters, and the abundance of sea life is hinted at in every tidepool. Dark spruce cling perilously close to the bony shorelines that define the margins between earth and sea. The region's first visitor to leave a record, Italian navigator Giovanni da Verrazano, was captivated by the sight of the bay's channels and islands, which he described as "all near the continent; small and pleasant in appearance, but high, following the curve of the land; some beautiful ports and channels are formed between them, such as those in the Adriatic Gulf in Illyria and Dalmatia . . ."

Penobscot Bay's topography is diverse. To the northeast, the islands are underlain by a complex of craggy, cliffy volcanics; to the northwest, they're characterized by a greenstone–green schist association. Stretching from the Muscle (probably a corruption of "Mussel") Ridge to Calderwood Neck on Vinalhaven is an evenly textured, coarse-grained gray-white granite. Such a massive outcrop of granite is called a pluton, after the Roman god of the underworld; in fact, the roots of Maine's coastal granite plutons, according to bedrock geologists, descend deep into the Earth's mantle.

After the Marquis de Vandrieul surrendered to Lord Jeffrey Amherst in Montreal in 1760 to end a century of warfare, land-hungry men and women from New England towns that had long since cultivated every available acre of land rushed to claim a piece of the eastern frontier. The amount of coming and going on North Haven Island between 1760 and 1775, for example, was phenomenal. Men came singly or with families or with groups of families. Some stayed; some went farther east; some gave up and returned to previous homes; and some went home and came back later. For the next several decades, scores of islands in the bay were settled by squatters who attempted to establish self-sufficient farms and independent fishing enterprises. Few succeeded.

Within fifteen years a new war broke out, this one a war for independence from British control of the natural resources—masts, lumber, and fish—upon which the livelihoods of Maine's settlers depended. Settlers moved to the islands for protection during the French and Indian Wars, but the process was reversed during the Revolution, when the British navy controlled the coastal waters from their stronghold in Castine, which they captured in 1779. Isolated island farms, particularly in Penobscot Bay, were easy plunder for British troops. Raids on saltwater farms by Tory privateers became so commonplace that the term "shaving mill" was coined to describe the boats that cleaned out these farms. Revolutionary patriotism among islanders seemed to be a function of their distance from Castine. The settlers on Islesboro, for example, conducted a thriving trade with the British at Castine, following the old belief that discretion is the greater part of valor, whereas settlers on the Fox Islands ambushed the British from the dense woods when patrols came ashore.

After the Revolution, the land rush resumed with the policy of paying off soldiers with land. Trees were cut and islands were burned to create pasture on even the smallest "junk-o-pork" island. By 1820, virtually every island greater than about twenty-five acres supported either people or livestock. The census for that year shows 207 hardy souls on the small islands surrounding North Haven and Vinalhaven.

After building a cabin, generally an island settler's next order of business was to build his own boat, which was indispensable for going to the gristmill or to the mainland to sell produce and obtain supplies. Eventually several families might join together to buy a coasting schooner, which was put in the charge of one of the families' sons, who would take farm goods to Boston's Haymarket.

By making do with the materials at hand, island fishermen earned a well-

Penobscot Bay

Isle au Haut Post Office.   C. Hunter, Island Institute files

deserved reputation for being supremely inventive. It was a Maine islander who invented the mackerel jig in the 1820s; another developed the seine for the mackerel fishery; a third islander figured out how to keep a huge catch alive long enough so the fish wouldn't rot before being packed or pickled in salt brine.

Beginning around 1870, island farming and fishing efforts were eclipsed by the granite boom, which swelled island populations to the bursting point. Immigrants from Scandinavia and Eastern Europe were brought to work in the quarries as the nation entered its first period of ambitious public works construction. Because granite could be transported conveniently on coastal schooners, island quarries developed earlier than those on the mainland. Most, however, persisted for relatively short periods—a decade or two to a half century, at most.

Today these granite-strewn islands are inhabited more often than not by various nesting seabirds and waterfowl. Penobscot Indian legends describe how their ancestors discovered islands by following birds. Even the most remote islands have huge colonies of fish-eating avians. Matinicus Rock, at the outer rim of Penobscot Bay, is the principal Maine residence of puffins and razor-billed auks. In 1977, only a single pair of eagles maintained an aerie in Penobscot Bay, having been pushed out of all other bays to the west; twenty years later there are five or six active nests on islands in the bay—proof of the slow progress being made to restore endangered species.

Isle au Haut, June 23, 1982, Seal Trap

Half-tide ledges make up from either side of the narrow entrance of the one-boat anchorage of Seal Trap, which means that precious few cruising yachtsmen will ever use it, and even writing about it will not alter its char-

*acter. We ghosted in on a dying southerly breeze just before sunset and put
up a dozen drake eiders in their brilliant black-and-white mating plumage. In
long, low profile, they passed so close to us at Seal Trap's narrow entrance that
we could plainly see the small patch of indescribably lovely pale green plumage
on the back of their heads—a rare sight unless you have the bird in hand.*

*Seal Trap might have derived its name from the use of this narrow,
watery cul-de-sac by Indians or early fishermen to capture seals for meat, for
the animals are abundant in the area. In fact, nearby Duck Harbor, just to
the south on Isle au Haut, was used as just such a place to capture sea ducks
during their molt, when they are flightless and gather in immense flocks that
could be herded ashore. But a local history is more poetic, if highly unlikely.
It suggests that Seal Trap was named by a French captain who was caught
off Isle au Haut's treacherous western shores during a fierce gale that threatened his vessel. Trying to claw his way off Isle au Haut's lee shore, he was
washed into Seal Trap, where he found not just any port in a storm but a
tiny harbor so completely calm that he could see the reflection of the sky.
Amazed, he named the place Ciel Trap (literally "sky trap"), and the name,
slightly corrupted, has stuck to this day.*

Today Penobscot Bay is the economic domain of a thousand or more working boats of every
size and description built to harvest everything from the delicate northern shrimp to scallops, lobsters, green urchins, red rock crabs, periwinkles, dulse, cod, haddock, hake, flounder, smelt, herring,
alewives, mackerel, pollock, pogies, skate, dogfish, salmon, tuna, eelpout, and wolf fish, to mention
some of the species that end up in fish markets throughout New England and, increasingly, the rest
of the world.

Merchant Row to Jericho Bay: The Center of the Archipelago

Although the islands in this stretch of water are not arranged in well-defined bays, when taken
together they constitute the most scenic landscapes of the entire Maine archipelago.

Year-round communities persist on Swan's, Frenchboro (Long Island), Isle au Haut, Deer Isle,
and Little Deer Isle (the inhabitants of the latter two isles still refer to themselves as islanders, even
though the suspension bridge to Sedgewick was completed in 1937). The sixty-five islands of the
Merchant Row group range in size from less than an acre to the two-hundred-and-fifty-acre
Merchant Island. All of the islands are underlain by coarse-grained pink granite, quarried in the
nineteenth century to build large public buildings in major eastern cities. With the many summer
cottages that have been built on islands in Merchant Row, this area continues to be one of the more
densely populated parts of the Maine archipelago.

One of the interesting historical patterns of settlement after 1760 on Deer Isle—a pattern that
was repeated on other islands—was that many north-facing shores were settled earlier and more
densely than southern shores. The determining feature for island farmers probably was the chilling
effect of damp fogs, which roll in off the Gulf of Maine and set back crops on seaward-facing
shores. On Deer Isle, the northern shores of Northwest Harbor and Smalls Cove were settled before
most of the island's southern shores, suggesting that the island settlers placed a higher priority on
growing crops than on catching fish. Even on Vinalhaven, a traditional fishing community from earliest times, the northern Thorofare side was settled before Carvers Harbor on the island's south side.
Another reason for this trend lies in the geological history of the area, which left the northern sides
of many islands gently sloped. Moreover, the harbors on these shores don't face open ocean or the
prevailing southwesterlies, thus providing more protection and better access.

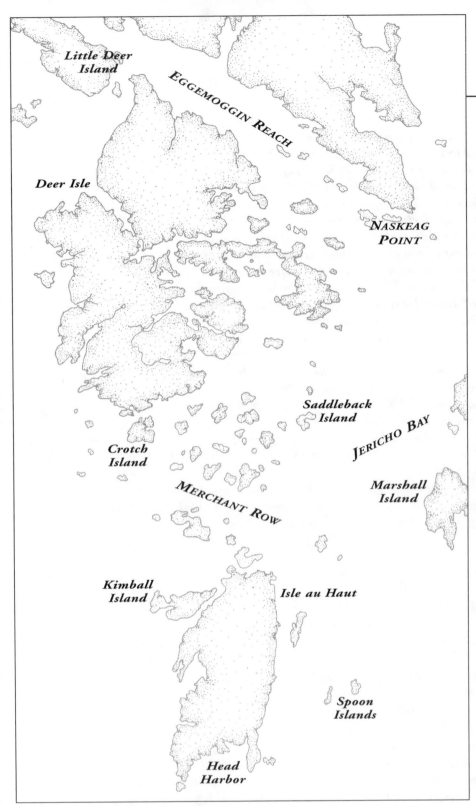

Merchant Row

The sea provided convenient access to neighboring farms and to distant eastern seaboard markets, and the islands in this region were settled earlier than most of the mainland. The settlers of Swan's Island, for instance—most of whom were sailors who served in the Revolution or the War of 1812 before becoming fishermen—used boats to visit one another's homes rather than go to the effort and expense of building a road across the island's rocky and rugged interior.

Between 1820 and 1845, many Swan's islanders were entirely engrossed in building ships, brigs, and schooners used either for fishing or to transport cordwood and lumber to market. James Swan, one of the early speculators in island real estate, offered to give ten acres of land to any fisherman who owned his own boat. The fact that Swan owned the island's tidal sawmill meant that he certainly intended to recoup his investment when islanders brought ship timber to be sawn.

As in Penobscot Bay, the islands of Merchant Row and Jericho Bay are underlain by granite. Because granite is resist-ant to the agents of erosion, which are also the agents of soil formation, the soils of these islands are among the most shallow and sterile on the coast. Some of the diversity of field and forest landscapes in Merchant Row is a result of the eighteenth- and nineteenth-century practice of burning islands to create pasturelands. The cycles of burning and overgrazing have run the shallow soils downhill, and the bleached, bare bones of the granite outcrops still poke through their thin grass skins.

In 1880, Merchant Row (like the rest of Penobscot Bay) became a world of boats carrying granite. Individual quarries, called "motions," were pounded out of hardrock on half a dozen islands in Merchant Row and Casco Passage, and major quarries were established on Deer Isle and Swan's and Crotch islands. The quarry on Crotch Island was one of the last to furnish granite to the cities of the Atlantic seaboard.

To yachtsmen today, the waters of Jericho Bay are a rock-strewn treachery, particularly in fog, when the exact location of any vessel is vague at best. To all but the herring fishermen, the silver lining is that these half-tide ledges are whelping and haul-out grounds for something like one out of every five seals that inhabit Gulf of Maine waters. Until recently, it was a rare fisherman who passed up an opportunity to practice his marksmanship on these pinnipeds, which allegedly dine on a strict and steady diet of fishermen's profits.

Johns Island (Bandit Island), June 25, 1989

We wanted to determine the status of the eagle's nest now that the island was advertised for sale, and so poked carefully along the back side of the boulder-infested lee to find a place to anchor. We skirted through a minefield of boulders to find a marker buoy at the edge of a surprising little uncharted channel, where we dropped the hook and rowed ashore.

Tucked in a spruce glade was a little log and tar-paper shack no more than twelve feet square, nearly invisible even from the shore and temporarily uninhabited. It was clear that we had stumbled onto what islanders refer to as a "bandit camp." Often built on land owned by others, these structures represent a semi-permanent pattern of survival use of Maine's islands by maritime people who live on the outer periphery of the law. Bandit-camp culture is rough and ramshackle; the condensed milk cans, the empty beer bottles, and the choice of calendar art hint of clammers who come on big tides to drink and dig. When they do, dinghies go missing from floats hereabouts.

Back in the woods, it is a good sign that eagles do not seem troubled by the outlaws—having produced a pair of young, to judge by the antic-looking head feathers that occasionally poke up from the aerie. That eagles and outlaws coexist here teases the imagination, especially because this island is up for sale. One suspects that its hosting both an endangered species and a clan of human bandits may make for a difficult real estate proposition on the island-dreams market.

Blue Hill and Frenchman Bays: The Arms of Mount Desert

No other stretch of Maine's coastal waters is defined so completely, so gigantically by the land that rises out of the sea, as are Southwest, Northeast, Seal, and Bar Harbors. So much has been written about Mount Desert Island that further attempts can only retrace old ground. Here it is enough to concentrate on some of the islands that ring the fractured granite shores of the Big Island. The bedrock of the islands surrounding Mount Desert is of a different composition than the granitic pluton that defines the rounded contours of Pemetic, Norumbega, Cadillac, and Champlain mountains. To the west, Long and Bartlett islands are primarily underlain by an ancient covering of the country rock into which the ancient volcanic vents of Mount Desert intruded. To the south, the Gotts, the Ducks, and the Cranberry Isles are composed of the hardened deposits that issued forth during millions of years of extrusive volcanic activity. To the east, the steep, austere topography of the Porcupines and Ironbound is defined by a massive inclined sheet of dark diorite that caps gently tilted older sedimentary layers. The formation looks like an inclined ramp because the islands are all truncated on their seaward sides—shaped by glacial ice, which plucked off boulders there, and undercut by the sea, which relentlessly erodes the softer sedimentary layers underneath.

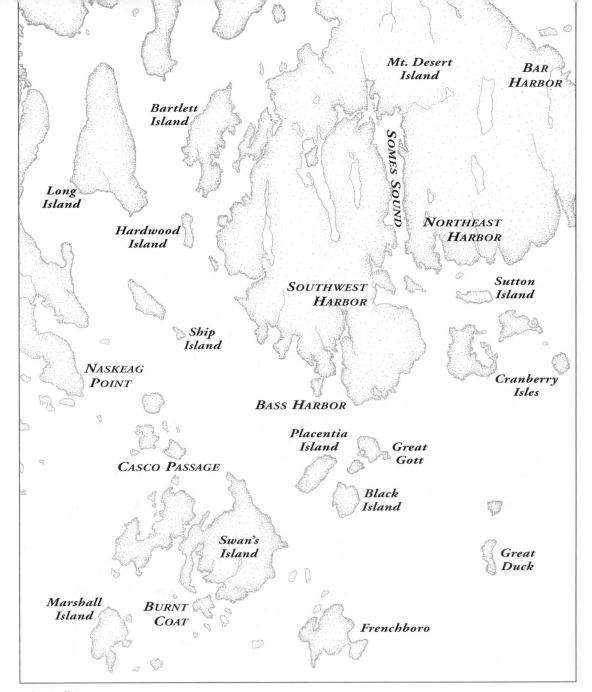

Blue Hill Bay

With the exception of Little Placentia Island, now called Great Gott, the islands of these bays were not settled until the conclusion of the French and Indian Wars. However, in 1688, when Sir John Andros, governor of the Massachusetts Bay Colony, sent a whaleboat along the Maine coast east of Pemaquid to survey French occupation, the expedition found Petit Plaisants ("Little Beautiful Island") occupied by two families. We assume this refers to the little cluster of islands around what is now called Placentia. We don't know anything about these settlers, but they must have been inconspicuous or politic enough to have avoided the enmity of both France and England, who spared no efforts to destroy each other's unprotected settlements along the coast of Maine.

Now, every May, these bays' largely uninhabited spruce forests are filled with warblers. Wave upon wave wheels in behind a change in the weather pattern, so much so that one day the woods will be alive with a thousand complicated descants when the day before all was silence enshrouded in fog. The warblers and other songbirds set up housekeeping in the dense canopies of the trees according to their flight skills and their abilities to exploit the different food niches found at given levels.

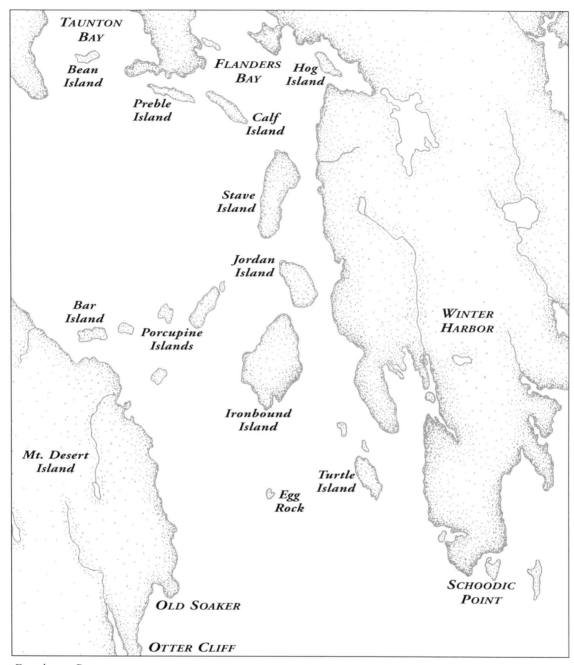

Frenchman Bay

In July, after the woods have been filled with the exacting songs of territorial males for several months, a less skillful choir takes up as the newly fledged young try to get the words right: "Old-sam pee-dee-b-d, sam-old-bodee-pee. I mean, old sam peabody, peabody, peabody," sings one enthusiastic but inexperienced white-throated sparrow.

Pigeon Hill, Narraguagus, and Pleasant Bays: "Kinda Thin"

East of Frenchman Bay one finally enters the region that can be truly called "down east." The climate here is more boreal than in southern Maine. Peat bogs and tamarack replace pine and oak forests; the fogs are more enduring and impenetrable; the society is more sparse and egalitarian. There are precious few lovely old sea captains' mansions like those in Searsport or Wiscasset. Pulp cutters, clam diggers, blueberry rakers, and Passamaquoddy Indians live on and off the land. They change occupations with the seasons and with the fluctuating prices of commodities, which are often set in distant places by people who have never been here, or if they have they knew they didn't want to be here for long.

RUNNING THE EASTING DOWN

Because the prevailing maritime winds blow from the west, it has been a linguistic convention for well over a century to say you're going "down east" when headed in the general direction of Canada, or to say you're going "up" to Boston or Portland when you're headed there or anywhere to the westward. One of the first things a newcomer to the Maine coast learns is that there is no north and south; there is only east and west. Some people think of Camden, Blue Hill, or Bar Harbor as down east, but these places are not what is meant by the term as it is used in Maine. Everyone agrees that along the shores of Washington County, where you are at the end of the line, you are down east: down east and at the raw edge of America.

Just east of Ellsworth, after passing the turnoff to Mount Desert Island if you're on Route 1—or after cruising under Acadia's sheer granite faces if you're offshore—you enter a region of increasingly strong tidal sets. The psychology of the coast changes; you not only leave one county and enter another (from Hancock into Washington), but you enter a different province of the mind. Along a partly wooded, partly barren landscape that has been worked hard for two hundred years are a handful of remote villages, each of which can be captured in the loom of a single street lamp. Offshore, narrow peninsulas finger out into the cold Fundy current to create cruel, treacherous pieces of water that force fishermen and mariners to maintain respectful sea room between themselves and the jagged shoreline. The eastern Maine coast does not open itself quickly to strangers; it lures you into the winter of its soul.

Pigeon Hill, Narraguagus, and Pleasant bays, whose waters spill back and forth into one another, are bounded on the main by Cape Split and Petit Manan Point. Petit Manan was named by Champlain, whose charts of the Gulf of Maine have given us more permanent place names—Grand Manan, Mount Desert, Isle au Haut, and Burnt Coat—than those of any other explorer. Champlain had a knack for coining appropriate descriptions of the natural features that mariners encountered for centuries afterward. Having said this, I must concede that Champlain's name for Petit Manan Island and its nearby peninsula's resemblance to Grand Manan is a little far-fetched. It looks nothing like the high, rugged shores of the Canadian island, but it must be a reflection of the relief felt by sailors after making a landfall on an uncharted and treacherous coast.

As you go farther east, even today, the settlements on the islands and along the coast get fewer and farther between. The same situation was true in 1760 when the British Admiralty began the painstaking process of charting the waters of Britain's newly expanded empire. The *Atlantic Neptune* was the first reliable marine atlas of the eastern coast of North America; it covered the waters from Florida to the Gulf of Saint Lawrence. The New England charts were produced by an engineer named Samuel Holland from on-the-spot surveys conducted between 1764 and 1773. In addition to showing water depths and the locations of all serious hazards to navigation, the *Atlantic Neptune* showed settlements and even ownership boundaries on the islands and along the coast of Maine. Obviously no expense was spared. It was virtually the only comprehensive view of Maine that existed for the next fifty years, and it gave the British an enormous advantage over the colonists in naval matters when the two countries fought the American Revolution and the War of 1812.

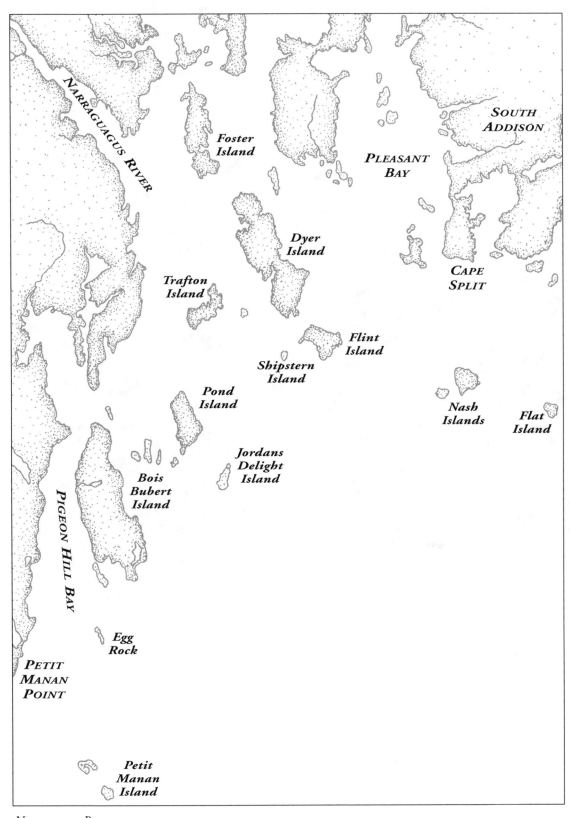

Narraguagus Bay

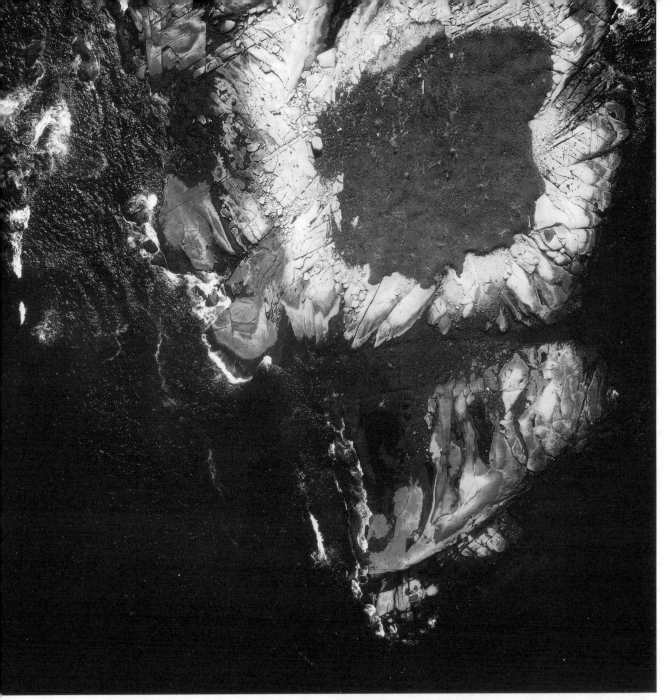

Eastern Island's broken granite shores, Eastern Bay off Jonesport.

COURTESY MAINE DEPARTMENT OF INLAND FISHERIES AND WILDLIFE

East of Schoodic Point, however, even the information from the *Atlantic Neptune* becomes rather sparse. In all of Narraguagus and Pleasant bays, the only islands correctly named in the *Neptune* are Petit Manan (Champlain's landfall), Bois Bubert (literally "the woods of Bubert," an unknown Frenchman), and Shipstern. Flint and Norton islands are misplaced, and the mariner's most important landmark, Pigeon Hill, is located on Dyer Neck, one peninsula to the west. Most of this confusion reflected the fact that the area was so sparsely settled that reliable information for local place names was hard to come by.

Cape Split, July 27, 1982

We rounded up into the small lobster harbor of Cape Split. On the eastern shore, Oscar Look, a lobster dealer whose family has sold fuel, lobsters, and groceries from a wharfside establishment for many generations, trades gossip with the few hundred people who make up the village of South Addison and dispenses wisdom to anyone who cares to listen.

After we fueled up, Oscar Look couldn't help himself and so volunteered a story from the day before. He'd been interrupted by an officious, overly shipshape yachtsman looking for ice and lobsters. In a place like Cape Split, almost an island unto itself, there is a fine art of presenting yourself on the water; if you don't know what you're doing or are in a hurry for service, especially during the lobster season when working boats are also exceedingly busy, you are subject to being taken down a notch or two, or more. The yachtsman had been rude. It was nothing so much that he said directly to Oscar, but he had yelled at the crew when landing at the float, had gotten in the way, had then become impatient, and had generally conveyed a feeling that he might not be quite as water-wise as he thought. After taking on his supplies, the yachtsman inquired about a mooring (there were none) and then asked whether there was enough water for him to anchor across the harbor in a little cove.

"Well," said Oscar, running the possibilities through his mind and calculating it all, "yes, plenty of water," knowing the chart read six feet and the boat drew five. But he also knew, as the yachtsman did not, that they were just coming on moon tides, which ran two feet higher and lower, and would be low at around 4:30 the next morning.

Sure enough, the following morning the yachtsman came back by Look's wharf, all steamed up, and complained about grounding out in the middle of the night. When Look nodded knowingly, the yachtsman said, "But I thought you said there was plenty of water."

"Sure, there's plenty of water there," said Look, "it's just spread kinda thin."

The three large river systems that empty into these bays are still critical runs for anadromous (Greek for "up-running") fish, such as alewives, smelt, and striped bass. But the Narraguagus River also supports one of the most famous Atlantic salmon fisheries left on the East Coast. As such, these fish are at ground zero for the future of the Endangered Species Act, which will be argued over issues of the genetic integrity of the remaining wild runs of salmon, such as the salmon on the Narraguagus. For decades, the U.S. Fish and Wildlife Service has been stocking the river with hatchery-raised salmon smolt as a stock-enhancement technique and a boon to an elite corps of put-and-take anglers who have invested tidy sums to be there fishing.

These fish runs explain not only the variety of homemade fish weirs or traps—which have in their day provided small fortunes for the fishermen who correctly guessed where to place them—but also the diversity of fish-eating birds that nest here. One small island halfway up Narraguagus Bay hosts no fewer than six nests of the normally territorial osprey.

Eastern and Western Bays: Subarctic Ecosystems of Beals and Great Wass Islands
The farther east you go, the more subarctic the coastal ecosystems look. Blueberry barrens are interspersed with tamarack swamps and bogs. Rare Arctic flowers occupy the extreme tips of islands and peninsulas, where the climate is raw, cool, and damp for all but one or two months of the year. Probably because of the long winters, the area was never rich or prosperous. Instead of lovely old mansions built by clipper ship captains, there are the small one-and-a-half-story Cape Cod houses of fishermen, woodcutters, and even some outlaws—men who keep alive their own traditions, feuds,

Eastern and Western bays

and private codes of justice. In the old days these men were called pirates, and there are still a few left, proud to use the appellation.

Champlain, who was so successful with his place names, stopped in these waters on his second coastal voyage. Naval historian Samuel Eliot Morison believed that Champlain dropped anchor in the Cows Yard between Head Harbor and Steel Harbor islands, which is still one of the few protected deepwater anchorages east of Schoodic Point. Champlain named the islands Cape Corneille, or Cape Crow, for the black birds that made their presence known to him in raucous fashion. Cape Corneille is now known by the less attractive name of Black Head. The birds he saw could have been either crows or ravens, which associate with each other on the islands; ravens are generally solitary, except on winter feeding grounds. Crows, on the other hand, use islands as roosting grounds and are occasionally seen in immense numbers. Flocks of more than a thousand crows are still seen winging their way across the waters offshore when the evening lights begin to flicker. Group after group heads for thick copses of island spruce, where they all roost in scores of little "murders," relatively free from two- and four-legged predators.

The waters of Eastern and Western bays surround four large islands—Beals, Great Wass, Steel, and Head Harbor—which together form the easternmost granite pluton of the Maine coast. Beals Island was the last coastal island to be ceded to the mainland when a bridge was arched over the swift tidal waters of Moosabec Reach in 1957. The smaller islands around Beals, like those in Merchant Row, have been burned and grazed for upward of a century, and many today still look bony.

The ledgy waters of Eastern Bay have remained important haul-out grounds for a large number of harbor seals. Most of the largest haul-outs used to be located just beyond the accurate range of a

The community launches a new lobster boat at Beals Island, 1984.   B. DODGE

rifle shot, but today they are nearly everywhere as a result of the Marine Mammal Protection Act of 1972, which made it a federal offense even to harass seals or other marine mammals.

THE REACH: THE WORLD OF SMALL PERFECTIONS

Moosabec Reach, separating Jonesport from Beals Island, is the location of one of the strongest tidal currents in North America. At peak flood or ebb on a moon tide, when celestial bodies line up to exert a pull on all biological rhythms as large as the sea and as small as the heart, the velocity of the seawater pouring through this narrow submarine canyon can exceed six knots. Few rivers near the sea run as fast or as strong. In the days of sail, six knots was a speed that coasting schooner captains dreamed of making on a broad reach in a fresh breeze; here on the Moosabec, a schooner clipping along at that speed could be brought to a standstill.

It is no surprise that lobster boats designed for power and speed reached perfection along these shores when dory and sloop were replaced by motorized craft in the pursuit of the world's most highly prized shellfish. Fishermen designed their boats to be powerful enough to negotiate the tides in the convoluted channels, guzzles, ledges, and eel ruts of the half-thousand islands and ledges in this corner of the Gulf of Maine.

More than the tides are at work here; a single-minded pursuit of small perfections runs deep in the traditions of many of these isolated communities, as I slowly came to learn. The centuries-old maritime attitudes are mirrored in activities such as the small-school championship basketball teams that Jonesport-Beals consistently fields or the neatly painted exteriors of fishermen's Capes that line the shores of Moosabec Reach and cluster at the head of the tide at Steuben, Milbridge, Harrington, Machias, Cutler, and Pembroke.

Today there are fewer boatbuilding shops on the shores of Beals Island than there were fifty years ago, and only one is devoted exclusively to building traditional wooden lobster boats. The rest are resigned to the steady if less satisfying work of finishing off the wooden pilothouses of fiberglass workboats. But the dominance of workboat fever in this small community is as pervasive as it was ninety years ago when Edwin Beal designed the first fantail-sterned boat with an enclosed cabin to chase lobster faster and better. Boatbuilding and lobster catching are still, after two hundred years of official history, the two passions of these twin towns along the Reach.

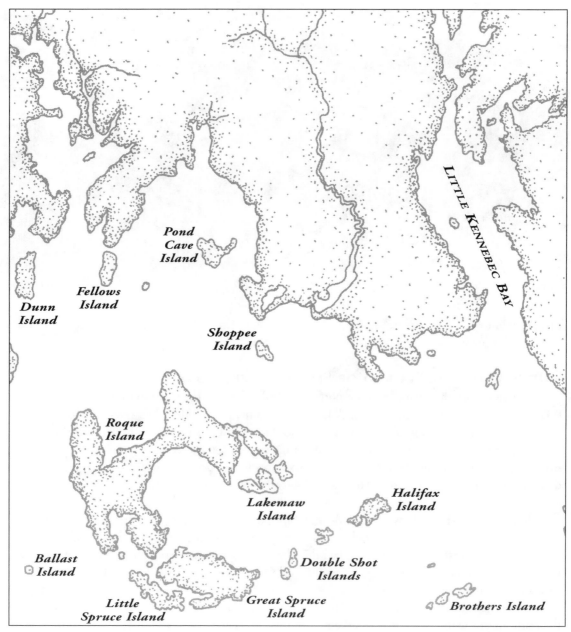

Englishman Bay

Englishman Bay: Puffins or Rogues?

No one knows the names of the first Europeans, English or otherwise, to settle on the islands in this bay, but by 1769 there were two log cabins on Roque Island, the largest island in Englishman Bay. Island place names often reveal something of the islands' history or ecology, but for most of the islands in the Roque group, the derivations are conflicting and obscure. Great and Little Spruce present no problems, except that they were called Parson's and Rough's islands in two different editions of the *Atlantic Neptune*. Double Head Shot is a topographic reference, and Halifax must have been named by an Englishman. Anguilla sounds more Spanish or Portuguese.

In the case of Roque itself, Morison has suggested that it may be an abbreviation of Isle des

Roque Island landing, Englishman Bay.   RICK PERRY

Perroques, a name that French explorers gave to places frequented by the "sea parrots," or puffins, they found on the islands of the North Atlantic. Although there is no doubt that puffins were once found on several other Maine islands beyond the few to which they are now confined, it is unlikely that they would have nested on Roque itself, because they are burrow dwellers and prefer exposed sea cliffs. Brothers Island at the outer edge of Englishman Bay or Libby Island at the entrance to Machias Bay would have served better. Another problem on Roque is its mainland connection by a low-tide gravel bar until 1805; this would have been an avenue of entry for all manner of predators, chiefly raccoons, which are deadly to puffins.

A more plausible explanation for the derivation of the name Roque is that it is a corruption of Rogue Island, referring to its use by pirates, known then as privateers, who raided passing merchant ships. In fact, there is a record of one John Rhoades, who headquartered his pirate fleet at Machias in the early 1700s and conceivably used the high headlands of Roque to post lookouts. On a clear day, Mount Desert is visible from the summit of one of the promontories.

Among today's yachting fraternity, Roque Island is most well known for its magnificent Great South Beach. There is also a belief among yachtsmen that upon completion of a successful passage east of Schoodic—where secure anchorages are difficult to find, fogs are more prevalent, and coastal towns are full of skeptical inhabitants—one has earned entry into an exclusive club. It is more a rite of passage than a sailing passage. Once anchored off the long, arcing, white, sandy beach, which stretches for nearly two miles between the shoulders of two immense headlands, you can congratulate yourself for a fine bit of navigating. Of course, in these days of fancy navigational gear, the challenge is not quite as real as it was twenty to thirty years ago, when the mystique of "Roque or broke" was prevalent. But the reward hasn't changed much: Great South Beach is as surprising and pleasing a landform as one could hope to find on this rocky, fog-bound coast.

No one has adequately explained why there is such a long, white, sandy beach here and not another one like it until Small Point at the mouth of the Kennebec, 150 miles farther south. A good guess, though, is that the two headlands of Roque trapped a massive tongue of ice as the glacier retreated across the landscape thirteen thousand years ago. The melting ice dropped its load of sand

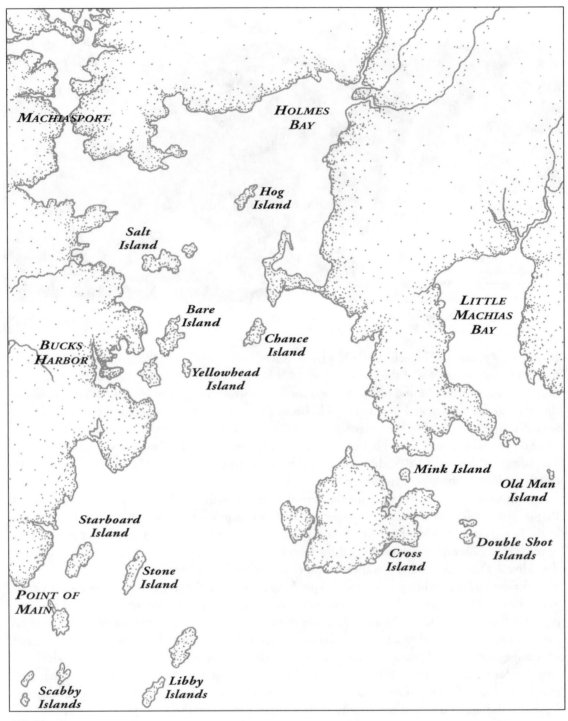

Machias Bay

and gravel, which has been held in place and protected from the onslaught of storm seas by the unique arrangement of the fringing islands. Although the sand moves up and down the beach over the years, transported by harbor currents, it is, if we can speak of shifting sand in such terms, quite stable. If the voyage from Schoodic to Roque is a rite of passage, Great South Beach is material for myth and legend.

Machias Bay: Volcanic Arches and Caves

Machias is an Indian word that describes the "bad little falls" of the Machias River, where the present town is located. Machias was settled earlier than many other parts of the coast because of the commercial possibilities afforded by the easily harnessed waterpower. It was used to saw enormous quantities of timber into boards, shingles, clapboards, shooks, and deals for the export market by the early settlers of Machias.

The names of the islands at the entrance to the bay derive from some of the town's earliest inhabitants—Stone, Libby, and Foster. It's hard to say how Scabby Island at the western edge of Machias Bay got its name, though it may have been given in the same spirit as Penobscot Bay's Ragged Arse Island, a wry fisherman's version of "Racketash."

The Machias Bay islands, like those of Englishman Bay, have a more rugged and forbidding topography than islands farther to the west, reflecting the change in bedrock that underlies the coast east of Jonesport. The southern shores of most of these islands show needle-shaped pillars of brittle, fractured volcanic rock cut through with dikes formed by later intrusions of other igneous rock. The softer rock of many dikes has eroded away, leaving narrow, vertical-walled crevices and a maze of arches and caves that discourages exploration on foot. In fact, the rugged terrain and difficult access to foot traffic along the shore of Cross Island, the largest of the Machias Bay islands, was a burden for the crew of the lifesaving station that was built there in 1879. The men who maintained their vigils along this exposed shoreline had long and time-consuming hikes to get back to the anchorage where their lifesaving boats were kept. Crews patrolled night and day, through rain and gale, watching for foundering vessels off the island's rugged perimeter. Telephone stations were located at various points along the shoreline of this fifteen-hundred-acre island to connect its farther reaches with the lifeboat station.

Cobscook Bay: Oil, Eagles, and Salmon

Cobscook Bay is distinct from other sections of the Maine coast. Here the old river valleys run northwest-southeast, or perpendicular to the trend of bedrock in Casco, Sheepscot, Muscongus, and west Penobscot bays. Cobscook is a system of concentrically curving bays, peninsulas, and islands formed from the partial submergence of these arc-shaped valleys and ridges carved in folded shales, slates, and sandstones. When the sea level rose following glaciation, it flooded a cross valley that connected the inner and outer longitudinal valleys to create the topography we see today.

Eastport looks over one shoulder at Canada and the other shoulder at Lubec across Cobscook Bay, separated by a ten-minute boat ride or a forty-minute looping drive through the unorganized townships of Whiting, Pembroke, Dennysville, and Perry. In the early years of the Republic, when Maine's merchant marine was recovering from the destructive privateering attacks of the Revolutionary War, the domestic fleet was crippled by an act sponsored by the nation's farm-oriented president, Thomas Jefferson.

The Embargo Act of 1807 immediately created an illicit smuggling trade down east, one that was headquartered in, but by no means confined to, Eastport. All manner of sailing and rowing craft carried cargoes across the border into British-controlled Canada. Captain Samuel Hadlock, of Little Cranberry Island off Mount Desert, dried his catch of cod on the coast of Labrador and sailed directly for Portugal, where he sold the fish for a high price and returned with salt and lemons. Hadlock made out so well on the enterprise that he ordered a new schooner, which he named HAZARD. In the future, whenever there was money to be made in an illicit trade, some mariners

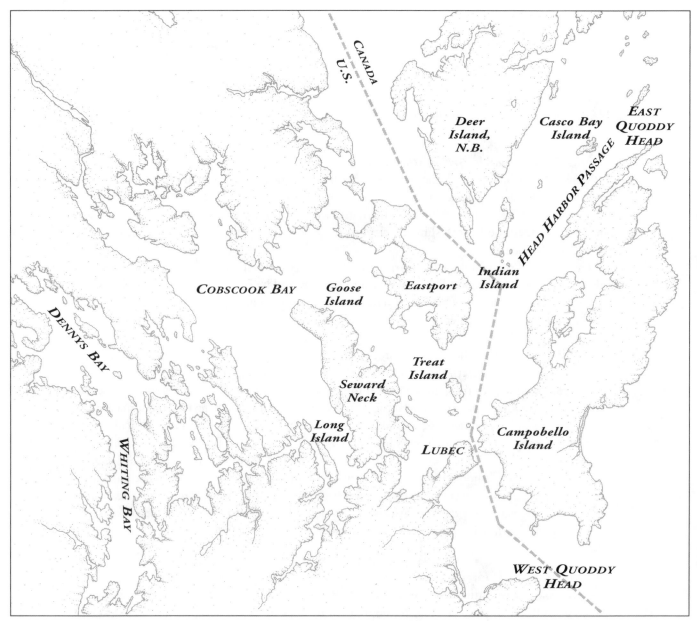

Cobscook Bay

would be at hand to take advantage of the quick profits to be made by those who knew the waters.

Cobscook Bay is an integral part of Passamaquoddy Bay, known for the power potential of its enormous tides—up to twenty-four feet when moon and sun line up twice a month. During the 1970s and 1980s, Cobscook Bay was front and center in the public discussion of whether or not the Pittston Company would build an oil refinery in Eastport. Of the many points of discussion in the heated public debate, none was more central to the outcome than the effect the refinery might have on Cobscook Bay's population of bald eagles. The eagle had been declared an Endangered Species—the first bird species in Maine to receive this form of federal protection.

Depending on the year, eight to ten pairs of eagles maintain nests along the shores and on the islands of Cobscook, away from the disturbances of civilization and near the productive fisheries that the waters of the bay support. During the lowest point in Maine's eagle population, in the 1970s, Cobscook Bay was the only area in the state where the eagles were reproducing fast enough to offset their annual losses. The fear, of course, was that a refinery—either by its daily presence or as a result of an oil spill—would harass this flourishing population. For its part, Pittston presented a disingenuous plan to protect the eagles in the case of a spill. They would not allow any of them to eat fish contaminated by the spill, but, like some kind of corporate Pied Piper, would lead the eagles off into supposedly uncontaminated areas and feed them there. You only had to imagine their technique: "Here, eagle, eagle, eagle . . ."

Falls Island, October 22, 1986

Shortly after the gray morning sky broke over the Island Institute's boat, FISH HAWK, we headed in through the narrow passages that separate the Fundian outer bay from the secret little shoal-draft gunkholes of South, Straight, and Whiting bays. Cobscook's unusual geomorphology and its hundred-isled interior, combined with Fundy's legendary tidal engine, produce watery landscapes and ecological assemblages like nowhere else on earth. The tide, at full flood running six knots past places like Falls Island, changes the landscape visibly almost minute by minute.

This huge lunar wave drives deep into Washington County's forested interior and touches on a corner of Moosehorn National Wildlife Refuge, which was purchased at the instigation of Franklin Delano Roosevelt, who probably coasted these same shores from his Campobello redoubt.

Uncounted acres of fringing salt marsh leach their nutrients over mudflats so vast that the hundreds of clam diggers who depend on this prodigious productivity actually travel by all-terrain vehicle from flat to flat and back to the main. Along the entrances of these huge flats are bolder promontories such as Coggins Head and Horan Head, where twenty-eight-foot tides wash

Matinicus Harbor, 1887, with fish drying "flakes" or "stages" and cordwood for the herring smokehouse. Off Wheaton Island, in the background, are fishing schooners. ISLAND INSTITUTE FILES

against sheer cliffs on which cling a marine biologist's bonanza of normally subtidal invertebrates and seaweeds exposed nowhere else at the earth and air interface.

And if all this grandeur were not enough to silence even the most restless soul, the cautious stewards that presently preside over air, isle, and water are seals and eagles that also live off the bounty of this system.

The full autumn days sped by too fast for us along this remarkable, almost unknown coast. The last day before heading back out into the Fundy Channel, while cataloging the wild eastern shore of Straight Bay, we saw the fluttering orange of surveyor's tape crisscrossing Coffin Neck. This discovery left us feeling that if we could have but one wish for this coast, it would be that some beneficent philosopher-king would declare the place a biosphere sanctuary where wildness would not be tamed and where our civilized souls could be turned out for momentary glimpses into the divinity of an enclosed, tiny, infinite wilderness.

Since the Pittston Company refinery was defeated, a new industry has grown up around the bay with the potential to pit environmental groups against a new breed of fishermen. Raising farmed Atlantic salmon in ocean net pens in the waters off Eastport and Lubec has become a huge business, employing hundreds from among Washington County's most isolated communities. Today the question is not eagles vs. oil but whether the millions of farm-raised Atlantic salmon that swim in pens endanger the native-run stock of Atlantic salmon that apparently still annually make their way up the Dennys River, at the head of the inner bay.

At the heart of the political debate here, no less bitter than the oil debate of two decades ago, is the arcane biological question of whether the Dennys River run of salmon is indeed a genetically distinct stock. If so, under the Endangered Species Act it must be preserved at all costs—the official position of the U.S. Fish and Wildlife Service and the unofficial position of anglers who still pull thrilling, silvery fish out of the river each year. Or have Dennys River salmon already been turned into a mongrelized subspecies after decades of publicly supported introductions of non-Dennys salmon to the river by the very federal agency, Fish and Wildlife, that is trying to force the aquaculture industry to pay for the agency's past mistakes? The latter has been the official view of Maine's Governor Angus King and industry heavyweights, who fear that recognition of a subspecies of any variety, from butterflies and other insects to salmon and wolves, will mean that vast sections of Maine will be locked up in wilderness-like reserves forever, while hungry people can only stare in from the boundaries.

Treat Island, September 23, 1986

Harris Point, on the back shore or eastern side of Moose Island (better known as Eastport), makes out into Friar Roads to create the kind of intricate point and cove geography where for millennia herring have mysteriously appeared inshore in huge schools to feed. And for about half a millennia, it seems, members of the Harris family have been devising all manner of means to catch the slippery herring, from brush weirs, to stop seines, and, lately, to large purse seines. Their catch has been smoked, canned, or salted on local wharves for either lunchbox fare or lobster bait. Now they are raising salmon and Donaldson trout (a steelhead trout hybrid) in ocean pens from tiny smolts to eight-pound adults.

George Harris, with his two sons, Lee and George Jr. (or "Butchie"), are

Herring catcher, Eastport, circa 1880.   COURTESY MAINE STATE MUSEUM

mending nets that are strung like holey laundry between the end of the house and the rear fender of their Ford pickup when we arrive to talk about fin-fish aquaculture. George says simply, "We've been in the fishing business for a long time, and we've done about everything you could do." Squinting his eyes in recollection, he recounts the family's fish fortunes.

"I started by going groundfishing—a little trawling, a little hand lining. But that's completely gone. Then we went into weir fishing forty years ago. Eleven sardine factories were here then, plus the places [where] they put up vinegar-cured fish—at least five or six places were here in Eastport and another seven over to Lubec." He gestures across to the other shore on the neck just north of West Quoddy Head. "Then there were all the smoked-herring places. Way back, every cove had a herring smoke shack or box; you'd skin them, smoke them, and trade them for groceries." He adds somberly that their fifteen weirs haven't seen a single herring in three years. With Lee and Butchie listening in to his recounting of "The Book of Harris," George says with finality, "We've come along with the times and changed with the fishing; and now we can see the change coming with aquaculture."

This debate about aquaculture's effect on native-run salmon is probably as good a place as any to underscore that during the past twenty years environmental issues are less and less about good guys and bad guys and more and more about larger issues such as what protecting biodiversity really means.

3

Island Vegetation:
Yew, Hazel, "Aspe," and Spruce

We stayed the longer in this place, not only because of our good Harbour (which is an excellent comfort) but because every day we did more and more discover the pleasant fruitfulness; insomuch as many of our Companie wished themselves settled here, not expecting any further hopes or better discovery to be made.

—James Rosier
True Relation of the Voyage of George Waymouth to the Coast of Maine, 1605

THE ECOLOGY OF FOG

The long fingers of the sea comb through island networks of air and soil to create special worlds not often found on the mainland. Fantastic forests, as from an *Alice in Wonderland* dream, are shaped by airborne particles of salt kicked up by a storm sea and implanted in the young bark of spruces. The bark swells in physiological tumult from the salt stress and produces burls—rounded globes that protrude from the trunks and limbs of trees like bowling balls.

The composition of island vegetation is dominated by the influence of cold Arctic-born water currents, which are described in more detail in Chapter 9. The Nova Scotia Current cycles up and over the Scotian Shelf and Brown's Bank from the east and is deflected first to the north by the Coriolis force, which derives from the spinning of the earth and deflects any body of water, air, or whatever in a trajectory to the right in the Northern Hemisphere. This Scotian current is then deflected southwesterly at Grand Manan Island, where it becomes the Eastern Maine Coastal Current and is discernible all the way to the tip of Cape Cod.

Where warm southerly air later in the season piles over the cold water, fog is generated. Day in and day out, somewhere in the Gulf of Maine there is fog. It rolls in when the winds are light and southerly, sometimes on the tide, to envelop the islands from the outer edge of the archipelago to its interior. The fog is more persistent and its eerie qualities increase against the gradient of the Maine Coastal Current and its source of cold waters off Grand Manan. The pea-soup fogs of the midcoast give way to down east Maine's "dungeon thick" fogs, which require master-mariner–level navigation to avoid the quirky ledges in the channels off Jonesport.

In ecological terms, fog provides an additional ambient source of water for a variety of lichens, mosses, and ferns, which are capable of extracting moisture directly from the air. Forming lambent emerald carpets atop rocky isles, these plants constitute an important part of island forests. Old-

Opposite: Burls result from salt stress on island spruce.   RICK PERRY

Boreal forest ferns and spruce.

RICK PERRY

man's beard (*Usnea* species), locally called Spanish moss, is a long, wispy, gray-green lichen that hangs from the limbs of fog-exposed spruce and gives them an ancient, battered look even when the trees are young and thriving. The forest floor on islands is carpeted with miniature cities of lichens, which are part algae, part fungi. Various shield lichens (*Parmelia* species) are set among gracile sprigs and rounded thalli (shoots) of reindeer, ladder, spoon, goblet, and scarlet-crested lichen (all species of *Cladonia—C. rangiferina*, *C. verticillata*, *C. gracilis*, *C. physiata*, and *C. cristatella*, respectively). One of these rock-encrusting lichens is the beautiful, vibrant yellow and orange *Xanthoria*, which looks like spilled paint from the tide line to the height of the land. Hairy cap, broom, pincushion, and sphagnum mosses are interspersed throughout the lichen growth. When this landscape is viewed on hands and knees, it looks Lilliputian and slightly dreamy.

Lichens perform a more important ecological function than merely making one wonder what it must be like to be little. The first growth of any sort to colonize bare rock, they secrete a weak organic acid that begins to dissolve the rock and initiate the process of soil formation. Little bits of soil collect in the crevices and crannies, facilitating settlement by a variety of other plants with more demanding requirements. Without lichens, many of the Gulf of Maine islands that support luxuriant forests would have remained as bare as the days when the glacier scraped them clean.

McGlathery Island Forest, May 12, 1982

McGlathery's interior is one of the true enchanted forests of the islands of Maine. The red spruce are tall and straight and almost completely close out the sky. The forest is carpeted with either a dense bed of spruce needles or lush lichens, mushrooms, and mosses. You can easily lose all sense of time and direction while wandering through these extensive forests and suddenly finding yourself in an extensive meadow amid the remains of a nineteenth-

century farm. Hidden from view, this meadow and farm site, complete with an old foundation and the same species of wildflowers that grew in the dooryard over a century ago (pearly everlasting and wild mints), bear silent witness to a way of life that has almost ceased to exist on the islands.

ARCTIC FLOWERS

The cold winds blowing off the Gulf of Maine create a boreal climate in May and June. Because Arctic species bloom earlier than other native species and can set seed more quickly under adverse conditions, they have leapfrogged down the chain of outer islands much farther south than on the mainland. In ecological terms, they have filled a vacant temporal niche. An ecological "niche" is just a concept, part of the accepted ecological doctrine these days, but it is useful for explaining certain phenomena.

It's easiest to explain with reference to animals. Take the passenger pigeon, which was a colonial-nesting forest bird that fed on forest insects until its habitat was greatly reduced and its numbers were decimated by market hunters. When the passenger pigeon became extinct, the seeds and insects that supported the original population were still alive and well. The concept suggests that sooner or later, something will utilize these resources—something will fill the passenger pigeon's niche. (In fact, the starling has most completely filled the niche.)

Arctic wildflower species are rare in Maine, where they are at the extreme southern end of their range. But they are among the most beautiful of island flowers. Even their names are lovely: pale oyster leaf (*Mertensia maritima*), bird's-eye primrose (*Primula laurentiana*), a small gentian (*Lomatagonia rotatum*), Greenland sandwort (*Arenaria groenlandica*), mats of astringent crowberry (*Empetrum nigrum*), and the loveliest, most delicate of all the Arctics, roseroot stonecrop (*Sedum rosea*). The pale blue-green leaves of roseroot alternate in closely packed layers up the stem of the plant, which grows in rounded clumps. The margins of the fleshy oval leaves are wavy.

There is an island east of Schoodic Point, Jordan's Delight, whose sheer, roseroot-covered, sixty-foot cliffs subtly change color as the flowers bloom and set seed. Roseroot is dioecious—that is, the male and female flowers are borne on separate plants. The yellow-tipped male flowers appear shortly before the red-tinged female flowers, which ripen into orange seed capsules. The cliffs on the island pulse in shades and combinations of yellows, reds, and oranges as the season progresses; it is indescribably beautiful.

Jordans Delight Island, August 28, 1996

Jordans Delight looms off the bow of RAVEN, *the Island Institute's thirty-seven-foot vessel, as the first sight in the scaling fog. The island is a quarter mile away on a bold shore. Along the west side of the island, the guillemot-inhabited cliffs are a splendor of unexpected color—the orange-gold* Xanthorium *lichen on the dark gray gabbro backdrop of sheer bedrock rises a clear fifty-five feet from the deep green waters below. On these outcrops and ledges, where the North Atlantic's smallest alcid, the scarlet-footed guillemot, tumbles off its nests most of the summer, the late-summer set of lush roseroot stonecrop's flowers are slowly fading,*

The sight of a second new house on this superb wildlife island is startling; the new house is even larger than the "boathouse" on the southern cliffs we first saw last year. A two-story, gabled, shingled cottage heaves up into view above the sea arch, hunched down and gigantic all at once. People here remember back fifty years or more when a stubborn peat fire got started and smoldered underground for years in the "mink soil" of the island's deep organic deposits. The slow burn extinguished itself only when it ran out of peat, having burned down to near bare rock. Only seabirds have cared to nest here. Now the seabirds have given way to newcomers, reminding us that to everything there is a season and that the season of seasonal development is also heading east.

THE BOREAL FOREST

The forests of the islands are composed primarily of spruce. White spruce, or "cat spruce" (because of the odor of the sap when the tree is cut), the most salt tolerant of the spruces, is found along the edges of the islands; red spruce crowds island interiors. Balsam fir, an important component of mainland conifer forests, dies young on islands. The forester's saying that "three foggy nights'll kill a fir tree" is an exaggeration, but the cool, damp, foggy climate does present ideal growing conditions for various wood-eating fungi that have a ravenous appetite for fir. As the fir trees die off, the spruce spread their branches and root network to occupy more and more growing space, until they eventually form a pure stand, which will persist for one hundred and fifty to two hundred years and, in exceptional circumstances, a century more.

Mature spruce forests now cover perhaps 90 percent of the islands east of Cape Small, although, if we are to believe the accounts of the mariners who sailed along the island shores and occasionally landed to cut firewood and replenish their water, island forests used to be significantly more diverse.

> *Turtle Island Spruce, August 4, 1976*
>
> *In 1964, the timber rights of Turtle Island were sold to the St. Regis Paper Company of Bucksport, the paper company most well known for its island harvests. Until the advent of the skidder, island logging was accomplished by teams of horses that would haul the wood to shore. From there it was loaded (by hand) on barges and taken up the Penobscot River to the pulp mill. Because of the unpredictable and difficult nature of island logging operations, islands were usually clearcut.*
>
> *When local residents on Mount Desert Island learned that Turtle Island was to be cut over, they contacted The Nature Conservancy, who negotiated with the owners to buy the island, but not until forty or so acres had been clear-cut. The old clear-cut, revegetating with hardwood shrubs, was evident for decades as a swath of lower vegetation across the middle of the island.*
>
> *The red spruce forest that dominates the southern interior of the island is exceptional in its age, productivity, and stability. Some of the tall, straight spruce are between one hundred and fifty and two hundred years old, the closest thing we have to a virgin coastal forest ecosystem. It is of great ecological interest to determine how such a forest adapts to periodic natural disturbances, such as windthrow and salt stress.*
>
> *The understory of the venerable forest is an otherworldly Emerald City. A deep, soft carpet of pleurocarpous mosses covers most of the forest floor. Tufts of bearded lichen hang in the muted, refracted light, an exquisite counterpoint to the pale clumps of reindeer lichen, the rich green woodland mosses, and the pale, spinulose wood ferns. Runners of the tiny snowberry, mountain cranberry, blueberry, and twinflower carpet the forest's lush understory.*

THE ORIGINAL ISLAND FORESTS

Knowing which explorers to believe and how to decipher their tantalizingly brief written descriptions gets you tangled in historical thickets if you're not careful, but a couple of ecological generalizations can be made. First, the vegetation of island forests, then as now, was the realm of the rugged, slow-growing, shallow-rooted, indomitable spruce. Nevertheless, island forests collectively were originally a good deal more complex—they were made up of many more species than we find today.

Many of the early explorers were tempted to gild the lily of their exploits. Glowing accounts of new lands made their voyages seem more significant. If their voyages were to be remembered through the centuries, the returning heroes needed to awaken interest in further exploration and investment—investment, more often than not, by merchants probably no less skeptical then than now of the prospect of spending money, even if it meant making more money.

John Cabot, who laid the foundation for England's claim to the entire northern half of North America, was one of the best at stretching the truth. He described the rocky Newfoundland coast as a land with fertile soil and a mild climate, suitable for the production of silk, and forests full of the valuable Brazilian greenheart tree. Others who followed were not as inaccurate, yet most of them described the new land only in terms of its "profits." Very few of them described its disadvantages. As early as 1524, Verrazano, who cruised nearly the entire eastern seaboard, described the coast of Maine as "full of very thick woods of fir trees, cypresses and the like, indicative of a cold climate." Not a bad description for the few words he devoted to miles of tidal coastline, but it points up the problem of determining when a rose is not a rose, or a fir not a fir. Common names for forest trees changed from place to place and from era to era. The British, who exhausted their supply of mast pines early in their history and began to import Scotch pine from the Baltic, more often than not referred to pine as "Baltic Firre." In fact, the word "pine" was almost never used to describe the various species of this family that were so important to shipbuilders, millwrights, and carpenters. Pine was called "firre" by Rosier, who listed it along with hazel and "aspe" among "the profits we saw." ("Hazel" probably meant hazelnut—a shrub; "aspe" referred to the aspen, or "popple.") Maine's bal-

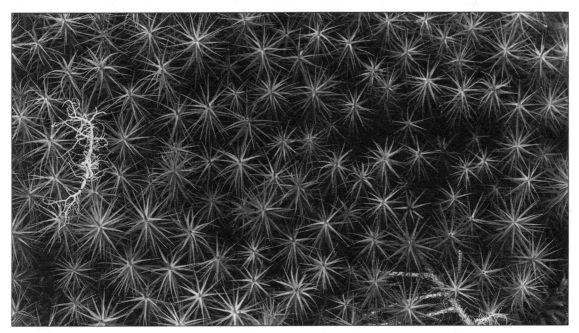

Hairy cap moss bed with reindeer lichen in a deep glade in the interior of Round Island, Merchant Row.

sam fir appears to have been called a "yew;" fir resembles yew, a common English tree species. (The native American yew is not a tree at all but an attractive shrub that is commonly used as a decorative planting around northern homesteads.) But it is equally possible that what was called a "yew" might have been a hemlock.

THE WOODWARD OF SOMERTSHIRE

The one notable exception to the lack of reliable accounts of the exploration of Maine was that of Christopher Levett, who wrote in the seventeenth century with a refreshing sense of humor.

> I will not tell you that you may smell the cornfields before you see the land, neither must men think that corn doth grow naturally or on trees, nor will deer come and look on a man until he shoot him, nor the fish leap into the kettle, nor on the dry land, neither are they so plentiful that you may dip them up in baskets, [or] which is no truer, that fowls will present themselves to you with spits through them.
>
> But certainly there is fowl, deer and fish enough for the taking if men be diligent. . . .

On first reading, Levett seems appealingly reliable; it turns out that he is even better than he sounds. In England, Levett served as the "King's Woodward of Somertshire," in charge of the harvest of timber from the large, intensively utilized king's woods. Many of the early eighteenth-century descriptions came from the pens of gentlemen of good estate, or of men of the sea (such as John Smith) who turned out to be skillful fishermen, or of adventurers who were bound for glory. But through Levett's eyes we have an unsentimental and insightful description of the vegetation of the islands and the coast of Maine. Levett was the first forester to cast an appraising eye on the value of the islands' timber.

Levett sailed for New England in 1623 and made a landfall at the Isles of Shoals, upon which he saw "neither one good timber tree nor so much good ground as to make a garden." One of these treeless granite isles is still known as Cedar Island, however; Celia Thaxter, the daughter of the innkeeper who turned this tiny archipelago into Maine's first island resort, described finding a cedar root imprisoned in a cleft of granite. It is entirely possible that parts of these all-but-barren Isles of Shoals once supported a ragged growth of salt-tolerant spruce, but most of this was undoubtedly cleared off by seventeenth-century fishermen who needed every available square foot of space for the production of salt fish from their extensive flake yards or fish stages. Levett called the Isles of Shoals good for "six ships, but more cannot well be there for want of more stage room." The presence of cedar trees would imply that there was once some swampy ground where wind-borne seeds of Atlantic white cedar had taken root.

From the Isles of Shoals, Levett made his way to the Piscataqua River, where he gathered his men and set off in late fall in an open boat to explore eastward along the coast. For the next several months Levett half walked, half sailed or rowed his craft between "Pannaway" and "Capemanwagen"—what would later be called Portsmouth and Cape Newagen on Southport Island. He was caught in gales and snowstorms. He rowed up the rivers that poured out of the forested interior, met with the Indians, cheered his often cold and hungry men, landed on many of the islands between the two ends of his journey, and built a fortified house on one of them in Casco Bay—perhaps House Island, perhaps not.

Along the way Levett carefully described the condition and value of the timber growing on the islands and the mainland, suggesting industries that might be developed from the harvest of the woods. It is notable that Levett described poor timber at several places he visited. He described Capemanwagen as a region of "little good timber and less good ground," most likely referring to the absence of pine and oak, the two most commercially necessary timber trees for all sorts of colonial enterprises.

Undoubtedly the long, rocky peninsulas and the exposed portions of outer islands supported forests dominated by spruce. Even today the distribution of spruce along the coast is strongly correlated with the degree of exposure to maritime climatic influences.

MURMURING PINES AND HEMLOCK

Hemlock was probably never an important island forest constituent, although the town histories of both Islesboro and North Haven mention tanneries, which would have presumably relied on local sources of hemlock bark for the curing of farm hides. The tanning industry seems to have died out quickly on both islands, suggesting that the local supply of hemlock was rapidly exhausted and other leather tanning agents were not available.

White pine was an important and valuable component of the original island forests. Clapboard Island in inner Casco Bay was one of the first islands named in the area. And as early as 1630, Jonathan Winter was writing enthusiastic reports to England of the supplemental income derived by men who cut clapboards out of Richmond Island's soft pumpkin pine for the export trade. James Rosier, the naturalist and "surgeon" who accompanied George Waymouth to Muscongus Bay, described the enormous pines he called "firres" growing on Allen and Burnt islands, from which "issueth turpentine in so marvelous plenty. This would be a great benefit for making tar and pitch." A local history of islands down east mentions that a white pine stand was cut on Bois Bubert, the large island east of the treacherous Petit Manan Bar; and the history of Swan's Island mentions that an early settler moved to the east side of the island and cut an immense growth of pines there.

White pine, though now rare on most of the islands where it was once found, is still the dominant species on islands of the inner coast, in such estuarine rivers as the Sheepscot, Kennebec, Androscoggin, Abagadasset, Sasanoa, Back, and Cross, and in the estuarine Merrymeeting and Montsweag bays. The tall pines, which create a minibiome of an exquisitely distinct look and feel, particularly attracted the notice of the British Admiralty, which had been perennially short of quality mast timbers for her Royal Navy. The British were, in fact, reduced to piecing together sections of masts from the much shorter imported Baltic pine.

When the Admiralty saw Maine's supply of white pine, they realized the advantage their navy would enjoy if they controlled this resource. In 1690, it became a crime to cut down mast trees that had been blazed with a "Broad Arrow," the old sign of naval property. All white pines two feet or more in diameter were marked by royal surveyors to be reserved as masts for the King's Navy. For nearly a century, local resentment grew over the "King's Pines" until it spilled over into a revolution.

Charles McLane, the Maine island's most prolific historian, notes that Sawyer Island in the Sheepscot estuary above Townsend Gut was originally known as Ship Island, where the Royal Navy cut and loaded mast pines. And Georgetown, originally known as Parker Island, was a major supplier of white pine masts. Maine's inner islands were blessedly accessible places to cut and load these trees.

The tax on tea had never fired the revolutionary fervor of pragmatic Maine frontiersmen. But when the king laid claim to all the best giant trees in the New World, now that was reason all along the Maine coast, and most especially way down east, to talk revolution. The Broad Arrow pines did more to tip Maine into rebellion than all the tea in China.

ISLAND HARDWOODS, FRAGILE FORESTS

Historical competition for hardwood trees in island forests was less severe, primarily because European forests were composed of many of the same kinds of trees. Christopher Levett, James Rosier, John Smith, and Raleigh Gilbert all mentioned the oaks found on both the islands and the mainland. "Oaks of excellent grain, straight and great timber" are the words that Rosier used. Many of the explorers noted the presence of other hardwoods besides the important oaks. When Champlain landed on the shore of Richmond Island in 1605, he was impressed by the luxuriant groves of oak and nut trees as well as vines of wild grape, which is why the Frenchman gave the name Bacchus to the island. It is not entirely clear just what the nut trees were, but five years later when Raleigh Gilbert and Sir John Popham were exploring the islands and nearby shore of Casco Bay for a plantation site, they described immense oaks and walnuts "growing a great space asunder, one from the other as our parks in England, and no thicket growing under them." Both Levett and Smith mentioned the presence of chestnut in Maine's forests; Levett found chestnut trees on the islands of Casco Bay, and Smith described them inland east to the Penobscot River. An account published in 1865 of a visit to the White Islands off Boothbay described the island forests as composed of spruce, oak, and hickory. It seems likely that chestnut, walnut, and hickory all were occasional components of the forests of at least a few of Maine's islands.

The 1805 *American Coast Pilot* gave instructions for coasting east toward Mount Desert as follows: "Steer east by south which will carry you between the Ship and Barge and 3 islands which you leave on your larboard which are covered with large rock maple trees." These three islands—Pond, Opechee, and Black islands of the Casco Passage, or Placentia and the Gotts at the western edge of Blue Hill Bay—are all notable today not for hardwoods, which have disappeared, but for their dense spruce growth. Incidentally, this particular Black Island is not named for its "black growth" of spruce, as are several other Black islands, but apparently for an eccentric hermit named Black who rowed to Somesville twice a year to buy supplies with golden guineas that he is supposed to have salvaged from the wreck of a British warship.

On a British Admiralty chart of the Maine coast published in 1760, the island now known as Hardwood Island in Blue Hill Bay was called Beech Island. Many of the early island descriptions note the presence, and in some cases the preponderance, of beech groves. American beech is a close relative of the European beech and would therefore have been easily identifiable. Swan's Island, according to a town history written in 1898 and the verbal recollections of the island's earliest inhabitants, was covered with a hardwood forest. Many of the town ancients could remember discovering enormous stumps where even in 1898 only spruce was found. The early records of both Baker Island off Mount Desert and Roque Island mention magnificent stands of the smooth gray-barked beech.

Ash and yellow and white birches were also found by the Europeans and early settlers on the islands. It is reasonable to guess that the Indians headquartered on Diamond and Chebeague islands collected ash saplings for basket stock on islands throughout Casco Bay. There is even a Basket Island. And James Rosier claims that Monhegan, lying three leagues out to sea and exposed to the severest of maritime climatic influences, once supported oak, birch, and beech along with its "firres."

Allen Island's Virgin Birches, June 5, 1979

In a cove on Allen Island's southeast tip is a small beach, accessible at high tide, that gives a bit of protection from the surge off the heaving Atlantic. If you time your approach carefully on the surge, you get deposited on the beach and can pull up your dinghy before the next sea does you any harm.

Crossing the wild south end are startlingly expansive fern glades, acres in extent, where little wakes of our footpaths trail in the pale green sea of waist-high growth. We stumble downhill into the midst of a grove of the most majestic trees I've ever seen. Huge, craggy, yellow birches four to five feet in diameter spread themselves up and down the slope. Massive, drooping

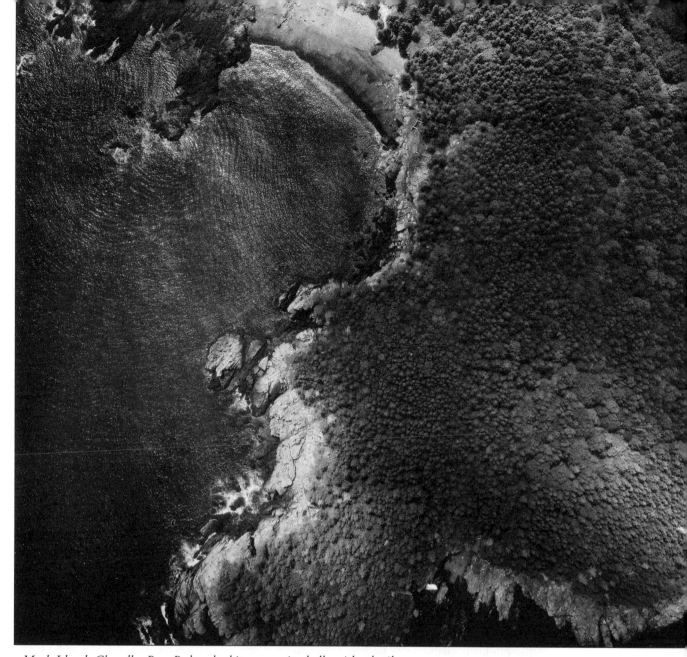

Mark Island, Chandler Bay: Red and white spruce in shallow island soils.

boughs hold up immense green crowns that grow into the light of the clear blue sky where two-hundred-year-old spruce have fallen away. The roots of these ancient birches cover the entire slope and must reach to the edge of the sea. Yellow birch trees have been known to live four hundred years and would have already been adults when Waymouth first landed on this island. Perhaps twenty of these trees are scattered among old-growth red spruce over the rolling five-acre slope, a piece of original island forest. It's like finding treasure, like time travel.

It is places like this where men in armor, glinting with sweat, first met men covered in seal hides, the fur turned in; where no one has felled the trees, dragged them into big piles, and set the pyres aflame for pasturage; where deer have tugged at green growth and huddled down to fawn; where hurt hawks have perched and waited out the long weeks for a broken wing to heal. This is where time passes in measurements not of human making; this is not his story nor mine nor yours. Here an epoch closes when one of these old monarchs falls limb by limb or in one thundering gale of a crash that no one hears. And nothing changes, because these great birches make in their own moldering wood a perfect bed for the tiny winged seeds of their own kind from which a new monarch springs and slowly casts its own deep shade over these glades. Whatever has happened here, or not happened, in ecological time, it's like nowhere else I've ever felt.

THE SETTLEMENT FOREST

No doubt the original forest cover increased in complexity as the explorers penetrated up into the bays from the exposed outer islands. A description of the original survey lots of Islesboro, laid out when the island was settled shortly after the Revolutionary War, provide a rare glimpse into the composition of the presettlement forest: "About twenty acres swampy spruce and hemlock. Eighty acres beech, birch, maple middling, good land but rocky hard land. Five miles to mill by water." And certainly as the explorers proceeded eastward, where the climate became cooler and fogs more prevalent, the forests were seldom much to write home about. At least this was the conclusion reached by Champlain, who described the cover of the Isles des Ranges ("islands in a range"—a good geographical description of the down east islands Cross, Libby, Brothers, and Head Harbor) as "covered with pines [probably he meant spruce], and other trees of an inferior sort." The name Ragged Island for two of Maine's outer islands—one at the edge of Penobscot Bay (originally known as Ragged Arse) and one on the outer rim of Casco Bay—suggests an irregular forest cover. As anyone who has looked at a wind-stunted spruce clinging to an exposed headland will tell you, they do look desperately ragged and poverty stricken.

From this rather exacting dissertation of the changing fates of forested islands, it is evident that many species that were earlier present and notable are now gone. Walnut, oaks, beech, hard maple, chestnuts, hickory, ash, yellow birch, hemlock, and white pine are conspicuously absent from all but a few island forests. No doubt the most significant reason that walnut, hickory, oak, and beech have almost disappeared from the islands is that their heavy seeds float out to and become established on islands rather irregularly. Once the last individual of a heavy-seeded species is harvested from an island, it may be an eon before time and tides interact favorably to reestablish that species there.

Although many island hardwoods were put to great and good uses, there is something about their demise that should give us pause. Cutting trees, especially on islands, can dramatically alter the composition of future forests. Perhaps the chief lesson to be drawn from the disappearance of so many island tree species is that although trees themselves might be rugged, forests are fragile.

HEATH ISLANDS

Although many more of Maine's islands were at one time forested, not all of them supported groves of trees. A colonists' petition for settling Fisherman Island off Boothbay in 1687 asked that Squirrel Island be included in the grant, because Fisherman was "void of wood either for fire or other use." Seal Island at the entrance to Penobscot Bay was described by Samuel Argall in 1610 as "nothing but rock, which seemed to be a very rich marble stone." Large Green Island, lying just to the west of Seal, was similarly bereft of tree growth.

It is worth stopping for a moment to consider the name Green Island, which is shared by no fewer than nineteen Maine islands. It could conceivably have been used to describe an island clad with evergreen forest but might also have referred to the brighter green of the shrubby cover typical of seabird nesting islands, whose highly acidic guano-laden soils inhibit tree growth. The 1760 edition of the British Admiralty charts of the coast of Maine shows several Green islands. One of them is the low, sprawling nubble lying between Isle au Haut and Marshall Island; it is chiefly distinguished as home to a colony of mixed-species seabirds, whose rich and copious excretions give the place a well-fertilized, luxuriant look. Without a doubt, many of the treeless islands of the Maine coast remained so by virtue of the nesting gulls, cormorants, and "shitpokes" (great blue herons) that inhabited them.

Sheep Island, September 18, 1989

> *Bold and treeless outer "heath" islands such as Sheep offer not only significant wildlife habitat but also, more to the point, in today's market present unparalleled seascape views for the would-be islander. In the case of Sheep Island, a building application has been wending its way through Vinalhaven's town approval process. Primarily on the basis of the fact that Sheep Island currently has no active seabird nests, the town's planning board narrowly approved (in a three-to-two vote) an application for a two-story house, a separate guest house, and a large septic field.*
>
> *The day we chose for a site visit was blustery but bright, although a steep chop had developed in both west and east Penobscot Bay. We were not sure we'd be able to land as we rolled and plowed our way down to the island, but there was a little lee at the north end of Sheep, where we anchored and launched the dink. Timing the landing on the slippery rocks in the surge required a combination of patience and a scramble, but we managed to avert a swim. As we started to make our way to the height of land, we could hear the gabbling of geese.*
>
> *Hand over hand and low to the ground, we moved like mink to a position where we could just make out the eyes of the sentry goose posted above the head-down feeding flock. The alarm was given in a crescendo of calls. Ponderously at first, but then in a rush of wings, ten, twenty, then thirty calling Canada geese stretched out into the steady wind, forming a long line of flight over the south end of Sheep before banking a slow turn back up the shore over our heads while we lay motionless on our rocky perch. They landed a hundred yards down the island, reposted their sentries, and slowly returned to their feeding among Sheep's thick, lush grass and heath cover.*
>
> *When we finally stood up in the center of the proposed building site, we could see the impressive view out over to Isle au Haut, Saddleback, Brimstone, and back to Vinalhaven. The question was who or what should enjoy these pricey and priceless benefits.*

SHIPBUILDING "BETTER CHEAP"

This coast was closer to India or China than the middle west.   —Mary Ellen Chase

It is unlikely that any industry or occupation has had such a significant and lasting effect on island forests as shipbuilding. Truly incredible numbers of vessels were hewn out of Maine's forests from the period after the Indian Wars until steel-hulled, steam-powered ships ended the Age of Sail. To estimate the numbers of trees that went into even the most humble of craft makes one realize that much of the original forest growth of Maine's islands could at one time be found sailing one of the world's seven seas. There are few coves, inlets, or tidal streams, however small, that did not at one time have a vessel of some description built and launched from its shores. In fact, because the cutting and sawing of lumber was the chief motive for settling Maine's forested shores, it was no exaggeration to say, as did one of Islesboro's shipbuilders, that a man could lay a keel and build his vessel on a timbered shore from which he cut both ship and cargo.

Three-masted schooner REPUBLIC *under construction at the Dunn and Elliot shipyard in Thomaston shows
the volume of timber needed for shipbuilding.*   F. CLAES COLLECTION

As most histories of Maine are quick to point out, the first vessel built in the New World was
the pinnace VIRGINIA, which was constructed during the winter of 1609 by the ill-fated Popham
Colony and launched from the shores of the Kennebec River. Shipbuilding moved slowly eastward
throughout the 1700s, but it did not really reach a critical mass until after the Revolution.

Though several British explorers recognized the military significance of Maine's supply of mast
timbers, it was again Christopher Levett, the King's Woodward from Somertshire, who saw the
value of the diversity and abundance of tree species that could make Maine the shipbuilding capital
of the world, as she indeed became. Wrote Levett:

> I dare be bold to say also, there may be ships as conveniently built there as in any
> place of the world where I have been and better cheap. As for plank, crooked timber and all
> other sorts whatsoever can be desired for such purpose, the world cannot afford better.

Although the island shipyards never came close to matching the commercial tonnage of ports
such as Bath, Wiscasset, and Thomaston, the numbers of small vessels built and launched from
islands is a good deal larger than the official records suggest. Unlike the launching of a large coasting
schooner, which was always a town event, a few men or fishermen launching a sloop or a pinky
schooner from the shores of an island was not a great deal more remarkable than someone buying a
new truck today. Probably neighbors were aware of it, but the rest of the world took no great notice.
In many island communities, almost every male inhabitant built a vessel of some sort.

Fishermen built vessels for their own use out of anything they could get their hands on for the
right price, which usually meant next to nothing. Enterprising islanders were part farmer, part fisherman, part logger, part what-have-you—so that boatbuilding simply became another skill that had

to be learned with the tools and materials at hand. Reuben Carver, the premier boatbuilder of Vinalhaven between 1820 and 1880, built a vessel almost entirely out of spruce—from a spruce keel and stem and stern pieces to spruce timbers and planks. As the story went on the island, when the vessel was launched, her crew hoisted a jib on a mast made of spruce and sailed to Boston with a deck cargo of spruce cordwood. It's probably not far from the truth.

Deadrise, March 6, 1982

In a few short weeks the last of the wooden fishing draggers to be built in Thomaston will slide down the ways from the Wallace boatyard on the banks of the St. George. Since the yard has been sold, no one is too fussy about people poking around to look her over, especially on weekends. All these graceful lines, scribed with a century's worth of knowledge, stare out blankly at you. The sheer and run of her decks, her plumb bow, and her tumblehome are lessons learned, one thinks, the hard way. Back aft, her deadrise can be appreciated by seeing a section transversely across a hull. If the bottom planking were flat, extending horizontally from the keel, she would fall off waves into troughs and would not hold her helm. With no deadrise there would be only the dead to raise. But how much round to build in her bottom . . . how much rise in the deadrise? This is the kind of knowledge that doesn't get much more local.

Shipyards on North Haven, Vinalhaven, Islesboro, Isle au Haut, Deer Isle, Swan's Island, and the Cranberry Isles produced one hundred and eighty five schooners averaging ninety to one hundred and ten tons, as well as a scattering of brigs, barks, and even full-rigged ships, such as the two hundred-ton vessels LUCY and NANCY.

As William Fairburn's monumental six-volume history, *Merchant Sail*, pointed out, few of the Penobscot Bay shipyards could be considered permanent; the builders moved as soon as the timber of an area was cut out, only to relocate in some new area in which the necessary stock of planking, knees, ribs, masts, and keels was still found rooted upright along the rocky shores. Some idea of the great weight of these trees comes from the fact that shipbuilders often chose to move a shipyard to a new location in the midst of a good growth of uncut timber rather than move the timber to the existing yard.

In 1790, a shipyard was built on Hupper Island in Muscongus Bay. By 1796, four schooners and a sloop had been launched from the shores of North and South Fox Islands. In 1800, David Thurlow settled on the island across the Thorofare from Deer Isle (which bore his name until it was changed to Crotch Island sixty years later), built a sawmill, and launched seventeen vessels, including a one-hundred-and-fifty-ton brig, before 1840. Similar efforts were under way at Vinalhaven's "Privilege," Deer Isle's "Privilege," Swan's Island, Isle au Haut, Islesboro, and the Cranberry Isles. In Casco Bay, it appears that the major yards were located on the rivers, whose waters were more protected, but the islands were used as sources of local raw materials.

Vinalhaven Boatbuilding, January 7, 1985

"You see," Phil Dyer explained to us one afternoon at his boat shop, "when you build a boat, it's like an artist painting a picture. His fingers are the tongue and they're speaking for him. His talent is coming out as a gift from God. It's the same way with building a boat. You gotta live it; it's part of you. Your hand is, so to speak, like your tongue. It's speaking for you. You're giving a part of yourself to that boat.

"I wouldn't build a boat if I had to slight it. I'm not interested. I want to give it man's best—my best. After all, you're dealing with a man's life. When a fisherman's down to the so'thard, and it comes off whistlin' forty, fifty knots, he wants to come home. And he don't wanna have to worry—did Phil Dyer put this boat together right?
"The boats I build, when I see them go by, I call them my children."

Keels, stems, and sternposts were cut from white oak as long as the supply lasted. Keel stock was always in critically short supply, because suitably shaped, large, clear white oak, free of defects, was not found everywhere, even in the so-called virgin forest. White oak is desirable as a ship timber chiefly because the integral arrangement of its water-conducting cells (xylem) inhibits the free flow of water through them once the tree has been cut—unlike similar cells of its relative the red oak. As a result, white oak is much more resistant to rot than almost all other ship timbers. Fairburn suggests that northern colonial white oak was so abundant in the early days of shipbuilding that often nothing but the heartwood of these trees was put into American-built vessels. White oak was never as common in Maine as red oak, but an 1816 report on the economic condition of the District of Maine, commissioned by the Commonwealth of Massachusetts, put the northern limit of white oak somewhere east of the Penobscot River Valley. Today white oak is rare north of Portland and almost unheard of on islands.

For the rest of a vessel, the materials were not as critical. Floors were of red oak or beech, their topping planks of almost any species that was handy: spruce, hemlock, white pine, or cedar. Ash was used for oars, rock maple for cabins and finish, tamarack (also known as hackmatack or larch) for knees, hornbeam (also known as ironwood) for hand spikes, and locust or spruce limbs saturated with pitch for treenails. Masts and spars were of white pine when it was handy, but spruce spars became more common as pine supplies dwindled.

It is difficult to estimate accurately how quickly ship timbers became in short supply, because the original island timber supply differed greatly from area to area, depending on bedrock, soils, topography, and the degree of maritime influences. But if you consider that the British Admiralty required at least two thousand oaks (not counting other trees) for one ship, it is easy to understand how whole forests could disappear.

After the Revolution, shipbuilders from Maine—because of the state's good harbors and seemingly limitless supplies of wood—constructed the majority of the nation's new merchant marine. Between 1830 and 1840, the South's cotton production nearly doubled, and the average size of Maine-built ships more than doubled—from one hundred and thirty to three hundred and twenty tons. Bath was traditionally the leading shipbuilding center of Maine, although small yards were scattered up and down the coast—and out on islands—wherever a concentration of pine and spruce grew. Half the vessels that would be built on Deer Isle, Vinalhaven, and North Haven had already been launched prior to 1830. Most of the shipyards continued to operate until close to the turn of the century, but their heyday had passed. On the mainland, however, the boom lasted at least through 1855, when fully one-third of the nation's entire tonnage of vessels for the year consisted of vessels built in Maine shipyards.

Seamen in the packet ship trade, it is said, would go belowdecks from stern to fo'c's'le to smell the conditions below before signing on. If the vessel smelled like a rose, it could only mean that she leaked badly, which meant that the crew would have to be constantly pumping. But if she were foul, then she was tight and the passage would be less difficult.

LUMBERING FOR CORDWOOD, KILNWOOD, AND PULPWOOD

Why are staves, clapboards, firewood, and kilnwood less noble products of island forests than the high-bowed, round-bellied, faired and true wooden hull of a ship, whether brig, bark, or schooner? Something in the asking hints at the answer. It may not be rational to conclude that wooden ships were a better use of island forests than the very products they were often built to carry, but it is hard to escape the impression that these products might better have been cut from mainland forests, where the effects of the cutting are repaired more quickly.

From the earliest times, red oak and beech trees were felled on islands to be riven into barrel staves. There are islands today in Casco, Penobscot, and Frenchman bays whose name "Stave" dates from this use, although their hardwood forests have long since been replaced by spruce. Levett, the practical forester, wrote that Maine's supply of beech and oak was "excellent timber for joiners and coopers. No place in England can afford better timber for pipe staves." (In Europe, staves were used to make great casks called "pipes" for the storing of wine.)

Later, when a brisk trade developed between the American colonies and the West Indies, cargoes of staves were sent south to be assembled and were returned full of molasses. As early as 1784, a Captain Parker of Yarmouth (as we are informed by William Rowe) complained: "I have this day seen the choicest timber cut down and sawn into staves. Transient men come down in gangs and cut from the islands, of which there are now nineteen on Chebeaggue [sic], and several vessels cutting their load."

Although Captain Parker may have known ships better than forests, you can hear him wincing through his description of the girth of trees felled for the stave trade that he probably would have preferred to go into his boat. One oak was so broad at its stump that a yoke of oxen could be turned around on it.

William Jones, a native of Maine, was sent to Cuba as a young man by a merchant to assemble the shooks of staves that had been jointed and crozed and were ready to be fitted in place. The record indicates that Mr. Jones returned to Peaks Island in Casco Bay to open up his own cooper's shop in 1840, but he had to close down fifteen years later because the supply of raw material was exhausted.

The cordwood trade was carried on from the time of the earliest settlements to supply Boston with winter fuel. Islands with good anchorages were visited routinely, and twenty to thirty cords were cut for a deck load to carry upwind to Boston. It was good winter work when fishing and farming were slack. One of Pemaquid's settlers, shortly after the conclusion of the long Indian Wars, related that most settlers' "whole living depended on cutting firewood and carrying it to Boston and other towns more than one hundred and fifty miles from them."

One of the situations that determined the speed with which islands were settled was the proximity of a tidal-powered saw- and grist-mill. At Roque Island the dam operated on both ebb and flood tides; in the small embayment known as Paradise Cove, the tide turned a gristmill on one bank and a sawmill on the other. The first settler of whom there is a record on Vinalhaven was one Francis Cogswell, whose name seems to have fit his occupation. He set up a tidal sawmill, no doubt attracted to the heavily forested shores, the steady surge of water in and out of the harbor, and the ease of shipping his product to a ready market. The name "Privilege," which was given to the small protected coves and inlets along the coast and islands of Maine where sawmills were built, gives an idea of the importance attached to such places by the original settlers.

We don't know when the timber supply of various portions of the coast was exhausted, but George Hosmer mentioned the abandonment of the Deer Isle sawmill in the early 1800s, "as the best of the lumber had been cut off in the vicinity." According to Morison, most of the original forest growth around Mount Desert Island had been cut off by 1870.

It is certain that in Penobscot Bay most of the forested islands had been cut over at least once prior to 1870, because the voracious kilns of the lime industry were headquartered in the Rockland area. Ever since limestone was first slaked into lime mortar in 1793, the expanding lime industry depended on an enormous and uninterrupted supply of wood to fire the kilns. By 1835, some one hundred and fifty kilns were producing three-quarters of a million casks annually. Several hundred vessels were ranging the coast for fuel for the kilns, which burned thirty cords at a crack. In the four midcoast towns of Thomaston, Rockland, Rockport, and Camden, there were seventy-five kilns being fired every two weeks for nine to ten months a year. That required at least twenty thousand cords of wood per year to be landed wharfside. The ragged-looking "kilnwooders," which delivered the wood fuel, often had their decks stacked so high with cordwood that it is said the helmsman steered by directions shouted from the bow.

Incidentally, it might be added that except for a cargo of granite, lime was the most dangerous coasting assignment. Lime burns when it gets wet; and, as any sailor knows, seawater has a habit of filling the bilges of even the tightest vessel. In such an eventuality, the only course was to head the craft to the nearest shore while trying to seal all the hatches and air passages into the hold with lime plaster, hoping that the cargo would not become hot enough to burst into flame. Once at anchor, the vigil began. If every crack into the hold had been sealed successfully, the fire went out. But as often as not, the fire could not be smothered, and the vessel had to be scuttled, which would swell the cargo in the hold to the bursting point, warping ship timbers and deck beams into unseemly and unseamanly shapes.

Lime Island Beach, May 4, 1984

Lime Island is the only island off the coast of Maine, with the exception of small parts of Islesboro, to be composed almost entirely of limestone. The bedrock is formed by the aggregates of skeletons of marine plants and animals that are deposited in oceanic waters near the edge of continents. These organisms were, no doubt, deposited at a time when Maine's waters were considerably warmer.

This small limestone unit did not escape notice by the lime industry; a small quarry cut sometime in the last century is gradually being reclaimed by forest.

The island's extraordinarily beautiful limestone beds have been slightly metamorphosed since they were deposited hundreds of millions of years ago. Superimposed upon the major folds in the rock are a great number of closely compressed minor folds. The alternating of unusually pure, nearly white limestone with bands that are blue-gray in color and much contorted creates a lovely marbled effect in the outcrops.

An unusual wave-built cobble beach extends along a good part of the north and west side of Lime. In between sections of the wave-polished cobblestones are sinuous twists of crenelated limestone. Most beaches slope gently seaward, but here, northeast storm waves periodically throw fist-sized cobbles high on the beach, creating a series of level terraces.

For perhaps six hundred feet along the top of the wave-built beach, wild columbine grows among the cobbles. The odd-shaped red-and-yellow flowers seem to tower above the scalloped, three-parted leaves. The name columbine comes from the Latin word for "dove," which the nodding, delicate petals resemble when they have just emerged from the green sepals. Columbine is one of the most beautiful and intricately shaped rare wildflowers growing on the coast of Maine.

The last serious wave of island forest cutting began around 1920 and lasted until the early 1960s. The paper mill in Bucksport, on the Penobscot River, then owned by the St. Regis Paper Company, was set up to off-load four-foot pulpwood from tug-driven barges. "Pulping" an island was a means of generating additional income where island populations and economic fortunes had begun to move slowly downhill. Several hundred of the larger islands were cut over during this time by crews who used horse teams or homemade tractors called skipjacks or jitterbugs to get the four-foot wood to the shore. A skipjack, still used in the woods to some extent, is nothing more than an old one- or two-ton truck stripped down to the frame and outfitted with welded log bunks and a two-speed rear end. Often a second transmission is mounted behind the original, facing the rear end, and is run in reverse to give the homemade vehicle a super-low gear to maneuver over uneven ground.

Probably no other island use did so much to generate the movement for island preservation than the last wave of pulpwood cuttings. A pulped piece of ground is unsightly, no question about it, and sensibilities had changed by this time; the coast and islands were beginning to become important areas for summer recreation.

In public discussions it is easy to get the impression that we want our forests to provide too many things for us. We want both inexpensive housing and uncut forests; we want paper and wilderness; we resist change while Mother Nature is busily harvesting what stands.

Allen Island Pulp Cut, October 24, 1985

Irving Smith, a pulpwood buyer for Champion International, stood looking over the two hundred cords of spruce piled at the edge of the woods on Allen Island. "Island spruce," he said, "is as good a pulpwood for high-quality paper as there is anywhere." Because Irving Smith was involved

Lime Island in west Penobscot Bay, with its beautiful limestone outcrops, has been both cut and quarried in the course of its history.   RICK PERRY

thirty years ago in island pulpwood harvests for the Bucksport mill and is now a buyer for the world's largest paper company, his opinion is of more than passing interest.

As we were discussing different ways that this wood might be moved to Champion's mill at the mouth of the Penobscot River, Smith recalled how island wood was sluiced into coves, boomed into rafts, and then loaded by conveyor thirty to forty years ago. Although the equipment, logistics, and costs of moving offshore spruce are daunting, Champion International is interested in helping to develop a wood-transport system, because, as Irving puts it, "The Maine islands have the largest concentration of old-growth spruce left in the state."

Today something like 90 percent of land on Maine islands is forested, although less than a hundred years ago a nearly similar percentage of acreage was cleared pasture. Collectively the islands have a standing volume of about five million cords of wood.

Those island forests, which began growing up from cleared pastures around the turn of the century, are reaching maturity over a large area all at once. The major problem that many landowners will face in the next decade is what to do when these even-aged woods begin to degrade: collapse in a heap from a windstorm or from the effects of a variety of heart rots, which thrive in the cool, damp climate of the islands. These are what trigger today's nightmare of twisted trunks and impenetrable thickets—without any help from us. And once the process starts, it is irreversible until the entire wood replaces itself; this takes ten to twenty years, which in the life of the forest passes as fleetingly as childhood.

On Allen Island, Irving Smith, joined by Don Rader and Joel Swanton

Allen Island pulpwood cut, 1982.   Peter Ralston

of Champion, gaze at the progress of the harvest where forest use is coming full circle. Approximately sixty thousand board feet had earlier been sawn in a wood contractor's portable sawmill to produce lumber for a spruce post-and-beam barn with spruce planking and flooring. By sawing lumber for the barn on the island rather than hauling it from the mainland, Allen Island's owner, Betsy Wyeth, has saved about 50 percent in lumber costs.

Our wood contractor, Konrad Ulbrich, of Warren, who owns a World War II landing craft, has calculated the costs and efficiencies of different methods of loading his fifty-six-foot, diesel-powered barge to move two hundred cords of Allen Island spruce pulpwood and logs to the mainland. Forest economists' predictions about the rising price of wood in the 1990s, when the mainland supply begins to get pinched, create an urgency to get the job started.

ISLAND FARMING: "PECULIAR SENSE OF PROPRIETORSHIP"

Other islands have one house and one barn on them, this sole family being lords and rulers of all land and sea girds. The owner of such must have a peculiar sense of proprietorship and lordship; he must feel more like his own master than other people can.

—Henry Wadsworth Longfellow

It will come as no surprise that several hundred years of harvesting wood from islands has changed the composition, complexity, and diversity of the island forests. But farmers also have had a hand in changing the face of island landscapes, and in some cases the changes they wrought have had more permanent and, in some ecological senses, more damaging effects; it is only because the effects of farming are more aesthetically pleasing that farmers are not more often called to account for their management practices.

It somehow seems fitting that the first island cultivator was a sea captain-turned-fisherman. In 1609, Captain John Smith planted a garden "on top of a rocky isle four leagues from the main [Monhegan] in May that grew so well that it served us for salads in June and July." But it is the farm on Richmond Island and the reports that Jonathan Winter faithfully wrote to Robert Trelawney that give the first and only detailed view of island farming in the early 1600s. In 1631, Winter wrote that "the island is a great priveledge [sic] to the plantation and at present very well stocked with all sorts of beasts that is needful. I take it to be the best plantation in the land, taking it every way both for sea and land."

One of the sorts of beasts with which this island (and soon others like it) was well stocked was hogs. Pork was one of the most important meats for the early colonial farms, but hog raising on the mainland was slow to develop because of the practice of letting the hogs forage in the woods during the warm months. As often as not, they ended up as a fine pork dinner for wolves. However, if the hogs were set out on islands, particularly those with oaks, the animals could feed in relative freedom and fatten on the fall acorn crop just before they were slaughtered. From Winter's account, it seems that hogs were also fed clams from the intertidal zone, which they soon learned to dig for themselves. After three years, Richmond Island had two hundred hogs.

Along the coast of Maine there are now eleven Hog islands. No doubt there were at one time many more.

On the subject of island names, we find the account of how Great and Little Hog were renamed Great and Little Diamond. For two and a half centuries they had been known as the Hog Islands; they were uniquely suited to raising hogs by having both clams for staple food and acorns for the fattening. But when an association of Portlanders bought up Great Hog Island at the turn of the century and built cottages there, the matter of an appropriate name came up for discussion in a public meeting. Many favored retaining the original name, but according to one record the matter was finally settled after a well-fed matronly resident rose and complained that her groceries delivered from the mainland always came labeled "Mrs. So-and-So—Great Hog."

There are several advantages to island farms. Owing to the influence of the surrounding waters, which act like a great thermostat, the growing season extends later into fall than it does on the mainland. There is an abundance of natural fertilizers. Seaweeds are always free for the taking; although the early records are in dispute as to how widely rockweed, oarweed, and kelps were used, no doubt they had their proponents then as now. One island farmer in Muscongus Bay described his method of increasing his corn yield: He harvested mussels in spring and set them in heaps along the upper edge of a cornfield to leach slowly over it during the growing season.

For those islanders who combined farming with fishing, and most did, fish were used well into the twentieth century as another source of fertilizer. The settlers learned how to use fish in this way from the Indians, who probably figured that sharing information during the growing season was preferable to sharing meager food supplies during the winter if the crops failed. Trelawney, ever the interested patron, was told that Richmond Island farmers fertilized corn with menhaden, or pogies—"One thousand fish to the acre owing to their rich oil."

"ONE ACRE IN A PIECE"

Island farming struggled along during the period of the long Indian Wars, but permanent family farms were as rare on islands as they were on the mainland. As soon as any island plantation got established during the brief years of peace, it was quickly snuffed out when hostilities were revived.

For almost a hundred years, the eastern frontier of Maine was left in limbo as the population along the remainder of the eastern seaboard swelled to the bursting point and land became scarce and expensive. At the end of the Revolutionary War, the eastern frontier reopened, and young and old alike picked up stakes and moved to Maine. Two hundred twenty-six towns were incorporated in Maine between 1783 and 1826, fully five times as many as before the Revolution. It was such a land rush that every available acre anywhere near the frail edge of civilization began to be cleared and turned under by rough horse-drawn plows.

One of the chief attractions of an island farm, aside from the sense of proprietorship that Longfellow described and the few ecological advantages that were, no doubt, lightly considered in any case, was that island titles were vague. There were many cases in which a persistent settler moved to an uninhabited island, cleared the land, built a dwelling, and was eventually, through one means or another, awarded its title. The period after the Revolution was one of feverish land speculation; often the cost of land was the chief limiting factor for would-be settlers. If a farm could be obtained cheaply or for free, it was all the more attractive, regardless of how poor the land was.

The census records of this period show that nearly every island greater than ten to fifteen acres (except for perhaps the completely "bald" islands) was settled for a short time, at least until wisdom became the better part of valor. Even the most bold, rugged, and steep-sided islands—which today seem like dangerous places to land, let alone attempt to farm—had their trees cut and the forests put to fields.

The original survey records of Islesboro, done at the time that the island was divided into approximately hundred-acre lots, describe over and over again the condition of the ground that would bring this farm era to a relatively quick end: "Forty acres ledgy, broken. Not more than one acre in a piece fit for plowing." The effort of clearing the stones from the discontinuous patches of fields on islands made Yankee industriousness not just a virtue but a life-supporting necessity. You can imagine the effect of descriptions of the new land that had just been opened up in Ohio on the folks back home on the island farm. Elisha Philbrook, from Vinalhaven, wrote back to the island that in Ohio he saw "one hundred acres of corn in one field so high that a man cannot hang his hat on them. Five acres of corn will cost not more labor than one acre will in Maine." And he added, "the land is free from stone." Hello, Ohio.

> ### *Lane's Island Raspberries, August 14, 1990*
> *One of the reasons that there are so many species of berry-producing plants on islands is that there are so many birds that fly among them. Birds are attracted to brightly colored sweet berries and carry them to various locations; ideally the berries will be dropped in a spot favorable for growth. Some species of cherries will germinate only after their outer seed coats have been broken down upon passing through a bird's digestive tract.*
>
> *Clumps of raspberries colonize thousands of acres of old fields around abandoned island farms and meadows along the archipelago. The thorns of red raspberry are smaller and less stout than those of black raspberry, but where they have taken hold they are a splendor of sweetness and a delectation for morning cereal and evening tarts, which a pair of field naturalists, ages six and eight, have collected from the outback.*

HAY FIRES: BURNING THE ISLANDS

Hay was the first island cash crop that was shipped aboard just about any vessel at hand to feed the burgeoning livestock population in and around Boston. Because horse and oxen were the principal means of transportation overland, prodigious quantities of feed were needed to keep things going. Massachusetts farmers who were raising livestock either for dairy products or to sell at market were no doubt reluctant to sell the crop on which their animals depended. Instead, at least in the early days, a good deal of it came from Maine islands. On a reaching wind, Boston's famous Haymarket Square was not much more than a twenty-four-hour passage.

One of the incidents that is still mentioned by residents of Matinicus Island was the murder of Ebenezer Hall by a group of Indians in 1724. It seems that Hall, a fisherman, also sold hay in Boston. To stimulate a flush of new growth, he was in the habit of burning over nearby Large Green Island, then as now an important seabird colony. Large Green Island was particularly important for the Penobscot Indians, who used the island to collect eggs and young seabirds for meat. Unhappy with Hall's peremptory use of their traditional hunting grounds, the Indians successfully petitioned the distant Court of Massachusetts to enjoin him from burning over the island. When Hall burned Large Green again, a party of braves, no doubt angered over the delay in enforcement, settled matters by ambushing and scalping him.

There are about seven Burnt islands on charts of Maine waters—a small percentage of the number of islands that were cleared either to raise a cash crop for Boston or later to pasture islanders' own stock. At least in the early days, all that was required to raise hay on a Maine island was an ax, hard labor, and a flint box. Over the course of a year or two, depending on the size of the island, the trees were felled. Large, valuable timber may have been rafted to a nearby tidal mill, but as often as not the timber was left to dry out, awaiting a hot spell to be torched off.

> ### *Allen Island, May 3, 1982*
> *Some evenings we watched meadow fires burning back on the mainland—a spring rite that seems positively Neolithic. On such nights there is a*

Harvesting the potato crop, Criehaven.   Island Institute files

> *red glow in the distance, and little Pentecostal tongues lick at the edges of the*
> *fields and disappear into the dark flanks of the woods. I have watched small*
> *groups of people of all ages standing with rakes, obscured in the heavy yel-*
> *low smoke, occasionally poking at a racing bit of fire, which then showers*
> *into a helix of incandescent sparks. It is a re-creation, a celebration, a ritual*
> *enacted since dawn's dawn. Other mysteries aside, it's a very good way to get*
> *a flush of new green growth.*

Where and when the process of clearing and burning islands began seems to have been a matter of historical happenstance. On the early charts of the Maine coast, Swan's Island was referred to as Burnt Coat, evidently a corruption of the French *brûlé côte*, or "burnt coast." Some have attributed the early name of Swan's to Champlain; although the name does not appear on any of his charts, it does appear on several of the other seventeenth-century maps. It's tempting to conclude that part of Swan's was burned for pasturage by an early independent fisherman trader who wished to leave a source of fresh meat on the island in anticipation of his return. Champlain, in fact, mentions that wild bullock and sheep were left on Cape Sable by Portuguese fishermen in the 1540s.

The illuminating *Atlantic Neptune* series of charts gives the name Grass Island to Black Island in Casco Passage. The *American Coast Pilot* presents this picture of eastern Muscongus Bay in 1809: "You may steer NE for Whitehead leaving Georges Islands (which are three in number) on your larboard. The eastern island has no trees on it." The Georges Islands are still three in number, but the eastern one, still called Burnt, has been reforested after a century and a half. Mosquito Island, which was described in the *Coast Pilot* as covered "with burnt trees," was described sixty years later by another eye as "a low rocky island covered with brush." The process of natural reforestation seems painfully slow.

Seal Island Fire, July 30, 1978

The Bermuda high had built over the normally cool waters of the Gulf of Maine and remained nearly stationary for weeks. The temperatures climbed into the high nineties and the mercury barely moved. The dog days of summer picked at the bones of the dead and dying.

From several miles off, even before the smell of the fire reached us, the island looked like a battleship aflame. As we got closer we saw that the air over Seal was dark with careening, screaming seabirds. Large rafts of eiders floated around Seal's shores in the confusion. I knew that the luckless petrels in their burrows in the turf would not survive this horror.

There was a group of Outward Bound volunteers with Indian tanks already on the island as we lugged the bigger fire-fighting gear ashore. But the fire had already gone deep into the peaty turf of Seal and was traveling underground and smoldering there. Although we quickly set up the pumps and the hoses and began to try to contain the fire, it would erupt over and over again behind the fire line that we had carefully laid out. Fresh groups of volunteers appeared at intervals throughout the late afternoon and evening, including a crew from the Thomaston prison. But the fire just kept going deeper under. All through the night the air was alive with the sound and feel of petrels circling through the shadows cast by the half moon and fire glow. I could hear petrel chicks in their burrows surrounded by fire; they were literally cooking at our feet.

We worked in shifts throughout the night and the next day amid the screaming gulls and other seabirds wheeling madly overhead. Near sunset, a large explosion rocked the island from a piece of ordnance left over from the days during World War II when Seal was used for target practice by navy ships and planes. Everyone was quickly evacuated. Before leaving, someone found the remains of a picnic lunch from those who perhaps had merely thought to burn off the hay.

For the next six weeks, when the air was southerly, you would occasionally inhale tiny charred pieces of peat dust that appeared above Seal as a yellowish smudge on the horizon. Every once in a while a dull explosion from offshore would rend the heavy air.

"PHANTOMS OF PURSUIT . . . AND THE ALMONER OF HUMAN LIFE"

During the initial period of Maine's settlement, farming was a distinctly less important occupation than fishing, lumbering, shipbuilding, or trading furs with the Indians. The Englishman Sir Ferdinando Gorges, who financed the Popham Colony, was a planter at heart. He hoped to sow seeds of settlement in Maine not only out of loyalty to his king but also, it appears, out of an abiding belief that farming was a good way of life. In a letter to one of his associates, he bemoaned the Maine settlers' interest in other pursuits: "Trading, fishing, lumber, these have been the phantoms of pursuit, while there has been a criminal neglect of husbandry, the true source of wealth and the almoner of human life." Although this sounds a little like a Masai tribesman who measures his wealth by the number of cattle he owns, Gorges had a point. Curiously enough, even after the attractions of farming for a living in Maine began to pale, husbandry continued to thrive, particularly on islands. Of the animals raised on island farms, none were better adapted to the Maine archipelago than sheep.

In most of the colonies, cows outnumbered sheep, because the settlers soon discovered that salt-marsh grass (*Spartina patens* and *S. alterniflora*) made passably good winter fodder for cattle.

The increase in cows for meat and dairy purposes was slow to affect Maine for a number of reasons. Maine had relatively little salt-marsh land to support cattle, cows were expensive, and on the islands cows needed water and were hard to move around. In fact, Hosmer's *History of Deer Isle* describes the death of a settler, his wife, three children, and a neighbor when their gundalow overturned as they tried to land a cow on Fog Island in Merchant Row. There are more Calf islands than Cow islands off the coast of Maine, which makes one wonder whether transportation wasn't another factor in limiting island cattle.

From the beginning, Maine islanders had little cause to interface with Boston's cash economy, with the exception of their need for cloth. Importing bolts of English cloth was an early necessity of life, but soon after sheep were introduced, the idea of making homespun wool caught on, which no doubt appealed to the isolated islanders.

According to Maine agricultural historian Clarence Day, the early sheep were "long-legged, narrow-breasted, light-quartered, coarse-wooled, roving and wild." After the Embargo Act of 1807 completely isolated the young nation from the cloth trade abroad, sheep raising became more and more significant to Maine's economy. For two generations, Maine was one of the leading grazing states in the country. During this time, flocks of the famed and prized Spanish merino sheep were introduced into Maine's local stock—in some cases selling for fabulous prices that only well-employed captains and merchants could afford.

The advantages of raising sheep on islands are almost too numerous to list. First, there was the matter of fencing, which was time-consuming both to build and maintain. No fencing was needed for pasturing sheep on small or middle-sized islands—say, up to two hundred acres. Then there was the need to water other farm stock—a chore wasted on sheep, because they were perfectly capable of providing for their own needs with what they could get from dew or intermittent rains. Not only were they capable of getting their own water, they could supplement their forage with seaweeds, notably kelps, from the islands' intertidal zone. Also, the island sheep were relatively free of parasitic worms, which on the mainland took a continuous toll. Finally there was the matter of their wool. Wool from island sheep was highly prized and brought a better price at the local mills than wool from mainland sheep. The exposure of the island sheep to cycles of sun, rain, and cold produced wool that did not shrink as much as other wool, was cleaner, and produced good staple, or "crinkle," for easy spinning. The president of the Knox Woolen Mill declared that the long-stapled island wool was superior in every respect.

Perhaps the only drawback that could be charged against island sheep was described in Hosmer's Deer Isle history, published in the 1800s. The sheep on uninhabited islands were subject to "such depredations committed . . . by a worthless class who have opportunities for plunder, and were it not for that, those islands would be of more value than they are now." Free mutton and wool aside, slaughtering a man's unguarded island sheep was one way to settle a score.

Transporting sheep back and forth to the island pastures was a considerable procedure and not without its dangers, but it was the kind of activity with which islanders were familiar and skillful— moving heavy items on and off rocky shores at the right time and tide. Most sheep were taken in flocks of ten to thirty to the peripheral islands from their winter quarters in May after they were sheared; if they were pastured before shearing, there was the risk of losing the long wool to bushes and brambles. In October, the sheep were driven and captured to be returned to their winter ground, a more tricky and difficult enterprise than getting the sheep to the island. They were wilder in fall, and a certain number were lost off the steep-sided island pastures. Stove-up leg of lamb and drowned wild sheep were trials of the trade.

Livestock were thus much more important than crops to island farmers. Undoubtedly more

Black face ram, Ram Island Ledge, off McGee Island in Muscongus Bay. K. ULBRICH

hay was imported to the islands than exported from them, to judge by the number of "hay land-ings" referred to in old deeds depicting those beaches where hay could come ashore.

Apples were raised on most islands from toughened, cold-hardy New England stock. Potatoes were probably the islands' most basic crop export, but by the early 1840s the potato blight had made its way to the shores of Maine, and the histories of both Deer Isle and Islesboro record the total failure of the islands' potato crops in 1845. Gradually, blight-resistant strains of potatoes were introduced, but in 1874 those few farmers who had not moved west were plagued by the potato bug, which for several years ate up not only cash and profits but also what had come to serve as winter hog feed.

Butter Island Sheep, July 2, 1989

We're back at Allen Island, in shirtsleeves, down and dirty, shearing forty-odd sheep and culling the spring wethers and durable ewes to start a new flock on Butter Island, forty miles north-northeast. With a dozen of less-than-thrilled sheep penned in the stern of FISH HAWK, *the Island Institute's twin outboard go-fast boat, we set off—at some pains to get up on a plane—and head for the lee of the Muscle Ridge and then the northern islands.*

As FISH HAWK *rounds up and throttles back at the southeast beach of Butter, preparing to unload our mixed ruminant cargo, picnickers from a nearby yacht stare in growing disbelief. The sheep, it must be said, are not in peak form, just shorn and covered with green excreta. The only possible means of debarkation is to get as close to the beach as possible and heave-ho, sheep by sheep, over the gunwale and into the brine as a proper and clean baptism into the animals' new island life. Twelve wobbly wethers and ewes thus make*

*their way out of the water and straight up through the cluster of pre–Fourth
of July beach picnickers in search of higher and more certain ground.*

SOME ECOLOGICAL CONSIDERATIONS

It is difficult to estimate the total number of sheep that were pastured on Maine islands when
the industry was at its peak (1830–40 was the peak for New England as a whole, but the peak did
not occur until 1860 in Maine, and perhaps even later on the islands). In 1858, there were two
thousand sheep on North Haven in contrast to approximately 250 cows and 25 horses. Kimball
Island and Isle au Haut each had four hundred sheep. In 1910, there were still five hundred sheep
on Great Duck Island south of Mount Desert; there were perhaps twelve hundred on Monhegan
and three hundred on Ragged Island—known as Criehaven—at the edge of Penobscot Bay. Even as
late as 1960, there were fifteen hundred sheep pastured on Maine islands, according to a state agricultural department estimate.

When the great ranges opened up out west, and sheep vied with cattle (and sheep men vied
with cattlemen), the science of range ecology was developed. It determined, among other things,
what came to be called the carrying capacity of the range—how many animals of any sort can be
grazed on a given piece of land without running it downhill and making it less able to support similar numbers in the future.

Early farmers' practice of burning islands periodically (fires were known to stimulate new green
growth), although practical and useful in some situations, usually had deleterious effects on island
soils. The problem is chiefly related to nitrogen. One of the most necessary but limited nutrients for
plant and animal growth, nitrogen is bound in soils mostly in organic compounds, which are

Allen Island virgin birches.

PETER RALSTON

released slowly to plant roots. The effect of burning is to oxidize the nitrogen to nitrates, which are widely used in commercial fertilizers. But nitrates are soluble in water, and although some of the fire-produced nitrates stay around to give a flush of new growth to undamaged roots, the greater amount of it, particularly on islands where rainfall and fog drip create high annual precipitation, is exported from the ecosystem. It leaches off the island into the Gulf of Maine—all well and good for marine growth but detrimental to island plant growth. The baldness and boniness of many islands today date from burning sheep pastures for "poor man's fertilizer."

One situation in which the practice of burning seems to have been mitigated is on grassy islands that also serve as seabird nesting sites. On these islands the effects of the seabird excretions may have offset the loss of nitrogen due to burning. At least the effects are less obvious, even to a practiced eye. Metinic Island in Penobscot Bay has had a herd of sheep on it continuously for two hundred years; one cannot argue with success.

Another consideration regarding the mutual interdependence of sheep and birds is a subtle effect that sheep are likely to have on island ranges. They feed selectively on certain delicate species of island flora and can build up a tough grass–dominated turf that burrow-dwelling seabirds are unable to excavate. The rare Leach's storm-petrel, which assembles in the offshore waters of Maine and comes in under the cover of darkness to nest on Maine's outer islands, may have been restricted as a result of the "golden age of sheep raising." No one seems to know for sure.

NATURAL LABORATORIES

The nature of particular island places is peculiar, local, and idiosyncratic. No matter where you go along this immense archipelago, you will be struck by the differences in the assemblages of plants and animals you encounter. I've seen the differences, ranging from dramatic to subtle, wherever fieldwork has taken me, from the gray granite ghost town of Hurricane Island to the Indian encampment or yellow birch grove on Allen Island to the heath mats of Jordans Delight or Seal Island's cliffs and ledges or the dark, deep spruce growth of Burnt, Turtle, Roque, and Cross islands.

Dramatic differences hardly seem possible; after all, these islands are within range of one another, are composed of thin soils stretched over bare granite, and are bathed by the massive currents of the Gulf of Maine. You would think that their natural communities—the numbers and variety of plants, birds, fish, and shellfish—would be remarkably consistent. Anyway, that was my belief, but I couldn't have been more wrong.

On the mainland shores, the amplitude of an ecological event that disturbs the community—a fire or a windstorm—is quickly dampened by the influence of adjacent communities that keep surging into the disturbed community, supplying new creatures to fill the gaps and compete with the species that remain. But islands are different; an island that was cleared for agriculture or quarrying or was flattened by a hurricane is set off on a new ecological trajectory, unmodified by neighboring influences by the simple fact of its isolation.

Striking ecological differences are etched into the island landscape and echo through time into the present. It seems to make little difference whether the changes were induced by the hands of man or the hand of nature; they all exert a visible influence on the complement of plants and animals that inhabit these isolated systems today. In this sense, Maine islands are natural laboratories where the effects of the past are indexed in the landscape.

Careful observers will begin to see island communities as an ensemble of historical motifs, resulting from minor or catastrophic events from human or natural agents that reverberate through time. The performances have the power to entrance their audiences, and any distinctions between islanders and their environments become naturally blurred.

4

Landforms: Island Cliffs, Caves, Cobbles, and Domes

And there in ragged grayness lay the quarry
"This pavin' motion," my companion said,
"Was goin' to make me rich and made me poor.
'Twas in the eighties I began to work here,
When the great cities paved their streets with blocks
A nickel a piece they were, and I could reel
Two hundred blocks or more each blessed day."
—Wilbert Snow

FIRE AND ICE: WHY THERE ARE SO MANY MAINE ISLANDS

The reason that there are so many islands off the Maine coast, and so few south of Maine, has almost everything to do with the glaciers that covered the Maine landscape before receding some thirteen thousand years ago. A wall of ice, flowing from the frozen Arctic, covered Maine and the Gulf of Maine as far as its outer banks with ice a mile thick over the highest point of land. Before this creaking, shuddering glacier scoured the landscape, the Maine coast had been much like the rest of the Atlantic coast: a gently sloping coastal plain with sandy beaches and salt marshes. What is now the Gulf of Maine was a rolling coastal lowland with an occasional granitic dome or an ancient crystalline pinnacle breaking the horizon.

The effect of the ice was drastic. Someone has taken the time to calculate that an acre of ice a mile high weighs on the order of seven million tons. The burden of the ice depressed the land along a weak zone in the crust that runs approximately northeast-southwest, corresponding to the present trend of the coast, warping the entire crustal block downward to form the bottom of what became the Gulf of Maine.

Then within a very short time—a few thousand years, at most—the ice melted. The resulting floods were not the little overflows we have every year, not the hundred-year floods that wipe out whole towns, but inundations of incomparable magnitude surging into the sea. These floods coursed out of lakes twice the size of Moosehead (today the largest lake east of the Great Lakes), through river corridors many times the size and volume of the Kennebec and Penobscot and Saint John, to fill the basins of the coastal lowlands.

At glacial maximum, about one-third of the world's total fresh water was frozen in the polar ice

Opposite: Cobblestone beach, Metinic Island.   S. St. John-Rheault

caps, compared with 3 to 4 percent today. The equivalent of nine million cubic miles of ocean was held as ice; then this water was released in a geological instant as the sea rose worldwide.

The rising sea sent long fingers into the land. It flowed up the old river valleys all the way to Millinocket on the Penobscot and near Greenville on the Kennebec; it flowed over the outer banks, which had been dry land, and completely submerged the coastal lowlands to form the Gulf of Maine. After several thousand years, the land, relieved of the weight of the ice, rebounded somewhat; most of Maine's islands emerged as the land rose. True, some of the highest island peaks had remained dry even during the worst flooding, but the majority of them must have been submerged; hills on Mount Desert that are now two hundred feet above sea level bear evidence of sand beaches that were once lapped by wind-driven waves off the Gulf of Maine.

Somes Sound, on Mount Desert Island, is the only true fjord on the eastern coast of the United States. The textbook definition of a fjord is a drowned valley, deeply scoured by glaciation, with steep sides and a deep bottom. All of the coast of Maine was affected by the last ice sheet, but only Mount Desert Island's topographic relief was actually increased by the effects of glaciation. From Cape Elizabeth to the Penobscot River, the direction of ice movement (from northwest to southeast) was transverse to the trend of the ridges and valleys (which run from northeast to southwest); consequently the landforms in these areas were subdued rather than accentuated by the glacier. In the Mount Desert area, however, the east-west–trending ridges of resistant granite formed such a formidable barrier that they changed the direction of the ice movement from northwest-southeast to a north-south flow. As the glacier crested the granite mountains here, it carved, plucked, and smoothed the sides of what must have been a much less impressive valley system. The resulting deep trench of Somes Sound was then filled by an arm of the sea as rising sea flooded the coastal lowlands.

The eastern wall of Somes Sound in several places rises more than a thousand feet above the bottom of the trough, which in its central section is more than one hundred and twenty-five feet deeper than where it opens to the sea at The Narrows.

THE DROWNED COAST

It is because of the Pleistocene glaciation that Maine has what is called a "drowned" coast. The name did not arise because, as my nephew recently surmised, many sailors had been washed overboard into her seas.

As to the question of whether the sea level off Maine's shores is currently rising or falling, there is, among the fraternity of geologists, no unanimous agreement. The sea, like the land, is restless and fickle. She may appear to be rising along one section of the coast and falling elsewhere. But a few records from the nineteenth century are illuminating. In the 1804 edition of the *American Coast Pilot*, which provided mariners with one of the few reliable sets of directions for navigating Maine's rock-strewn waters in the era before charts were widely available, there is the following note for sailing east of Schoodic:

> In standing in [from "Skutock Hills"] for this island, you will see a small place called Titmanan's Island [Petit Manan]. There is a bar that runs from the shore to this little island which is about one league from the land and has a few bushes on it. The bar is covered at high water but bare at low water.

Anyone who has crossed the Petit Manan Bar when a falling tide is kicking up short, steep seas against a smoky sou'wester will agree that it would almost be better if the bar were still uncovered at low water so that everyone would have to go around it rather than smash through those violent waters.

Petit Manan Point, May 9, 1973, Ghost Ships

The moment you are out of sight of the end of the road, the last vestige of the human world melts away. From a slight rise, Petit Manan Point stretches out forever in the slanting afternoon light. I glimpsed the silhouetted dihedral of a marsh hawk careening low over the heath. Little stands of spruce and wind-gnarled jack pine gave foreground perspective to a new world that I had lived near for over a year but had never really seen from coveside. The white curl of the surf around treacherous Petit Manan Point combed back over the heaving deep green sea. And just offshore was a world farther out, a world of small islands, their tall trees like masts astride their craggy decks. Ghost ships.

LONG ISLANDS AND ROUND ISLANDS

If you ignore the borderline cases, Maine's islands come in two shapes: either long and narrow, such as the islands of Casco and Muscongus bays, or rounded and domed, such as Mount Desert, Deer Isle, Swan's Island, Isle au Haut, Vinalhaven, and Beals Island off Jonesport. The bedrock underlying these islands controls their topography. The region from Casco to Camden is primarily underlain by the rootstocks of ancient fold mountains; the remainder of the coast is dominated by the remnants of volcanic activity.

To understand how these shapes come about, you must understand that over the immensely long periods of time by which geologists measure these things, the earth's surface has been plastic. Mountains rise and disappear; rivers flow off the highlands and carve intersecting networks of valleys; oceans fill, flood the land, and drain away. The study of the rise and fall of landforms is called geomorphology. There are few places in the East where geologists have such a field day studying the restless movements of the earth's surface as along Maine's shores.

To study geology is to dream the big picture, and to observe the dramatic rock tableaux on Maine islands is a geologist's heaven. It is better by far than geologists' other favorite haunt—roadcuts along interstate highways, which reveal otherwise invisible cross sections of the earth's crust.

The big picture of rock history is sometimes revealed in small details. I have spent many pleasant days with geologists as they plinked away at island shorelines with their picks. I recall an afternoon spent with a geologist who had been bent over a small outcrop on a Casco Bay island for half an hour or more. When he stood up, he pointed to a series of lovely, sinuous crenellations in the outcrop and said, "This is a third-order fold of an ancient mountain chain and is good evidence of a continental collision."

EASTERN MAINE VOLCANICS

The crustal events that pushed the western Maine coast into fold mountains and configured the rocks of eastern Maine into complex and fantastic volcanic shapes resulted from the collision of two ancient tectonic plates. We'll get back to this in a minute, but first let's concentrate on the beauty of rock shapes and forms.

Brothers Islands, August 7, 1982

The Brothers Islands loom out of the water—steep, barren, and spectacular—near the eastern edge of this archipelago. The rounded dome on Western Brothers Island, composed of volcanic tuff, has an absolutely sheer, east-facing scarp that is a miniature of Yosemite's Half Dome. The center of this dome is cut by a diabase dike, most of which has eroded away, leaving a deep chimney. It is difficult climbing in the twenty-foot cut that runs half the width of the island. At the shore the dike has been eroded into distinct, regular steps; looking up from the bottom is like seeing Jacob's stairway rising into the heavens.

The south-facing cliffs on Eastern Brothers Island rise vertically sixty to seventy feet out of the deep green water. The needlelike, jagged peaks look like the hardened remnants of an ancient sand castle; they provide a place of unequaled beauty from which to watch a rising or setting sun. On a clear day, you can see twenty miles across the Bay of Fundy to Grand Manan Island.

THE LITTLE PICTURE: THE GEOMORPHOLOGY OF PLACE NAMES

The study of the origins of place names can be a riveting form of entertainment. The Maine coastal islands present an unlimited challenge to someone who will one day provide the definitive explanations for how 4,617 discrete pieces of island real estate (not to mention innumerable submerged features of the Gulf of Maine) were named by generations of Maine sailors and islanders. If none of the islands had names, no doubt they would come to be called by some of the same names they were first given. An island with a bold granite southern shore that shimmers in summer sunlight should rightly be called White Island. There would be a number of Long and High islands, a few Sand islands, a scattering of Washerwoman ledges where the surf foamed up over a half-tide ledge, perhaps one or two Crotch islands if this didn't cause too much blushing—although around the turn of the century this was reason enough to rename more than one Crotch Island. The lovely metasedimentary formations of Shipstern Island off Milbridge leave no doubt as to how the island got its name.

Shipstern Island, June 23, 1978

Shipstern, an eight-acre island, is almost impossible to land upon. It is capped by a dark gray dome of gabbro, a granitelike rock whose resistance to wave attack helps explain the island's steep precipices.

The alternately layered ochre and white sedimentary units at the western end of Shipstern are among the most beautiful rock outcrops anywhere on the Maine coast. The sheer wave-sculptured rocks at this exposed end of the island resemble the stern of some abandoned galleon afloat at the entrance to Pleasant Bay; they whisper of pirates and treasure and Spanish doubloons.

Many of the islands and ledges of the Maine archipelago that were named for their geophysical features would receive different names now. Who has even heard, in these days of imported textiles and polyesters, of a thrumcap—a round hat made of four leftover pieces of homespun called thrums? Would we still call the myriad of smooth-rounded ledges by these whimsical names: Sugar Loaves, Junk o' Pork, Ladle, Colby Pup, or Virgin's Breasts? Probably not.

Big Garden Island, July 11, 1981

On Big Garden's well-named shores, a full salad bar from a garden of earthy delights is laid out. Here is an abundance of edible beach pea, orach, sea celery, and goosetongue. From the little inner bar you can collect sea blite and glasswort to go with steamers and mussels. But the best part comes from the cobble beach, where a profusion of sea rocket grows.

Brimstone Island beach, the only one of its kind in the Gulf of Maine.   GEORGE PUTZ

Sea rocket is the ultimate colonizer, an islander always looking for a new island. When an underwater volcano erupted off the coast of Iceland in 1972, the first plant to colonize the newly created island of Surtsey was sea rocket. It grows along the temperate and polar coasts of the Atlantic and distributes itself by an ingenious adaptation of its seed capsules. Each flower matures into a two-part capsule, the larger of which has an air pocket that allows the capsule to float great distances to new habitats. The other part of the capsule, though smaller, is actually heavier; it drops in place to germinate a new plant the next season. A real bet-hedger, like all islanders.

The tiny four-petaled flowers of sea rocket are lavender, with centers of bright yellow. The plant's stems and spatula-shaped leaves are fleshy and succulent, which is one adaptation to conserve water in the dry strand environment. Sea rocket has hot, sharply flavored leaves reminiscent of horseradish, which is also a member of the mustard family.

POPPLESTONES, COBBLESTONES, AND KILLICK STONES

Long before Maine's rocks were quarried for lime and granite, the shores of her rocky coast provided more humble products. One of the first was ballast for vessels serving the early coastwise trade. One island off Jonesport is still known as Ballast Island. Another, Great Spoon Island off Isle au Haut, was no doubt named for its high, inverted-spoon-shaped hill and long, trailing handle, which makes up the cobble beach. On the early British Admiralty charts, however, Great Spoon Island was called Fill Boat Island. Ballast and Great Spoon islands both have exposed beaches where smooth, round rocks were easily collected to ballast the holds of homemade sailing vessels.

Somewhere along the line, someone realized that large, wave-smoothed stones, free for the taking off Maine's shores, could be sold to city merchants intent upon having clean streets. Dirt, in a matrix of horse manure, hardly made city streets pleasant to negotiate. The smooth round "popplestones," as they came to be called, were the first (but not the last) Maine rocks used to pave the streets of East Coast cities. Popplestones were probably also the first ballast ever sold for profit, and collecting them provided employment to Maine islanders in the early 1780s.

Isle au Haut, Boom Beach, August 22, 1981

The road from the north end of Moore Harbor leads eventually to both Eastern Head and Western Head. At Western Head, five hundred feet beyond where the road ends, is a path that leads to the head of a deep chasm called Western Thunder Gulch. Here, storm waves kicked up in a good southerly will crash into the rock canyon, compress the air inside, and produce an explosion of sound and spray.

During an easterly or northeaster, Boom Beach, in the small bight below the road that skirts the south end of Long Pond, is the place to be. The beach is a collection of smooth, rounded boulders mostly one to two feet in diameter (with a few enormous boulders up to five feet), which make an awesome sound when breaking storm waves move them rudely about. A tympanic crescendo.

Islanders' ingenious use of the materials at hand was simply another case of making a virtue out of necessity. Illustrations of this could be multiplied indefinitely, especially on the islands where specialized occupations were slow to catch on; men and women were expected to be good at everything or at least able to cope with what they had.

Maine's rocky coast had not only an abundance of cobble-lined coves for popplestone streets but also provided here and there just the right-shaped rocks that could be fashioned into small anchors known as "killicks." (Using iron for anchors was almost unheard of; in any case it was too expensive for the self-sufficient island economies.) Rather long and thin stones were necessary for these handmade anchors, which were used chiefly in the western bays from Casco to Muscongus, where the bedrock had the correct trend. One island on Muscongus Bay whose shores are covered with just the right-shaped rocks is still called Killick Stone. A neighboring island is called Stone Island—named for the island's first family settler, though this island, too, has ideal killick stones.

POCKET BEACHES AND ROCKY HEADLANDS

Of Maine's 7,039 miles of shoreline, perhaps 60 miles are sandy beach, mostly in the southern part of the state. This is a biogeographically distinct part of the western Gulf of Maine, almost more a part of Massachusetts. There are more sandy beaches on Casco Bay islands than elsewhere because the Androscoggin River used to empty its sediment load into Casco Bay before its course was altered hard-left into Merrymeeting Bay. But these beaches are unfortunately sited on the north sides of islands, so that sunbathing has never been as enticing here as other places.

Maine's most remarkable and beautiful island beach lies far to the east of Casco Bay, however.

Roque Island Beach, July 22, 1982

The Roque Island beach is the longest sandy beach in the archipelago. Its two-mile stretch of fine-grained white sand is what remains of a large glacial deposit trapped between Roque's parallel headlands. As the sea rose following the melting of the glacier, wave energy sorted and reworked the original deposit. The beach is remarkable not only for its extent but for the uniform size of its sand particles, indicating a stable wave climate over hundreds of years. During storms, any sand washed off the beach is not carried out to sea but is caught at one end of the horseshoe-shaped beach. Depending on the subtle yearly changes in the beach profile, the beach is scooped out at one end and built up at the other until redirected wave energy reverses the process. Through a pattern of constant change, the beach is maintained.

In place of sand beach fantasies, the littoralists in Maine have had to make do with the hard, cold facts of life. The shores of Maine islands are made for solitary pursuits, such as taking yourself quite seriously on an exposed promontory during a gale after being spurned in love. Or dancing at midnight just out of reach of the breakers that surge in and out after a front has passed and the moon lets your life come shining.

> ### *Brimstone Island Beach, August 28, 1975*
> *Beyond the ragged southern fringe of Vinalhaven are a half dozen islands in a group, all treeless and burnished a tawny gold in the late summer sun. The largest of these islands, Brimstone, is named for its beautiful, peculiar bedrock that pokes like dark bones from beneath its thin skin of heath. Brimstone's bedrock has been quarried into a billion tiny pieces by pounding sea and prying ice and piled onto a pair of steep cobble beaches on either side of the island. On a calm day you can land and prospect for the indescribably smooth blue-black lucky stones that the sea's swash has polished to a high sheen. With a little oil from the nearly vestigial gland beside your nostril, you can add a three-dimensional luster to a brimstone. And if you can find one without so much as a hairline fracture, you have a lucky piece as old as time itself.*

The coast's rocks are also made for children, or those who can think like children, who can remember what it was like to be small and overwhelmed by the enormity of the world around them. It is true that Maine's sea cliffs are in places startling, even to the most jaded eye—Monhegan's White Head and Mount Desert's Otter Cliffs, each of which has been called the highest sea cliff on the East Coast of the United States—but almost every other mile of shore also has precipices for a childlike eye.

SEA CLIFFS, CAVES, AND SEA ARCHES

Like a street fighter, the out-thrust jawbone of a rocky headland or peninsula dares something to hit it, and a storm sea is only too willing to comply. A point of land focuses wave energy at its outer edge, whereas coves are treated more gently. Waves bend around promontories and headlands. As they bend, they lengthen, become less steep, and spill some of their energy, so they can be quite tame as they curl into a cove.

If the cove is fronted with a deposit of glacial till—a mixture of sand, silt, gravel, and cobbles scraped off Canada and transported to New England—waves will rework the deposit. They will transport the silt offshore, leaving the larger rocks nearly in place and distributing the sand along the horseshoe arc of the cove to form a "pocket" sand beach. The particle size on the beach is a good index of the average annual wave climate; as the particle size shrinks from cobble to gravel to sand or mud, it indicates that the fury of the wave energy is more and more dissipated. In this sense a beach is really a kind of natural recording anemometer. Slight currents transport silt; a two-and-a-half-knot current transports inch-round stones; wind-driven storm waves pack three tons of power to a linear foot of shore; and so forth up the Beaufort scale. A granite boulder on Matinicus Rock, calculated by a stonecutter to weigh a hundred tons, was moved twelve feet during the lifetime of one of the island's lightkeepers.

Sea caves, rock arches, and other architectonic rock renderings exist in a number of well-visited places at Acadia National Park, including Anemone Cave and The Ovens. But these most delicate and ephemeral of all rock formations exist in dozens of other places on the islands and along the rocky shores. Even as the forces of time waste at the walls of caves and arches, the masterful hands of the sea are busy carving more.

Cross Island Sea Cave, August 5, 1981

Midway along this outer coast, we see far below us a little beach of fine stone. We decide to climb down to it, because it is near low tide and the sea is calm at the the cliffs' base. When we arrive on the beach, like a dream from Mysterious Island, the narrow maw of a sea cave opens before us. We walk in cautiously, listening to the restless beating of the ocean outside; it is a large, muffled roar, pulsing here, everywhere. Sea anemones of pale and vivid colors are attached to the back wall of this sixty-foot-deep cave; we are in a space that feels like the interior of a chambered nautilus, like the inner ear of the sea.

There is a story among the nearby fishermen of an island cave from whose entrance you can see clear through to the other side. Low tide is the only time when the entrance of the cave is exposed, the story goes, and if the surge is not too strong and you have calculated your timing right, you can enter the eerie sea vault, which opens up above like the lifting of some Jules Verne proscenium, and head for the heart of this mysterious island. It might be compared to falling Alice-in-Wonderland-like into a hole in the sea. The farther back you go, the more you wonder what you are doing there. Ahead may be a pinpoint of light. If you have enough nerve to make your way along the cool, wet walls of this tortured fault chasm bisecting the island, you'll suddenly have the feeling you have reached the other side of the island. And then you want to get out, because you cannot help but reflect that should the winds and seas begin to build, this might be the place where you'll pass an eternity.

Seal Island Cave, September 5, 1992

After years of hearing about this sea cave, it was thrilling to stumble upon it. On the far side ramparts of this outermost island is a little cleft called Squeaker Guzzle, where red-footed guillemots still tumble into and out of the skree slope late in the season. If you climb down a fault zone where two massive halves of the granite island have let go of each other, using hand-holds to get down into the zone of sea foam, where the energy of the breaking waves makes the air heavy and stringent, and look back over your shoulder, you'll suddenly see the entrance of the cave. It looks like nothing at all at first, but when you climb up and in, onto a little tabletop, it is almost pitch black except for the slanting light at the entrance. Higher still is another ledge where two people can press side by side, hugging their knees. It is close and peculiar, not a place you want to spend the night. But sitting on the ledge, with the tide coming just right, you hear the air tumble into the cave in a rush and a slow, uncurling boom . . . pfruump, whoosh. You feel that you are inside something very big.

THE GRANITE COAST

Beginning at the western edge of Penobscot Bay, along a seam running from Monhegan to Burnt Island and up the Muscle Ridge Channel all the way past Rockport, Northport, and Belfast to Cape Jellison, the bedrock changes to formations dominated by granite. Granites of all textures, shades, varieties, and colors (including reds, pinks, grays, blues, and whites) form the basis of a chain of islands that continues down east all the way to Beals, Great Wass, and Head Harbor islands—some ninety miles away.

Granite is really nothing more than frozen magma, and magma is rock that has melted beneath the earth's crust. All this melted rock is the result of collisions of continental plates, but the more easily visualized results were volcanoes—immense, violent, eruptive volcanoes that were pushed up to the earth's surface by the force of increasing quantities of molten rock. Two-thirds of the Maine coast is composed of the remnants of a long period of volcanic activity, when the coast was figuratively a ring of fire—so much so that the coast is technically described by one of Maine's best-known geologists as "the bays of Maine igneous complex."

THE HARD FACTS OF LIFE ON A HARD ROCK ISLAND: QUARRYING

There is some urge within most of us to dignify the hardships of work by speaking of it in terms of its past glory. Enormous stone vaults were pounded and blasted from the unflinching granite on some thirty-three Maine islands from Friendship to Jonesport, but there are precious few histories of the Maine island quarry years that included what these men of hard rock thought of the work. More often historians have written about the large towns and workforces of two thousand or more men, most of them immigrants, who appeared almost overnight (and in many cases disappeared as quickly) on islands such as Clark, Dix, High, and Hurricane. The Scots, Italians, Finns, Swedes, and Welsh who came to the American shores of opportunity were probably happy enough to be here and have paying jobs, but the cost in labor and lives was high, just as it was in previous human eras of constructing monuments to a forgetful future.

Cross Island's sea cave in outer Machias Bay can only be entered at low tide. LOLLY COCHRAN

The granite communities ran just like the granite from the Muscle Ridge islands across to Vinalhaven, up through Stonington and the islands of Merchant Row, to Swan's, Black, and Mount Desert and eastward to Head Harbor off Jonesport. This hundred-mile section of the coast was the center of an enormous trade in stone: granite for bridges and breakwaters; for paving blocks and public places; for libraries and the Library of Congress; for monuments and memorials; for foundations, sills, lintels, curbstones, and a hundred other uses. And everywhere went millions of cobblestones, the bread-and-butter work, to pave the muddy streets of burgeoning cities once and for all. In 1900 and the preceding few decades, more men were employed in the Maine island granite business than in fishing and farming combined.

Driving this industry was a dynamic American machine: men with big appetites and bigger visions who dreamed of huge new buildings and then built them for a nation come of age. Formed and faced with granite from Maine were Boston's Customs House and Tower and the Boston Museum of Fine Arts, the Massachusetts Institute of Technology in Cambridge, New York's capacious Public Library and a grandiose post office building in lower Manhattan, the Philadelphia Post Office, the hospital of the University of Pennsylvania, and the Naval Academy buildings in Annapolis. Elegant structures such as New York City's Metropolitan Museum of Art and the Cathedral of Saint John the Divine, and the Lincoln and Jefferson memorials in Washington, were once silent, solid hefts of rock on the shores of Maine islands.

Although small island quarrying operations had begun as early as 1792, the first commercially quarried granite in Maine was cut in 1826 on Vinalhaven to build the walls of a prison in Massachusetts. With access to inexpensive water transportation, island quarries had a natural advantage. In the Vinalhaven area, which would become the center of this trade, a second quarry opened in 1846 on Leadbetter Island, just across the Narrows on the west side; a third, the so-called East Boston Quarry, opened in 1849. There were three more by 1860 and seven others by 1880.

The early quarries primarily provided rough granite for breakwaters, forts, and lighthouses—many of the latter to mark the unforgiving Maine coast itself. With the end of the Civil War, contracts were let for public buildings of all sorts, sizes, and descriptions: post offices, customs houses, libraries, train stations, and the like. By 1890, Maine led the nation in the production of granite.

Granite with subtle blends of whites and grays came from the exposed plutons of Mount Desert Island, particularly from Hall Quarry. The same colors came off of Hurricane, High, Dix, and Clark islands, and from Vinalhaven's dozen massive quarries, including one on Norton Point which also cut black granite for monuments and facing stone. From Jonesport came a bloody red granite; other quarries advertised blue and cinnamon hues. The flecks of quartz and mica within the feldspar mineral matrix of granite also produced a variety of textures, from fine-grained granodiorites to massively textured, great, gray granites with individual crystals as large as a thumbnail. Sometimes in a dome of granite with a different cooling history, individual crystals of dark micas remelted to produce patterns of frozen swirls like those in a chocolate pound cake. Pattern upon pattern could be bought depending upon a buyer's whim or the job to be done.

Crotch Island Granite, September 20, 1980

One of Crotch Island's three quarries was owned by the same company that operated the Hurricane Island quarry. The Crotch Island quarry was most famous for the shade of its granite—lavender pink and milky white with occasional flecks of deep red caused by the presence, in unusually high concentrations, of a particular variety of feldspar, one of the mineral constituents of all granites. The Museum of Fine Arts in Boston was built with Crotch Island pink, although the rough blocks were first taken to the famous cutting shed on Hurricane Island to be cut and polished. A few of these blocks are still lying around on the south end of Hurricane Island where the polishing sheds once stood.

To carry the granite blocks to Boston, Philadelphia, and New York, where they were in high demand, the Crotch Island Company commissioned a shipyard in Bath to build them a four-masted, steam auxiliary, one-hundred-and-seventy-foot schooner, the FRANCIS HYDE. *Later, parts of the George Washington and Triborough bridges, Rockefeller Center, the Smithsonian Institution, and the Chicago Art Museum used Crotch Island granite. In*

1966, a new project on Crotch got under way when granite for the Kennedy Memorial was ordered by the Kennedy family from this most famous, and only remaining, island quarry on the coast of Maine.

THE TECHNOLOGY OF QUARRYING: THE RIFT, THE LIFT, AND THE HARDWAY

Granite lies in sheets of varying thickness over the surface of the land. Because of the structure of granite's mineral constituents, granite fractures along right-angle planes. There is something within us that likes a right angle.

An experienced stonecutter is able to tell how the grain runs in an unbroken piece of granite. Quarrymen used to speak of the plane of granite in terms of its "rift," which runs perpendicular to the horizon and in most Maine granite was oriented along an east-west axis. The "lift" of the granite (what geologists call the "sheeting") runs parallel to the horizon. The "hardway" runs at right angles to the rift.

The earliest attempts to cut granite in homemade quarries, called "motions," involved locating a "toe," where the lift thinned to an edge. There a man could trace out straight lines on the surface, chisel along them, and drill a series of quarter-inch holes, which he would then fill with dry pine plugs and pack with mud. If he had calculated the rift correctly, he would return the next day and the swollen pine plugs would have split the stone. Of course, using soft "pumpkin pine" to cut hard white granite was not the most efficient method of quarrying the stone, and more modern means of using feather and half-round wedges quickly replaced the older system.

Crotch Island, Deer Isle Thorofare, with granite schooners loading paving.   ISLAND INSTITUTE FILES

When the demand for rough blocks for the busy city harbors of the eastern seaboard created the Maine granite industry in the 1850s, quantities of rock began to be shaken loose with charges of black powder. "Lewis holes" were two four- to six-inch holes drilled side by side and filled with blasting powder, packing, and a fuse. Blasting in the early days was notoriously unreliable; when a charge failed to go off, someone had to find out why and, in finding out, frequently earned an obituary in a local newspaper.

The division of labor in a quarry usually involved a blast-hole team and a drilling team. The top drill holder was one of the quarry elite; his steady hand and nerve held the finely tempered star bit in place while two other men whaled away with sledges, taking turns and counting out a cadence. One slip of a sledge and the top drill holder joined the company of the three-fingered people. A correctly tempered drill did not bounce when struck by a sledge; it rotated perhaps a quarter turn in place and slowly bit into the granite.

The sheets of granite widened toward the center of a main quarry face due to the natural jointing patterns in the rock. This trend of the lift, as quarrymen spoke of it, allowed them to cut single pieces of enormous dimensions. The four rough columns for the interior of the Cathedral of Saint John the Divine were sixty-four feet long and eight feet in diameter and weighed three hundred tons. An earlier piece of granite cut for the monument to Major General John Ellis Wool weighed half again as much as the cathedral pillars and was at the time the largest single piece of granite ever cut from solid rock. Because granite quarrying everywhere has fallen on hard times, the best guess is that this record still stands.

Although all the early cutting was done by hand, the stones were hauled by wagons, called "galamanders," driven by yokes of oxen. By 1900, steam-driven air compressors were used to replace some of the more grueling handwork; with the introduction of machinery, fewer men were needed to run a quarry.

One of the interesting historical sidelights of the island quarry era is the complementary role played by another island community to the west. On Chebeague Island in Casco Bay, boats were built to carry granite; for the initial period, Chebeague supplied all the boats that worked the coast of Maine. Before this, Chebeague Island sloops had carried rock ballast from the shores of Casco Bay islands to the expanding Portland shipyards. So it was only natural that the island should have gotten into the business of hauling granite to build coastal forts and breakwaters. By 1870, about fifty Chebeague Island craft coasted among the islands carrying granite. The vessels, originally rigged as sloops but later rerigged as schooners, were beamy, full-bellied craft manned by crews who knew how to handle rock and, most important, how to stow cargoes. In the early days, paving stones were sluiced aboard the sloops, but later they were loaded by derricks. A load of sixty thousand paving stones headed for Boston, New York, or New Orleans was not uncommon. The record is that in one twelve-day period, 320,465 paving stones cut on Hurricane Island were shipped from its stone wharves.

At the height of the granite era, there were quarries on thirty-three islands along the coast of Maine. Not even the industrious crews from Chebeague Island could handle the daily quarry production. George Wasson, one of Maine's maritime historians, has written, perhaps with more poetry than truth, that when a vessel became too creaky to carry lumber from Bangor or cordwood to the Rockland lime kilns, she was considered "none too ripe for the stone business" and was often loaded to the scuppers with huge blocks of granite. For many granite schooners, and the crews who slept on deck, their destination lay only a matter of fathoms away.

Carvers Harbor Cemetery, July 30, 1979

It is said of the stonecutters of Vinalhaven's dozen large quarries that when they began coughing blood from quarry dust, they started carving their own gravestones. If the monuments they left in the Vinalhaven graveyard are any indication, these hard men had a long time to consider their deaths. It is both eerie and moving to wander through this small cemetery where a half dozen of the most individualistic gravestones give mute testimony to the makers whose bones lie somewhere below. Their proud work and intricate carving still cling to the hillside overlooking a magnificent scene of tidal bore. Though the rocks stand in solid ceremony, the words carved into their headstones are not as sharp as they were seventy years ago.

THE END OF AN ERA

The first concrete house in the United States was built in Port Chester, New York, in 1874. Although there is no record as to whether it was a tasteful piece of architecture, the handwriting was quickly visible on the walls made of this new material. Cement making was a skill that had been familiar to the Romans, although it was lost during the Dark Ages. It was rediscovered in 1824 by an engineer in Portland, England, and the product is still known to many as Portland cement.

The introduction of this building material, which was less expensive and easier to handle than granite, was probably the ultimate cause of the decline of granite quarrying on Maine islands, but it was not the only cause. The end of lucrative government contracts, the construction of railroads on the mainland, and labor unrest all laid blows on an increasingly moribund industry.

Nowhere was the end of the era more dramatic than on Hurricane Island. The island had been bought in 1870 for the preposterous sum of fifty dollars by a retired Civil War general who had fought at Bull Run. Davis Tillson had a reputation for being a petty tyrant, probably all the worse for owning his own island, which he ran as he pleased. When Hurricane Island separated from the Town of Vinalhaven in 1878, it had its own post office, bank, pool hall, bowling green, bandstand, ice pond, ballfield, boardinghouses, and forty cottages. Hurricane was justly famed along the coast for its cutting and polishing shed. It was said that no granite took polish as well as Hurricane's fine-grained, gray-white granite.

For forty-five years the superintendents of works on Hurricane were named Landers. First John Landers and then his son, Tom, had run the day-to-day activities on the island, where the population at one point reportedly reached fifteen hundred. The Landerses built a beautiful house at the top of the slope above the main pier along a steep cart trail called Broadway; it was the only house on the island in which a cistern was carved into the granite foundation. The Landerses were brilliant engineers; they laid out a set of dendritic channels across the broad, east-facing slope of Hurricane, turning much of the hillside into a catchment basin where rainwater was channeled to a reservoir for watering livestock and servicing the steam-powered engines that drove the drills on the massive active face that looked out to sea.

But when the last Landers died on Hurricane in 1915, it was excuse enough for the Hurricane Island Granite Company, in financial difficulties anyway, to announce that it was closing the company store and ceasing regular runs to the mainland. A kind of panic ensued among the quarrymen, stonecutters, blacksmiths, paving cutters, tool sharpeners, tool boys, lumpers, stone boxers, and teamsters and their families, who were given only short notice to pack for the last boat. Many of them were forced to leave some of their possessions behind, and most never returned. The houses were taken down and sold wharfside; the church pews, organ, and altar went to the North Haven Catholic church, and the remainder was floated across Hurricane Sound to Vinalhaven.

*Unquarried granite shoreline, Vinalhaven, showing the "lift" (natural fractures in the horizontal plane),
and the "rift" (fractures in the vertical plane).*   RICK PERRY

For years Vinalhaven people who visited Hurricane described the eerie pall that hung over the
island. Tools were literally set down in place; huge, half-carved stones stood where they had been
hauled into sheds or set down on their way to the wharf. Everything was as if hundreds of people
had disappeared overnight, which is precisely what happened.

Hurricane Island Stone Ghosts, August 2, 1979

*I caught a whisper of one of the thousands of Hurricane's untold stories
one night with just enough moon in the night sky for walking around the
island paths without a light. I was sitting in a little clearing among the
spruce that had invaded what once had been the quarriers' "town." Deep in
conversation with a couple of friends, I was idly running my hand over the
moon-bleached bare granite when my fingers felt a straight ridge in the
smooth surface. Leaning down to adjust my eyes to the moon glow, I could*

just barely make out four letters: R, P, L, and N. Initials on the rock, surely a century-old sign of a tryst. But the most remarkable feature was that the letters had not been carved into the rock; rather the granite surrounding the letters had been lovingly worn away—perhaps worried away—leaving these four initials to rise in bold relief from the hard surface. In some ineffable way those initials encapsulated all the poignancy of this island town that disappeared along with all its stories and dreams and personal histories scattered to the wind.

RESHAPING THE STONE MYTHS

Of all the human purposes that islands have served, none has left such permanent marks as the brief granite era. Scores of islands were cleared of trees and cut up for projects big and small, supremely beautiful and thoroughly utilitarian. Perhaps no island along the Maine coast has been so completely reshaped as the ten-acre dome of granite off Vinalhaven lately and accurately called Bald Island. During the first decade of the twentieth century, the island was literally blasted out of the water and hauled across Penobscot Bay to create the Rockland Breakwater. Bald Island now looms up, particularly out of an early-morning fog, like a piece of lunar landscape that has fallen out of orbit and landed in west Penobscot Bay.

Among other unanticipated benefits, abandoned quarries provide fine swimming holes and skating ponds in a good number of island communities. For the greatest part of the summer, the remnant Scotian current makes ocean swimming a character-building exercise, as the Hurricane Island Outward Bound School has proven to several generations of disbelieving students. But for teaching young children how to swim or for lying around in the water like a fat frog or manatee, nothing quite matches an island quarry swim in August or September. The best island quarries are deep and full of dark, still water and have little hidden niches along their sides—perfect for sitting motionless as stone and watching the birds make trips back and forth along the cliff face or observing the comings and goings of island sylphs playing along the shore with little children. The Boom Quarry, off an unmarked trail on Vinalhaven—which, if you have to ask, you won't find—is reserved for people who look better with their clothes off, and God bless them, too.

For me, the era's enduring legacy is to be found on Hurricane. A scant fifty years after a massive industrial enterprise had cut most all its trees, removed its soil, housed huge numbers of immigrant workers to cart off its bedrock, Hurricane became a premier setting for a world-famous wilderness program. Here is the true and lasting nature of Maine islands: Hurricane's cut and blasted granite faces are covered again by obdurate spruce, which grow out of fissures in bare rock; its motions are carpeted beneath thick mats of luxuriant mosses; and a few of its monuments are scattered about on the shore or just split from a fresh seam on the active face, frozen in a green and blue bower.

5

Birds of the Islands: Mews, Medricks, Hawks, and Hernshaws

The civilized people have lost the aptitude of stillness and must take lessons in silence from the wild before they are accepted by it. The art of moving gently, without suddenness, is the first to be studied by the hunter, the more so by the hunter with a camera. Hunters cannot have it their own way, they must fall in with the wind, and the colors and smells of the landscape, and they must make the tempo of the ensemble their own. Sometimes it repeats a movement over and over again and you must follow up with it to be part of it.

—Isak Dinesen, *Out of Africa*

For all of the short island spring and long island summer, and deep into fall when the winter ducks come, birds are it. To appreciate anything about the coast or the islands, you must take some time from whatever else you are doing to observe the habits and behavior of birds. You'll be glad you did. This sounds categorical, but there it is.

Along Maine's seven thousand–plus miles of shoreline, from the low-water mark to a hundred miles out to sea, there is not a strand, copse, mudflat, skerry, or shoal that is not regularly haunted by winged visitors. On the islands birds are everywhere, doing everything: birds aloft on wings or alight on water; birds beating their way north or south, soaring on silent feathers, wheeling in brilliant bursts of life; birds with tiny beating hearts and huge wingspans; birds hatching on ledges or in down-lined nests; birds hunching over craggy barren aeries; birds flying, dying, dancing, fishing, fighting, singing, mating, nesting, eating, excreting, and calling their insistent songs over the tympani of the restless sea where benumbing quantities of school fish lurk, every day all around you.

Summer and winter, they are the coast's living, beating heart. In spring and fall the sight of their vast migrations is as powerful an influence on the spirit as the march of the equinox across the heavens. Islands are among the few places on earth where the air is invested with such a palpable force.

Flint Island, June 6, 1975
The flint and shingle shore of this island way down east gives way to the craggy island edges over which spruce boughs are combing tiny droplets of water from the wet breath of fog. The sea hardly seems to move; it just murmurs on the beach at slack tide. At such times the universe is narrowed down

Opposite: Seabird hunter Cyrus Rackliff, who hunted and fished off the islands of western Penobscot Bay during the late nineteenth and early twentieth centuries.

to a few feet, compressed into a tiny field of view. The air is silent, heavy, and still.

Then suddenly, not twenty feet off the island edge, navigating by the shore just a wingspan off the spruce, two magnificent adult bald eagles burst into view: one a female, slightly larger than her mate, who follows off her outboard wing. They fly by, wing tip to wing tip, out of the fog—looking as startled to see me as I them, and then career sharply away and are gone in an instant. But I hear, and in the damp air imagine I feel on my face, the rush of heavy air off their wings. In that frozen moment I feel a sensation telescoping itself outward, beyond Flint's outermost realm, into a foggy white light far beyond boat times and lists of names of things I had left a world away at the campsite. On their wings' winds I am swept off the island and transported to the outer edge of the universe.

Through all the years it took for me to form the notion that islands are a kind of archetypal landscape that we carry around in our minds, that image from Flint Island never faded. It is important to consider carefully how to keep this kind of place balanced between accessibility and inaccessibility, because in one single moment of solitude, it could provide our callous, name-collecting nature something as precious as insight—inner-sight—itself.

Toward the close of the last century, during the period of the highest human occupation on islands, populations of birds reached all-time lows—not just along the Maine coast but throughout the East—as they became a source of everything from food to feathers and oil to eggs. Before the worst of the abuses were checked, several species were driven to extinction. That these are gone forever makes our lives poorer. Several other species of birds that were hunted too relentlessly no longer found the shores and islands of Maine to their liking and are only recently beginning to return. For the most part, however, the birds have recovered their original territory and populations, with only a few deleterious side effects. It could have been much worse; for most of the coast from Massachusetts to Florida, it was much worse.

INDIAN USES OF BIRDS

James Rosier describes the remnants of an Indian encampment on the shores of Allen Island in Muscongus Bay where "fire had been made; and about the place were very great egg shells." The importance of birds to the Indians has already been alluded to in Chapter 3, in the serious matter of the burning of Large Green Island by an early Matinicus fisherman.

The Indians appear to have been concerned about the management of the seabird resource. There is a record of an annual spring meeting held by sagamores and sachems near Yarmouth to determine on which nesting islands in Casco Bay each group would concentrate their hunting. They decided that they would return to a given colony only once every three years.

Seventeenth-century naturalist John Josselyn described how the Indians around Saco Bay harvested the cormorant (which he referred to as a "shape" or a "shark"): "Though I cannot commend them to our curious palates, the Indians will eat them when they are flayed. They roost in the night upon some rock that lies out in the sea; thither the Indian goes in his birch canoe when the moon shines clear." The Indian then quickly dispatched "the watchman," whereupon he was able, by "walking softly [to] take them as he pleaseth, still wringing off their heads; when he hath slain as many as his canoe can carry he gives a shout which awakens the surviving shapes, who are gone in an instant."

This remarkable description of Indian seabird hunting techniques compares closely with the methods employed for six hundred years on the Outer Hebridean island of Saint Kilda, the only European community that lived exclusively on the meat and eggs of cliff-nesting gannets, murres, puffins, and guillemots. An account from the seventeenth century describes the islanders' fowling methods: "If the sentinel be awake at the approach of the creeping fowlers and hear a noise, it cries softly 'grog, grog' at which the flock moves not; but if this sentinel see the fowler approaching, it cries quickly 'bir, bir,' which would seem to import danger, since immediately after, all the tribe take wing, leaving the fowler empty on the rock."

With the Saint Kildans, as with the island Indians, if the seabird sentinel could be killed, it was comparatively easy to go through the remainder of the sleeping birds to collect a good store.

FISHERMEN AND BIRDS: "AS IF THEY HAD BEEN STONES"

Seabirds represented an important source of protein for the European fishermen and explorers, who often were suffering from scurvy by the time they made a landfall on this side of the Atlantic. Jacques Cartier described the harvest of the hapless and flightless great auk from Funk Island off the coast of Nova Scotia: "We came to the Island of the Birds . . . whereof there is such plenty that unless a man did see them, we would think it an incredible thing . . . they seemed to have been brought thither and sowed for the nonce. In less than two hours we filled two boats full of them as if they had been stones."

Recorded observations by visitors to the Maine coast invariably included remarks on the concentrations of waterfowl and seabirds. Birds were one of the important reasons that the idea of permanent settlements could even be seriously entertained along the cold northern New England shore. Perhaps part of the attraction lay in the fact that hunting in England was a privilege restricted to the king and his attendants; one of the first colonial laws passed in the New World was the 1641 ordinance giving everyone the rights to "clamming and fowling."

Unlike fish, all birds apparently were considered edible. One colonist in the mid–nineteenth century wrote: "There is nothing that swims the water, flies the air, crawls or walks the earth that I have not served upon my table." He then goes on to describe the meals he has made of boiled owls and roasted crows. The directions for roast puffin were to slit the carcass down the back, open it flat like a kipper, then prop it upright on the hearth and grill it in front of the fire.

Seabirds were taken by shooting (which was expensive and inaccurate before the percussion cap gun came into wide use) and by netting and driving. Netting seabirds involved setting stakes in the mud of a cove frequented by diving waterfowl and stretching a net between them to entangle the birds as they swam away.

Without a doubt, the most devastating means of procuring eiders for the table, for the market, or for their feathers was through a "drive." Unlike most seabirds, which shed their feathers one by one to replace the worn-out flight suit, eiders molt their feathers all at once. There is a period, usually toward the end of August, when they are flightless and raft up in extraordinary concentrations. When this occurred, a great number of boats would assemble from island and coastal settlements and station themselves so that the birds could be driven on shore. Duck Harbor on the southwest shore of Isle au Haut was one of the places selected for such drives, because it is narrow at the mouth and extends a half mile into the island's interior. George Hosmer wrote that the drives would begin in upper Penobscot Bay near Eagle Island, from where the flightless ducks would be driven south, "narrowing the flock. When the fowls reached shore they were taken and killed and everyone engaged could have all he needed." The Ducktrap River in west Penobscot Bay presumably served a similar purpose.

A single drive on Vinalhaven took 2,100 birds, which may have been half the nesting population of eiders for the west bay that year. After the 1790s, the drives became less and less successful as the eider population declined.

Apart from the meat that the ducks provided, which could either be salted down or sent straightaway to market, feathers were also an important commodity. Eider down, as well as the wing and tail coverts of geese, swans, and winter ducks, brought a ready market in the city for quilts and bedding. Although there is no better natural insulator than eider down, which fetched a premium price, other species were hunted and sold as well. Charles Eliot's biography of the John Gilley family of Baker Island south of Mount Desert gives a good description of colonial island occupations. One winter Gilley's sons sold a hundredweight of feathers from winter sea ducks. It took six to eight duck skins for a pound of feathers, which reveals the intensity of the hunting pressure placed on the ducks.

The other serious colonial pressure on the bird populations came from "egging," probably a harmless enough activity when island populations were small but more and more damaging when everyone got into the act. Islanders would row out to one of the various Egg Rocks in the early spring after the birds had begun to nest. The islanders were careful to take a bucket of freshwater, which would determine how far along toward hatching the herring gull, eider, or cormorant eggs were. If the eggs floated, they had been incubated too long and were returned to the nest; if they sank, they were fresh enough to be sold and were taken back by the party. Farther east, the Halifax eggers harvested 750,000 murre eggs in a single season—a yield that could not be sustained.

AUDUBON'S VOYAGES ALONG THE MAINE COAST

It is difficult to come by an accurate description of how fast bird populations declined along the coast of Maine. It was probably connected to the increase in human populations, which accelerated rapidly until approximately 1830, leveled off, and hit a new peak with the beginning of the labor-intensive quarrying era in the 1870s.

One glimpse into the state of affairs in the early part of the nineteenth century relates to what did not happen. John James Audubon, an aspiring American ornithologist with an exquisite eye for painting, had been traveling around the country collecting specimens. After nearly a year in the South, culminating in several feverish months of collecting and painting in the Florida Keys and Everglades, Audubon returned to his wife, Lucy, in Philadelphia and quickly planned another collecting trip. This time he wanted to go north.

Audubon left Boston on August 14, 1832, aboard a steamer for Portland, intending to continue up into the Bay of Fundy. A week later he wrote back from Eastport: "Birds are very, very few and far between." The next May, Audubon returned, sailing downwind for Eastport again, where he arrived after a three-day passage. He chartered a cutter and prepared an expedition, not to Maine waters but to the Canadian waters eastward. Among the islands off Grand Manan Island, Audubon searched hard for gulls. For gulls! It is obvious that in 1833 the Maine coast was not what it is now. Today, an early May expedition would expect to sight, almost anywhere east of Cape Elizabeth, not just two or three species of gulls but terns, cormorants, eiders, guillemots, herons, ospreys in great concentrations, and, with a little local knowledge, even petrels, razorbills, puffins, and perhaps an eagle. For several of these species, Audubon had to go all the way to the desolate Labrador coast to find specimens to draw.

LIVES OF BIRDS

Island birds can be viewed through many different lenses. You can look at the daily behavior of the birds of the islands and consider their evolutionary relationship to one another. An evolutionary approach considers first those species that are represented earliest in the fossil record and on up through the evolutionary record of increasingly specialized bird families. Or you can view species from a habitat point of view—pelagic (oceanic) birds, seabirds, beach birds, night birds. Then you would consider that if birds exploit similar prey species or live together and share habitat islands, they should be considered as elements in an ecological community. But if you can't decide which is the best way to look at birds, then you just go back and forth between different lenses and try to put it together later, which is what I have done.

Tube-Nosed Swimmers: *Procellariiformes*

The tube-noses, or albatrosses, as they are more commonly known, belong to an ancient order of birds known in the fossil record as far back as 40 million years. They are all strictly pelagic—that is, oceanic—birds. This order of seabirds is distinguished by the hollow tube on the top of the bill that functions, depending on which wholly unsatisfactory explanation you believe, as a means of excreting salt and locating the oily matter on which they feed or as a directional wind sensor that allows them to sleep on the wing while riding out gales. To this group belong the largest living species of bird in the world, the wandering albatross. Its impressive twelve-foot wingspan far exceeds that of the next nearest competitor—as well as the smallest of seabirds, the swallow-sized petrels, which are seasonal residents of Maine's outer islands.

Leach's Storm-Petrel: *Oceanodroma leucorhoa*

Pelagic birds are forever a source of mystery and revelation. How do they weather the fierce gales that can shred a vessel? Where do they rest when the sea gives no quarter? What do they eat in the huge, awful expanse of lifeless water far off the coasts? If numbers were the only measure of such things, the Leach's storm-petrel would be called both common and abundant in Maine. Though it nests in large colonies numbering in the thousands, it is rightly considered a rare species. Few people have ever seen this secretive and delightful small seabird, which dances during the day like a butterfly over the sea's surface with its wings held aloft while feeding on all manner of floating bits of marine life.

In the Gulf of Maine these small petrels, no bigger than a robin, stage in the gathering dusk in unknown waters offshore and arrive under the cover of darkness on perhaps no more than a dozen mostly treeless lumps of rock at the outer fringes of the Maine archipelago. Here, after exuberant nighttime mating flights, they crawl into a rocky crevice or perhaps a burrow they have excavated in the soft peat to lay and incubate eggs and raise a single, fat, downy chick.

But there's much more drama and mystery to the lives of these unassuming gray birds than this description suggests. First, they are nocturnal on their breeding grounds because they are altogether too easy prey for greedy gulls during the daylight hours. As many a gull pellet of tattered gray feathers and a pair of protruding webbed feet gives evidence, the life of a petrel can be quickly and wholly circumscribed by a single swallow of a great black-backed gull. Even moonlit nights are dangerous, because gulls are sharp-eyed hosts waiting, waiting for the dinner guests to arrive. Island nesting refuges are few and far enough between that mortal enemies must share the ground and pay the price.

But on dark nights, when the moon has set early or risen late or is new and therefore altogether faceless, it is a different world for petrels on their remote breeding grounds.

Seal Island, June 5, 1977, "Little Jesus Feet"

From the cliffs of Hurricane Island, you can just barely see the white ribbon of Seal Island's outer shores. We sought and ultimately secured permits from the U.S. Fish and Wildlife Service, which owns Seal, to construct a tent platform to serve as a temporary base for mapping the vegetation

*communities and for sampling the flora to make permanent herbarium spec-
imens for the College of the Atlantic.*

*We locate our tent platform in a slight depression near the center of the
island that provides some measure of protection from the beating of the
winds, which always seem to be blowing half a gale. Last night was partially
moonlit. Several hours after crawling into the tent, I wake to a strange,
melodic, whirring noise overhead. After listening intently for a time, while
the sound mixed with other more unworldly calls, I crawl out of the tent and
sit next to it, surrounded it seems by the voices of lost souls stirring at this
late-early hour.*

*In and out of the stark shadows of the lunar light I feel the flicker of
flight wings amid overhead whirring sounds. Stranger still, from a boulder
field beyond the ken of the tent comes another call—a slow purring noise,
punctuated by a soft clucking sound that has me on hands and knees, ear
down amid the granite boulders. As I kneel rock-still, a robin-sized bird drops
out of the moonlit sky to land near my feet and scrambles into a crevice
between some boulders. Another and another follow, seemingly oblivious of
my presence, whirring down like rain and disappearing into the ground.*

*They are petrels, arrived from nowhere to relieve their mates in the bur-
rows. First the wings whirring in the dark air. And then the song. It is like
nothing I had ever heard—a low, faintly musical sound that moves by in
waves and is answered in a moment, at first softly and then with more insis-
tence, maybe relief, from the burrow. The air and the ground are alive with
the song.*

*When the whirring calls cease, all is silent for a few moments until a
new call—a deep, throaty chuckle—rises from the sea of rocks and reverber-
ates underfoot. Then one or two more chuckles, then more, until an entire
chorus of laughter erupts underfoot. The hard jumble of rock filled with
thrilling pulses of mirth, of reunion, of fluttering hearts racing in the
moment of dark danger defeated. A pure ode to joy.*

*When petrel chicks are well developed, you can extend your arm into
their burrow and cup your hand. Your warmth attracts the little night bird,
which nestles into your palm and looks like a little gray ball with large
webbed feet big enough to walk on water. Sailors all over the world have a
special place in their hearts for petrels, which remind them of gentle Mother
Mary and which, in a Cockney play on words, they call Mother Cary's chick-
ens. But here on these windy spots in the Gulf of Maine, the fishermen call
them "Little Jesus feet," because they seemingly walk on water and carry the
souls of the dead to new life.*

*I went to sleep last night a careful researcher, counting patches of Arctic
vegetation on the island's bare bones. But I awake this morning filled with
the certainty that such careful measures, though respectable science, can
never divine creation.*

Full-Webbed Swimmers: *Pelecaniformes*

Among ornithologists, this order of less than fully seagoing birds is distinguished chiefly by
four toes united with a single web. To bird-watchers, the cormorants and gannets are better known
for their gaudy throat pouches, called gular sacs. These pouches are most colorfully developed in
tropic birds and frigate birds, where they serve not only for transporting fish but also for elaborate

Cormorant nesting site on Old Man Island, Machias Bay.

sexual displays. Most members of the order have large wings, short legs, and large bills. They are known to be strong flyers, but they are rather ungainly on land.

Double-Crested Cormorant: *Phalacrocorax auritus*

It's not easy to love a cormorant unless you overflow with the milk of human kindness for all living creatures. After all, a bird that was known since colonial times as a shark, or to fishermen as a shag, for its habit of pilfering fish weirs, hardly inspires feelings of respect. It's not a matter of the reasonably small number of fish that cormorants could consume that would make otherwise reasonable men think nothing of shooting them at each and every opportunity; it is their habit, when entering a weir, to chase (or shag) the fish, which breaks up the school and allows the fish, in their confusion, to find the way out.

The fishermen-sponsored pogrom directed against the cormorant grew in intensity as coastal fisheries became commercially more important than the bank fisheries. The fairly detailed descriptions of the period between 1880 and 1925 indicate no records of any cormorants nesting in Maine. They were simply eliminated as a breeding species for forty-five years.

In more recent times the wardens of the U.S. Fish and Wildlife Service have participated in the vendetta. Salmon smolt are stocked in some of the estuaries of the state's major rivers in an attempt to augment natural populations or reestablish them where they have been driven off by the long march of civilization. This usually happens during the second week of April—which, as it happens, is when the cormorants descend on Maine, voracious after their long flight north to their nesting grounds. What ensues, as anyone could have predicted, is that the sluggish, hatchery-raised smolt

Double-crested cormorant juveniles.

are consumed in great numbers until the larger, more desirable alewives arrive, thus angering not only the salmon fishermen who come to Vacationland to catch fish and spend money but also the hatchery personnel, who have taken great pains to raise these temperamental salmon.

The effort to control Maine's cormorants seems almost timeless; it is at least as old as Indians paddling canoes out to cormorant colonies, or bank fishermen collecting the birds for bait. Surely these large, dark birds deserve better than to be salted in barrels for fish bait. For years, wardens would motor out to the various Shag, Pulpit, or Smutty Nose rocks and take turns blowing the big birds out of the sky. It was an expensive and time-consuming method of control and is no longer practiced.

One of the wardens, who headed the Pest Control Division of the wildlife service, was an actor in this drama, although he had no great love of visiting the offshore colonies for the hunt (which never worked anyway; no matter how many breeders were slain, there seemed always to be enough nonbreeders to take their place immediately). The warden found that patrolling a short section of the river where the sluggish salmon smolt were dropped was enough to discourage the greatest number of cormorants from their estuarine easy street; he actually became fond of the birds, who seemed day by day determined to make his work easier. All he had to do was arrive in the morning towing the same outboard-powered boat behind the same station wagon and the cormorants would take immediate flight and be gone all day. When you think about it, cormorants get easier to like.

During most of the season, cormorants feed on commercially valueless sculpin, cunner, alewives, and gunnel, which they dive for in waters of less than thirty feet. Of a more primitive stock than other diving birds, cormorants have fewer oil glands to keep their feathers dry, which explains their habit of standing with wings outspread on buoys or ledges as if they are drying out their laundry. They build nests on the most exposed, least desirable pieces of colonial seabird real estate, nesting frequently on the same rocks with gulls, eiders, and guillemots. Occasionally they nest in trees, but their habit of fouling their nests spills over onto the trees and strips them of needles. Many a treeless Maine island has the double-crested cormorant to thank for its grassy green look, but before the trees fall, arboreal rookeries look like ghost towns in the making.

The cormorant young are born without feathers; in fact, they are covered with reptilian-like scales and have a distinct tailbone protruding from their sterns. They look for all the world like little black lizards until they grow a juvenile plumage. Anyone who has doubted the truth of Darwin's theory of evolution should have a closer look at the homely young of the cormorant before insisting that birds are not descended from reptiles.

Herons and Their Allies: *Ciconiiformes*
The Ciconiiformes are the long-necked, long-legged wading birds that inhabit every ice-free coast of the world. Their telltale toes are long, slightly webbed, and arranged three in front and one at the rear. The flight of most wading birds is lumbering and strenuous, but they travel great distances in migration once they get airborne. Almost all of the one hundred and fourteen species belonging to the Ciconiiformes have long and often peculiarly shaped bills that are adapted in some way to persecute finny creatures swimming in shallow waters.

Great Blue Heron, Ardea herodias
The great blue heron, measured tip to toe, is the largest bird of the Maine coast, though it relinquishes its primacy to the bald eagle when the measurement is taken wing tip to wing tip. Herons are colonial nesters, which means they are in the habit of nesting in squawking, honking, flapping concentrations of their own kind and their near relatives.

There are perhaps a half dozen Maine islands with the name of Heron. The birds have been part of the coastal scene since the white man arrived, and for a time long before, no doubt; herons are known in the fossil record for forty million years. Rosier and Josselyn both mentioned them, calling them "hernshaws"—a more polite name than "shitpoke," which is what fishermen call them.

It seems likely that the short-term effect of the herons' copious droppings is to fertilize the island forests, where they become established in colonies that range from fifteen to two hundred nests. But the longer-term effect—over, say, a decade—is to kill the leaves and needles of the trees in which they nest, forcing the birds to evacuate to another island, a process that happens more quickly when they have been nesting in spruces.

Before the feather-seeking milliners arrived on the Maine coast in the 1880s, the population of this large heron was already declining from what appeared to be wanton human vandalism, particularly within mainland colonies, which have all but disappeared. By 1850, great blues were already scarce, which helps explain why the plume hunters, who were so relentless in their exploitation of herons and egrets elsewhere, were not even more destructive to Maine colonies.

Great blue heron returning to Mark Island heronry.   RICK PERRY

Mark Island, August 20, 1975, The Long-leggeds

Mark Island lies at the end of a long chain of narrow islands at the southern terminus of the Turtle Head Fault—a narrow sliver of upcountry rock that has somehow wedged its way a hundred miles southward into Penobscot Bay over the past several hundred million years the way a seed squeezes itself out of a pod. Not particularly remote, Mark lies just three miles out in west Penobscot Bay, but it is nearly inaccessible because its steep, craggy shores lack any good landing spots.

Picking a narrow cut in the shore bedrock you can squeak in, and, timing the approach between the surge and swash, you can land a peapod on the steep beach.

The shore rocks are completely different from Vinalhaven's massive granites: greenish gray, they are cut with long, vertical fracture planes that have been riven away from the edge of the island, leaving large, columnar slabs all akilter like pieces of an ancient temple. Often fog has rolled in, and the shore spruces have a gauzy dew dripping from the tips of their branch combs. You have to crawl up and under the spiny lower branches of the white spruce that ring the periphery of the shore to stand up in the emerald-lighted interior, where a deep, soft soil supports a rich complement of understory flowers I've found nowhere else: red and white dolls eyes, trailing yew, and dense patches of aromatic wild leek grow in profusion around the bases of beech, birch, and maples. I'm in an ancient hardwood forest surrounded by these old monarchs measuring two to three feet in diameter. The deep leaf litter, dampened by the fog shroud, seems soft and centuries old. Except for the muffled heave of the bay, everything is quiet. Walking slowly through the gray-green filtered light to the height of land toward the south end of this thirty-five-acre Oz is to be completely transported. Mark Island, with no cellar hole, with virtually no possibility of supporting human life, is still as the Indians knew it.

Into this reverie, an alarming and completely unrecognizable sound cuts the stillness and halts you in your tracks. From the top of an understory birch, a large, gangling great blue heron fledgling stares down its lanceolate bill and emits another challenging alarm cry. Soon another great blue lets forth from off to the left and higher up. The notes seem to start somewhere within the recesses of the birds' sinuous bodies but are amplified by the sharp, reedy bills and sound like nothing so much as a blast from an oboe that Shostakovich might have scored.

Egrets and Ibises and Other Herons

One of the most interesting behavioral adaptations of herons and their allies is what ornithologists call "postbreeding dispersion." Most birds raise their young and then, keyed to the changing length of day and night, begin to get restless in late summer. Ducks and geese, as well as cormorants, terns, and some gulls, begin staging in bays and protected waters in anticipation of the day when they will all of a sudden get up and go south. But wading birds at the end of summer fly off in all directions to all points of the compass; many fly hundreds of miles north. The young, in particular, often pay for this behavior when frozen flats cause starvation. But the advantage of this behavior is the discovery of new breeding habitats by those who go off prospecting.

In recent years, the Maine coast has benefited from the dramatic and sudden northward shift of the breeding range of snowy egret and glossy ibis. Before 1970, these birds were rare visitors to the Maine coast, but in 1972 not only did they show up on the islands in Saco Bay, they settled down and raised young in an increasingly large, multi-specied heronry at Stratton Island. In an era when we have become used to the sad litany of human incursions into the number and diversity of wild creatures, it is reassuring to realize that nature is still capable of striking back with a pleasant surprise.

Waterfowl: *Anseriformes*

The birds we call waterfowl and lump together into a single order are called wildfowl by the British. Both names are an indication of the service the birds have rendered to mankind. It seems likely that no other group of birds has provided as many meals to as many different societies as the ducks, geese, and swans, which together account for the greatest number of this order's members. These birds were among the first to be domesticated, although the most meritorious service in this regard now rests with the relatives of the Asian guinea fowl, whose chicken descendants make it the most abundant species of bird on earth.

Ducks, geese, swans, and their relatives are semiaquatic birds that are strong divers and flyers, have well-developed oil glands that protect their plumage from becoming waterlogged, and possess for the most part downy feathers for insulation.

Common Eider: Somateria mollissima

The eider is the second most common species of nesting bird of the coastal islands of Maine (the common herring gull is first). This is remarkable, because a census of breeding birds on Maine islands in 1904 turned up only four eider adults, and those were only at the extreme eastern end of the coast, on Old Man Island off Cutler. Thirty years later there were still only two dozen nesting pairs. Today, on some three to four hundred Maine islands, between fifty and sixty thousand eiders pair off to mate in April; this number does not even include the immature or nonbreeding adults.

Male eiders have stunning black and white plumage with a faint green crown; the females are uniformly dull brown, presumably a protective coloration, because they alone incubate the eggs on the nesting islands. Once the brief mating period is over in early May, the brightly colored males raft up and hang about the edges of the nesting islands, cooing and moaning at their now totally disinterested mates until they give up, swim off, and form bachelor groups.

The hen eiders eat little during their month-long vigil over the eggs, although on sunny days they occasionally mound up the down they have earlier plucked from their breasts to line the nest and arrange it quiltlike over the eggs while they take a break. More often than not, the nesting islands chosen by the eiders are inhabited by black-backed and herring gulls. This seems somewhat curious behavior on the part of the eiders, because the gulls are the most ruthless predators of young eider chicks and are not above gorging on the eggs of a temporarily vacated nest.

The dynamics of the relationship of gulls to eiders are illustrated in dramatic terms during the early weeks of June, when the greatest number of downy eider chicks hatch. Although the four to seven eggs are laid over a period of as long as a week, the sounds or sympathetic vibrations of early-hatching chicks stimulate the whole brood into a feverish attempt to break through their calcium incubators, such that they will normally emerge within minutes of one another. Without this synchrony, the losses to predation would further decrease the number of eiders that survive.

A few hours after the hatching, the chicks are mobile enough to be shepherded by the hens down to the water. The opportunistic gulls are intimately aware that a procession of duck dinners will be attempting to make its way through the nesting ground. They watch and wait. The eiders also know this, and a fair number of them wait for the cover of darkness to make their way through the gauntlet. With the hen in the lead and the chicks keeping close behind, constantly peeping and cheeping, which seems certain to give away their location, the family makes its way down to the sea. Some 25 percent are lost or stranded in the underbrush or in the gullets of gulls before the first day of their life is over. In sheer numbers, the mortality is immense. There are on the order of 30,000 nesting hen eiders in Maine, which together produce something like 100,000 to 150,000 chicks within perhaps a three-week period. It is literally a field day for the gulls, who will prune these numbers down to between, say, 75,000 and 150,000 chicks within the first week after hatching.

Once the chicks and hens have reached the water, the losses are fewer, because the young are precocious; they can dive and feed themselves from birth and are afforded protection from the cruising gulls by their response of disappearing underwater when a shadow passes close by. Gulls can still pick the unwary young out of the water, and it is in this selection of the unwary that gulls and eiders seem to coexist for each other's benefit. The eiders produce enough young to supply part of the diet of the gulls with whom they share nesting space, and the gulls cull the least well-adapted chicks before they reach breeding age and pass unfit genes on to the next generation. It's not a sentimental arrangement, but it seems to work pretty well.

Winter Ducks

Maine's nesting eiders start to move south in late September and October. Although some of their species are present in winter, they are the breeders from farther north. These northern eiders arrive with squadrons of other migratory waterfowl, including Canada and blue geese, brant, and teal, to name a few. These are birds of passage that are mostly headed for the great salt marsh estuaries of Massachusetts and the southern Atlantic coast.

The winter ducks spread themselves out along the protected coastlines of every island shore from Stratton on the west to Old Man on the east. Among other places, the ducks congregate around the offshore ledges where the pounding surf loosens the holds of a variety of marine creatures on which they feed. Goldeneye, buffleheads, scoters, scaup, and old squaw—known to hunters as whistlers, butterballs, coots, bluebills, and pintails, respectively—swim in and about the various Gunning rocks from October to April.

Of all the winter ducks that have been residents of the coast during the bitter months, none is more rare and beautiful than the harlequin duck, which inhabits one of the most violent ecological niches of the bird kingdom. The incomparably colored and appropriately named harlequin feeds on the small crustaceans and marine snails kicked up by violent surf breaking on a half-tide ledge. For the last eighty years at least, these uncommon northern ducks have been arriving and wintering off the Brandies and Roaring Bull Ledges off Isle au Haut. The harlequins, which are called "squeakers" locally, are in the habit of scurrying in the "gutters" or "guzzles" formed just in front of a breaking wave, then reappearing in its train. One nineteenth-century hunter remarked that he had collected no other species that showed more mended broken bones than the harlequin duck. Bless their turbulent souls.

Vinalhaven, December 19, 1979, Christmas Bird Count

George Putz organizes a Christmas Bird Count with a lobsterman nicknamed Sneak and another retired lobsterman known as Muckle. There are probably more Maine lobstermen who participate in Audubon's Christmas Bird Counts than workingmen in any other place along the eastern seaboard. Part of the reason is that lobstermen are unusually adept at observing shifts and cycles in nature, because their livelihoods depend upon recognizing and recording such things. And they take their cues wherever they can find them.

Most fishermen like to watch seabirds simply because they're good company on the water. They're also good luck; lots of bird activity generally means there's lots of marine life, and birds help define areas where the fishing will be good. Besides, many seabirds make for good hunting during the fall duck season.

Sneak says he uses gulls as signals around Seal Island to tell him if someone is disturbing his traps. "The bitch is we get hauled a lot down there; they steal a lot of our lobsters. You can be pretty sure when somebody is out there. You can tell by the birds, by the gulls. Anybody that knows anything can tell in a minute. If the birds are uneasy or setting off in the water, you know."

On the appointed December day a week before Christmas, we pick up Muckle in town and drive to Sneak's house out on Calderwood Neck. There we pile into the cab of Sneak's four-wheel-drive pickup. It snowed a few days earlier, but it hasn't turned really cold yet, so the ground is still soft where the frost hasn't worked its way down the two to four feet that it will later in winter. We negotiate the long driveways that lead down to Vinalhaven's grand summer places around Seal Bay, Winter Harbor, Vinal Cove, the Mill River, Perry's Creek, and Crockett Cove. We prospect every headland and beach, however unprepossessing, whether it is named on the charts or is just part of local knowledge.

The flocks of sea ducks begin adding up: bluebills (surf scoters), whistlers (American goldeneye), butterballs (bufflehead), and old squaw. Sneak, who's given up hunting them, knows where they're rafted up out of the wind or feeding in tide rips or on productive bottom. We even surprise an old great blue heron up on the Thorofare. It is a unique record for this

big wading bird, which usually moves out of Maine completely when the last
flats have frozen. Muckle says that often old males do not migrate at the end
of their lives.

Birds of Prey: *Falconiformes*

One of the distinguishing features of birds of prey—the order to which hawks, eagles, and falcons belong—is that the females are larger than the males. There are many possible explanations for the adaptive advantages that this arrangement might convey, but none of them explains why a larger female body size hasn't arisen in any other orders of birds.

Birds of prey are also distinguished by their diurnal habits, keen vision, sharp talons, opposable hind toe (useful for grasping prey), and strongly hooked bill. Up close, the bills look imposing and threatening, but they are less lethal than the talons, which are strong enough in the eagle, for instance, to break a human neck—not that this is known to have ever happened.

Bald Eagle, Haliaeetus leucocephalus

In 1979, there were forty-eight nesting pairs of eagles in Maine, a pathetically small population, except that their numbers were then greater here than in any other state east of the Mississippi (with the possible exception of Virginia and Maryland, where eagles move back and forth across state lines often enough to confuse the issue). Two-thirds of Maine's eagles nest on the coast rather than on the large inland lakes, and most members of the coastal population maintain their aeries on islands, where they are less likely to be disturbed.

Estimates of precolonial eagle numbers vary, but it is likely that there were on the order of four to five hundred pairs before the Europeans arrived. Josselyn reported that in 1668 a great shoal of eels was stranded in upper Casco Bay and that an "infinite number of Gripes [eagles] thither resorted insomuch that, being shot by the inhabitants, they fed their hogs with them for some weeks." Herbert Spinney noted the decline of eagles nesting in the midcoast area because of lumbering in the late 1800s. Large pines near the coast, favored as nest trees by eagles, were among the first to be cut and exported for ships' masts. Some islands were cleared entirely.

Sheepmen throughout the world consistently have a dim view of eagles, national bird or no. By the mid-1800s, the great increase in the flocks of island sheep could only mean trouble for eagles, which have an appetite for dead, dying, small, and newborn lambs. In 1806, the town meeting on Vinalhaven placed a bounty of twenty cents on an eagle carcass.

By the 1830s, eagles were all but gone from Casco Bay, where one naturalist had a few years earlier described being surrounded by a flight of thirteen of them as he climbed a nest tree on Peaks Island. In the early 1800s there were fifteen occupied nests on the Kennebec River below Bath, but they were gone by 1908. By the 1940s, the population for the entire state was estimated at sixty pairs. If the decline has been slower than for other persecuted species, it is because eagles live twenty-five to forty years in the wild. But it seems clear that for the past twenty-five years, eagles, although protected by law, have not been reproducing at a rate sufficient to offset the annual mortality.

Because eagles, like humans, eat at the top of the food chain, they tend to concentrate environmental poisons that have been introduced in trace amounts to their food supplies. In the nineteenth century, island sheepmen realized that a measure of eagle population control could be accomplished by lacing the carcasses of dead animals with strychnine. In the latter part of the twentieth century, eagles have suffered from the introduction of persistent pesticides into the food chain that, in the case of DDT, interfere with their calcium metabolism such that, in the worst cases, eggs are laid in jellylike masses. As DDT has begun to decline in tissue samples, polychlorinated biphenyls, known as PCBs, have begun to show up in alarming concentrations in the bodies of dead eagles. For species

Peregrine falcon with prey, Wooden Ball Island.   S. BAIRD

at the top of the food chain, it takes decades to begin to repair the ecological damage of centuries.

In 1970, there were still five or six eagle nests left along the Kennebec River and a progressively greater representation of this largest of birds of prey in the coastal waters eastward. By 1980, the westernmost concentration of breeding pairs was found in and around Mount Desert Island, with the westernmost nest in Penobscot Bay. But slowly, slowly their numbers have increased, and they are expanding their range both westward and eastward. In 1997, ninety-five pairs of nesting eagles produced one hundred and forty-one young. Another one hundred and eight nest sites were occupied but produced no young. When eagles nest again on Casco Bay islands, maybe we will have turned the corner.

One pair took up a nest in a heronry in Narraguagus Bay, which must present all sorts of uneasy dilemmas for the great blues, whose defenseless and ungainly young are almost too easy a target for the pair of eagles that stare down at them daily with unsentimental eyes. Because the eagles maintain an awesome presence there, the scavenging gulls, crows, ravens, and their kind are less likely to cause mischief. But the herons apparently pay for this protection, if the picked bones of young herons found in the eagle nest are any indication. It's like a Mayan custom of sacrificing virgins to propitiate the hungry bird gods.

American Osprey, Pandion haliaetus

Perhaps no other bird is so characteristic of the Maine coast as the osprey, whose numbers, unlike those of the eagles, have increased after their bout with DDT. Osprey inhabit every continent of the world except Antarctica and nest up and down the East Coast. But somehow their brilliant brown and white plumage and harsh "kree-kree-kree" cry is a more appropriate addition to the dark contours of a spruce-lined cove. Captain John Smith thought so when he visited these rocky isles three and a half centuries ago: "Yet you shall see the wild hawks [who] give pleasure in seeing them stoop six or seven after one another, at the schools of fish in the fair harbors."

Although the osprey is large, it is not exceptionally strong for a hawk. Most of the time it has no particular need for strength, because it feeds on relatively small fish, which it catches by dropping out of the sky and into the water feet-first. Eagles are in the habit of intercepting these slightly smaller cousins as they return with a fish to share with mate or young. When this happens there is no contest; eagles win, wings down.

Osprey have never been persecuted to the same extent as eagles. To most fishermen, it is bad luck to kill an osprey. During the quarrying years, however, the superstition from which osprey had benefited did not deter the coast's new immigrants. The late Arthur Norton, founder and curator of the Portland Museum of Natural History, reports that after the Hurricane Island Granite Company fell on hard times in 1890, nine of the twelve pairs of ospreys nesting throughout Hurricane Sound, mostly on Green's Island, were shot by unemployed quarrymen "whose primitive conception of hunting was abetted by an abundance of cheap fowling pieces and ammunition."

Most of Maine's osprey migrate to Central and South America for the winter and return to this rocky coast during the first week of April to reoccupy the same nest used in previous years. If winter gales have wreaked havoc on their platforms of sticks, potwarp, and seaweed, they begin anew. Most build nests in the tops of shoreside spruce, but some birds appear to prefer nesting on the ground. One population of eight to ten pairs in northern Penobscot Bay nests exclusively on inaccessible rocky shores. This population, which has increased over the past two decades, occupies the needle-shaped ledges that are characteristic of the volcanic rocks of the northern end of the bay. A good number of these ground-nesting pairs are no doubt related to untold generations of osprey that for almost a century occupied a nest on a ledge at the entrance to Pulpit Harbor on North Haven.

Other Hawks, Falcons, and Owls

The coastal islands of Maine form an important part of the flyway for northern-nesting hawks and falcons. The fall migration is more spectacular than the spring arrival, because hawk and falcon movements are closely tied to changes in the weather. When the wind veers into the northwest after a September gale, cold, clear air pours over the ribbon of land and water, bringing high pressure, which means it's time to fly. Suddenly every variety of winged creature seems to be slicing south-west, and the hawks are close behind to pick up the pieces.

The soaring hawks, such as the red-tailed hawk and the broad-winged hawk, avoid the islands and the water in between, but the accipiters—the mid-sized Cooper's hawk and the smaller sharp-shinned hawk—will fly by your head all day if you stand on a high hill where the wind rises up and over. During the fall migration of these low flyers, small piles of flight feathers mark the spots here and there along the islands where the hunted have become fuel for accipiters on their winged wanderings to the so'th'ard.

Along the outer rim of the islands, if you have sharp eyes and sit still, it is possible to see merlins—magical falcons that stoop to conquer the slow of wit and wing. In an earlier era, the merlins were accompanied by a larger number of peregrines, the fastest-flying bird, which is known to dive out of the sky at speeds approaching two hundred miles per hour. Their numbers are increasing along the islands where they used to nest, and the outer islands are an important part of the flyway for Arctic peregrines.

Wooden Ball Island, September 28, 1985, Peregrine Watch

Wooden Ball seems like a piece of rock dropped from outer space into the sea. Because fishermen from the nearby island of Criehaven once fished "the Ball" from camps they built here, the island has a little more of a settled feel to its stark, rocky beauty than the more austere Seal Island, which we can see lying awash in the northwesterly driven sea. Looking at the white rollers combing all over the surface of the deep blue sea reminds me of the description that fishermen use for such days: "white horses are galloping down the bay."

On the fourth day after another cold front, we spot our first peregrine. It's a sight we're not likely to forget. This one came in fast and low over the dome of the east end of Wooden Ball; its speed and strength of wing, its mastery of the air immediately marked it as singular. Peregrines are birds of open heaths, of tundras stretching to the horizon, of wild fringing beaches of uninhabited coasts, and, lately, of bridges and skyscrapers where a nearly inexhaustible supply of pigeons is apparently too alluring to ignore.

We watched this peregrine worry some migrating warblers and sparrows that are flitting along Wooden Ball's central pasture, but the falcon does not appear to be hunting seriously. A pile of yellow-shafted flicker feathers at the other end of Wooden Ball, however, looks like what might be left after a midair explosion. At the end of the day we have tabulated thirty-one sightings of peregrines careening along this outermost edge of the archipelago during this first week.

As the peregrine network grew and our observation skills were honed, peregrine sightings increased to fifty-five to sixty birds per season. Most of these birds were the darker color phase, indicating that they are Arctic migrants. The observations of this small, shifting group of field biologists provided five years of data that elegantly supported the notion originally proposed by Bill Drury (of the College of the Atlantic) that these tiny heath islands are critical feeding stations for one of the globe's grandest and most endangered species.

Owls, particularly the great horned, are frequent island denizens, easily recognized by their nightly hooting from the boughs of giant spruce. They mostly hunt rodents—sumptuous pickings—leaving the regurgitated remains in furry pellets to ease an island biogeographer's task of enumerating the rodent complement. But great horned owls have also been known to be a murderous presence on even the outermost nesting islands, where they come under the cover of darkness to find and feast on young terns and petrels.

Allen Island, February 13, 1983, Snowy Owl

No matter how much snow falls on the coast during a northeaster, it is never enough to cover the bedrock bones that protrude from the windswept northern pasture at Allen. And because the wind never relents, most of the snow that does fall is blown into pockets where the wind spins into little eddies. Allen Island is a stark landscape of browns and whites against the backdrop of a gray sea.

Out over the pasture, the moon is a quarter full and on her back. A few of Orion's brightest stars are visible along with a scattering of others in the dark firmament of space. From the spine of the point that looks back to the few scattered lights of Port Clyde, a huge, silent shadow glides a few feet overhead in the eerie lunar light. Somewhere the mind knows this presence to be an owl cruising the bare pasture for signs of meadow voles, but the size of the bird, caught as a long-winged shadow on the ground, is a shock—the more so because not a whisper of sound trailed off the wings of that ghostly gray streak. There is only the silent ground and, off in the distance, the faint rote of the sea.

(The following week I found the body of a beautiful snowy owl, dead apparently of starvation, out on the point. I took it home and carefully mounted it. It was the most beautifully feathered bird I had ever held.)

Gulls, Terns, Auks, and Shorebirds: *Charadriiformes*

It is maybe a little unfair to put shorebirds at the end of the list of birds that make up the order Charadriiformes, because they account for most of its species. But a great many of the shorebirds—the plovers and sandpipers that nest on the wide expanse of Arctic tundra—fly directly across the mouth of the Gulf of Maine on north-south trips and are most typical on the vast mudflats fringing Cape Cod and the embayments farther south. Maine gets a fair representation of turnstone, dunlin, curlew, willet, and godwit—to mention a few of the larger shorebirds—but along our coast they are on the move, toward either their northerly breeding grounds or sandy southern beaches. When they stop on a half-tide ledge or an indented muddy cove, it is often just for a quick periwinkle and go.

Gulls, terns, and auks, on the other hand, are more comfortable in and around Maine waters and have been associated with the Gulf of Maine in mariners' minds ever since the first Biscay shallop whitened the horizon. These birds are divided into two families: the Laridae (the gulls) and the Alcidae (or alcids, including auks, murres, and puffins). They are colonial breeders, which means that their reproductive hormonal balance is synchronized to a critical mass of the group; they don't get into the mood to pair, mate, and incubate until the air is full of their darting shapes.

Greater Black-Backed Gull, Larus marinus

The black-backed gull is the largest member of its family in the world. The greatest concentrations of black-backs are found in Arctic waters, along the barren coast of southern Labrador. In Maine, the first twentieth-century breeding records of this huge black-and-white bird date from the early 1930s. During the next fifteen years, black-backs extended their breeding range into all Maine bays. Theirs is one of the most surprising and rapid range extensions recorded in the twentieth century.

Black-backed gulls nest in mixed colonies with herring gulls, cormorants, and a variety of other seabirds, but they always command the highest ground on an island. They are generally not as gregarious as terns and other gulls. Their breeding colonies seldom exceed fifty pairs on an island that may support several hundred pairs of herring gulls and perhaps five hundred to a thousand pairs of terns. In flight a black-back resembles a bald eagle as it soars and wheels in great circles, showing a brilliant white head and tail at either end of its great dark back. It's a good enough resemblance to carry over to its habits in and around a colony. No other bird exerts as strong a presence or is as aggressive a predator of other birds. Black-backs can swallow whole the chicks of gulls or eiders that are big enough to be immune from the harassment of all other appetites, with the single exception of eagles.

Herring Gull, Larus argentatus

It is hard for many ornithologists to embrace wholeheartedly this opportunistic feeder that hangs around fish-packing plants, lobster boats, and garbage dumps getting fed on and occasionally

Gulls have adapted well to life around the edges of fishing villages.   PETER RALSTON

entangled in the excess of our throwaway lifestyle. It's not just a case of familiarity breeding contempt; there is a resentment against a species that has driven some of the smaller and rarer terns and laughing gulls out of places where they were once common. Even though herring gulls now nest just about everywhere and eat just about anything, a century of egging and a few decades of feather collecting had reduced their breeding territory to a handful of Maine islands. For a period of time in the late 1800s and early 1900s, their southern breeding limit along the entire eastern seaboard was No Man's Land near Matinicus at the outer edge of Penobscot Bay.

Great Spoon Island, July 19, 1993

The deep, throaty chuckle of gulls signals all is well. Anyone who has spent time on the shore also knows other gull calls—like the more highly pitched and triumphant one sounded when food is located that signals other gulls to assemble. These were all in the air at the southern end of Great Spoon Island. Skirting the hiding spots of the young black-backs and herring gulls, I hear yet another call, more wild and scary and different from any of the other calls. Out to sea from one of Spoon Island's headlands are a half-dozen herring gulls wheeling and screaming over the water where a lone black-back is floating on the glassy surface of the sea. Near this large, glossy-

Herring gull predation.   CHRISTOPHER AYRES

backed gull is a nearly full-grown herring gull chick, haplessly paddling its way back toward shore. The black-back rises out of the water and lands on the chick, grabs its neck, and holds its head underwater for a while. Surprisingly, the struggling chick wriggles free, rights itself by waving its pink-webbed feet in the air, and tries to paddle away.

Overhead the wheeling herring gulls do their best to distract the black-back by swooping down and screaming out the call that I had just heard. The urgent meaning of the call is clear: There's going to be a murder. Again and again the black-back rises up and lands on the chick. Again and again the chick struggles free and tries to right itself. But then the black-back has a final go, and the chick's pink-webbed feet cease kicking altogether. For five to ten minutes the black-back tries to eat its quarry, but can't tear through the skin. It abandons the lifeless mass of feathers, and they float slowly out to sea.

The experience of watching these endless cycles of birth and death unfold has a grim hold on the memory. I can think of no other ecosystem so close at hand as Maine's mixed seabird colonies, where five or six species share small breeding territories and are so intricately bound to one another. Seeing such places makes it impossible not to wonder about the evolutionary significance of these cycles. Why would the black-back have expended so much energy killing this young herring gull, which was too big to eat? Didn't it know? Was this simply a gratuitous murder? What triggers such intense aggression when herring gulls are already relegated to marginal breeding territories off the headlands in the low-rent areas on Great Spoon's shores?

Aside from what such episodes may indicate of seabird diversity offshore, they serve as a powerful reminder that nature is full of the dark chaos of excess and brutal instinct. We are left with the disquieting notion that our own inner natures may not be immune from these cycles.

Terns: Common, Arctic, and Roseate, Sterna hirundo, S. paradisaea, S. dougallii

Terns, or sea swallows, or medricks, have never fully recovered from the effects of the millinery trade during the brief, brutal years that their feathers fetched a fine price in the garment district of New York. Hunting winter ducks for feathers to use in feather beds had been an important way of generating cash for islanders during the nineteenth century, but collecting feathers for ladies' hats was an entirely new business.

Terns were the chief objects of interest when plumage collecting began in earnest on Maine seabird islands in 1886. By 1896, after terns had been virtually exterminated on their nesting grounds, the breast and wing feathers of gulls were collected. Keen competition among the milliners drove the price of a dozen skins from four dollars to twelve. The few tern colonies that were not exterminated were located on lighthouse islands, such as Matinicus Rock, where keepers and their families protected the creatures that were often their only company from early May to September.

The excesses of the millinery trade generated the first widespread public outcry against the habits of those who thoughtlessly exploited wildlife resources for personal profit. Overhunting had been a serious problem for several decades in America, particularly for species such as the passenger pigeon, which migrated in compact flocks and made attractive targets for market hunters. The slaughter of birds, not to eat but to decorate ladies' heads, was simply insupportable to many who were willing to overlook the excesses of hunters. Suddenly it was possible to prick the consciences of enough people not only to stop the milliners in their tracks but to initiate a spate of national bird protection laws. The lobbying was brief and intense. Frank Chapman, a distinguished American ornithologist, conducted a survey during the course of two afternoon walks through the streets of New York. Five hundred and forty-two heads out of a total of seven hundred had been decorated with feathered hats from twenty-odd species, including terns, grackle, owl, grouse, and green heron.

In 1898, William Dutcher, of the American Ornithological Union, hired several Maine fishermen and lighthouse keepers to protect terns and gulls from the milliners. The same year, Dutcher reported that he had extracted an agreement from New York City milliners that they would not buy the skins of any birds shot after 1899. Two years later, the Maine Legislature passed a model bird law, making it a crime to sell or ship bird skins. By 1902, Dutcher, who had personally seen to the protection of Maine bird colonies on Great and Little Duck islands, No Man's Land, and Stratton Island became the chairman of the newly formed National Association of Audubon Societies. Fait gradually accompli.

Before the widespread slaughter of terns was initiated in 1886, Arthur Norton had counted seventy-five tern colonies on the islands of Maine. After the turn of the century, terns continued to decline, even though they enjoyed protection. In 1900, there were twenty-three colonies between Saco and Machias bays; thirty years later Norton found a total of twenty-one colonies. A 1977 count reported twenty-eight colonies; today there are thirty-eight colonies supporting some 11,315 pairs of three species of terns.

It appears that herring gulls, whose numbers were equally reduced during the plume-hunting years, recovered more quickly and have increased at the expense of terns. In a mixed gull and tern colony, terns are forced to occupy smaller and smaller territories, and in some cases they have been driven off nesting islands altogether.

Metinic Island, June 16, 1989, Dread Flight

The high rampart of Metinic trails into Penobscot Bay like a ramp descending into the bay's cold waters. All around, everywhere you look, you feel like a speck on the expanse of open water that curls around distant low islands—Large Green and Little Green to the northeast, Matinicus and Criehaven to the southeast. But dead ahead twenty miles away on the mainland, distant and alluring, loom the mountains behind Camden and Rockport. Closer in, little white curls of water on the deep blue ocean surface hint of the heartache and horror of running aground in the thick of fog or at night on Roaring Bull, Black Rock, and the Northern and Southern Triangles, where sharp teeth gape just below the surf's smiling white lips.

At the most distant northern tip of Metinic, beyond the frail, weathered, abandoned houses, a small flock of terns wheels above the beach. A lone cruising gull triggers an instant reaction from the terns that rise as a single keening, careening organism of many parts. The terns ascend into the air as if shot from guns, screaming in a confusion of targets, a disturbing "dread flight" of delicate-winged fish hunters protecting their nests and young from marauders.

The Alcids

The alcids—auks, puffins, and guillemots—which are at the southern end of their breeding range on Maine's offshore islands, are the Northern Hemisphere's equivalent of penguins. They even look like penguins in their formal black-and-white plumage. One of their extinct numbers, the great auk, stood three feet high, and was, like all Southern Hemisphere penguins, flightless.

The processes by which similar ecological habits and habitats channel evolutionary change into a limited number of morphological options is called convergent evolution. Auks and penguins show similarities because they prey on the same kinds of species and live in the same kinds of habitats; in other words, they occupy similar ecological niches, such that the demands that their environment imposes upon them, even though they come from different ancestral stocks, cause the same kinds of random genetic traits to be naturally selected. Favorable traits in later generations frequently show the species looking more like one another.

Great Auk, Pinguinius impennis

The great auk was the first species to become extinct in the New World. It is still an open question whether these flightless black-and-white seabirds nested on Maine's islands, but they were most certainly regular visitors. They swarmed along the outer islands diving for fish on their way south to winter along the barrier islands of Cape Hatteras and on their way north to mate on the coasts of Labrador, Newfoundland, and Iceland. Their bones have shown up in Indian shell middens with enough regularity that the arrival of this bird full of oil and meat must have been an important event for coastal tribes.

Awkward on land, the great auk was the fastest and most powerful diving bird in the evolutionary record of life. It used short, tapered wings to propel itself down to forty fathoms in pursuit of schools of smelt, herring, or capelin. The few observations of the auks' fishing techniques made by naturalists before the birds disappeared described rafts of twenty to fifty birds that would dive to surround a large school of herring, actually driving the fish to the surface. This school would feed not only the young and less adept auks but also the flocks of gannets, murres, kittiwakes, and puffins that would gather for a piece of the action.

For several hundred years after the Funk Island colony was discovered by early Newfoundland fishermen, the great auk provided one of the few reliable sources of fresh meat that an expedition could expect to find after a North Atlantic crossing. After the turn of the nineteenth century, the ease with which these large feathered birds could be driven down to the shore and clubbed to death made them attractive targets for those who had a market for their oil, meat, and feathers. The tiny islands of Hamilton Inlet off the coast of Labrador, for instance, supported a colony of some five hundred thousand great auks before it was virtually wiped out in one season.

The adults mated for life, an apparently common trait for many of the world's large birds. If one of the pair died, the other would neither pursue nor accept another mate. As exemplary a behavior pattern as this loyalty might seem, it no doubt hastened the species' downfall. The one egg that the mated birds produced could never replace the loss of those two, and the single birds whose mates had fallen victim to the market hunters' clubs no longer contributed to the population. In 1844, the last known great auk was collected by a naturalist for a museum collection.

In 1995, a sixty-year-old Massachusetts man, Richard Wheeler, decided to retrace the migration of the great auk from its once massive Funk Island colony off the east coast of Newfoundland, southward and westward along Nova Scotia, and across the coastline of the Gulf of Maine to Cape Cod Bay. All along the outports of Newfoundland, Wheeler's story of the auk haunted the cod fishermen, whose fishery had collapsed and closed for the first time ever in five hundred years.

Wheeler left Funk Island on July 4 and four months later paddled his kayak into Penobscot Bay.

Rockport Harbor, October 12, 1995

In late afternoon, getting on to dusk, Dick Wheeler's kayak is still in the water at the float. He unpacks his gear, which has been carefully stowed in various watertight sea bags, showing us the camera that he mounts on the forward deck and speaks into as he paddles. On the prow of the kayak a carved head of an auk points directly ahead.

When Wheeler stands next to his kayak, his shoulders seem huge and his hips and legs have shrunk. In fact, says my wife, he looks like a hermit crab come out of a seashell. It has not been clear until now why Wheeler has set off on this quest to chase the ghost of the auk, paddling nearly a thousand miles across open water, except that the frightening ghost of extinction haunts him and those of us who cluster around his fragile craft long enough to listen to his tale.

Atlantic Puffin, Fratercula arctica

The Atlantic puffin is one of the most common birds of the North Atlantic—with a total population of perhaps fifteen million birds—but it is now, and has always been, a rare bird on the coast of Maine. Before some of the excesses of hunting, egging, and feathering were halted at the end of the nineteenth century, puffins were eliminated from four or five islands where they had once nested. The largest of these colonies, on barren Seal Island at the entrance to Penobscot Bay, supported some fifteen hundred pairs of puffins. Sometime during the 1860s, they disappeared from Seal. Their numbers were decimated by herring fishermen, who draped nets over their burrows at night to catch them in the morning.

Matinicus Rock, the thirty-acre dome of granite twenty-eight miles offshore, is the location of Maine's largest puffin colony. One of the minor historical ironies surrounding this colony is that it survived the millinery years not so much because people were fond of this little seabird filled with the look of preposterous self-importance but because the rock supported one of the few protected tern colonies at the end of the nineteenth century. Without the protection of the terns by the lighthouse keepers, it is anyone's guess whether Maine's puffin population would still exist at all.

Like other members of the alcid family, the puffin has wings that are a hopeless compromise between the conflicting morphological demands imposed by flight through both air and water. When puffins fly toward Matinicus Rock, they look like "toy doodlebugs," according to one turn-of-the-century naturalist, but their lack of grace in the air is more than made up for when they beat their wings through the denser medium of seawater to catch darting schools of fish. Someone has taken the time to count the most fish ever seen hanging out of a puffin's bill: twenty-eight. This was quite a feat, because the birds catch the fish one at a time. This bird must have figured out how to hold twenty-seven slippery, squirming bodies while it snared the twenty-eighth.

On a mostly bare, eight-acre piece of granite at the outer edge of Muscongus Bay, an unlikely group of interns recruited from all walks of life, funded through the patronage of the National Audubon Society and directed by a witty traveling ornithologist, has reintroduced puffins to one of their for-mer colonies. Steve Kress's effort to reestablish puffins in Muscongus Bay is one of the most likable research projects ever conceived. You cannot look at a puffin, or even a picture of a puffin—with its ludicrous posture and its most magnificent bill—without liking it immediately and unreservedly.

Eastern Egg Rock, July 14, 1982
"It's well known that birds will land near decoys," says Steve Kress, the man who pioneered the use of decoys for seabird restoration projects on Maine islands. "Duck hunters and shorebird hunters have known that for years. But I don't know if anybody's ever used decoys for stimulating breed-ing behavior. But when you think about it, of course it makes a lot of sense that birds, particularly colonial birds, would be keenly tuned into very spe-cific shapes."

Atlantic puffins' billing display at Eastern Eagle Rock, Muscongus Bay.   PETER RALSTON

Partly because the puffin decoys showed initial promise and partly because Kress knew from historical records that all Maine puffin colonies were located on specific islands that also supported populations of fiercely protective nesting terns, he chose Eastern Egg Rock in outer Muscongus Bay to experiment with decoying techniques to attract both species of birds. Like puffins, the three species of terns found in Maine waters—Arctic, common, and roseate—have suffered a long decline on the Maine coast throughout most of the twentieth century due to the explosion of black-backed and herring gulls, which have displaced them on their traditional nesting grounds.

After working and waiting for almost a decade, on the Fourth of July in 1981 the future arrived for Kress and company, and for anyone concerned with restoring natural populations to the wild. It must have been a sweet sight indeed when Kress picked up the careening flight pattern of a puffin beating furiously toward Eastern Egg Rock. But this time Silver Engraved Number 38 had its bill crammed full of herring. "Beautiful herring," Kress exclaimed over and over again. The fish were tangible proof that hidden away in a rock crevice at the south end of the island for the first time in a hundred years a new generation of puffin chicks had hatched.

Songbirds: *Passeriformes*

The passerines, the order to which swallows, wrens, robins, and wood warblers belong, are the most numerous and most intricately speciated group of birds in the world. Of the eight thousand–odd avian species scattered across the globe, about five thousand, or 60 percent of them, are passerines. This means, among other things, that no matter where you are, if you see a small, colorful bird and identify it as a passerine, you will be right more often than you are wrong (a highly comforting happenstance in an age of uncertainty).

Another distinction accorded passerines is that the great majority of their species have only recently diverged from ancestral types—as recently, in many cases, as the end of the Pleistocene era, about ten thousand years ago.

The wood warblers of North America are perhaps the best example of bona fide new species to appear in the recent record of life. The prodigious intercontinental migratory flight of the tiny black-and-white warbler that wings between northern coniferous forests and South American tropical forests has demonstrated to evolutionary biologists how difficult a task it can be to maintain a species gene pool. If some subtle change should reduce the warbler's food supply so that it wintered in Florida rather than completing its spectacular annual journey to the Amazon River basin, it would be isolated from its congeners in the Southern Hemisphere and would slowly diverge to become a new species.

Apparently processes similar to this have been occurring over the past few thousand years (and surely for many thousands before that), which in part explains the wonderful proliferation of gaudy-colored warblers that annually nest in northern spruce forests.

The myriad spruce-clad islands of Maine provide convenient resting and feeding spots during the semiannual migrations for what seems like every small bird that uses the Atlantic Flyway. The islands also provide nesting habitats for the bewildering variety of warblers that would confuse us with their subtle wing-bar and eye-stripe markings: the black-and-white, the blackpoll, the yellow, the Cape May, the myrtle (or yellow-rumped), the black-throated green, the parula, the bay-breasted, the pine, and the Canada—to name just the common species.

When the first waves of passerine fellow-traveling swallows, thrushes, sparrows, and warblers

Matinicus Rock seabird warden, part of a century-long tradition at the edge of the Gulf of Maine.

PETER RALSTON

hit the islands in late April or early May, the spring air is suddenly charged with new tones and pitches and with a million possibilities of new life. Soon the birds settle in amid the lichen loft of spruce limbs (if they are warblers), or in the banks of some soft island side (if they are swallows), or in bushes and shrubs around an abandoned field or homestead (if they are redstarts or humming-birds) and begin to sing as if their lives depended on it. In fact, not only do their lives depend upon it—because mate selection is a function of their sonority—but certainly ours do, too.

LOOKING BACKWARD AND FORWARD

What are we to make of the history of our relationships with birds along the coast of Maine? One thing is apparent: In sheer numbers there are now more nesting birds on the islands than there have been at any time since shortly after 1800. As in the rest of the country, the past has left a mixed legacy. It is true that we will never again see the likes of the Labrador duck or the great auk, which disappeared from the earth before we knew what hit them. Other species, such as the Eskimo curlew, may or may not have been rescued from the brink of an irreversible genetic event: extinction. Their fate is still hanging from an excruciatingly thin thread.

Although the toxic contaminant dilemma still casts a dark shadow over the fate of top preda-tors, there is wider public recognition that in ecological matters there are no free lunches; protecting the forests from endemic insects such as the spruce budworm also contaminates food supplies and eventually the health of those who eat at the top of food chains. And you don't have to have feathers to be a target. But this is not the whole truth. The most silent spring, to use Rachel Carson's worrisome phrase, as far as the songs of birds on Maine islands have been concerned, happened before the turn of the twentieth century, and the springs for twenty to thirty years afterward were pretty quiet.

But we enter the twenty-first century in much better shape. Many of the birds that totally disappeared from our shores have returned to nest in great numbers. Presently hundreds of volunteers and professionals help monitor upward of three hundred and fifty island nesting sites, ensuring the continuity of protection that first began in this archipelago when Matinicus Rock lightkeepers from nearby Matinicus Island were first drafted into service. This multifaceted seabird protection effort is one of the most remarkable conservation stories on the entire Atlantic seaboard in the twentieth century and continues to the present. It is a lasting contribution sustained by the traditions of local pride and cooperation that continue today.

Brimstone Island, July 30, 1995

Landing on the outer beaches and skerries of Brimstone Island is ideally accomplished in a calm sea.

Today under south-side cliffs, alive with seabirds careening into volcanic crevices overhead, the sea has not yet gotten up when "the Mayor" of Brimstone heaves into view. This Vinalhaven lobsterman has fished the surrounding waters for some decades, but this particular Sunday he steams out to Brimstone in a heavy outboard skiff and rounds up into a brisk southwesterly onshore breeze with a boy on the bow. The boy, his son, hops off and holds the bow in the surge on the steep beach while the Mayor grabs a small anchor, sets it on the forward gunwale by the fluke, and spurns offers of help from those ashore. "Prob'ly won't work, anyways," the Mayor says. His son runs the painter high up on the beach as his father pushes the bow off the face of the beach. The skiff slides easily down, running back on the swash toward the cliffs, where a foamy rind lies just outside the breaking surge. Then at the appropriate moment, the Mayor jerks the painter taut, flipping the bow anchor off the gunnel into the waters just beyond the surge, where it catches and brings the skiff up snug, short of the cliff but outside the breakers, and in full view of a wide-eyed summer audience.

The beach is small and receding as the tide boils up and around. We arrange ourselves like the gulls overhead, adopting our postures, settling in, straining a look at the shimmering southerly sea. In addition to bringing lunch for him and his son, the Mayor carries a small handful of signs from The Nature Conservancy. The signs, which are deployed on the trails leading up off the beach to replace an older set, inform visitors of the nesting seabirds and ask us not to trample through the colonies on the grassy bluffs. High above our little beach, the Mayor, in a dark hooded sweatshirt and white T-shirt, shares the ramparts with the black-backed gulls.

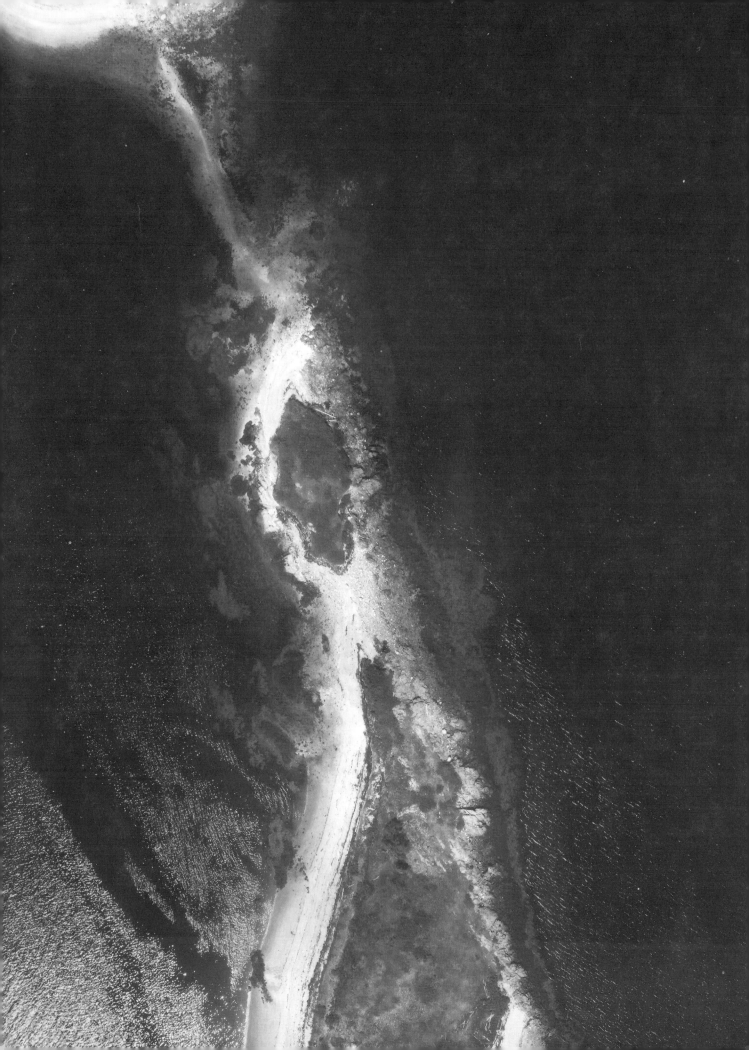

6

Mammals Great and Small: Whales, Sea Hogs, Stags, and Coney

I remember a remark made by a girl about her father, a businessman of narrow sensibilities, who, casting about for a means of self gratification travelled to Africa and slew an elephant. Standing there in his new hunting togs in a vast and hostile silence, staring at the huge, dead bleeding thing that moments before had borne such life, he was struck for the first time in his headlong passage through his days by his own irrelevance. "Even he," his daughter said, "knew he'd done something stupid."

—Peter Matthiessen, *The Tree Where Man Was Born*

Most of Maine's common species of mammals are missing from the islands. For the greater number of these creatures, long-distance water travel to islands is not a great temptation. Those mammals that have moved back into the sea, such as otters, seals, and whales, or have learned to negotiate the tricky channels of the air, such as bats, have found vacant ecological niches in and around the coastal islands of Maine and are represented in greater numbers than their landbound cousins.

For the nesting birds, whose lives are largely poor, nasty, brutish, and short enough anyway, the limited variety of carnivorous mammals found on islands makes their existence more secure. It could be said that there are so many birds on the islands simply because, by comparison, there are so few mammals.

James Rosier, the observant seventeenth-century naturalist, compiled the first species list of Maine mammals during a two-month exploration of the islands and coast with George Waymouth's expedition. On his list of "Beasts We Saw the Country Yield in the Small Time of our Stay there," Rosier included reindeer, stags, fallow deer, "wild great cats," dogs—some like wolves, some like spaniels, coney (rabbit), hedgehogs, and polecats (skunks), as well as the expected bear, beaver, otter, and hare. Unfortunately Rosier does not describe which species they sighted on the islands and which they saw on the mainland, but it is possible to piece together some of the original picture.

The original explorers were most impressed with the marine mammals they saw—especially the whales. Rosier's account of an aboriginal hunt in his 1604 account has left us with one of the few eyewitness descriptions of how Maine's Indians captured whales:

Opposite: First Chain Link Island, part of a tidal land bridge from island to island, in north Penobscot Bay.
COURTESY MAINE DEPARTMENT OF INLAND FISHERIES AND WILDLIFE

He bloweth up the water and . . . is 12 fathoms long; they go in company of their king with a multitude of their boats and strike him with a bone made in the fashion of a harping iron fastened to a rope, which they make great and strong of the bark of trees. . . . Then all their boats come about him, and as he riseth above water, with their arrows they shoot him to death.

A decade later, Captain John Smith was so impressed with the number of whales and porpoises encountered during his voyage that he thought to pay for his trip by capturing whales. But after several days in fruitless pursuit, he turned instead to cod fishing.

The species accounts that follow are an attempt to understand the patterns of island and marine mammal distribution when colonists first arrived and to trace the mammals' fates since.

Marine Mammals: Blackfish, Grumpus, and Sea Dogs

Ever since amphibians first wriggled out of a warm, epicontinental sea, a general progression of life forms has followed them onto land. In some ways this migration is surprising, because life on land is certainly more harsh. Temperature extremes are greater from day to night and from season to season; and in the early days of life before a thick atmospheric shield evolved, ultraviolet light was an intense stress to which land animals had to adapt. But land offered a huge variety of niches to occupy, once successful strategies evolved for coping with its wildly fluctuating environmental conditions. One of the most significant of these strategies is warm-bloodedness, which allows animals to regulate their body temperatures rather than be regulated by the whims of the weather.

In comparison to land, the environment of the sea is much more stable. Perhaps it is not surprising, therefore, that some mammals have moved back into the sea, having acquired the advantages of live birth and regulation of body temperature. In fact, four different groups have reversed their ancestors' sea-to-land voyage and now live primarily or exclusively in saltwater. Sea otters completed the marine transition approximately two million years ago; the sirenians (manatees and dugongs), from whom tales of mermaids (or mermen) may have developed, re-entered the sea almost eighty million years ago; and the cetaceans (whales and dolphins) returned almost one hundred million years ago—scarcely after they became warm-blooded mammals in the first place.

No doubt the ancestral stocks of these groups first became coastal dabblers, jumping into the water to look for food and climbing back out to eat it or rest. But gradually they began to exploit food resources farther and farther from land. The oldest marine mammals—the whales and dolphins —are full-fledged seagoing creatures; the youngest—the sea otters—come ashore to rest and bear their young. The seals are somewhere in between. A few are truly seagoing; the rest occasionally have to come ashore. It seems to be a matter of how much evolutionary time they have had to adapt to their watery environs.

Original Accounts of Whales in the Gulf of Maine

Unless international events take a sharp turn for the worse and we are all thrown back to a primitive reliance on inexpensive animal oil and protein, we are watching the end of a millennium of humans hunting whales. For a thousand years at least, and probably a lot longer, men of some courage and daring have been paddling or rowing small boats offshore to chase and spear the largest living creatures in the evolutionary record of life—the great whales. Now there is an international moratorium on the taking of all species of large whales. The few smaller species that continue to be killed are the price that the great whaling nations of the world (Japan, Norway, and Iceland) demanded for reasons of maintaining cultural identity, as their moribund whaling industries slide into their long-overdue grave.

The species of whale that the Indians most likely hunted around the islands of Maine may have been the pilot whale. Compared with the swift rorqual whales (finbacks, humpbacks, seis, and minkes), which tend to be farther offshore, pilot whales move along the inner rim of the Gulf of Maine, appearing in late April or early May. Captain John Smith described them as appearing in great numbers and "easy of approach," though he turned aside from his original intention of taking whales to catch cod, which were even easier to approach. Right whales, which the Europeans had learned to slaughter, were abundant in the Gulf of Maine, but mostly they traversed it along the outermost islands, where Indian canoes could travel only under the best of conditions in the summer.

John Josselyn writes that the Indians and colonists alike hunted dolphins and porpoises, species of small whales that inhabit Maine waters. Called "sea hogs" by the English, they were cut into thin pieces and fried. "It tastes like rusty bacon or hung beef, if not worse, but the liver boiled and soused with vinegar is more grateful to the palate," wrote Josselyn. Perhaps so, but it is a little harder to trust Josselyn's judgment on marine mammal matters after reading his description of ambergris, the waxy substance formed within sperm whales and occasionally found washed ashore on the Maine coast. Josselyn took it "to be a mushroom . . . that riseth out of certain clammy and bituminous earth under the seas, the billows casting up part of it on land and fish devour the rest." Maybe it's unfair to pick on Josselyn's ambergris mushroom, because almost no one else at the time had any idea where this valuable substance, used as a perfume fixative, came from. Nor would anyone else be able to say

Finback whale vertebrae, hauled up in a fisherman's net.   Peter Ralston

for sure until New England ships had harpooned and slit open enough sperm whales on their Indian Ocean and Antarctic feeding grounds to lay that particular mystery to rest.

William Wood, the "Lord of the Isles," in his comprehensive listing of marine life around the Isles of Shoals, mentions the "shouldering whale" and the "snuffling Grampus," perhaps the twenty- to thirty-foot pilot whale (also called the blackfish), which is a common inshore species.

By the time New England towns such as New Bedford and Nantucket had established themselves as the centers of the world's first great whaling empire, the costs of fitting out a whaling voyage had become prohibitively expensive for other coastal towns that wanted to get into the trade. Even wealthy Wiscasset ship owners were reluctant to refit their ships with all the costly and specialized equipment necessary to capture whales and render the blubber into valuable oil. A few expeditions were sent out from Bath and Wiscasset in the 1830s, but they were not overwhelmingly successful.

Beached pilot whales in the western Gulf of Maine.   COURTESY COLLEGE OF THE ATLANTIC

Tightfisted, conservative Maine merchants elected to pass up the extreme risks and extreme special-ization of the whaling era almost before it began. Occasionally, someone would gear up from an island town such as Vinalhaven to hunt whales in the Gulf of Maine, but until the harpoon with an explosive head was invented in Norway in 1925, and fast steamships were designed, catching whales was not easy, and the coastal stocks had long since been depleted from shore stations.

One of the benefits of the international effort to preserve whales is that their numbers have slowly increased in the Gulf of Maine, where many are resident for the better part of the year and where some northern right whales appear to reside year-round. Researchers at island whale-watching stations such as Mount Desert Rock, thirty miles off the coast, have documented the yearly increases, even cataloging the rare appearance in the Gulf of Maine of the blue whale. The blue whale uses the entire Atlantic Basin, north and south, as its cruising grounds, communicating with other individual blues in deepwater acoustic channels that can apparently connect individual whales that are a thousand miles apart. But during the last two decades of whale watching there have been only five blue whale sightings in the Gulf of Maine, two of them on Jeffrey's Ledge in September and October of 1993.

Mount Desert Rock, July 9, 1975
In the late afternoon sun we are provided a rare bonus aboard the fish-ing vessel JESSE. A huge humpback whale surfaces nearby. While we throttle back to drink in the spectacle, in no hurry to go anywhere, the humpback repeatedly raises its massive white flukes clear of the ocean and then smacks

them down emphatically on the surface. Called "lobtailing" by whale biolo-
gists, it is a most emphatic means for announcing, "Whale here!"
Out beyond the shadow of the rim of the mainland, where the ocean
drops off to secret shoals and deeper feeding grounds, we sense another
realm. Shearwaters and petrels are more common than gulls and terns, and
the creatures of the deep rise to meet us in the awe and doom of man's world.

During the past decade, a significant new industry, whale-watching, has developed to harvest the rising public interest in what is referred to in the trade as "charismatic megafauna." As we learn more about the habits and behavior of these long-lived marine mammals, we have come to realize that they are not just large, dull creatures; nor are they dumb. In fact, recent research indicates that most cetaceans have elaborate means of communicating with one another in forms and terms that are indistinguishable from language and song. New high-speed whale-watching vessels operating throughout the Gulf of Maine from Gloucester to Bar Harbor to Grand Manan are adding to our knowledge of whale distribution and behavior, even as their presence undoubtedly alters the very phenomena we are trying to understand.

Baleen and Toothed Whales: You Are What You Eat

The toothed whales—dolphins, porpoises, pilot whales, and orcas (the so-called "killer whales")—frequent the Gulf of Maine too, but they are all smaller than the baleen whales and usually travel about in a great hurry while trying to locate their food—schools of fish. The filter-feeding baleen whales are rarely short of food, because they utilize smaller and more abundant forms of marine life, so they are in general less hurried than their flesh-eating relatives.

In an ecological sense, whales do something that no other creatures can: They transform tiny plants and animals that float in the nutrient broth of the sea into complex and compact animal proteins and oils. A calf of a baleen whale, named for the comblike modified teeth that strain sea life from a single five-thousand-gallon gulp, will put on fifteen to twenty thousand pounds in a single year. When you compare this to the time and effort of raising grain or forage for beef cattle, which convert plant life into animal protein at a ratio of ten pounds of vegetable to one pound of meat, it's easy to understand why many whale species have been hunted to near extinction. They are almost too successful at the way they make their living.

Another way to look at it is that humpback, finback, sei, minke, and right whales—to mention the baleen whales (*Mysticeti*) that are common in Maine waters—eat lower on the food chain, two levels lower, in fact, than the toothed whales (*Odontoceti*). In an ecological sense, you are not so much what you eat but where you eat in relation to the different energy levels of a food chain. The size and numbers of a predatory species are limited by the ecological principle that there is only roughly a 10 percent efficiency of energy conversion as you move up from one level of the food chain to the next—for instance, from copepods to herring. Baleen whales strain out tiny but abundant forms of life and can therefore be larger and more numerous than their fish-eating relatives.

It is difficult to overstate the effect of seeing a whale for the first time. The familiar large land animals are chiefly interesting to us because of their fearlessness, at least where they are not intensively hunted. In the days when it was still possible to watch grizzly bears feeding at the Yellowstone National Park dump, I remember the shock of seeing one walk past our parked Volkswagen bug at dusk, its shoulder filling the window for one shuddering moment. It was obvious from its taut, edgy demeanor that this creature was capable of doing a lot of damage in a very short time.

But the baleen whales are different. Fear is a reaction wholly alien to an encounter with a great whale—whether you are in a kayak or a large boat, or in the water with them. They are absolutely graceful in their movements—which is difficult to believe, given their size—and they move effort-lessly through the water. A slight wave of their flukes and they are thirty to fifty yards away. They appear from below or out of nowhere, changing buoyancy like a living submarine.

If it is a humpback playing with you and all is right with the world for this moment, a large, long white flipper might break the surface and stretch toward the sky. Ah, sun, sea, and whale between; ever after, worlds without end. Homo sapiens have finally agreed to take their fingers off the triggers of cannons that explode into the great dark backs of cetaceans and churn them into a sea of red froth. We will now leave them in peace.

Seal Island, July 29, 1978

After the long night on the fire lines, three of us stand on Seal Island's central bluff transfixed in the early light of dawn while the blood-red orb of the sun looms out of the water. The island ground is hot, scorched, and smol-dering. The fire has burned off all of Seal's rank vegetation, revealing the deep scars of bomb craters. In the acrid air of burning earth, I sense the vague and indistinct odor of petrels—musky, mysterious, and carrying the incense of some far-off place. The blackened earth, cratered by bombs and twisted metal, looks like a war zone—the charred, scarred earth and the stench of the hapless dead birds.

About a half mile from shore, between sun and sea, a whale's spout catches the light in the shimmering orange path. Then another spout and another spout hang like willowy breaths from Neptune's deepest lungs. Humpbacks traveling in a pod. We had thought that the sounds and smells of the burning night had drained off every ounce of feeling, but the appear-ance of the whales blunts the sharp despair of the hairless ape, whom deso-lation follows around the globe. In the sight of those silent shrouds catching

Humpback mother and calf surface off Seal Island feeding grounds.   J. MORTON

the glow of the ever-rising eastern sun, a lightness begins turning, turning
toward the morning on the bare, bleached bones of Seal's rocky carcass.

The Northern Right Whale and the Endangered Species Act

The story of the northern right whale, which spends spring and fall in the great curving arms of Cape Cod Bay, at the southwestern end of the Gulf of Maine, is more bleak and complicated than that of any other great whale. Because it is the slowest of all the great whales, because it gave a great amount of oil, and because it floated when dead, it was the "right" whale to kill. Between 1530 and 1610 Basque whalers killed twenty-five to forty thousand northern right whales, mostly from a single station on the Labrador coast at Red Bay.

Red Bay—The End of the Road—September 23, 1985

We pulled into Red Bay, Labrador, last evening after driving up and over some of the most stunning Arctic highlands one could ever hope to see. The cranberry and blueberry have turned wine red and the long, low, slanting, late afternoon sun lights the tundra vegetation, which carpets the landscape everywhere except where pink granite boulders are frozen in tumbling poses.

The road into Red Bay is an isolated piece of highway running from Port Sal, where the ferry lands after crossing the Strait of Belle Isle, north for twenty miles to connect these Labradorean outports with a lifeline of fuel, health care, and government highway jobs. We drove quite literally to the end of the road at the north end of town, where there is a small turn-around, and pitched our tents.

Red Bay is where Basque whalers set up a large base on the modest sized island that protects the harbor entrance. From this station, the whalers chased down northern right whales and perhaps bowheads, too. The town got its name from the abundant terra cotta tiles the whalers used to ballast their ships on tempestuous voyages across the North Atlantic to the Labrador whaling grounds before returning with casks full of whale oil. The tiles, discharged in the harbor, still cover the bottom and give an eerie red hue to the waters of the bay, which seem to have been permanently bloodied by the whaling.

The location of the station on the island rather than on the mainland shore suggests that relations with the Tulle Eskimo, who lived mainly further north, were tenuous at best. Nevertheless, with relatively primitive hunting and sailing methods, this single Basque whaling station, which might have employed as many as two thousand men at its height, put a huge dent in the population of northern right whales. Near the end of the sixteenth century, before the rest of the North American continent had even been explored, the Red Bay whaling operation simply disappeared into the mists, seemingly overnight. Like so many other resource crises hinted at in the archeological record, we'll never know exactly why.

Because the natural rate of reproduction of right whales is low, they have recovered ever so slowly since they became the first officially protected species in 1933. In fact, the entire North Atlantic population may be derived from only a few mature females that escaped persecution. Today the population of the northern right whale hovers at around three hundred individuals, and is the most endangered whale in the North Atlantic.

All of the more than twenty years of networked observations by responsible reporters show that right whales transit the Gulf of Maine in spring as they migrate to their summer feeding grounds in the deep waters off Grand Manan Island. Along the way they appear on Stellwagen Bank and other offshore locations, but they only occasionally stray into coastal waters. A few individuals show up off Matinicus and Isle au Haut, but the ecological data demonstrate that they have been found feeding primarily in one portion of the Gulf of Maine in Maine's state waters—the region immediately surrounding Mount Desert Rock.

Mount Desert Rock is also virtually the only place within Maine's territorial waters that is adjacent to the very deepwater regions of the Gulf of Maine, where depths of six hundred feet are close to shore. Biologists know that right whales feed heavily on a single prolific species of zooplankton known as *Calanus finmarchicus*, which ecological research has shown are notably absent in coastal waters but are abundant offshore, especially in the areas of vertical upwelling the right whale targets during the summer.

Farther off the coast, where the northern right whales share the ocean with gillnet fishermen and offshore lobstermen, the animals occasionally become entangled in fishing gear. Virtually all right whales sighted in the Gulf of Maine show the battle scars of entanglement on their skin, according to New England Aquarium researcher Scott Kraus, although mortality is more frequently caused by oceangoing ships that collide with the whales while they are sleeping at the surface. In Maine state waters, however, only once in the past twenty-five years has a northern right whale become entangled in fishing gear, and it was successfully freed without harm.

Harbor seal pup.   PETER RALSTON

Because there are so few northern right whales, the loss of even a single individual is serious. Killing a northern right whale violates the strict provisions of the Marine Mammal Protection Act. In 1996, responding to a lawsuit brought by an ecological activist, the National Marine Fisheries Service (NMFS) was forced into a difficult corner. Effective lobbying by shipping interests in Congress had already exempted them from additional regulations aimed at reducing whale mortality from collisions at sea, so the full weight of the regulatory burden was placed on the fishing industry. In Cape Cod Bay, which is critical for the northern right whale, NMFS banned gillnets during spring and fall and severely limited lobstering. When they proposed extending these regulations to the whole coast of Maine, all hell broke loose. Maine lobstermen, the vast majority of whom have never seen a right whale, were faced with potentially devastating costs, which were initially estimated to total $70 million for the state's lobster fishery as a whole.

An ecological approach to the dilemma of reducing right whale entanglement in fishing gear would logically focus on seasonal restrictions of gear in specific habitats where whale sightings have been backed up with biological data. The proposed regulations created a huge firestorm of protest from Maine lobstermen that had the sad and unintended effect of turning fishermen from potential allies in whale conservation into an adversarial block. Even Maine's normally even-tempered governor, Angus King, was incredulous when he read the proposed regulations. "These lobstermen are your friends," he said at a NMFS public hearing in Rockland attended by seven hundred angry fishermen. "They are the ones who will see and can help free any entangled whales. Don't piss them off!" In unnecessary confrontations such as these, marine resource managers at both state and federal levels have their credibility eroded by their attempts to establish regulations, which in this case are broadly understood to be completely inappropriate for the coastal waters of Maine.

Whatever modifications might reasonably be made to fishing practices, there is no certainty that any of the recent or potential restrictions on fishing or shipping, undertaken at great cost to these industries, will ensure the survival of this ancient species still hovering on the brink of oblivion and seemingly not designed for the modern world.

Harbor Seal, Phoca vitulina

If you like dogs, particularly water dogs such as Labrador retrievers, you are likely to be an easy touch for seals. Their large brown eyes, with no visible iris, make them one of the chief attractions at zoos and aquariums, where they entertain for hours on end. The analogy with dogs goes further. The young seals are called "pups," and their vocalizations are best described as "barks." But adult seals, which are awkward on land, apparently remind naturalists more of farmyard bovines, because they are known as "cows" and "bulls."

Harbor seals are the most widely distributed of the thirty-three species of seals in the world. They inhabit the waters and half-tide ledges of the shores of Japan and China in the Pacific, the west coast of North America from the Bering Sea to Southern California, and both sides of the North Atlantic. The world population is at least one hundred and fifty thousand, although it may be twice that number.

To the extent that scientific minds have any adequate means of measuring nonhuman intelligence (in a kind of interspecific insecurity, we are forever trying to figure out how "smart" other mammals are), harbor seals are said to be highly intelligent. They are capable of recognizing individual boats from which people have shot at them in the past; they often "know" whether a fisherman has a gun before they can see it; and they can judge rifle range more accurately than can most other quarry. In the Gulf of Maine, some fishermen used to shoot at harbor seals primarily to test their marksmanship.

Harbor seals are true seals—their hind flippers drag aft—whereas the eared or walking seals have flippers that are turned forward, making them more mobile on land. As true seals, harbor seals

Harbor seal populations have quintupled off the Maine coast during the last two decades.

CHRISTOPHER AYRES

are better adapted to water than land and rarely struggle far from the water on ledges or beaches. Harbor seals mate in spring, along about May, either in the water or, on sunny days, on half-tide ledges. They are not faithful to one single ledge, but they have group ranges that a bull and his harem and their pups use throughout the summer. The whelping ledges onto which cows crawl in June to give birth to shiny-eyed, ten- to twenty-pound pups are generally tucked into the inner reaches of the bays, where the waters are more protected. There is some evidence that seals can control the timing of their parturition, particularly when a storm makes it difficult and dangerous to crawl onto a ledge. If harbor seals are born in the water, the cows can sometimes cradle the pups between their flippers, but they must get them to land quickly or the youngsters will drown.

The pups suckle from mom's retractable teats and totally depend on their supply of fat-rich milk for the first several weeks of life. If the pups are separated from their mothers during this time, they usually starve, because they have not yet learned how to catch fish. Mortality is high among seal pups. Storm seas and tides often come between mothers and pups, disease strikes others, and angry bulls defending their right of access to the harem cows will crush a few more pups in their clumsy fury. After the pups are capable of feeding themselves, they make all the mistakes that young children make; annual mortality figures during the first year are about 60 percent. It's dangerous out there.

As Harry Goodridge, the legendary trainer of Andre the Seal, demonstrated in Rockport more than two decades ago, harbor seal pups are one of the few species of marine mammals that can be raised successfully by humans and reintroduced to the wild. It is an arduous process, now all but illegal. What was learned from the remarkable relationship between Harry and Andre has deeply enriched the scientific understanding of the habits and capacities of these clever creatures. Andre's migrations from his winter home at the New England Aquarium and elsewhere in southern New

England to Rockport Harbor became the stuff of legend and were intensively covered by local newspapers. When Andre finally succumbed at age twenty-three, his passing was mourned throughout the region and even internationally.

Some may not remember that Andre's predecessor, Basil, the first harbor seal pup that Harry Goodridge raised, was swallowed whole by a shark while Harry was out lobster fishing. Harry was so infuriated that he raced ashore, rigged up a harpoon, and like the mythical Ahab hunted down the beast and struck it with full force. He was towed for hours by the shark before it succumbed. Harry in turn towed the shark back ashore, where it proved to be a great white shark; it had pieces of the unfortunate Basil within. Great white sharks, incidentally, are occasionally sighted in the Gulf of Maine, but

Rare northern harp seal crossing the road in Tenant's Harbor.
D. GRIMA, *COURIER-GAZETTE*

they were much more common in west Penobscot Bay when the Belfast chicken processing plant used to discharge offal directly into the bay. The plant's discharge had all sorts of unintended biological consequences, including increasing the carrying capacity for great whites.

> ### Johns Island, June 20, 1989
> *The high-tide entrance to the slot between Johns and Opechee, marked this year by tiny styrofoam floats, emerges out of the radar chatter, and we ghost into another hole in the fog where the islands make just enough heat to part the vapors. This is seal country. The ledges are thick with russet, gray, silver, and tan pelages of more than forty fat and grunting seal mothers, pups, and bulls. As we drift our way into the gut, the seals roll heavily into the water, pop up all around* FISH HAWK, *and stare with dark, liquid eyes at the intruding motor-driven two-leggeds. At some unknown signal, they begin to move easterly in unison. Slowly gaining momentum in the Johns Island aquarium, the fast males porpoise through the shallow channel at bursts of twenty knots in a sheer, exuberant display of spray, spiral, and flipper slap.*

Gray Seal, Halichoerus grypus

The horse-faced gray seals are much less social than their smaller relatives, the harbor seals. Gray seals confine themselves to the outer ledges of offshore islands such as Matinicus Rock, Frenchboro, and Great and Little Duck islands. At the southern end of their range in Maine, gray seals are a rare sight for all but a few lobstermen who haul in these waters. It is thought that no more than one hundred and twenty-five of these occasionally gigantic marine mammals—the bulls of which weigh more than eight hundred pounds—inhabit the Gulf of Maine. They are not just uncommon in Maine; their total worldwide population probably does not much exceed one hundred thousand individuals, which makes them one of the rarer mammals on our globe.

One of the reasons, if we can speak of nature as rational, that gray seals are rare is simply that they are less gregarious than harbor seals. They do not fish cooperatively, which is one means by which wild species can reduce their unit level of energy output in relation to the food they eat. It's a matter of efficiency of effort. The same is true of a pack of wolves or African hunting dogs, which can chase down moose or zebra that are both larger and faster than they are. One or two animals take the lead in a chase, burning up all available energy until they drop to the rear, and another pair that has been loping along moves up—sometimes transecting the arc of the fleeing quarry until predator and prey arrive exhausted at a standoff, where the superior numbers prevail.

Seals and the Marine Mammal Protection Act

In 1975, Maine's island shores hosted between five and six thousand harbor seals; two decades later an estimated thirty thousand of them are long-term residents of half-tide ledges in the Gulf of Maine. Recent studies of female harbor seals demonstrate that their reproductive rate has not begun to level off, suggesting that the population in the Gulf of Maine has not yet reached the natural carrying capacity with respect to food supplies.

The phenomenal increase in harbor seal populations during the past twenty years—a five- to six-fold increase—corresponds to the enforcement of the Marine Mammal Protection Act and is ample evidence, if you needed it, that their numbers in the past were controlled by their primary predator, Maine coast fishermen. Many people forget that through most of the 1960s, the State of Maine paid a bounty of five dollars to anyone who took the time to bring the nose of a harbor seal to the Department of Marine Resources headquarters in Hallowell. More than a few individuals made a seasonal living off this pursuit, turning in hundreds of noses per year for decades.

The explosion of seal populations around Maine's islands is a good or bad thing depending on how you earn a living. If you are in the rapidly developing sector of "ecotourism," showing the folks from away a slice of island life, the abundance of seals sunning themselves around the edges of islands is a great boon. But if you are in the salmon farming business, you tend to view the increasing number of seals around ocean pens the way ranchers view coyotes. The depredations can be serious, particularly in winter when seals are their hungriest, and particularly when Canadian harbor and gray seals, from farther north, move into eastern Maine, where salmon farms are concentrated. Under the language of the revised Marine Mammal Protection Act, however, the vastly increased herd of harbor seals in Maine waters is as fully protected as the truly endangered right whales, for instance. So-called "lethal taking" of harbor seals is a serious criminal offense even if, as one fish farmer officially was informed by the National Marine Fisheries Service, the seal is inside the pen eating his Atlantic salmon. Such federal protection, not surprisingly, does little to improve the climate of discussion between this important sector of the coastal and island economy and the environmental community.

TERRESTRIAL MAMMALS

When you come up out of the water and consider the mammals of the islands that live above the tideline, the whole picture changes. The large terrestrial mammals are, with the exception of deer, widely dispersed and uncommon. A significant number of species have been hunted to extinction on the islands.

Wolf, Canis lupus

It is only within the last two decades that anything like a significant minority of public opinion has warmed to the wiles of wolves. Almost from Day One of settlement in Maine, wolves were a problem. "Their hideous howling made night terrible to the settlers," Edward Trelawney, of Richmond Island off Cape Elizabeth, wrote to his brother, Robert, in England. Because the early mainland settlements were huddled along the coastline, the colonists in effect had placed themselves between the deep forest, where the eastern timber wolf sought cover, and the shore, where the wolf sought food. The outlying pastures where land was cleared for livestock became increasingly tempting targets for these meat eaters. One of the chief reasons that Casco Bay islands were cleared for pasturage was that hogs and cattle here were less subject to depredations from wolves than they were on the mainland. Eight to nine months of the year, a colonial farmer who pastured livestock on the offshore islands could rest easier at night in the knowledge that none of his livestock had provided a wolf its dinner. But come winter and the freezing of the bay out to the islands, the peace was broken.

According to several accounts, the wolves possessed a sixth sense about the ice. Year after discouraging year, Casco Bay farmers waited for an early spring breakup to get even with wolves trapped on the islands when the ice gave out. But no matter what day, week, or month the ice bridge lifted, the farmers would find tracks of the wolves that left the islands at the last moment, depriving the farmers of certain revenge.

"The wolves are of divers colors," wrote John Josselyn in 1667 in his usual informative manner, "some sandy colored, some griseled, and some black." Because the diet of the wolf had an immediate and direct effect on the fortunes of colonial farmers, the animals were hunted down more intently than were bears. In 1739, a bounty of five pounds sterling was paid for a dead wolf; a few years later it was eight, and then sixteen "if a man should kill three." These figures, almost unheard-of sums in colonial New England, illustrate how diligently the colonists tried to eliminate the wolf from its domain.

Several town histories of coastal Maine relate the stories of settlers as they were returning home, usually in winter after dark, and at some point realizing that they were being trailed by a wolf or a pack of wolves that were beginning to close on their quarry. The terrified settlers would start walking faster, break into a trot and finally into headlong flight, sometimes dropping a piece of clothing to interrupt the wolves' pursuit for a few moments. No doubt these events took place much as they were related. But what is interesting in these accounts is that no one actually gets attacked, much less eaten; they just get chased—often right to the farmhouse door, which they close just as the wolf hurls itself against it. For the wolf, perhaps the chase is the point; it evens the score a bit to chalk up a moral victory for the canines, which frequently end up on the losing side in an encounter with two-leggeds.

Cyrus Eaton, a historian for the Saint George River Valley, describes the last wolf hunt along the shores of west Penobscot Bay. In the spring of 1815, a she-wolf and five whelps were spotted. The alarm went up, and soon some twenty men and their dogs took up the chase, which lasted three days and ranged through Waldoboro, Thomaston, and Saint George. At the end of it, the last wolf, one of the pups, took to the water and headed out toward the islands of the Muscle Ridge. Whether the pup made it we are not told, but no wolves were ever seen again in the area.

Wilderness activists in western states have successfully petitioned government wildlife and land management agencies to undertake wolf restoration programs in places such as the Yellowstone ecosystem. Similar suggestions for northern Maine trip over objections from private landowners, not to mention deer hunters and other sportsmen, so the restoration idea has not yet gone too far here, but the wolves have, at least in other parts of the country. In a major eastern range extension during the past decade and a half, wolves have gradually and naturally expanded into vacant territories in boreal forests in Michigan, southern Canada, northern New York, and Vermont. After confirmation from DNA analysis of a specimen collected in 1993, we are officially informed that wolves are residing in Maine for the first time in nearly two centuries.

Coyote, Canis latrans

There's no question about the presence of coyotes; they've arrived and are here in large numbers.

Almost exclusively a species of the western parts of the North American continent when European settlers first arrived, coyotes have undergone a major range extension eastward during the last quarter of the twentieth century. Smaller than wolves and unable to compete with them in the long run where their territories overlap, coyotes have undoubtedly benefited from the absence of wolves in much of their former range. But wolves have been gone for a long, long time, so why have coyotes rather suddenly moved east into the North Maine Woods, and even more recently the edges of towns and out to the islands?

No one really knows the answer. The end of the extensive pogrom that western ranchers and the federal government carried out against coyotes for decades until the 1970s to protect livestock certainly reduced the pressure on western coyotes. It is likely that this reduced pressure has resulted in larger coyote populations, which over time are expanding into new territories.

The eastern coyote is subtly different from its western kin. For one thing, eastern coyotes tend to be slightly larger, and their skull shape is somewhat distinct, almost as if evolution were occurring on the order of decades rather than millennia—which some evolutionary biologists, notably Stephen Jay Gould, believe to be the case.

Although Maine law allows year-round trapping of coyotes, and some are taken each year, there seems to be little danger that this wily woodland canid will shrink back into oblivion at the hands of hunters and trappers. And wolves are unlikely to become so numerous as to drive coyotes from all their haunts, especially because coyotes are more clever at living at the edges of human settlement, where they are more warmly received by all who neither hunt deer nor raise sheep.

Allen Island Shearing, July 9, 1991

Mollie is the shepherdess contracted to oversee the Allen Island annual sheep roundup. As she steps back from the heap of sheep fleece, redolent with lanolin at her feet, Mollie hangs her shears on the fence and sits down to discuss the island sheep business. The proprietress of Offshore Sheep Services, Mollie probably knows more about the practices and pitfalls of raising sheep on Maine islands than most others—except perhaps for Jenny Cirone, of Nash Island off Cape Split, who has an additional half century of experience raising island sheep.

We recount the recent visit we made to York Island off Isle au Haut, which has had a flock of sheep for at least a hundred years. One morning shortly after this spring's lambing season, the owners were alerted to the possibility of problems in the northern pasture by the presence of an eagle, which generally signals that a lamb is down. When the owners hiked to the north end, they found that twenty-eight lambs had been slaughtered overnight. Immediately suspecting coyotes, they called in a U.S. Fish and Wildlife animal control officer and drove the island with dogs to try to flush out the beast that had wreaked such havoc. Their efforts were to no avail; the murdering creature was gone, but judging from the teeth marks, it was certainly a canid.

Mollie nods throughout the retelling of the horrid details; she had seen and heard it all more times than she cares to remember. But she also knows some things that no one else had mentioned. "Could be coyotes," she says. She had seen coyotes go "kill crazy" in a flock of sheep. But dogs could not

Sheep Island, Southeast Harbor, Stonington, could support either sheep or bears, but not both.

be ruled out. Either dogs or coyotes could have picked up the scent of new-born lambs and crossed the quarter mile from Isle au Haut to York. The only way to tell, Mollie says, is from the tracks. The middle two toes of a dog tend to be longer than the outer two; in a coyote, the middle toes are shorter. "It's not real easy to tell," she says, "but you take a piece of grass and lay it so it just fits in the print of one of the outer two toes; then set it in one of the center toes. If the grass fits inside the toe print without touching the end, it's a dog; if it doesn't, it's a coyote."

Although no one will ever know just what happened that terrible night on York, few people understand what apparently docile pet dogs are capable of doing when they get loose on an island where sheep are raised.

Red Fox, Vulpes vulpes

Almost everyone who has taken a moment to listen to the history or folklore of the islands knows that the Fox Islands—now called Vinalhaven and North Haven—were named for the sly canids that were sighted on their shores by English explorer Martin Pring in 1603. Pring's voyage was underwritten by a group of wealthy London merchants who were eager to get their hands on a load of sassafras, a tree whose medicinal qualities could supposedly cure all ailments. They made their landfall at forty-three degrees north latitude on the Maine coast and rode at anchor on the southwest side of Vinalhaven, probably in what is now Old Harbor. They found the shores "pleasant to behold, adorned with goodly grass and sundry sorts of trees," and named the largest two islands for "those kinds of beasts [we saw] thereon."

Somewhere along the way, the foxes that Pring saw came to be called silver foxes, although they were not so described in the original account of the voyage that Pring wrote for Richard Hakluyt, England's compiler of New World discoveries. Silver foxes make a better story, and it is certainly possible that the tree-climbing gray fox (*Urocyon cinereoargenteus*), which had a more southerly distribution throughout the United States, could have thrived on Maine's larger islands. It is also remotely possible that a population of red foxes had been genetically isolated on Vinalhaven and North Haven for a long enough period of time that their pelage changed from reddish brown to silver gray. Apparently such a situation has occurred on the Channel Islands off Santa Barbara, California, where a dwarf species, the island fox (*Urocyon littoralis*), now lives.

The possibility of a separate species on Vinalhaven and North Haven seems unlikely, because even these islands, which lie four to eight miles out to sea from Owls Head, are in winter periodically connected to the mainland by ice. We are told by various island historians that 1816 was the first time in thirty-five years that west Penobscot Bay was completely frozen over. Again in 1835, by early February the bay had frozen to the outer islands. Horses and sleighs crossed the bay until mid-March to transport hay to island livestock in danger of starvation, although few undertook the dangerous trip with any relish.

No doubt the foxes, whatever their precise lineage, also used the ice for winter travel, following the trails of rabbit, hare, and small rodents, which sneaked off into the white unknown looking for better things to eat. When and if the Maine climate grows gradually colder so that the islands are again briefly connected by frozen seawater, we may expect to find small populations of foxes on the larger islands they once inhabited. Until such random climatic events occur, foxes are unlikely to make island voyages, because there is enough for them to eat around their mainland hideouts.

Bear, Ursus americanus

Isolated and rugged islands no doubt once furnished more than a few secure denning sites, but bears completely disappeared from island ecosystems in the early decades of the 1800s, when serious island settlement began. Both Marshall Island in Jericho Bay and Bradbury Island in north Penobscot Bay were originally called Bear Island. On today's charts, an island adjacent to Bradbury is still called Bear, as is a smaller island in the passage known as Western Way off Mount Desert, though neither of these islands has recorded the massive paw print of this mammal in more than 150 years.

Various island histories record the dates when the last bears were shot, as if their deaths—as those of the Indians who fell before—meant that the community was safe from evil. Two bears were shot on Swan's Island before the turn of the nineteenth century, and no others arrived to take their place. On Vinalhaven, a solitary bear persisted within the confines of the large swampland northeast of Carvers Pond until 1825, when it, too, was shot.

Maine's islands appear to have been ideally suited to these individualistic, somewhat ornery and antisocial creatures. Because bears find their meals lower on the food chain than do wolves, they do not rely chiefly on meat and do not need as much operating space. Within forested areas they can sustain themselves in a range of between one and five square miles, and on an island they can get by on less because they also have the benefit of the intertidal zone. Writing of his experiences on the coast of Maine in the mid-1600s, John Josselyn describes bears fishing for lobsters, which were plentiful enough to be stranded in tidepools: "The bear is a tyrant at a lobster and at low water will go down to the rocks and grope after them with great diligence."

Bears are unquestionably strong and single-minded enough to swim the waters between most of the forested islands of Maine. Except for a brief fall mating season when they are captive to the fury of their hormones, bears do not seek one another's company. It is easy to imagine a grumpy bear retiring to the peace and solitude of an island for the winter, lumbering around until he gives in to a long sleep.

Maine supports the East's largest population of black bears, but most of these are found in the northern woods. However, Cross Island, a fifteen-hundred-acre forested island in Machias Bay, supports at least one shy bear—or else someone has gone to a lot of trouble to make paw prints around several of the island's waterholes. If bears are indeed on Cross Island, they may also appear elsewhere on large, uninhabitable islands someday.

Reindeer, Stags, Fallow Deer—and Moose

Was it significant that James Rosier mentioned three species—reindeer, stags, and fallow deer—in his list of mammals of the New World? Because reindeer, also called caribou, exist in great domesticated herds in Lapland, it seems likely that Rosier would have had an accurate picture of them in his mind. Rosier's and Waymouth's exploration of the islands of Muscongus and Penobscot bays and of the Saint George River Valley was conducted during early summer (and in the company of a local band of Indians whom the naturalist's party first befriended and then betrayed), so Rosier and Waymouth may well have seen some of the big forest ungulates. We know that two-thousand-year-old bones of caribou, which were extirpated in Maine by sport hunting about a hundred years ago, show up in shell middens along the coast of Washington and Hancock Counties, but their remains have not yet been unearthed farther west.

Perhaps Rosier's "stags" are in fact moose, which would have been prolific in the low, swampy areas of the Saint George peninsula, where they reside today. A half century after Rosier, Josselyn describes the moose (which he calls "elk") as "a monster of superfluity": the tips of their antlers "are sometimes found to be two fathoms asunder." Rockland and Thomaston historian Cyrus Eaton wrote that in 1750 a group of six moose was sighted on an island in north Penobscot Bay. One feeble calf was captured and made into a pet.

Evidently moose were not strangers to islands—after all, they swim well and move about considerably in search of browse—but they make such obvious targets and provide so much meat that they likely disappeared early. In the last few decades, aided by the transformation of much of the North Maine Woods into large acreages of the young hardwood shoots that follow most clear-cuts, the moose population has increased substantially. When the Maine Department of Inland Fisheries and Wildlife conservatively estimated moose numbers to be in excess of twenty-five thousand, it was enough, in the department's opinion, to support a limited hunting season. Because moose are not hunted in southern and eastern Maine, their numbers have also increased substantially on the coast, and they have once again begun to appear on the large forested islands, from Cross Island down east to Hog Island of Bremen.

Allen Island Moose, June 26, 1982

Two of the loggers saw what they at first took to be a horse in the field, but it was actually a young bull moose with spiked antlers. It plodded over the rise and disappeared into the woods. The next day we found moose tracks on the north point. Two days later someone spotted the floating carcass of a young male moose off Western Egg Rock, southwest of Allen, and

Postcard of young moose ashore in Fox Island Thorofare.   <small>Courtesy Jamien Morehouse</small>

hauled it ashore. Having stuck its neck out to get to the island, the hapless yearling didn't have a long enough neck to keep it out of an offshore sea. The incident stimulated plenty of conversation among Friendship lobstermen, most of whom would have been happy to come across four hundred pounds of meat to stock the larder.

Later we heard the story of a Southwest Harbor man who was tuna fishing off Mount Desert Rock, thirty miles out, when he saw a moose swimming farther out to sea. Knowing that the animal's chances of getting back to the mainland were less than zero, the fisherman dispatched the hapless creature and winched it aboard. Heading back to shore, he debated whether to call the Coast Guard, figuring that things would get complicated, but finally relented when he thought about some of the unpleasant consequences of unloading in daylight at the public landing. He radioed the Coast Guard in Southwest Harbor and explained the situation. There was a long pause on Channel 22. Then the voice came back on and said, "Let me get this straight. You went out for bluefin tuna, for which you have a license, but you're coming back in with a moose. . . ."

Ten-four.

Deer, Odocoileus virginianus

Virtually every forested island along the Maine coast that is larger than ten acres shows signs of occasional visits by deer. Some people find it hard to believe that deer can get around among the islands as well as they do, but it should not come as a great surprise. Like most mammals, deer float naturally without any great effort. (Additional buoyancy is provided by their hair, which is hollow for better insulation value.) Healthy deer are reasonably good swimmers, perhaps not as strong as moose in the water but certainly capable of the across-the-bay marathons they occasionally under-take. Their center of buoyancy is slightly forward of their center of gravity, which has the effect of allowing the front quarters to ride a little higher as they swim. That, in addition to a long neck, helps them keep their head in the air. The only part of the deer's body that leaves a bit to be desired in terms of water travel is its tiny hooves, which provide only modest propulsion. The splayed feet of the moose allow it to swim a little faster.

No doubt it is the young bucks that, as in other mammalian groups, do the greatest amount of traveling. In summer when food is plentiful, the young bucks are looking not so much for adequate forage as for a population of does to impress. Several summers ago off Bluff Head, a granitic promontory on the eastern shore of Vinalhaven, we saw what we assumed was a bird with a broken wing making its way toward us from the middle of east Penobscot Bay. It turned out to be a young buck, which set itself ashore unsteadily after what must have been a six-mile trip from the shores of Isle au Haut.

> ### Bradbury Island, July 12, 1975
> *Moving across this densely forested island through the woods with note-book, binoculars, and camera in hand, I sense a shadowy presence. The longer I am here, the more certain I am that something is watching me, some part of this wild island. After several hours of carefully cataloging the island flora, I see, like a trick of the imagination, the trees dissolve to reveal glimpses of tawny outlines of several does and fawns that materialize out of the brown and green forested background.*
>
> *The deer are alerted to my every movement, not only by the incredibly acute hearing of their constantly twitching ears but by the derisive cries of three or four crows who follow me from above the deep canopy of the woods. They make such a raucous noise that a child would know where I lurked. The crows and deer act for all the world as if they are in league with one another, as indeed they are.*
>
> *All hunters know that deer are the distilled essence of wild places close to home, the more so for hunters with a camera.*

There are places down east where local hunters swear that groups of four or five deer move out to the large islands for the duration of the hunting season and then return to the mainland either at the onset of colder weather or when the ice builds a temporary bridge.

On the larger islands farther off the mainland, deer don't move but choose to overwinter. Island winters may be more raw than those on the mainland, but they are less severe in terms of the degree of cold and the depth of snow. (Snow is the great winter killer in a food-stressed deer herd. A snow depth of more than eighteen inches effectively limits a deer's movements in search of food. In all but the tallest, the snow catches them just below the brisket and causes them to "yard up" and wait it out. Once the food is gone from the yard area, the grim starvation dance begins, because it takes more energy to search for food than the deer have in reserve.)

Island deer are able to supplement their diets with kelps and other seaweeds. But islands also present special problems for deer: after a certain point in December they are isolated by the frigid water. In winter, deer need to eat six to eight pounds of woody vegetation per day; once that supply is exhausted, they cannot withstand a frigid inter-island swim to find a new supply. Inevitably, in the absence of predation or significant hunting pressure, deer populations gradually increase even as their food supplies remain constant or decrease.

Starvation can occur over the course of a single severe winter, but the cumulative effects of food stress usually take several years to become acute. One of the first responses to chronic food stress is that does drop a single fawn instead of the usual set of twins in spring. Fewer fawns survive, disease increases, and the average size of the younger individuals declines. On islands where these effects continue for years, herds of tiny deer are produced; the adults are sometimes not much bigger than dogs. This is what has occurred on Isle au Haut—where, on its Acadia National Park land, no hunting is allowed—and more recently on Monhegan, where introduced deer were considered by many to be part of the island scene and not to be hunted. Eventually a sanctioned deer hunt by a trained stalker had to be instituted.

Ultimately all populations are limited by the supply of food that is available to them; the question is how quickly the natural controls intervene to bring a population back in line with its food supply. In the case of island deer herds, we have eliminated their predators. Hunting prohibitions often turn out to be ill-conceived efforts to freeze systems that are constantly changing in nature. Sooner or later something has to give.

On Maine's year-round islands, an overpopulation of protected deer generally pits wildlife and animal rights folks against gardeners. Deer are also hosts to ticks whose bites can spread Lyme Disease. In recent years, island communities have increasingly had to wrestle with the emotionally charged issue of authorizing deer hunts to thin a herd. These discussions, whether they have occurred on Monhegan, the Diamond islands in Casco Bay, or Great Cranberry off Mount Desert, seem to have the same cast of characters: those whose attitudes are primarily influenced by Disney's Bambi pitted against those who cultivate private flower or vegetable gardens. Resolution is never easy.

Mink (and Minkholers), Mustela vison

The mink belongs to a distinctive group of carnivores called mustelids, all of which possess specialized anal scent glands that serve primarily as a means of olfactory communication either among individuals of their species or close competitors. Just a squirt on a rock or a stump is so much easier than a testy confrontation. In the case of the ponderous skunk—called a "polecat" by Rosier and Josselyn after a similar species common in the Old World—the scent glands can convey a particularly emphatic message to a harassing predator: Don't bother; the meal is not worth it.

Mink are the most common carnivore and the only mustelid found on the islands of Maine. They are almost as quick on land as in the water, where they can swim fast enough to catch small fish. In their diets they are both opportunistic and omnivorous, as even a casual examination of one of their calling cards—a scat, or dropping—will confirm: raspberry and strawberry seeds mixed with bits of crab and eggshell, rodent hairs, and even small feathers. There is at least one record that a mink climbed the trunk of an osprey nesting tree and carried off a helpless nestling.

A slightly larger, separate species, called the sea mink, was known only to the coast of Maine. Because the sea mink was about 30 percent larger than its riverine cousin, and had a longer and softer coat, it was a prized trade item among Indians. There is evidence that Maine coast sea mink skins were traded as far north as Labrador by aboriginal inhabitants of the archipelago. The various Otter islands lying off the mainland must have been named for the sea mink, because Maine's real otter is restricted to a freshwater habitat. The sea mink's presence probably was behind the naming of the Otter Ponds on several of the larger islands. The sea mink disappeared by about 1860, a casualty of overtrapping. Its north woods relative moved into the vacant niche.

The island niche occupied by the small, agile mink appears to have benefited significantly from the effects of the quarrying era. The huge piles of granite tailings on the quarried islands provide literally thousands of opportunities to pull a disappearing act, as well as hundreds of miles of underground tunnels and innumerable burrow sites in which to raise young. Mink swim from island to island looking for food, but no islands are as hospitable as those that have been cut for granite. Occasionally you can find fresh mink scat on a seabird nesting island, but this situation is rare enough to make you wonder whether open water intimidates even this highly aggressive package of speed and stealth.

During the rash of strikes that shut down operations on many of the granite islands just before the turn of the century, the derogatory term "minkholer" was coined and applied to scab labor brought in to break strikes. No doubt the furtive and opportunistic activities of this breed of men resembled in the minds of union men the habits of the mink, which today still emerge hungrily from tailing piles and scurry about the shore when a granite island falls to silence.

> ### *Shipstern Island, July 31, 1982*
> *Shipstern's steep sides and nearly impossible access make for ideal eagle habitat. The island's pair of northern bald eagles maintains an alternate nest on one of several nearby islands. Seeing no activity on Shipstern on this rare day when the seas are flat calm, we are able to get ashore.*
>
> *Near the north end of the island is another pile of sticks that one might assume belongs to the eagles. However, it is the work of another animal. Hard as it is to believe, a beaver swam out to the island and built a lodge, partially out of small birch trees it felled. The stumps of some of these gnawed trees are plainly visible. What the beaver thought it was doing on Shipstern, which has no flowing water, is hard to imagine. Like other rodents, beavers produce a large number of young, most of which disperse downstream from the area where they are born. In fact they are usually driven out by their parents as soon as they reach maturity. This beaver apparently reached the end of the line—where the stream on which it was born reached the ocean— and just kept going until it reached Shipstern. However the beaver got to the island, it soon exhausted its food supply of the inner bark of small birches and probably swam away, unless of course the pair of eagles made a meal out of it.*

Rabbits and Raccoons: Island Introductions

These creatures belong to separate families of mammals, occupy different niches, and have evolved from different ancestral stocks. In fact, they have little in common except that they are about equally uncommon on Maine islands.

Raccoons are handy at fishing in freshwater streams and are also often seen along saltwater shores foraging for crabs, clams, and mussels. This is all very deceptive, however, because raccoons avoid at all costs any water that is deeper than they can wade in—and with good reason, for they are poor swimmers. If hunger drives them to it, raccoons may be able to negotiate narrow channels that separate the mainland from any nearby islands, but for the most part they are found on larger islands only because someone thought they were improving island fauna through their importation. Several years ago, a sporting club on Vinalhaven did just that, with the idea that hunting raccoons with dogs in winter would be fun. After a season or two of such diversion, the sport died away. Now partridge, or grouse, are nearly unknown on Vinalhaven, and farm fowl disappear in ones and twos over the winter.

While on the subject of island introductions, it is appropriate to mention a population of red foxes released on the thirty-acre No Man's Land in 1916, probably by a Matinicus fisherman. Though the record of this release does not indicate the purpose, if any, one imagines the foxes were to be raised for their pelts. Whether or not the foxes were a successful business enterprise can only be guessed. It is certain, however, that the effect was felt chiefly by the burrow-nesting Leach's storm-petrels, which

Racoon on ledge, Roberts Harbor, Vinalhaven.
PHILIP CONKLING

apparently provided the foxes with most of their food until the colony was exterminated.

Among the many terrors of a rabbit's life, water must rank near the top. Every once in a while a population of rabbits or hares (which are a different species) appears on islands near the mainland, but their access routes must certainly be over a temporary ice bridge that forms in a quiet channel. There is a lot more to the lives of rabbits, but not much that relates to islands. Like people who simply will not set foot on a boat, rabbits appear on islands only in unusual circumstances. One of these that deserves passing mention is their presence on quarried islands. During the granite years on islands such as Vinalhaven, rabbits were raised as an additional and inexpensive source of red meat. Italian stone carvers, in particular, were in the habit of setting up hutches to raise rabbits for Sunday dinner.

Over the years some of these potential Sunday dinners wandered off and have intermixed with other rabbits introduced for the wilder purpose of hunting. Someday an energetic soul will conduct a study of Maine island rabbit blood and be surprised at the number of exotic strains that are co-mingled within the island populations.

Criehaven, July 20, 1990

Criehaven, designated on the charts as Ragged Island, was perhaps named for the condition of its wind-ravaged spruce that cling to the rocky fastness of this outermost inhabited island of the archipelago. A dozen lobstering families maintain the fishing privilege around the island shores. They interact easily with one another and with the few summer families that have been coming since Robert "King" Crie died and his heirs divided up his fishing empire.

But lately Criehaven has been cursed by a plague of rabbits—a little piece of Australia-like experimentation that someone apparently thought would add a pastoral dimension to the island's complement of wildlife. In the absence of predators, the rabbits have overrun and underrun every niche on the island. We disembark from FISH HAWK, *the Island Institute's field research boat, to discuss ecologically sensible strategies for reducing the rabbit impact. During the previous winter, rabbits unhappily crawled into several of the island's dug wells. The rabbits' carcasses were recently salvaged from the well by the still-trim wife of the island's largest property owner because he himself could no longer fit down the well. The feat of his wife, however, still provokes a good deal of commentary among the admiring lobstermen. "He got her young and trained her well," said a lobsterman, to the general amusement of the rest of the fishermen.*

MERCHANT ROW MICE AND THE THEORY OF ISLAND BIOGEOGRAPHY

Although it might seem unlikely at first glance, voles—the country cousins of city mice—are the most common mammal on the islands of Maine. Their presence is unlikely because they are so small, can about fit in the curve of a tablespoon, don't regularly take to water, and are usually thought of (to the extent that we think of them at all) as timid and unassuming. There can be little truth to this prejudice once one realizes that voles come to Maine's islands either as clever stowaways or, when a particularly high tide catches them unaware, as castaways on little wooden boats otherwise known as driftwood. It's what ecologists call the "sweepstakes route."

No one has ever introduced meadow mice or voles to an island to raise them as a source of fur or to hunt—no one, that is, except Ken Crowell, who did it more than thirty years ago. As a zoology student, Crowell wondered what kinds of small mammals were distributed among the scattering of Maine's islands. From this modest wonder came an elegant idea that over the course of many years was part of the groundwork for what has come to be known as the theory of island biogeography.

As Crowell began trapping small animals on Deer Isle and the smaller islands of Merchant Row, he soon discovered that of the three species commonly encountered on Deer Isle, only one— the ubiquitous meadow vole, or field mouse (*Microtus*)—inhabited the smaller offshore islands. The species that were "missing" from the other islands were the deer mouse (*Peromyscus*), recognized by its large ears and long tail, and the red-backed mouse (*Clethrionomys*), which has a rusty red back, as its name suggests. The fact that both of these forest-dwelling species were absent from the islands where the field mouse had arrived and maintained itself led Crowell to speculate on one of the most fundamental questions of ecology: What determines the number of species living together in a natural community?

Over the next fifteen years, Crowell introduced the missing species to various small islands off Stonington, which were like distant oceanic islands to the mice, and recorded their fates. One by one, most of the introduced populations of deer mice and red-backed mice slipped into extinction. Through patient observation, Crowell discovered that the reason for the extinctions boiled down to the specialized feeding habits of the deer mice and the low reproductive potential of the red-backed mice. Whereas the meadow vole is one of the most prolific rodents—producing six to eight young every two weeks—its not-very-closely-related cousin, the red-backed mouse, is one of the slowest rodent reproducers. In the time that a single meadow vole can produce 233 offspring, her red-backed cousin produces only 25. In the matter of the roulette probability of survival, meadow vole populations have a greater chance of pulling through simply by virtue of their greater numbers.

The deer mouse, however, has as impressive a reproductive potential as the meadow vole, but its disappearance seems to be a matter of a preference for seeds and fruits of plants rather than stems and vegetable parts, which the meadow vole eats. Because there are fewer meals of seeds and fruits per acre than there are of stems, the deer mouse needs more space on islands. With a less abundant and more unreliable food supply than the meadow vole has, the deer mouse became extinct on the smaller islands. It *is* able to maintain itself on the larger islands, even if they are farther offshore. Observations from Crowell and other island naturalists were translated into one of the most powerfully significant ecological ideas of the century, as propounded by E. O. Wilson, Harvard's well-known "ant man," and Robert MacArthur, who was Cornell University's greatest ecological thinker until he died as a relatively young man.

Essentially, Wilson's and MacArthur's theory of island biogeography suggests that the number of species that inhabit islands is a balance between the colonization and extinction rates that populations naturally undergo. Because larger islands have more niches, extinction rates are lower and more species are found. And because islands closer to the mainland have higher colonization rates, more species are likely to be found there. When you consider all the mathematics, it gets down to something like this: The number of species on any island is proportional to the cube root of its area divided by the linear distance to the mainland.

The power of this simple model has grown since it was introduced by Wilson and MacArthur in 1967, because it has been subject to all sorts of field testing and because it is easy to grasp its conceptual essentials contained in the acute balances between extinction and immigration, between distance and area, between life and death. In recent years, ecologists have been more concerned about the slow extinction of biodiversity, partly as a result of this theory. Increasingly, we see habitats all over the globe being transformed into "habitat islands" in the midst of an inexorably rising sea of human expansion, development, and occupation of the terresphere. Terrestrial habitats have shrunk, from rain forests to savannas to the coastal edge—which the beast that walks upright inhabits more tenaciously than any other ecological niche.

In recent years, the theory has been extended to predict the number of species likely to be found in any discontinuous habitat. Ecologically speaking, mountaintops, caves, and ponds are really islands in space and time, and the numbers of species that make up these communities can be predicted with some accuracy on the basis of the Wilson-MacArthur model.

Island Biogeography and Rare Species

The Song of the Dodo: Island Biogeography in an Age of Extinctions (1996), by David Quammen, takes up the story of a handful of dedicated island field biologists who are applying the predictions of Wilson and MacArthur to present-day environmental questions. Quammen chronicles the story of how western explorers found and destroyed island cultures and drastically altered island biology throughout the Atlantic, Pacific, and Indian oceans during the past four hundred years.

Quammen's book is highly instructive because it suggests how important islands have become to our understanding of the future. Islands are important not just in and of themselves, he argues, but because they are critical to understanding how people can interact with natural ecosytems. Islands force us to address such questions as how many isolated habitat islands make a whole? What are the minimum viable areas that can support, say, a mountain lion or a right whale? Will migration corridors work? Can we learn how to restore pieces of biodiversity by reintroducing species that have been lost or are on the brink of extinction before our headlong flight into the future precludes the possibilities of fully functional and wholly integrated ecosystems?

LOOKING BACK AND LOOKING AHEAD

Looking back over three hundred and fifty years of our relations with island mammals, we see that the record is not pretty. Almost all of the big game species on the islands were hunted to early extinction. But now bears are back; moose, too. Wolves and what are most likely mountain lions have miraculously reappeared in places such as coastal Washington County, and the wily coyote—never before part of Maine fauna—has also taken up residence. We'll never know whether the original island foxes were red, gray, or silver, but as long as the islands host a food supply of voles, mice, and birds, a few foxes will walk out on the ice in cold winters, or get caught on an ice floe and drift to an offshore home.

Deer live on islands occasionally in numbers too great for their own good. Only caribou, among the original faunal complement, are missing and will continue to be after a recent ambitious reintroduction effort failed. Now and again, rabbits and raccoons have made the trip out to the islands, often helped by man. The mink has moved into the habitat once occupied by a separate species of sea mink to give new life to what were once called "Otter" islands.

The situation in the marine environment is, as usual, murkier. Seals, now protected for almost three decades, have continued reproducing and have recolonized areas with an astonishing rapidity. They haul out on an increasing number of ledges to watch our activities and to raise their bewhiskered pups.

In a sense, whales are the great disappointment. After all these years of protection—since the 1930s for the northern right whale and almost as long for the humpback and others—there are still so few. We should be grateful, I suppose, that in the Gulf of Maine the most ancient, and some say most highly developed, mammals of the world still sing, splash, and dance in the blue-green water. But there are precious few compared to what our forebears saw and slew.

Even though there is today a less diverse and reduced abundance of island and marine mammal fauna than we wish for, there is hope for recovery of the ecosystem. Our real challenges may not be how to deal with scarcity, but how to balance the conflicting interests that will be increasingly created by any resurgence of our wild finned and furred legacy. If the recent imbroglio between defenders of the northern right whale and the Maine coast lobstermen tells us anything, it is that although we need to see the system as a whole, we still need to know where and how the pieces fit together.

7

Submerged Islands: Clams, Scallops, Lobsters, and Urchins

There is much temptation to stay [in], the truth of which true men avoid by going out no matter what. The worst of it is not in gale or storm but when it is plainly severe and cold: early mornings when sea smoke works its way into every man's and boy's blood and bone. At least a dozen compulsive workdays a year it creates a dwarf world where those on the water work in clouds, and those ashore watch mastheads come and go like dorsal fins of extinct fish.
    —George Putz, *Island Journal*

ISLAND BOUNDARIES

Where does an island end and the rest of the world begin? Some islands lose their distinction, become mere peninsulas, appended extensions of the mainland at low water; while new ones, treacherous ledges at high tide, uncover their gleaming teeth as the tide recedes. Thus in order to begin to appreciate Maine's island endowment, they need to be defined in relation to the tide. The accepted convention is to count an island as any piece of land totally surrounded by the sea at mean high tide.

Even so, this neat tidal convention doesn't begin to define the real boundaries of an island in the Gulf of Maine. For starters, islands are mountains in the sea or, in the case of Cape Cod's islands, huge glacial till and outwash plains left by receding ice sheets. Their long, sometimes steep slopes or gently shelving shoals extend the domain of islands outward from the shore and downward over the shadowy bottom to nooks, crannies, and crawls in the shallows and depths, out of sight and mind.

Here is a whole other hidden world of islands. The sea creatures that live on and about these subtidal island slopes and shoals—scallops, lobsters, mussels, urchins, starfish, kelps, and a thousand other pieces of treasured sea life cast ashore when a sea gets up—are inseparable parts of the essence of any Maine island. Not to pick a quarrel with Noah Webster, but there is more here to a Maine island than meets the conventional definition.

Out among the islands, town boundaries tend to peter out and be subsumed mostly under the jurisdiction of "harbor gangs," as anthropologist Jim Acheson has described the lobstermen who control these territories. So, too, for the scallopers, musselers, urchiners, and others who prowl patches of subtidal sand, gravel, and cobble plains among and about the islands. It takes time to recognize that many Maine islands are surrounded by a quasi-legal invisible boundary within which certain rights are conveyed to harvest fish and shellfish from island flats, coves, guzzles, bottoms, and waters. This island-marine realm generally extends about two miles from the hard edge of the

Opposite: Lobster cannery owner, Isle au Haut.   STANLEY G. FRENCH

shore, or about the ecological distance over which a fisherman in a small boat can maintain control. You won't find these marine metes and bounds recorded in deeds, but you can be sure the boundaries are nonetheless fixed and real.

To understand island ecology, you must understand the underwater worlds of islands, where a great deal of their commercial value, and hence contention, is focused.

Barnacles feeding at high water.
ISLAND INSTITUTE FILES

ISLANDS AND MARINE BIODIVERSITY

Without islands the Maine coast would not be just aesthetically less distinct but also biologically less productive. The immense number of islands here sets up conditions for enhanced nearshore productivity; the higher the density, the higher the level of productivity, all other factors being equal.

As Gulf of Maine waters circulate among the islands, the islands help mix, oxygenate, and enrich the water. Tide-induced vertical water currents around islands bring an astonishing abundance of nutrients and marine life up from the sea floor. Tide-driven currents also surge through passages between islands, creating funnel effects that increase the volume of feed available to filter feeders as well as the species that prey on them. Individually, islands support thousands of wetlands, large and small, and the nutrient-rich runoff from them also enriches the surrounding waters. These factors help explain the inshore movement of lobsters, crabs, and fish during spring and summer and the high density of lobster traps around the margins of islands during the shedding season.

Marine ecologists measure productivity in part by estimating the yearly amount of carbon fixed by plants through photosynthesis. Ecologists at the Bedford Institute of Oceanography in Nova Scotia have been measuring the primary production of seaweeds in the shallows of the Gulf of Maine for more than two decades. Data on nearshore productivity is crucial to understanding how islands lead to enriched coastal food chains. The estimates are made by studying the growth of seaweeds and by harvesting them. Studies in Saint Margaret's Bay, Nova Scotia, show that as much as one thousand grams of carbon per square meter per year is captured by the seaweeds along the shores there. This compares with estimates of only one hundred and twenty-five grams of carbon per square meter per year for the open ocean adjacent to the Gulf of Maine and translates to three hundred and seventy kilograms (eight hundred and fifteen pounds) of carbon produced per year for every meter of shoreline around a substantial portion of the Gulf of Maine.

The islands of Maine contribute about twenty-five hundred miles of collective shoreline, a total of over seven thousand miles of Maine's entire salt water coastline. Along this complex, perhaps two

Eaton Island's pocket salt marsh boosts nearshore subtidal activity, Penobscot Bay.

and a half billion pounds of carbon are produced annually just by seaweeds, forming the base of a food web that could sustain about a hundred million lobsters. These values are among the highest for coastal productivity recorded anywhere. In part, these high values are due to the large and intricate topography of the shallows around the many islands in the bays of Maine. Without these islands the nearshore zone would be a much simpler place, without the biological richness we currently enjoy.

SLIPPING SEAWARD: INTERTIDAL ENVIRONMENTS

Not just ecologically, but also legally, the domain of Maine islands extends beyond the high-water mark into the half-land, half-sea realm between the tides. Unlike most other states along the Atlantic coast, Maine deeds have extended ownership to the low-water mark since colonial times, a legal convention designed to increase colonization by encouraging fishermen and other shorefront owners to improve their properties by constructing wharves and fish-drying stages.

A great deal has been written about Maine's rocky intertidal zone ever since Rachel Carson's elegant descriptions of tidepool life and the ecological zonation that she studied on the shores of Southport Island at the edge of the Sheepscot estuary. Small wonder! The rocky intertidal zone is one of the most diverse and productive habitats found anywhere at the oceanic-continental edge,

Ecological zonation in rocky intertidal environments was brought to popular attention by Rachel Carson, who wrote extensively about Maine's island shorelines. RICK PERRY

where hundreds of easily recognized species of plants and animals are commonly found at your fingertips.

If life in the ocean is so good, why, then, have the last several hundred million years of evolution seen some marine forms struggling out of their watery pastures and onto the land, which is hotter and colder and drier and in almost all ways less habitable? Survival in the sea is tenuous until a creature gets big enough so that it does not make a convenient mouthful for something bigger. The intensity of predation and competition for inevitably scarce resources must be twin driving forces for land colonization.

This dynamic is certainly visible in the intertidal region, where the common marine plants and animals stratify themselves into the neat zones that Carson described, including the barnacle zone, the periwinkle zone, and the rockweed zone. Recent studies of the way these creatures maintain such a rigid stratification indicate that the upper boundary of each zone is primarily determined by a creature's physical tolerance to drying out. The lower limits of the zone, however, are determined by competition and predation. When you look at a diverse marine intertidal zone, you can almost hear the struggle for a foothold slightly above and beyond the reach of the snapping mandibles of competitors and predators below.

The dominant species of the rockweed zone are the brown seaweeds, which attach themselves directly to the rocky shores. Two species—sea wrack and knotted wrack (*Fucus* and *Ascophyllum*, respectively)—dominate this immense community around the edge of rocky islands. The seaweeds' long, thin fronds, with conspicuous float bladders, hang limply over rocks when the tide is out, protecting large numbers of marine snails, crabs, and brine shrimp, then float upward as the tide rises to form dense pastures that provide shelter and feeding areas that are especially critical for juvenile fish.

Beneath the rockweed zone lies the kelp zone, named for the constellation of red algae that spread their fronds across the rocks like a carpet. Throughout rocky intertidal areas of the world, Irish moss is collected to extract carrageenan, an important emulsifying agent and food additive that is used in toothpaste, gels, ice cream, puddings, and a host of other products. The largest carrageenan facility in the United States, Marine Colloids, maintains a processing plant on the Rockland waterfront, although it now imports all its raw materials from other regions of the world.

Two Bush Island, July 11, 1992

This little granite island thrusts into Penobscot Bay's upwelling, which surges from two-hundred-foot depths to wash the immense fronds of kelp around the edge of the island. Kelps are reddish brown seaweeds found growing at the lowest places of the intertidal zone—those that extend through the light zone to the toe of the island slope. The sweeping coastal currents, underwater canyons, and tidal forces stir a rich broth of nutrients through these kelp forests where the leatherlike fronds sweep and grow.

Two of the commonest species—Laminaria, with wide, flat fronds, and Alaria, with a distinct round midrib—can grow to ten to twelve feet along the Maine coast. Perhaps that's modest when compared to a West Coast kelp, which grows more than a hundred feet long, but our kelps can grow inches per week, feet per month. They are of enormous interest to biologists, because they are able to grow fast even in winter, even down to zero degrees Celsius and at low light intensities. And no one knows what value their store of complex biological molecules might be to, say, the pharmaceutical industry or the biotechnology field.

These kelps are the most difficult seaweeds to collect, because they are exposed only at the lowest of low tides—the so-called moon tides. But after storms, you often find fresh fronds of these species that have been torn loose from their holdfasts. They are fun to look for. If you dive, kelp forests signal areas of high biodiversity and pull you into their dreamy interiors.

The Short, Sweet Life of the Clam

Perhaps it shouldn't be surprising that the first marine conservation law that was passed after Maine became a state invested the regulation of clam harvesting to towns along the coast, ensuring that the inhabitants of the community could take these shellfish at any time for personal and family use and fishermen could take them for bait.

According to Dana Wallace, Maine's distinguished clam biologist emeritus, a clam "industry," as such, didn't develop until freshly shucked clams began to be used for bait during the heyday of the offshore fishing fleet. Between 1850 and 1875, clams were steamed, salted, and barreled during the winter for sale to fishermen heading to the Grand Banks for spring or summer dory fishing. Buyers included European boats fishing for cod on the Banks.

According to Edward Earll, who researched Maine fisheries for the newly formed U.S. Fisheries Commission during the 1870s, the clam flats in the Town of Deer Isle (then a bridgeless island) produced the largest volume of clams and employed the largest number of diggers on the Maine coast. Following the decline of offshore fishing after 1875, soft-shell clams, or "steamers," became an increasingly important product harvested from local flats and transported throughout New England for clambakes and shore dinners.

Hurricane Island Clams, June 1, 1982

The encircling ledges at the north end of the island trap sediment from waves that undercut the shore deposits of mixed sand and silt, spreading them out in a small, shallow bed captured between the tides. The evidence of an Indian encampment is still visible from shell fragments leaching out of a layer of burned soil at the shoreward edge of the slope; it hints at an intertidal clam community. Little holes suggest where you can carefully dig at dead low tide; an occupied burrow sends a stream of seawater squirting vertically into the air, and poking around, you find where the hard shells of clams are worn smooth by wave energy. If you're quick, you can outdig them as they burrow deeper to escape.

Because these are clams from a mostly sandy deposit, their stomach contents are not packed with mud and their meat is almost unbearably sweet to the taste of salt-parched lips and tongue, particularly when steamed in a pot covered by rockweed and served with fresh beach peas.

In the 1980s, with new federal public health laws to prohibit the sale of shellfish harvested in polluted places, almost half of Maine's clam flats were closed either due to pollution or to the absence of verifiable water quality data showing that the flats were free of bacterial contamination. But in the last few years a host of volunteer groups of clammers and local activists have mobilized to collect data that might allow closed flats to be reopened. In 1996 alone, ten thousand acres of clam flats were reopened along the Maine coast. Perhaps more significantly, a clam hatchery has been established on Beals Island that has begun to supply seed clams and expertise to towns interested in reestablishing clam populations and harvests. Down east, where historically 40 percent of the state's clams were once harvested, the continued absence of clams from flats long closed to digging is mysterious and disturbing.

The history of this intertidal fishery, an important adjunct to islanders since the dawn of Maine civilization, suggests that failure to find the reasons behind the depletion of local clam flats has been among the most serious, most prolonged, and most neglected of all of our marine resource management failures to date.

SUBMARINE PLAINS OF SAND: COBBLE, GRAVEL, AND BOULDER BEDS

The edges of islands are good places to imagine the shape of the seabed just below the surface. Extend your mind's eye outward and downward through the intertidal zone to the green-filtered-light worlds of sand and mud plains, where burrowing creatures hide from the predatory fish patrolling overhead, their large mouths gaping wide.

Here and there along the subtidal channels of islands, where wave energy is too intense for sand or mud to settle out of the water column, are habitats composed of particles varying in size from gravel to cobble to boulder. Most of these subtidal communities—ecological extensions of intertidal mud, sand, shell, cobble, gravel, and boulder deposits—were laid down by river meltwaters powering massive loads of suspended particles off the receding continental glacier fifteen thousand years ago. Then waves from the rising sea reworked these deposits; the smaller particles were carried off and laid down in quieter waters, and the heavier gravel, cobble, and rounded boulders were left behind. To understand the distribution of gravel and cobble habitats subtidally, it is helpful to remember that the average size of the particles is a rough index of the force of waves or currents affecting that part of the shore: the larger the size, the more intense the wave climate.

Bass Harbor Blue Scallops, December 11, 1994

RAVEN *heads across Bass Harbor Bar, where an ebb tide and an easterly wind have driven up a steep and opposing sea.* RAVEN*'s bow rises to meet each new wall of water, and her hull shudders momentarily with each sharp crest. Green water piles around the pilothouse, but the deep and steady pulse of the Caterpillar diesel gives an unusual sense of security across this narrow piece of unfriendly water. We round up past Bass Harbor Head Light and into quiet waters framed by a world of rounded grayness, with all of Mount Desert's mountains arrayed on a foreshortened horizon.*

Just around Lopus Point, we can see two shrimp boats and several rerigged lobster boats dragging for scallops. Mo Rich, the proprietor of the

wharf and the owner of the seafood packing plant where we stop to refuel
RAVEN, *is waiting for the boats to return. He remarks laconically that both*
the supply and prices are holding up, except for the mysterious "blue" scal-
lops that have been showing up from some locales, such as those down off the
Spoons. Blue scallops are a harmless alteration of unknown origin in the
color of our favorite bivalve adductor muscle, but the color renders them
unmarketable because they look like they're old, tired, and rotten to boot.

Later we learned that research conducted by the University of Maine sug-
gests that the blue color (actually a suffused blue grayness) results from a glu-
cose deficiency that occurs when the scallop has pulled all of its carbohydrate
reserves into its reproductive system. Spawn till your adductors turn blue!

THE RISE OF LOBSTERING

To colonists arriving in the Gulf of Maine, the American lobster was surely one of the most
abundant resources, so much so that it is worth repeating the well-known saw that indentured
servants were known to insist in contracts that they not be fed lobster more than three times a
week. A resource so common and abundant that it could be collected at low tide from virtually
any rocky shoreline from spring to fall seems to have been taken for granted during the first two
centuries of settlement.

A trade in lobsters and an appreciation of their commercial value did not develop until the
problem of how to transport this highly perishable cargo was solved. Beginning sometime in the
1840s, specialized inshore sailing vessels from Massachusetts began to appear in isolated Maine fishing villages with a so-called "live well," which allowed seawater to circulate through a compartment
in the hold. These "lobster smacks," as the vessels were called, bought lobsters caught locally for a
penny or two apiece and sailed back to Boston, where the live catch could be sold for ten times as
much. The commercial significance of this markup was not lost on local entrepreneurs, and soon
fishermen, including Elisha Oakes from Vinalhaven, had entered the trade. Oakes sailed from island
to island in Penobscot Bay to collect a boatload before heading upwind to an eager market.

Lobstering, Maine's most lucrative fishery today in terms of the value it brings fishermen,
began as a pastime for those too old, too young, or too feeble to make the trips to the offshore
waters for groundfish. Some say that catching lobsters for a commercial market began in Cundy's
Harbor in eastern Casco Bay in the 1840s. On Swan's Island in outer Blue Hill Bay, lobsters were
not sold until after 1850. Occasionally a fisherman might collect some small lobsters from along the
shore—the larger ones were thrown back as unfit for family use—but no one thought of lobsters as
a commercial species.

During the old-men-and-young-boys days, lobstering was done from dories or wherries of the
Gloucester and Swampscott types. With the decline of the cod fishery after the Civil War, and the
disappearance of mackerel after 1885, more and more fishermen invested in their own boats and
worked for themselves. Friendship sloops soon became the most popular lobstering boats; they were
weatherly and would stay pointed up into the wind when the lobsterman left the helm to haul and
rebait his traps.

Lobster Canneries and Short Lobsters

The lobster resource around Maine islands began to experience the first signs of overfishing
after Portland mercantilists perfected the technology of canning. William Underwood began canning lobsters in Harpswell as early as 1844. Vinalhaven was one of the first island towns to see a
cannery; one operated in Carvers Harbor between 1851 and 1858, then was reopened in 1870. By

Mudflats on Vinalhaven, including Mill Creek (bottom right), Vinal Cove (top), and inner Seal Bay.
JAMES SEWALL COMPANY

the 1870s, there were a dozen canneries in operation around the midcoast region, and prices paid to fishermen had increased from a nickel to ten cents a pound. The Burnham and Morrill Company (later famous for their baked beans) and others began building canneries up and down the Maine coast, many of them on islands, including North Haven, Deer Isle, Isle au Haut, Head Harbor, and Beals. Enormous quantities of lobsters were caught. "Shorts" brought a penny each.

By the end of the 1870s, prices were high enough for lobsters that, according to Edward Earll, of the U.S. Fisheries Commission, many cod vessel fishermen had "gradually drifted into the lobster fishery, finding it more profitable than any other branch of the fisheries of the region." North Haven's lobster cannery opened in 1857, according to Earll, and of the 180 "boat fishermen" on the islands, "170 are engaged in the lobster fishery from early spring to the first of August." These lobstermen tended sixty pots each. Isle au Haut's lobster cannery was built in 1860 but closed in 1873 "owing to an unpleasantness between the owners and fishermen."

Earll noted that along the western shores of Penobscot Bay in the Town of Saint George, "lobsters are perhaps more abundant in this district than any other locality east of the Penobscot River. The Muscle Ridges have been continuously fished since 1850, and have probably furnished more lobsters than any other grounds of similar size on this portion of the coast." The striking abundance of lobsters in this small area of Penobscot Bay is equally apparent a century and a half after the original observation.

The vigorous trade in canned lobsters spawned debate, especially in the legislature, about protecting future supplies of this increasingly important local resource. In 1872, Maine passed its first lobster law, prohibiting the taking of egg-bearing, or "berried," females. Two years later the legislature weighed in again by establishing a closed season for lobsters from August 1 to October 15 and establishing the first minimum size for all harvested lobsters at ten and a half inches.

Although the fresh lobster market could realistically sell only those lobsters big enough to make a meal (ten and a half inches and up), the canneries bought lobsters of all sizes and sold them primarily to the foreign market. By 1886, there was enough concern over the decreasing size and numbers of lobsters caught in Maine waters to induce the Legislature to pass another "short-lobster law" increasing the minimum size of lobster that could be landed. But most lobstermen took a dim view of the effort to regulate their fishery, and bitter howls of protest went up. The coastal town of Saint George went so far as to pass a local ordinance that any fines levied by the state for taking short lobsters were deductible from a fisherman's next property tax bill.

By 1889, approximately two thousand Maine lobstermen harvested twenty-five million pounds of lobsters, a record that would not be equaled again for almost a hundred years. In 1885, an energetic lobsterman would fish between a hundred and a hundred and fifty traps. The early traps were made of spruce boughs and lath; after the destructive marine teredo worm invaded Maine waters, traps were constructed of oak. In 1885, lobstermen already were complaining about the bitter competition in the fishery—how a man used to be able to make four to five dollars a day hauling lobster traps but was reduced to a dollar a day as more men went lobstering.

By 1900, a Vinalhaven lobster pound, located in a little embayment on the island's western shore, was handling two hundred thousand pounds of lobsters annually, and steam smacks were hauling the catch to Boston fish markets. With the introduction of the first make-and-break gas engines around 1903, lobstering came of age. Although the early engines were considered dangerous—a sternman who wanted to smoke, for instance, was encouraged to get in a dory that was towed behind—auxiliary-powered sloops soon dominated the business. Originally, the two-cycle, four- to ten-horsepower engines were meant to be used when the wind failed, but "it was only a short time before we saw all sail set and the engine running wide open," according to one of Vinalhaven's historians.

After a decade of argument, the evidence of declining catches simply could not be denied. In 1906, after ten years of occasionally violent controversy, the lobstermen recognized that the taking of "shorts" had to stop, and they formed the Lobstermen's National Protective Association.

LOBSTER TERRITORIES: "MUTUAL COERCION, MUTUALLY ENFORCED"

Beyond the hard edge of an island shore is hard bottom. For most of this century an island's actual marine boundaries have been determined by the history and natural history of the American (really the Maine) lobster. Here is the domain of the most venerated and valuable near-shore species to be hauled out of these cold waters. Lobsters occupy cobble and boulder fields, rock shoals, ledge, kelp forests, canyons, and gullies, as well as soft bottom when nothing better is available. They are territorial creatures that occupy most of the hard bottom out to a depth exceeding three hundred feet and thus have the potential to exist in fantastic numbers.

Because lobsters have been economically valuable for more than a century, lobstermen long ago staked out individual territories in lobster habitat to reduce potential conflict over who has the right to harvest where. This territory, especially around islands, increases patrimony and used to pass down from one generation to the next with title to the island proper. Even when islanders "removed," they didn't necessarily give up their proprietary lobster fishing territory around an island. Today the few families with proprietary fishing territory around islands that they originally settled maintain what to outsiders almost seems like feudal control over large areas of public resources.

But make no mistake about it: You and I cannot put lobster traps or a herring weir or other structures around any Maine island without the permission of the "owners" and expect much of what we put there to be where we left it when we get back. These marine "lands," circumscribed by boundaries hard won over time, are essential historical, cultural, and economic facts of island life.

The state laws governing the lobster fishery are easy to understand. But the most important rules of all, upon which the astonishing success of the fishery depends, appear in no Maine statutes. These are the unofficial, unwritten, and universally applied rules of territoriality that give the world of Maine lobstering its unique structure. As anthropologist Jim Acheson has described in his classic *Lobster Gangs of Maine,* any resident of the state can get a lobster license, although not everyone can go lobster fishing. Understanding this paradox is the key to understanding the vast complexity of the informal means that Maine lobstermen have used to limit entry and regulate effort.

A prospective new lobsterman (or woman, and there are a few) has to be "invited" or apprenticed into the fishery by other lobstermen in the harbor, often when another lobsterman is about to retire. Lobstermen agree to make room for the new gear in their territory, even though their landings and income might not be expected to increase as a result. The fundamental principle at work here is to find a balance between the number of lobstermen who can profitably fish the harbor's waters and the number of lobstermen needed to maintain the territory at its edges against the pressures from lobstermen from adjacent harbors who keep "testing the line." The tension among fishermen from adjacent harbors is palpable, particularly when the fortunes of one harbor are in decline relative to the next, which can excite attempts to adjust boundaries.

When someone sets gear in someone else's territory, a polite reminder might be issued—a couple of half hitches on the spindle of the offender's pot buoy. If the gear is not moved, sometimes a second warning is issued—the doors of the trap are found open when it is next hauled. Then the pot buoy goes missing, along with those of its similarly painted friends. A lobsterman's work thus takes not only a keen sense of the ecology of local lobster population dynamics, but also careful timing, opportunistic use of fog, knowing where other boats are at all times, a knife, and, above all, teamwork from other members of the harbor "gang." Acheson and others have referred to the territorial system of Maine lobstering as "mutual coercion, mutually enforced."

"This Is My Ocean"

Sherwood Cook is an island fisherman whose father and grandfather lived on the lonely but beautiful north end of Metinic Island before they bought another smaller island, Little Green, several miles to the east, where the family has maintained the fishing privilege ever since. Like so many lobstermen, Sherwood is a well-spoken, well-read man.

Sherwood Cook, Little Green Island, June 2, 1985:

I don't know what you want to know about Metinic, except that both my father and grandfather went lobster fishing from there for years before they got Little Green. My grandfather was short, with a great big handlebar mustache, and, like most small men, had a chip on his shoulder. When he was fishing one time, two men from Port Clyde came over and cut some of his traps. So he went out with a shotgun and blew a hole through the side of their boat. The two men had been drinking when they left Port Clyde and had bragged that they were going over to cut old man Cook's traps off. We proved that in court, and of course my grandfather got away with it.

Metinic is owned by two families, and they have fishermen who fish on the share basis there. Large Green Island's done the same way, and there's three of us fishing like that on Little Green. On a share basis I furnish all the traps, as much as they want, and I have the bait in tanks in my fish house. And of course [I have] the island. It's good for them and good for me. And I don't mean just financially either. It's been fun working with these people. But there's hardly any justification for somebody saying, "This is my ocean." However, it's been done this way for a hundred and fifty years, and it's a system that works.

I don't come inshore and bother any of the fishermen, and they don't come out and bother me. Oh, a few times when somebody wants to come in, I take two half hitches over the spindle and say, "Come on, fellers, you're over the line. Move!" But if I didn't do this, this territory would be fished as open territory, and I don't think it would be good, because fishermen would move in with hundreds of traps. At least we've maintained a lobster farm there. We haven't exploited it; we haven't overfished it.

LOBSTER CAPITAL OF THE WORLD

Lobstering is not only Maine's most valuable fishery, it defines the coastal and island culture in a way that none of the other many honorable ways of making a living on our ragged littoral edge can quite claim. The ethos of lobstering is carved in scores and scores of lobstering communities along the Maine coast—144 to be exact—where independence, individualism, intense competition, attention to detail, and invisible cooperation are daily facts of life. These are values that work more often than not and, wonder of wonders, are consistently well rewarded.

Although lobsters are trapped from around the edges of every Maine island from the Isles of Shoals to Moose Island off Eastport, the center of their distribution has always been the islands of Penobscot Bay. Today almost 40 percent of the lobsters landed in Maine are caught in the bay, mostly from around the spectacularly productive islands. This region has truly become what local boosters have been claiming for decades—"the lobster capital of the world." Within the bay, the islands of the Muscle Ridge, the island waters surrounding Vinalhaven, and the island-studded waters off Stonington are, acre for subtidal acre, the most valuable lobster grounds in the world.

What began as a way to employ old fishermen and young boys became, by the 1970s, a lucrative way to earn a living, replete with tax-deductible radars, four-wheel-drive pickup trucks, and Caribbean island vacations.

The Maine islands are especially good places to listen to older fishermen's stories of the cycles of abundance and scarcity to which they, like gulls, have adapted over centuries of storied time. The history of the inshore fishing boats of the Maine coast as told by many island fishermen provides a powerful "sociobiological" description of the seemingly inexhaustible supply of different species that creates an adaptability of Maine coast fishermen to the natural cycles of species on which they depend.

"There's an Old Sea Going"

Around Carver's Harbor on Vinalhaven are families of men who have lobstered off the island's edge for generations and who have either profited from its riches or been broken trying. John Beckman, one of Vinalhaven's high-line lobstermen, has not just survived, he has thrived.

Beckman was maybe sixty-five years old when I first met him, but he looked a decade younger. He's not tall but he has huge, broad shoulders, and his hands have a way of making even large lobsters look frail. Yet the first things anyone notices about John are his eyes, blue as the winter ocean, and deeply creased around their edges, it seems, from laughter and humor, from a life well lived on the water. Of all the fishermen whose stories I've listened to, John Beckman's cast a deeper spell; the

Lobstering in Matinicus Roads with the new generation of make-and-break engine. FRANK CLAES COLLECTION

words just tumble out of his mouth in pure cadences that sound almost like the sounds of the sea itself.

Although the fall lobster run was on, Beckman was staying put that day, because he knew there was a big sea outside, however calm it might seem in the harbor. "There's an old sea going," he said. "It ain't the wind, it's an old sea from somewhere, and with this wind you'd have all the pounding you'd ever want." It was a good day to stay in and talk about the Seal Island grounds.

John Beckman, October 14, 1989:

One thing about Seal Island lobsters, because it's an outside place, you wouldn't get them soft goddamn shedders that ain't worth nothing, like you get up in the mud—like you get on the back side of Vinalhaven and up the bay. Lobsters don't need a very good shell where the water's warm, the water's calm, and ain't that many predators after them. But Seal Island is altogether different kind of country. Christ, if a lobster's going to crawl out of his hole, he'd better be in good shape. A storm can come on in no time. Down there, you catch hard lobsters all summer.

I always had gear down there. Even when I was a young man, I'd say, "Well, I'm going to take a vacation next couple of days. I'll haul my gear up inside around Vinalhaven." I'd get rested up in here. I'd haul all day long, but it was like a rest compared with hauling down there. And it still is. It's always rough down there. Your pots is always hung down, and the tide runs harder, and you gotta fight them snarls when your gear gets all balled up.

To fish at Seal back then, you had to be a young, strong man and you had to have a pretty good boat. PANDION, that was my boat then—it's the Latin name for fish hawk. She was a big boat then—thirty-four feet. (Christ, we never would have dreamed there'd be thirty-eight- or forty-foot lobster boats.) See, there's deep water all around Seal. It's fifty-five, sixty-five, seventy fathoms up to northwest in them tows. I've seen wicked lobstering in there. You wouldn't need to haul more than a hundred pots and you'd have a boatload—eight hundred, nine hundred, eleven hundred pounds. Jeez, there was some monster hauls!

And you'd catch lobsters there late into the winter, where the cold'll get them up here [around Vinalhaven]. Being down there, they get that deep ocean water circulation, even around shore. You could fish there until January, then you'd lengthen out again and go off outside, offshore. But you knew you wouldn't get many hauls from then until spring. A man like me, and Bert Dyer—Christ, we was young and had young families—we had to keep going all winter. Which we did. But nights coming home from there, there'd be some hard pounds of it.

You know, all the men in my time that I've known that was lost was lost in nor'westers. Fall nor'westers, freakish nor'westers—they was the ones that seemed to get men. You wouldn't think it would be. But the seas are just so steep and deep, they wash you all the time.

I went pretty hard all through my young years, all winter on long warps, and I loved it. I loved to get out on nice pretty blue days in the winter, like you get, snow on the ground. Christ, as long as it don't shriek too hard, why, it seems awful good to get out on the water on a cold day. It ain't cold on the salt water.

I've always loved Seal Island. It's a different place; a world unto itself. I've seen fabulous lobstering there. The lobsters just seem to crawl toward Seal in the spring. You can see it happen. You set your traps out there in April and you won't catch hardly anything but them old groundkeepers, we call them—lobsters that have been right there all winter. But then you'll start getting these pretty lobsters coming in over the bottom off the edges in thirty-five, forty, forty-five fathoms. And then, Christ, after a couple of weeks, you'll get 'em in twenty-five fathoms, and the next thing they're gone from there and they're up in the rocks. By June, they're pretty much gone off the edges. They go fast, especially going off in the fall.

You see, a lobster's pretty sensitive in his world. I'll go out there sometimes in a northwest wind and take lobsters out of the trap in the morning and they'll be, oh Christ, all numb; they won't reach up and grab you. That afternoon, after that wind would go sou'west, and you go to take them out of a trap, by Jesus, they'd all be going at you, right feisty. And the wind ain't got to be so it's blowin' on them, either. It's just the weather pattern coming around sou'west. They'll respond just to that wind shift. And if it's going to go 'round sou'west, even before there's any wind blowin' at all, they'll start. People say, "I don't believe that," but it's true. You ask other lobster catchers. It's just that sou'west wind. So think how sensitive they are!

You know, your environment makes you what you are. I believe in that. I don't hold with luck; I think you steer your own ship throughout life.

LOBSTER WARS

"Lobster wars" occur when one harbor's fishermen challenge another group's control over its waters, usually at the traditional but invisible lines that separate communities on the water. Such confrontations can be triggered when a group of young and vigorous fishermen senses an advantage —an edge to be gained—over a declining or aging population in another harbor.

Thus boundaries on the water are fluid; they are maintained by informal agreements until one group can no longer adequately occupy and defend its territory. When this situation arises, traps are cut in an escalating confrontation, which has from time to time involved gunplay. But mostly lobster lines are redrawn between harbors by a more discreet form of economic warfare, where one group of fishermen "nickel and dime" another group—if not to death, at least to retreat.

THE DAWN OF LOBSTER CONSERVATION

In 1907, the Maine Legislature passed a law increasing the minimum size of lobsters that could be harvested from the original minimum that had been established in 1874. According to many contemporary reports, the new lobster conservation law was ignored by lobstermen up and down the coast for several years after its passage. State figures show a collapse of lobster landings in 1913; fewer than six million pounds were harvested from the coastal waters, one-quarter of the average harvest of the previous decade. There was a similar disastrous decline in the local herring fishery. Maybe bait was scarce and expensive, which would have had a secondary and reinforcing effect in the decline in lobster landings. But after a few years landings rebounded somewhat; although no lobstermen got rich, they got by.

For most of the 1930s, lobster landings were lower than at any other time before or since, apparently reflecting a population decline from unknown causes. Because the low landings occurred during the Depression, it is worth asking whether this was the result of a lack of a market for a luxury seafood. But such an explanation can't account for the fact that the low landings began as early as 1928 and lasted through the early 1940s. Between July 1, 1934, and June 30, 1935, fewer than five million pounds of lobsters were landed along the entire Maine coast, less than a third of the harvest of earlier decades. This must have represented a severe hardship on local families already stressed from the effects of the collapse of the national economy.

> Bert Dyer, Vinalhaven:
> I remember before I got out of high school in 1940, lobsters was only fourteen cents a pound, right in the dead of winter. And there wasn't any! I used to skip school and go with the older fishermen, with Birger Magnusson and them. We'd fish off Isle au Haut and down to Seal Island in a little twenty-six-foot boat. Colder'n a bastard. Christ, we'd haul all day and he'd give me fifty cents. We'd haul all day for forty pounds and it damn sure wasn't overfished. It's just their natural cycles.

Beginning in the mid-1940s and continuing to the 1980s, reported lobster landings along the Maine coast and islands were remarkably stable, varying less than 10 percent from the half-century average of twenty million pounds per year.

THE MYSTERY OF LARVAL LOBSTERS

According to lobster biologist Bob Steneck of the University of Maine's Ira C. Darling Marine Center, the steady increase in lobster landings since 1990 is not just a result of increased fishing pressure but represents "a real expansion of the population." Furthermore, according to Steneck, "the vital signs look good. There are lots of small lobsters in the water, and the broodstock appears to be healthy."

Steneck's research into the life cycle of the Maine lobster fell into the middle of this pleasant surprise. Since the late 1980s, Steneck had been trying to figure out the central mystery that has confounded lobster biologists for more than a century—how do tiny new lobsters recruit into the population? For a long time we've known that the pound-and-a-quarter lobster that most of us would recognize on our dinner plate is between seven and eight years old, the age at which most females spawn for the first time. We also know that large spawning females can carry a prodigious number of eggs—between fifty and sixty thousand on average—which hatch into tiny larvae that float in the water column before molting into something we would recognize as a miniature lobster and settling on the bottom.

But there the mystery begins. The next phase of development that biologists had observed in natural conditions wasn't until the lobsters reached four to five inches or so and could be found in rock crevices in plentiful numbers. Where did they live between the time they settled on the bottom at a quarter of an inch and the time they reached four inches? Where, in other words, were their nursery areas?

Steneck began looking for tiny lobsters in a variety of habitats: in mud bottom, in sand, on ledgy or hard bottom, in gravel and cobble bottom, and in boulder fields. Laying out sample plots in each habitat and using a suction device to sample what lived there, Steneck could get accurate counts of each species inhabiting these different bottom environments. And he discovered the location of the lobster nursery grounds: cobble fields with rocks two to four inches in size in relatively shallow water—a habitat that far surpasses all others he investigated. Here the young lobsters are able to scramble into crevices that provide immediate shelter from predation at a stage when they're good eating for a wide variety of marine animals.

In a follow-up series of experiments, Steneck showed that the time that elapses after a tiny new lobster reaches the bottom before it is eaten is, on average, fifteen minutes. Lobsters that land on mud bottom (not sand) are capable of excavating a burrow to get out of harm's way. The problem is that it takes these newborns approximately two hours to construct a burrow. Before they are secure, the vast number of them have provided meals for fish or crabs or other voracious marine life.

Steneck and his colleague Lew Incze, at the Bigelow Laboratory of Ocean Studies in Boothbay, also showed that, during a two- to three-week period at the end of August and the beginning of September, lobsters almost literally "rain" out of the water column onto bottom habitats after their floating larval phase. As with so many inexplicable events in nature, the drama is over quickly; if you're not at the right place at the right time and looking hard, you'll never see it before it's over.

One of the most arresting features of Steneck's research is that cobble habitat, according to marine geologists, is relatively rare, making up only between 2 and 10 percent of all subtidal environments off the Maine coast. In addition, this bottom habitat is not uniformly distributed offshore. Because of different glaciation patterns in eastern and western Maine, subtidal cobble habitat is much more prevalent in eastern Maine and decreases as one proceeds "up" the coast to the sandier

Wooden lobsterboats built by J.O. Brown and Son, Inc., North Haven, rafted up during the 100th anniversary celebration at the shop, 1989.
                                                                    PETER RALSTON

portions of southern Maine and Massachusetts. Steneck calls these cobble nursery areas a "reproductive bottleneck."

For years, lobster biologists have been aware that these crustaceans do not molt in water temperatures cooler than fifteen degrees Celsius (fifty-nine degrees Fahrenheit). They simply float around in the water column for a longer period of time and are diminished in numbers by predation. From satellite images of the Gulf of Maine, oceanographers have recently documented what a few intrepid swimmers have long understood. A plume of cold water comes down out of the Bay of Fundy and along the Maine coast, curving offshore near Mount Desert Island and running somewhere in the region between Swan's Island and Frenchboro. Steneck describes it as "a thermal threshold that may act as kind of a gate at the mouth of Penobscot Bay."

Putting these disparate observations together, Steneck theorizes that the dramatic increase in lobster landings is a function of a ten-year warming trend in summer water temperatures in the Gulf of Maine that began in the early 1980s. Because it takes a lobster seven to eight years to reach the size at which it can be legally landed, it wasn't until late in the decade that the higher percentage of molted lobsters began to be reflected in the landing statistics. Steneck also proposes that the limiting factor for lobster populations in eastern Maine is relatively cooler summer water temperature, which inhibits the first molt and reduces the number of new recruits, whereas the limiting factor to the southwest may be the relative scarcity of cobble habitat for the critical nursery phase. But the great stretch of Maine coast, say from Casco Bay to Islesford off Mount Desert, has both favorable water temperatures and ample cobble nursery areas—conditions that maximize recruitment of new lobsters into the population and ultimately into the pot.

Lobster Biology: The Impossible Has Happened

Lobsters, unlike most other creatures of the world, including the marine world, exhibit indeterminate growth, meaning that with each successive molt of their old shells, they become larger and larger, apparently never reaching an age when their growth stops. One of the interesting sidelights to the natural history of the Maine lobster is the question of the largest one ever landed. According to anecdotal records, the largest lobster ever landed weighed fifty-seven pounds, which is roughly one hundred thousand times as large as a first-year lobster.

Even if the growth of individual lobsters is nearly indefinite, you don't have to be a lobster biologist to wonder whether the catch can sustain the vast increase in effort that lobstermen have directed to the pursuit of this venerable crustacean in recent years. The stability of the lobster harvest from the late 1940s to the 1980s was achieved by a steady increase in fishing effort. Lobstermen were buying and rigging more traps, investing in faster and bigger boats, and equipping them with computerized navigational equipment for precisely locating lobster habitat. They were, in short, going longer, farther, harder (and probably smarter) than ever before in the history of the industry. As a result, ever since the end of World War II, there has been an impressive increase in economic prosperity for lobster fishing families on Maine islands and ashore.

Then the impossible happened. Beginning in the late 1980s—in contrast to virtually every other fishing resource in nearshore or distant waters, which have been decreasing—reported lobster landings began to rapidly increase in Maine. The year-by-year increases in lobster landings were not small increases of a few hundred thousand pounds but millions of pounds a year. The landings increased by twenty million pounds, a doubling of the harvest. Prosperity has not only been sustained, it has actually accelerated during the past decade. On islands from Chebeague and Long to the midcoast islands of Vinalhaven and Swan's and all the way down to Beals, the leading economic indicator is the number of new Ford or GMC pickups lined up at the harbor landing. There are so many, you can't find a place to park, especially if you don't own one.

This, of course, cannot last. Since 1960, the number of lobster traps in Maine waters has increased by about 300 percent. Seven thousand Maine lobstermen now fish more than 2.5 million traps. As anyone who has stood on the shore of one of Maine's lobster ports can tell you, the number of brightly painted lobster buoys dotting the surface of small areas of the ocean astounds the eye and mind and leaves you to wonder whether the lobster will survive.

John Beckman, October 14, 1989:

These lobsters are going way up into the bays now. When I was a young feller I don't remember it happening, but I've heard people say that happened before, and I imagine it has. They get lobsters and give 'em hell way up in Castine and Islesford, way up there where lobster catchers mostly starve to death. North Haven, too. Christ, it used to be you could never be a lobster catcher in North Haven. They always had to be part-time, with some kind of old boat or little boat that they fished through the best of it and never got no lobsters. They had to work for summer people. They hated it, but they had to, to live. And now, you see a nice fleet of lobster boats up in North Haven. Because those lobsters took that change and that's where they are.

Official lobster biologists, many of whom have been in a thirty-year running war with lobstermen, point out that something like 90 percent of the female lobsters that mature in any given year are harvested before they develop eggs, leaving precious few females to carry the species into the future. Yes, the response goes, but Maine law prohibits the taking of "berried" lobsters (females with eggs underneath their tail). And every Maine lobsterman who catches a berried female (an "egger") cuts a V-shaped notch in her second tail fin from the right; whenever she is recaught, she goes back to the sea as a known spawner. V-notching is fine, say scientists, but it can't have a measurable impact on egg production in the Gulf of Maine. Says who? Says you, just because you can't measure it. There are those few who dip the berried females in Clorox and try to eliminate all trace of eggs. In response, the "fish cops" have developed a test that reveals minute traces of Clorox. So goes the thrust and parry of these oratorical debates, which have such a finely honed pattern to them that they have been elevated to the level of arch-ritual.

The increase in landings, however, is a testament to the effectiveness, at least in part, of the various conservation measures that Maine lobstermen have imposed on themselves. In addition to V-notching all egged or "berried" females, they have adopted and rigidly observed the so-called "double gauge law," which prohibits the harvest of large brood stock lobsters; they added escape vents to all traps to release juveniles; and they ruthlessly enforce sanctions against those who deal in "shorts." They have recently added biodegradable panels to prevent "ghost" fishing (in which lobsters in lost traps become bait for succeeding lobsters). It seems that the more conservation measures they have imposed, the higher the landings.

Trap Limits

Twenty years ago, most Maine lobstermen fished two hundred and fifty traps; today eight hundred is closer to the norm. Before recent trap limits went into effect, a small number of Casco Bay lobstermen were fishing gangs of trawls of between two thousand and three thousand traps; the resulting territorial snarls have led to that area being known as "the Bay of Pigs."

Twenty years ago the Maine Department of Marine Resources estimated that there were half a million traps in Maine waters; today that number is estimated to be five times greater, although there has been no official tally because for most of the twentieth century there was no official trap limit in Maine waters except for those surrounding Swan's Island.

Lobster chatter along the working waterfront.   PETER RALSTON

Swan's Island Trap Limit, September 14, 1984

In this unusually progressive fishing community six miles south of Mount Desert Island, more than three-quarters of the island's forty lobstermen have just successfully petitioned the legislature to create a unique trap limit in a two-mile-wide zone around the island's shores. Swan's Island lobstermen fish four hundred and seventy-five traps. According to Sonny Sprague, first selectman and lobster catcher, who led the legislative campaign, "the trap limit will work for the fishermen of Swan's Island." The logic is simple: The same number of lobsters will be caught but in fewer traps, and this reduces a lobsterman's basic costs. The three hundred traps not needing to be replaced at $40 per trap is a savings of $12,000 every two to three years.

Several other Maine island lobstering communities, such as Monhegan and Criehaven, have observed unofficial trap limits, mostly because mutually enforceable limits make good economic sense. But because efforts to promote trap limits and regulate entry into lobstering conflict with deeply held beliefs that no single set of licensing requirements and trap limits can work for the whole of the coast of Maine, various trap limit proposals were regularly advanced and debated for two decades. However, in the face of increased fishing pressure on lobsters from many different directions, even this hallowed tradition has changed: In 1996, Maine adopted a statewide limit of twelve hundred traps and instituted localized management zones; in 1998, the state placed a moratorium on the issuance of new lobster fishing licenses and mandated an apprenticeship program for future entrants.

CONSERVATION FROM THE BOTTOM UP

The economic news is not all bad on the eastern rim of the Gulf of Maine. In fact, some of the news is extraordinarily good. The value of the 1994 Maine lobster catch exceeded $100 million for the first time in history, surpassing the 1993 total by a cool $28 million. Although lobster landings declined slightly in 1995 and 1996, the value of the harvest continued to hover around the $100 million mark and it went up again in 1997. That's a lot of pickups.

The value of the catch reached historic levels due to a happy confluence of several events. Actual landings of forty million pounds in 1994 were the highest in more than a century of record keeping, and the demand was strong enough to keep prices to lobstermen firm, averaging for the year at around $2.60 a pound. No one believes that the news can stay this good for long, but along with large landings from the urchin fishery (which have since declined), a good supply of shrimp, and high scallop prices, the coastal Maine fisheries economy got a nice boost through the first half of the 1990s. According to the United Nations Food and Agriculture Organization, 70 percent of the world's fishery resources are overfished, in decline, or under severe restriction to allow rebuilding. Yet one of the most intensively fished marine species in the Gulf of Maine has appeared in record abundance. How could this be?

If you answer this riddle, you can either proceed directly to heaven or get elected to any town office anywhere along Maine's coastline. If you start collecting opinions about these observed facts, you could spend half a lifetime trying to sort them out and never get anywhere at all. Maine lobstermen have undoubtedly benefited from the increasing trend of summer water temperatures, which for the past several years have crept farther east and increased the marine ecosystem's basic growth rate. Some lobstermen believe that the absence of predatory cod, which prey on juvenile lobsters, can explain the trend. But then seals, another noted omnivorous predator of benthic habitats, have also increased rapidly during this past decade, so the suggestion that basic alterations of predator-prey relationships have accounted for lobster abundance seems inconclusive, at best.

Beyond finding any immediate explanations, becoming familiar with the way the lobster industry is structured and managed is fundamental to any understanding of why the Maine lobster fishery is thriving. To begin with, basic common-sense principles of biology have been slowly and carefully structured into a few simple and universally accepted conservation regulations that Maine lobstermen rigorously enforce. The conservation ethic of the Maine lobsterman is, of course, easily obscured amid the sight of pot buoys so dense over "shedder bottom" that you could practically walk across a bay on them. But Maine's lobster conservation rules do protect small lobsters before they spawn for the first time and large breeders that carry immense numbers of eggs. It is a sore point among most Maine lobstermen that no such law exists in Massachusetts, where a lot of females that have been protected in Maine end up being caught and landed. Maine also requires that an escape vent be built into each lobster trap, to ensure that juvenile lobsters can easily exit without becoming lunch for larger lobsters in the same trap.

The effect of these conservation measures, originated in intense negotiations among lobstermen, is to increase the proportion of females to males in the population as well as their average fecundity, thus enhancing the reproductive potential of the entire population.

Broodstock Lobsters

The abundance of lobsters has of course not gone unnoticed among other fishermen. A large number of them are shifting out of groundfishing to go lobstering. Who wouldn't, if you had the boat? In addition, a significant number of large draggers, unable to fish on Georges Bank now that major areas have been closed, are starting to target lobsters instead of cod and haddock. Dragging for lobsters in Maine waters (within three miles of the coast) or landing lobsters from draggers in

Maine ports is prohibited, but in federal waters and in the waters of New Hampshire, no such pro-hibitions exist. Massachusetts, however, is moving toward tighter restrictions.

Although lobster "by-catch" (that is, a relatively small quantity of lobsters unintentionally caught by fishermen dragging for cod and haddock) has been a minor part of lobster landings for decades, it is clear that draggers from Gloucester and New Bedford have recently discovered where to find large concentrations of lobsters migrating in spring and fall. The volume of lobsters landed in Gloucester and New Bedford exceeded a million pounds for the first time ever in 1995. One boat landed nine thousand pounds in one trip. But even more disturbing was the ratio of females to males that National Marine Fisheries Service personnel have documented from dragger landings. One large haul topped out at ninety to one—that is, ninety females for every male caught. Clearly, large aggregations of sexually mature females have been located by draggers for the first time ever, and successfully fished. "That's our broodstock," said David Cousens, president of the Maine Lobstermen's Association (MLA).

The MLA appealed to the New England Fisheries Management Council to take emergency action to limit the number of lobsters that draggers may catch, citing the ecological effects of drag-ging on bottom habitat and the effect on lobster broodstock. According to Patten White, executive director of the MLA, large numbers of female lobsters that serve as the broodstock for the Gulf of Maine move across sandy and gravel "plains" during late fall on their way to deeper water for the winter. These are the females that shed their eggs in spring and sow a new crop of larval lobsters that are carried in current gyres around the shores of the Gulf of Maine during the summer. Cousens adds, "Every once in a while you get into a bunch of females, and you might see a few catches with ratios of sixteen-to-one, females to males. I think the highest ratio they've ever recorded in twenty-five years of sea sampling is twenty to one. But ninety to one, no way; something's wrong here. They're indiscriminately scooping up our broodstock."

The governor of Maine intervened in the delicate matter of making a suggestion to the then-governor of Massachusetts. Angus King picked up the phone and called William Weld for a heart-to-heart conversation about lobster conservation. The wheels of government began turning. After half a century of complaint from Maine, Massachusetts in 1996 finally banned the landing of lob-sters from draggers, except as incidental by-catch.

> ### Beals Island Lobster Chatter, August 27, 1996
>
> *At the end of the day, we steer toward Beals Island, where we are to meet with one of the most respected island fishermen, Herman "Junior" Bachman. The founding president of the Downeast Lobsterman's Association, Junior Bachman has been participating in Maine's effort to design local lob-ster management zones.*
>
> *The new law that creates the mandate for local area management is an attempt to codify and provide structure for successful, time-honored practices among Maine lobstermen: common-sense conservation principles applied in community territories, along with unique forms of limited entry that are locally refined and self-enforced.*
>
> *The applications of these principles of lobster management may not be the sole reason for the lobster industry's astonishing success, but neither can they be dismissed. During the past six to seven years, lobster harvests have approximately doubled in volume and more than doubled in value.*
>
> *The public landing in Jonesport where we are tied up waiting for Junior to return from a meeting in Augusta is filled with newish pickup trucks. On*

this mellow August evening, between twenty and thirty trucks come and go, driven by wives, uncles, kids, girlfriends, and grandparents. Here also is a constant reminder of the diversity of marine products that are crossing the wharf at the end of the day. Musselers, quahoggers, urchiners, clammers, whelkers, and lobstermen without access to one of the dozen or so private wharves lining the reach are all hauling the day's bounty ashore.

When Junior arrives, we talk lobster politics over a cup of coffee in the pilothouse. Junior is in a lather over how the federal government is managing lobsters beyond Maine's three-mile territorial limit, where state authority ends and regulations promulgated by the National Marine Fisheries Service begin. Lobster scientists say that Maine's lobster resource is exploited at too close to its limit of sustainability and that so-called fishing mortality needs to be curtailed. Maybe yes and maybe no, depending on whom you talk to, but most lobstermen we've asked say they are seeing an awful lot more small lobsters in their traps than ever before. What really has lobstermen stirred up, says Junior, is the way federal biologists and managers refuse to recognize the value of Maine's most important conservation rules—those that have been developed by lobstermen in the first place.

The five-inch limit on taking broodstock lobsters, the marking and release of egg-bearing females, and an escape vent in all traps to reduce ghost fishing are measures that were developed and adopted by Maine lobstermen long before they were codified into law. If the federal managers are so fired up on how to make Maine lobstermen control their fishing inshore, why don't they impose these minimum regulations in the Gulf of Maine beyond the three-mile limit, asks Junior. This is especially galling to fishermen down east, because so much of their territory is in federal waters, where lobstermen from out of state now regularly fish, taking lobsters back to their home ports that cannot be legally landed in Maine. Therein lies the nub of the issue as to where the line between state and federal fisheries management policies should lie.

The question of whether state lobster conservation rules or federal law should prevail in the waters of the Gulf of Maine is not an idle academic debate. According to the federal government, the American lobster is overfished throughout its range, which extends from Eastport, Maine, to Cape Hatteras, North Carolina. According to the National Marine Fisheries Service, sweeping new cutbacks in fishing effort are urgently required to save the fishery from collapse. Federal scientists base their "overfished" determination on their annual trawl surveys, supplemented by information gleaned from landings data. But because landings data is collected at dockside, after V-notch females and other large broodstock lobsters have been returned to the sea, there is a near universal belief among Maine lobstermen that they have gotten no credit for decades of hard-earned conservation investments in their fishery. And to add to the injury, federal trawl surveys are not conducted anywhere near the Maine coast, where 80 percent of the lobster stock is thought to reside, creating a huge blind spot in our knowledge of the status of lobsters in the Gulf of Maine. Partly to redress this problem, a group of lobster scientists, under the leadership of Bob Steneck, chartered a large oceanographic vessel from Florida, one of the few equipped with a submarine, to conduct eight days of surveys to evaluate the abundance of broodstock lobsters in the deep waters of the Gulf of Maine where no one has ever looked.

ABOARD THE *JOHNSON SEA LINK,* OCTOBER 29, 1997

"We have a seal," radios Hugo to his counterpart in the front chamber of the four-man submersible vessel, as we begin our descent to a place three hundred and twenty feet beneath the surface of Blue Hill Bay. Hugo is a technician from the Harbor Branch Oceanographic Institution. We are in a submarine equipped with video cameras and a laser measuring system to count and measure any lobsters we encounter in these deep waters.

The ballast tanks blow a silver stream of bubbles past my porthole as we begin our vertical descent. Soon the silvery light gives way to pale green and then quickly to an emerald green world of refracted light in the dense, plankton rich water of Blue Hill Bay. At eighty feet, barely a quarter of the way to our destination, the rich green algal glow gives way to black-green and then to inky darkness. This particular dive occurs at one of eight locations between South Bristol and German Bank, Nova Scotia, that the submersible will survey along the edge of the Gulf of Maine. Bob Steneck wants to see whether these deep locations are refugia for large reproductive lobsters, which may explain the amazing resiliency of Maine's lobster population despite the intense fishing pressure to which it is annually subjected.

The JOHNSON SEA LINK, one of the earliest submersibles designed to travel through the far reaches of oceanic depths, resembles nothing so much as a lunar landing module, with thrusters mounted fore and aft and arrayed to provide mobility in the strange world of the bathysphere, the lightless depths scientists have only begun to explore in the last decade or two. Up on the deck of the 181-foot mother vessel, EDWIN LINK, are a handful of lobstermen and their families who have

Urchin sorting at a processing house.   D. GAVRIL, *SALT MAGAZINE*

been invited by Steneck to take the plunge to the bottom in another unprecedented part of this research program—part expedition, part classroom, and almost pure thrill. The lobstermen who do not elect to make the dive themselves are nonetheless eager to view the videos SEA LINK sends to the surface showing the realm of the crustacean they have spent their lifetimes chasing.

The SEA LINK begins to make its way along a transect, its lights carving out a window of visibility only six to eight feet ahead of our track as we hover a few feet off the soft bottom only three hundred and nineteen feet below the surface, but many worlds removed from light and air. We soon see a whole field of sea anemones, waving to and fro like a meadow of poppies in the underwater currents. Here and there on this underwater plain are boulders encrusted with filamentous algae and festooned with thick-stemmed anemones. Little translucent shrimp skitter off the bottom as we approach.

At the second boulder we disturb our first lobster, which has probably not seen light since it was a tiny floating larvae many years earlier. It gathers itself up on its eight pairs of spindly legs and begins to move away. In profile, the segmented joints of its body plan, like some creature put together with Legos, show up eerily in the light. Little pinpoints of red laser light get a measurement of the carapace on the front of this large lobster, which is over the limit for landing and thus part of the broodstock. We have our first data of the dive, sending the news aloft to the pilothouse of the ship hovering somewhere above us.

Every once in a while during the two-hour dive, we hit bottom with a thump and must rise up a few feet and maneuver around the uneven surface. It is comforting to see so many translucent white anemones, soft-bodied animals that are the first to be destroyed when the bottom is dragged. Danny Lunt, one of the participating fishermen from Frenchboro, says its been about a decade since scallop draggers cleaned out the beds here in this deep pocket of the bay. But for the most part we are looking at a seemingly benign, stable environment: no climate, no waves, just the endless conveyor belt of the currents sweeping food endlessly by these creatures, which have adapted to an almost timeless life in the benthos.

I think to myself: all my life I have dreamed of this, the moment when the bubble of air overhead shrinks away and disappears while I descend into an entirely new world. I feel I could stay here a long time. In fact, Hugo had carefully informed us at the beginning of the dive that we have enough food for five days and enough air to last two weeks if ever we should become stranded. But all too soon our time is up and we begin our ascent to the surface, carrying a trove of data that Bob Steneck will share not just with his scientific colleagues, but with others whose fortunes rise and fall with the health of the populations of lobsters hidden in these briny depths.

THE URCHIN GOLD RUSH

Many fishermen will remember 1989 as the year that the Japanese taste for sea urchin roe first began to influence their annual fishing strategies. Simply by hiring a diver and making a small investment in totes for boxing the spiny creatures at sea, virtually any fishing boat owner could get into the "virgin" sea urchin fishery. The development of an export market for this abundant but under-utilized species is the most compelling example of the globalization of valuable marine resources in the 1990s.

For decades, sea urchins have been called "whore's eggs" by lobstermen, who despise the creatures that clog their traps and drive their spines through gloves. But the urchin's reproductive organs, the roe, is prized in Japanese sushi bars, where it is called "uni." It is associated with important religious and cultural celebrations throughout Japan, which is the world's leading importer of urchins.

By 1991, urchins had become a million-dollar fishery almost overnight. Fabulous amounts of money were made in a short period of time. Since then, urchin harvests from Maine have quintupled, and the average price received by fishermen has more than doubled: in 1995, urchins represented a $40-million fishery, second in value only to lobsters. But it did not last long. Predictably, a gold rush mentality gripped fishermen, who rushed into the fishery before someone else could clean up first. The tragedy of the commons played itself out again as hapless marine resource managers and the legislature dithered over regulatory strategies.

The Department of Marine Resources ran hard trying to catch up with this explosive industry. They divided the coast into two urchin management zones, slapped a moratorium on new urchin licenses, and shortened the harvesting season on both ends, in fall and spring. Nevertheless, in a clear sign of overfishing, urchin landings declined (although the value went up) for the first time statewide in 1995, especially around the islands of Casco Bay, where the pressure was the most intense and where there were reports of large areas that had been stripped of urchins. The 1995 harvest from around Penobscot Bay's islands also declined, but less than that along other parts of the coast. In 1996, urchin landings dropped again, although value per pound increased again. But the following year both prices and landings dropped steeply.

Urchins feed on kelps and appear to favor high-energy subtidal environments, which suggests that the windward shores of islands and the exposed island coastline provide ideal habitat. Not a great deal more is known about the basic biology of the urchin, although surcharges on urchin harvesting and buying and processing licenses have recently yielded more than $625,000, which will be used to study the urchin's reproductive biology, larval settlement, and growth rates, now that the species has been severely overfished.

Harvesting blue mussels, Deer Isle Thorofare.   V. DeLucia, *New York Times*

ECOSYSTEM MANAGEMENT FOR LOBSTERMEN, URCHIN DIVERS, AND KELP HARVESTERS

You cannot spend time on the water or in harbors, or around fishermen or their wives, without hearing stories about the linkages between the species that are commercially exploited. Lobsters have been harvested intensively for a century; they went through a long decline in the 1920s and 1930s but have rebounded to once unimaginable levels. Urchins used to be so abundant that large underwater "barrens" existed where urchins scraped the kelp beds clean. Now urchins have been pounded hard, and kelp forests have quickly reestablished in many formerly barren sites. As kelps grow, lobster shedding habitat improves, providing an additional boost for the lobster fishery. Many lobstermen believe that there are more lobsters around the islands and up the bays because the cod are gone. And there may be some kind of relationship. But large spawning cod have been gone from most of these waters for between thirty and fifty years.

Communities of fishermen have long memories for the cycles of the sea. They believe that populations of commercially important fish and shellfish have an ebb and flow to them, that fishing of some sort will always be an option, and that, in the end, opportunistic flexibility will prevail. In spite of the conflicts between mobile-gear and fixed-gear fishermen, these are the values shared by most of the fishing community members in New England. But of all the resources of the Gulf of Maine, few are as watchfully contested as the Maine lobster, and few fisheries can boast such a history of successful management, from the harbor up.

That we are essentially clueless as to how the abundance of lobsters might be integrally related to the cycles of species such as urchins, kelps, or cod is only the latest example of the dire need to rethink, to reinvent, almost the entirety of our fisheries management system. It must be brought closer to home and harbor. New lines must be drawn in the Gulf of Maine, separate from the offshore banks. Traditional fishing territories tied to specific communities must be given the recognition and protection of law. Fishermen must be brought into a real-time, scientific data-gathering process. Hardest of all, because it requires an enormous leap of faith for all involved, we must somehow create an ecosystem-based framework of management that has not been implemented anywhere else on the watery globe before.

The alternative to these strategies is abundantly clear: failure and more failure. The future is not just upon us; it is flowing through our lives as we stand hopefully by, wondering whether there isn't a better way to understand the cycles of life around the productive edges of the archipelago.

Junior Bachman, Beals Island, November 18, 1996:

I got into fishing by being born in a small fishing village and being with my dad when I was a small boy. Of course, I was like everybody; every kid in a small fishing village always has a few traps and a small punt when he's going to school. That's a way of life. Life in fishing villages wasn't all that bad. Nobody had money, but eating was never a problem because you went fishing, hand lining, lobster fishing. Nobody went hungry. Kids went barefooted anyway, so that was no problem. We had as much as anybody else, and in fact, being on the shore, the fishermen fared much better than the people inland that lost their jobs and lost everything they had.

These small fishing villages work differently than [communities] in other places. Village is like a family. Fishing villages don't work like Portland. We care for each other. It's the difference between the down east heritage and other heritages. The dividing line of territories was just a matter of how far you wanted to row. Beals fished in one place basically. We looked out for each other. Rockland and the islands east, the industry is fishing. If we lose the lobster fishing, the way groundfishing has gone, all these villages will become ghost towns.

8

Four Centuries of Island Fisheries: Herring, Mackerel, Tuna, and Cod

I believe that in relation to our present modes of fishing, a number of the most important fisheries, such as the cod fishery, the herring fishery, and the mackerel fishery, are inexhaustible. And I base this conviction on two grounds, first, that the multitude of these fishes is so inconceivably great that the number we catch is relatively insignificant; and secondly, that the magnitude of the destructive agencies at work upon them is so prodigious that the destruction effected by fishermen cannot sensibly increase the death-rate.

—Thomas H. Huxley, 1883

FISH WEBS: YOU ARE WHAT YOU EAT

The most basic law of fish ecology is almost a cartoon of itself. Little fish are eaten by bigger fish that grow to become food for yet bigger fish—simple in concept, amazingly complex when applied to a fishpond as large, diverse, and dynamic as the Gulf of Maine. But stay with this image for a moment. Although food chains in nature are not based on simple, deterministic relationships among species, the mouths of fish tell us almost everything about how they live and die.

School fish such as mackerel, pogy, and herring, which are the chief food for larger fish, feed on floating masses of small animal and vegetable life, which form the basis of the food webs in the Gulf of Maine. Yet for the most part, these smaller fish each target different kinds of food. The oily menhaden, or pogy, which appear seasonally in massive schools, have a diet so unlike that of mackerel and herring that they do not compete with them. Pogies strain tiny diatoms (a type of phytoplankton with a silica cell wall) through a series of intricately layered gill rakers, which act as a fine-mesh net as the fish swim through the water. The microscopic sea vegetables are then processed by the fish into oil and protein.

Both mackerel and herring feed chiefly on copepods (from the Latin, meaning "oar-legged," referring to the way these tiny oceangoing crustaceans "row" through the water). Fishermen often find mackerel guts packed with "red feed," or "cayenne," a species of plankton copepod known by its scientific name, *Calanus*. Herring more commonly eat a smaller copepod known as *Pseudocalanus*, but neither mackerel nor herring confine their diets exclusively to these two plankton species. At the right time, and in the appropriate locale, they will consume prodigious quantities of most of the other species of floating crustaceans and their larvae. Because most mackerel are caught in the south-

Opposite: Dragging for shrimp with small mesh resulted in a "by-catch" of juvenile groundfish. Shrimp nets now use a special device, the Nordmore grate, which greatly reduces bycatch. PETER RALSTON

west corner of the Gulf of Maine, and herring predominate in the northeast corner at the mouth of the Bay of Fundy and in Passamaquoddy Bay, they seem, for the most part, to have divided up the spoils geographically, except where their schooling overlaps off the midcoast in the Gulf of Maine.

Herring, the most abundant fish in the Gulf of Maine, swim through the pastures of the sea until they are discovered by, say, a silver hake or a score of other common predators that make a meal of them. Small hake, in their turn, become a meal for a cod or a haddock, which becomes a meal for the giant Atlantic bluefin tuna, at the top of the food chain, which fishermen harpoon and air freight fresh to Tokyo.

But there's a catch: The reality of ecological energy dynamics tells us that, on average, there is only about a 10 percent transfer of energy from one food level to the next. Thus for a giant bluefin tuna to put on a pound in weight means it will need to eat ten pounds of bluefish, which have eaten a hundred pounds of pollock, which have eaten a thousand pounds of hake, which have eaten ten thousand pounds of herring, which have eaten a hundred thousand pounds of crustaceans, which have eaten a million pounds of smaller animals you cannot even see. We who eat at the top of the food chain usually fail to appreciate the stupendous quantities of other feed on which we also depend.

It seems likely that the abundance of both the mackerel and the herring, and for that matter almost all other commercially important species of finfish, depends less on the food that is available to them when they are adults than when they are small fry. It's all very mysterious, because microscopic fish larvae are the most difficult to find in the expanse of the sea, and the outlines of their movements from the time the eggs hatch to when they reach commercial size are only dimly perceived. But a few facts are suggestive. The annual production of mackerel eggs is usually sufficient to create a new age class, but for this species in certain years there seems to be an inverse relationship between the number of adult mackerel present and their breeding success—that is, the more adults, the fewer the fry; counterintuitively, the fewer adults, the more fry that survive.

SCHOOLING BEHAVIOR

What makes fish school? The question has mystified naturalists and scientists for centuries. About three-quarters of the ocean's twenty thousand species of fish form schools as juveniles, but only about one-fifth spend their adult lives in schools. Schools of cod and herring are some of the best-known examples of this behavior, and exploitation of this knowledge has made commercial fisheries possible in northern seas since mankind first learned to weave fishnets. From close observations, fisheries biologists know that when fish move forward in a school, they maintain a geometry all their own. They orient in parallel fashion and swim at the same speed while maintaining a fixed distance between themselves, as if polarized by a magnetic field. Then suddenly the school changes direction, seemingly all at once, although in large schools this appears almost as an electric shock wave that takes only fractions of seconds to travel through the school.

Schooling behavior has evolved for complex reasons. Predators are no doubt confused by the innumerable prey targets in schools and selectively feed on individuals at the edges of a school, particularly when the school is disturbed and temporarily disaggregates. Predators that aggregate in schools, such as cod and tuna, can spread over greater distances and more easily locate prey. Also, school fish conserve energy, much like geese in flight, by riding the vortices of individuals ahead of them. Sightless fish cannot school, so one of the mystifying questions is how schooling fish have light enough to orient themselves to one another in the black of night. Apparently light from a crescent moon, or even the stars on a moonless night, is enough, but the phosphorescence of creatures that cling to fish scales may play a role as well.

Early herring weir, constructed with woven birch brush, near Eastport. COURTESY MAINE STATE MUSEUM

COD, HERRING, AND HISTORY

Henry Bryant Bigelow, the oceanographer who, more than any other single person, painstakingly contributed to our knowledge of the ecology of fish in the Gulf of Maine, supposes that the number of both mackerel and herring in any given year may be most directly related to the kind of winter the fish experienced. If they emerge from their deep winter hideouts in good physiological shape (which seems to be related to the number of adults that have been competing for the copepod food supply), their eggs will be fatter and a higher proportion of them will hatch to produce stronger fry that are better able to elude the snapping jaws of other hungry marine creatures with a temporary size advantage. Of course, even in a good hatch, the young fish can be decimated by killing temperatures or salinities, or they can perish from a simple lack of food. In the telling, it's sometimes hard to believe that we ever get a chance to eat a fish stick or a sardine sandwich.

Because fish such as herring, mackerel, and cod were the raison d'être and chief economic preoccupation of the original island settlers, a good deal of anecdotal information can be drawn upon in island communities where the cycles of abundance and decline are felt in the effects of poverty and prosperity during acutely memorable periods. Understanding the natural history of the fish common to the islands helps unravel the human history and drama of these rocks surrounded by the sea.

And because herring are the smallest fish to support a major fishery over a century's worth of time, we'll start there and work our way up the food chain.

HERRING: YOU GOT THE SILVER, YOU GOT THE GOLD

Fishermen will tell you that once you've fished for herring, it spoils you for any other kind of fishing. Catching herring has always been a "clean" activity compared to the fishery for cod, haddock, flounder, and other groundfish, which during this century has always depended on dragging an otter trawl rigged with heavy bottom chain and massive roller gear that roils a cloud of sediment and sweeps up everything in its path,

During the summer months of most years, Seal Island is one center of prodigious activity for herring and herring catchers. Like the seabirds that return to Seal year after year to breed, immense stocks of herring also appear on selected bottoms off Seal Island from late June to October to feed and spawn. During daylight hours, herring congregate on the bottom; then, in the gathering darkness of summer nights, just past the equinox, they begin to rise toward the surface, following tiny shrimp and shrimplike copepods that also ascend in the water column under the cover of darkness to feed. One legendary spawning run of herring, in 1946, was measured at more than seventeen miles long.

For almost half a century, one might see as many as two dozen seiners and carriers slowly circle-dancing around Seal's shores long after the far western light had faded, stalking the great schools of herring as they moved to the surface and toward the shoals to feed. By daybreak, this whole city of bobbing lights, like the herring, had disappeared from sight, having run shoreward to markets with holds bursting and scuppers plugged to keep the engorged vessels afloat.

Seal Island, August 1, 1982

One night on the dark of the moon, we gained a glimmer of what the herring fishermen must know in their bones: that the immeasurable richness of these waters is mysterious and godlike. The phosphorescence in the water fired the night mind as it lit the waves curling in on Seal's shores. While looking out to sea we watched a streak of eerie, pale light shimmer beneath the sea's surface, then begin moving shoreward in a slow, ponderous surge that changed direction, flanked, disappeared, and reappeared.

The sinuous, luminescent light flashed on and off in networks of neural activity. It was a huge school of herring, firing the rich waters, but glowing, like a single mind.

Mending herring nets at House Island.   Courtesy Maine State Museum

The Gulf of Maine Herring Grounds

The earliest observations of the Gulf of Maine region give a vivid picture of herring abundance. In 1675, naturalist John Josselyn, who lived at his brother's plantation on the shores of Saco Bay, wrote, "The herring, which are numerous, they take of them all summer long. In 1670, they were driven back into Black Point Harbor by other great fish that prey upon them so near the shore that they threw themselves (it being high water) upon dry land in such infinite numbers that we might have gone half-way the leg amongst them for near a quarter of a mile."

"Torching" for young herring, or sperling, was one of the earliest methods employed to take this fish. (It is now prohibited.) When the herring move into coves at night at high water to feed, they are attracted to light, which in the early days was provided by burning pitch-pine boughs and, later, rags soaked in kerosene. When the herring rose to the surface, they could be scooped out of the water with buckets. Fishermen have also employed a variety of other low-technology harvesting methods, notably stop seines or twine to shut off coves, trapping small schools that have moved there under the cover of darkness.

Ever since colonial times, herring traps or weirs (fish traps made of nets attached to wooden stakes) have been used to snare herring inshore. The earliest weir was simply a brush fence strung across the mouth of a cove; it was low enough that the fish could swim over it at high tide but then be trapped when the water ebbed. In subsequent years, weirs constructed of spruce spiles woven together with birch brush were built along the shores of islands and in mainland coves. Consider for a moment the productivity of these inshore waters where a fishery could develop that required little else but small trees cut from nearby shores and tended from boats that could be rowed a short distance to where the weirs were located.

Some of the herring caught in weirs were sold to smokehouses on Matinicus, Vinalhaven, Deer Isle, Islesford, and other islands, there to be preserved for shipment in the coastwise trade. But herring did not become big business in Maine until after the introduction of canning technology following the Civil War. Even as bait fish, herring were of only marginal importance, because stocks did not appear among the Maine islands until much of the salt fleet had already loaded and left for distant fishing areas.

The center of the herring fishing effort throughout the first half of the nineteenth century was located off the Magdalen Islands in the Gulf of Saint Lawrence. Maine vessels could sail around Cape Breton in April, catch a "trip," return in late May, then turn around and fit out for fishing voyages that would last throughout the summer months. The first American vessel to go to the Magdalens, according to Wayne O'Leary, a historian who has carefully researched Maine coast fisheries, was a schooner from Isle au Haut that made a voyage as early as 1822. Finding that cod was scarce, the ship made a virtue of necessity by returning with herring. Records show that several vessels began making the voyage the following year, illustrating a recurring pattern of small fishing villages exploring new fisheries and developing niche markets.

Herring weirs became increasingly sophisticated over the years, not only in their placement to capture the maximum number of fish but also in their construction. Today most stationary weirs consist of a long leader of net hung on stakes. The net leads the school of herring to the "bib pound," which has a hook-shaped opening; this leads into another smaller pound and finally into a "pocket." When a school of fish has been trapped, the weir tender closes the doors to the pound as he rows in, driving the herring into the pocket, where they can be taken out of the water.

In 1825, the purse seine was introduced in Gloucester, where it was first used to catch mackerel. A net that encircles large schools of fish, the purse seine was slowly adopted for herring and after 1850 revolutionized the herring fishery. Like all fishing vessels, herring purse seiners have gotten steadily larger. This fishing system has one important biological feature, namely that herring spawn on or near the bottom, then rise at night to the surface to feed. The surface is the only place that purse seiners can catch them. As a result, many observers believe that purse seining takes a smaller percentage of spawning adults than other forms of fishing, such as midwater trawling.

Flat Island, August 9, 1995

The Island Institute's field crew set up a research station on Flat Island, down east off Cape Split, to field-test new satellite image data. Because we are on new moon tides, we want to be there close to dawn, when the maximum amount of the intertidal area will be exposed. The difference in acreage between high and low tides gives a hint of their enormous ecological effect in the Bay of Fundy. The island nearly doubles in size, revealing massive kelp beds waving fingered fronds just beneath the surface and exposing a whole new island along its outer shores. Dulse, as good as Grand Manan's, is everywhere, and we forage on it along with strands and sheets of another species similar to what is imported from Japan as "orami" and "nori."

As we stand on the island's outer shores, just off dead low, the tide begins to work its magic. Slowly, dimly, we are aware of tiny floating eggs washed along on the building current, first one and then another, then more and more until in transfixed amazement we watch what must be thousands passing by us. Floating eggs, thicker than frog spawn, are the deep stirrings of life reborn passing silently by. Herring eggs sink, but some other fish species—as prolific as a biblical miracle—carried on a new moon tide in a timeless dream pass these rugged, silent shores. O holy, o floating tide, this saltwater river will carry ten thousand thousand parts of our past and future directly by our sea boots if we have the care and patience to wait and watch like ancient midwives.

Herring spawn in late summer in "three to thirty fathoms," according to Henry Bigelow, and they are laid over many different types of bottom—rock, pebble, and gravel—but never over soft mud. A single gravid female lays between ten thousand and thirty thousand eggs, which sink to the bottom and cling in clumps to everything from seaweed to pebbles to pot warp or anchor rode. The fry will grow to be four to seven inches long during their first two years, when they are called sardines. By the end of their third year, they are larger than ten inches and frequent deeper waters.

The largest herring catch ever recorded from the Gulf of Maine occurred in 1946, when two hundred and nineteen million pounds were taken. Most of these weighed about half an ounce, which meant that something like six billion fish were caught. That's six thousand million individual creatures produced in two to three years of growth from this rich green sea.

Ever since the beginning of serious fishing for herring, Eastport has been the center of the industry, because the particular combination of environmental conditions around the mouth of Passamaquoddy Bay attracts these fish in greater concentrations than along any other section of the coast. In 1808, the first herring were smoked in Eastport, primarily for an export market. By 1900, the smoked herring industry had grown to six million pounds a year. That same year, seventy-two million pounds were canned as sardines, and another 2.5 million pounds were salted for bait. Just before the turn of the twentieth century, there were sixty-eight sardine factories in Eastport.

Vinalhaven, August 22, 1995, Starlight V

Alfred Osgood, herring catcher from Carvers Harbor, Vinalhaven, is a legend throughout the Gulf of Maine. Ever since fishermen began catching the silver-sided herring in the Gulf of Maine more than four centuries ago, no other fisherman has landed anywhere near the volume that Osgood has pumped out of the sea night after night, month after month, year after year. Handpicked crews from this island town roam the herring grounds off Seal Island in outer Penobscot Bay, out to Halfway Rock and Jeffreys Ledge off Portland, and up to Cashes and Stellwagen banks off Gloucester. Every fisherman in these ports and a hundred others in between are familiar with the name of Osgood's boat, STARLIGHT, and the legendary successes of its owner, captain, and crew.

When STARLIGHT V, the fifth and largest of Osgood's herring seiners, made its initial appearance one day in the summer of 1995 in Vinalhaven's Carvers Harbor and tied up at the old crab plant wharf, few people aware of the fishing pulse of the harbor could fail to take notice. From her white pilothouse, STARLIGHT's pale green hull sweeps aft to measure seventy-two feet overall. Her six holds can pack three hundred thousand pounds of herring.

The sun is still a blinding bright orb in the western sky as the crew of the seiner slips its lines off the wharf. With a high bow and long sheer, STARLIGHT glides into the dying southwesterly sea rolling into west Penobscot Bay. Jason Day, twenty-nine years old, Osgood's alternate skipper, is at the helm. Billy Guptill and a crew of four others, including two of Alfred Osgood's sons, David and Justin, are busy checking the lines, nets, rings, buoys, hydraulics, and miscellaneous gear that this most modern and efficient purse seiner carries neatly on her stern.

It will take almost six hours of steaming time to reach the herring grounds, so at four o'clock most of the crew eat a quick supper and retire to

Threading adult herring on racks for smoking, Eastport, 1920.   FRANK CLAES COLLECTION

Electronics on bridge of STARLIGHT V, *1995.*   PHILIP CONKLING

> *one of the ten berths scattered belowdecks. For me, the slow heave and roll*
> *of* STARLIGHT *in the dying southwesterly is too intoxicating, and the late*
> *afternoon summer sun is too full and entrancing to admit sleep, although I*
> *know there is a long night ahead. When the sun slowly rolls below the west-*
> *ern rim of this world and its glow is finally extinguished, there will be time*
> *enough for sweet rest in the arms of a serene sea.*

In the Gulf of Maine, sardines account for well over three-quarters of the commercial landings of herring. The sardine industry began in 1875, apparently after an Eastport entrepreneur decided to experiment with packing small herring rather than lobsters in cans. Wrote George Brown Goode in his monumental work on America's fisheries, *Fisheries and Fishing Industries of the United States,* "By far the greatest consumption of herring for food is in the shape of so-called sardines, packed for the most part in cottonseed oil, and in cans made in imitation of those imported from France."

Earlier, in the eighteenth century, smoked herring had been shipped from Eastport to Boston, New York, and Philadelphia "to serve for the food of the poorer classes during Lenten season," wrote Goode, and to supply "the demand from the slave owning states." But the Civil War had disrupted the trade, "and most of the smoke houses remain abandoned to this day." Sardine canneries revolutionized employment prospects along the Maine coast, and by the turn of the century there were some seventy-five canneries, including several around the periphery of Penobscot Bay in Stonington, Belfast, Rockland, and Port Clyde. Today six sardine processing plants remain in Maine, most having fallen victim to changing consumer demand.

Observing the Herring Cycle

For centuries, the vast abundance of herring in the Gulf of Maine has astounded fishermen, casual observers, and scientists alike. About a hundred years ago, the movements of herring from offshore areas in winter to local coastal spawning grounds around the rim of the Gulf of Maine was described for the first time in detail. American fisheries biologist Spencer Baird in 1877 wrote, "One principal spawning ground of the herring in the Bay of Fundy is near the southern head of Grand Manan; and by a very wise provision of the New Brunswick government, a closed [season] was enacted, extending from the 15th of June to the 15th of September, during which the capture of these fish was forbidden. They now resort to that portion of the coast in considerable numbers, and the quantity of eggs deposited is said to be something almost inconceivable."

This simple spawning area closure that Baird described more than a century ago was in effect for approximately sixty years, during which time landings in the eastern part of the Gulf of Maine, although they fluctuated annually, were reliable enough to support a major export industry of canned sardines and smoked herring. This provision for spawning area closure was dropped in the 1930s. Canada has since evolved a different method of management based on an elaborate system of quotas, but it has not prevented local population crashes. The system appears to have worked less effectively than nineteenth- and early twentieth-century measures in protecting important local spawning stocks.

It appears that a single age class that has a poor spawning year can affect population levels for many years to come. An 1881 study of a particular group of Bay of Fundy herring showed that these fish received no recruitment of young fish for about ten years and finally seemed to have disappeared from the area after the last ones died of old age. Likewise, during exceptionally good spawning years, when environmental conditions are optimal, billions of new young fish are added to the population and will continue to produce some young until the next big spawning year occurs. The reason that herring catches are so difficult to predict from year to year appears to be largely a result of the greatly fluctuating survival of the spawn. This survival is in turn determined by the interaction of such factors as water temperature, salinity, the effects of tides and currents, and the physiological condition of the adult females when the eggs are laid. All of this makes understandable why marine biologists can quickly get into trouble when they try to predict the levels of fish populations.

Outer Pumpkin Ledge, August 22, 1995, Starlight V

While most of the crew sleep, Jason brings Starlight *in between Large and Little Green Islands, up underneath Monhegan's dark cliffs, all the while monitoring the crackle of radio traffic from other herring boats. Shortly after nine o'clock, when* Starlight *suddenly throttles back in the darkness, the crew members appear instantaneously and suit up in full foul weather gear. We are off Outer Pumpkin Ledge, southeast of Bantam Rock, and Jason is staring intently at the patterns of color on the forward scanning sonar. Jason, whom I've known since he was fourteen or fifteen, has not volunteered much all evening, but now he quietly observes, "This is the most fish I've seen in quite a little while."*

The loom of instrument light casts an eerie glow throughout the pilot-house as he begins recording Starlight's *slow turns on the chart plotter. The herring appear as a bright wall of red on the sonar from the top of the water column to the bottom, but the school is in water too shoal to deploy* Starlight's *deep net, which is also the largest in the fleet.*

Off to port and starboard the lights of four other boats bob and blink in the inky night. All warily circle the fish, the ledges, and one another. After the radio crackles intensely in a quick, intense interchange, Starlight *begins to move ponderously off to the northeast toward one of the other boats.*

Fifteen minutes later we come up alongside the Anna Lisa, *a forty-eight-foot seiner out of New Harbor. Jason carefully backs down as the skipper of the* Anna Lisa, *Paul Paulino, hands the ends of his seine net to* Starlight's *crew. In the pocket of his net we watch approximately one hundred and sixty thousand pounds of silver-sided herring flipping near the surface. This is more than Paulino can load aboard his modest vessel, so he is proposing to give the rest of the fish away. I stare incredulously at Jason, who explains that, recently, most of the Gulf of Maine got together to form the Independent Seiners Association, and that one of the things they agreed to do was to share catches that were too big for one boat to handle rather than tolerate the waste of herring dumped overboard, dead.*

Before Starlight *can load, another boat, the* Sarah McKay, *out of Port Clyde, comes alongside* Anna Lisa's *port rail. Her seine net, too, is loaded. After both the* Anna Lisa *and the* Sarah McKay *are loaded to their scuppers,* Starlight *takes on some four hundred bushels; at $8 per bushel, we have just received a $3,200 gift, with little fanfare.*

Herring Spawning Grounds

For more than a hundred years, the annual progression of spawning of herring around the rim of the Gulf of Maine has been studied and documented. The first comprehensive study of American fisheries was published by the U.S. Fisheries Commission, edited by George Goode, in 1887. This report, printed in five volumes, was a massive undertaking that involved the nation's foremost fish-

"Drying up" the seine net at Monhegan Harbor, 1926.   Frank Claes collection

eries biologists, including Spencer Baird, of Massachusetts, the first commissioner of Fish and Fisheries in the United States. One of the principals of this undertaking was Joseph Collins, of Islesboro, a noted vessel captain and crusading official of the U.S. Fisheries Commission, who got his start in fishing as a ten-year-old jigging for mackerel off Mount Desert Rock.

Even a century after its publication, this report stands out as a unique research effort. The study contains not only the first detailed picture of landings of all commercially important fish and shellfish by region but also excellent descriptions of local fisheries and fishing grounds based on interviews with experienced older fishermen from every harbor between Eastport, Maine, and Galveston, Texas, including detailed descriptions of all the fishing activities in Penobscot Bay.

Shooting the Net, Outer Pumpkin Ledge, STARLIGHT V

Although the four hundred bushels of herring are gratefully received, it is a small contribution to the three thousand bushels, or three hundred thousand pounds, of herring that STARLIGHT *needs to satisfy its markets ashore. Jason returns his gaze to the chart plotter.* STARLIGHT*'s net runs to an astonishing forty fathoms in depth, and Jason needs an additional few fathoms of margin to avoid tearing the bottom out of that $140,000 investment.*

Jason says that in summer the herring congregate in loose schools; but in fall, after cold weather sets in, they bunch together, and a small spot of fish on the image can fill STARLIGHT*'s holds. Meanwhile, on the stern,* STARLIGHT*'s crew waits. Two men are perched on the bug boat—the short, fast boat that will carry the twine in a large circle around the herring when and if the captain gives the word.*

We circle round and round in the eerie, inky void. It is disorienting to be constantly changing direction in the blackness of the night. For Jason to give the signal, STARLIGHT *must be uptide of the fish to avoid fouling the net in the propeller as the net shoots off the stern. In addition, the fish must be in forty-five to fifty fathoms of water to protect the net, the sonar signal must indicate a large and dense enough bunch of fish to make the set worthwhile, the location of other boats must be monitored, the compass heading must be remembered, and the movement of the feeding fish as they graze on the floating zooplankton pasture must be factored in. It is apparent that few people are equipped to keep all this information in mind at once, much less keep it constantly updated as one or more of the variables changes. It is not clear why, in spite of all the sophisticated electronics, sets often fail to produce much.*

Soon a half moon will rise, which can spook the fish, and Jason begins to monitor this, too. In addition, he is responsible for the safety of the crew and vessel. You begin to understand why captains receive a larger share of the night's returns.

After circling for well over an hour in intense concentration, Jason swivels in his chair, takes the mike that is wired to a speaker on deck, and quietly says only two words, "Let's go." The brake on the winch cable holding the bug boat on the stern lets go with a riflelike crack. Then it all comes down to how quickly that small craft can haul two thousand four hundred feet of forty-fathom twine in a long arc around this body of fish before they spirit away. Perhaps three minutes pass before the leading ends of the net are handed up over the rail and Jason hastens back to the sonar. A slow smile spreads over his face as he peers at the image of a bunch of fish neatly circumscribed on the screen. A whole village's-worth of halogen lights go on as

*the bottom of the net is pursed and we gaze out at two acres of white corks
lazily floating on the surface.*

In late spring as waters warm, herring aggregate in large schools and move onto spawning
grounds first in Minas Basin and the upper Bay of Fundy, then around Grand Manan Island, into
Passamaquoddy Bay, and then westward bay by bay, to reach Penobscot Bay in early summer.

An 1898 report of the U.S. Commission of Fish and Fisheries by H.F. Moore provides a comprehensive description of the spawning grounds along the Maine coast. Moore wrote that "until about
1880 spawning herring were unknown at Matinicus Island, but now they come regularly about
September 1 and remain for three or four weeks. No herring are known to spawn at Monhegan
Island, but on the opposite shore in Penobscot Bay they arrive in September and remain until the
end of October, although it is probable that a few are spawning during the latter part of their stay."

For more than a century, Maine fishermen, especially between Moose Island (Eastport) off
Passamaquoddy to Vinalhaven at the edge of Penobscot Bay, have built and maintained weirs to
intercept the surges of herring moving shoreward and along the rim of the Gulf.

Drying Up the Fish, STARLIGHT V

*As the net comes up, the herring flipping in the water sound like a hard
rain. The heave and surge of this massive school is enough to roll STARLIGHT
on her starboard side. As the herring continue to thrash in the diminishing
confines of the net, their scales, once collected for pearl essence, shine in the
water, in the twine, and in the drying pocket, suffusing the whole scene in
an opalescent glow that is serenity itself. Meanwhile, just outside the net the
shadows of a pair of sleek seals cruise the perimeter of light. The seals roll in
lazily for a meal, and out of the night sky herring gulls suddenly appear and
swoop in for scraps. You understand why they say that fishing for herring
spoils you for other fishing.*

*The fish pump is lowered into the pocket of the twine, and a waterfall
of herring begins cascading into the first hold. This is quickly filled, and the
second and third shortly afterward. We have taken on several hundred thousand bushels—maybe one million individual silver-sided, blue-backed
Atlantic herring—in one set.*

Economic Significance of Gulf of Maine Herring

In 1875, the technology that a handful of American businessmen had applied to canning vegetables and farm products was applied to canning Maine herring. They were marked as "French sardines." Although the Maine sardine industry has shrunk from its glory days of past decades, the
industry still employs a thousand packers, mostly part time, in the six remaining factories on the
coast. In 1997, the plants packed thirty-two hundred metric tons of herring, which translates into
$40 million worth of product and a $10 million payroll. Lobstermen bought an additional thirty
thousand metric tons for bait, to round out the domestic harvest in Maine.

Rockland, August 23, 1995, STARLIGHT V

*The chilly bleat of the Owls Head light foghorn registers in the deep
folds of sleep. Outside, a dripping fog clings to the twine and rails and to the
spars of other vessels that are beginning to stir along Rockland's waterfront.
Jason brings STARLIGHT alongside Prock's granite wharf beyond the ferry
terminal at the north end of the harbor. On the wharf a crew member starts*

the cranky fish pump, which will lift close to three hundred thousand pounds of herring up thirty vertical feet and into the fleet of O'Hara Corporation trucks lined up and waiting.

One by one, the O'Hara trucks pull up under the chute of the fish pump while thousands of pounds of lobster bait are steadily sucked out of the holds and dropped into their trailers. Five tractor trailer loads from STARLIGHT, *plus the smaller haul of the* WESTERN SEA, *another purse seiner, are just about enough bait to satisfy midcoast Maine's August lobster market demand for a day. No wonder lobstermen think of themselves as maricultur- ists who feed Maine's population of lobsters.*

Then STARLIGHT *must still make stops at North Haven to unload bait, as well as resupplying several lobster stations around the shores of Vinalhaven. If Jason and the crew are lucky, they will get back to Carvers Harbor in time to see their families briefly before resupplying and heading back out before the sun goes down. Billy Guptill and Alfred Osgood both have strings of lobster gear that they must find time to tend. But for the crew of* STARLIGHT, *when it comes to another round in the elaborate dance of a herring chase, everything else is a sideshow.*

MACKEREL SNAPPERS

D. H. Lawrence was referring to love rather than fish when he wrote, "There are many fish in the sea, but most of them are mackerel," but the picture is accurate enough, because mackerel is probably the most abundant species of fish along the Atlantic coast, although in any given year in the Gulf of Maine they may be outnumbered by both herring and menhaden (pogies).

In 1816, Abraham Lurvey, of Mount Desert Island, invented the mackerel jig—a small hook with a shiny pewter sinker for its shaft—and initiated the era of jigging for mackerel. It would last until 1865, when Southport Island fishermen began to catch them in a seine. For fifty years the jiggers and elegant gaff-rigged mackerel schooners would whiten the bays of Maine in a silver age of fishing.

Eighteen hundred thirty-one was the high-line year for mackerel jiggers, whose boats had to be faster and more trim than the pinkies, because schools of mackerel arrived unpredictably and disap- peared as quickly. In years when the mackerel were abundant, a masthead lookout could spot upward of fifty separate schools at one time. The wake of mackerel is less compact than that of either pogy or herring. They spend more time at the surface, so from his high position a lookout could recognize their shadowy movements even at depths of eight to ten fathoms. Mackerel jiggers chummed the school to the surface by throwing ground-up oily herring and pogies (alewives) in the water. When the mackerel started feeding, the jigs were dropped into the sea and the voracious mackerel were pulled in as quickly as the lines went over.

In 1837, Isle au Haut became the first town on the Maine coast to send a vessel, the PORPOISE, to the Magdalen Islands in the Gulf of Saint Lawrence for mackerel. The PORPOISE then spent the remainder of the year hooking mackerel off the United States coast. Other towns around Penobscot Bay soon followed suit. According to Edward Earll, one of the contributors to the U.S. Fisheries Commission report, during the first half of the nineteenth century, North Haven islanders primarily built—and fished from—small boats for cod in spring on inshore grounds, "after which they fitted for the 'Bay' mackerel fishery." Although pickled mackerel fetched a higher price than salt cod, it was a chancier enterprise, and "broken" voyages when hardly a mackerel was hooked were not uncommon.

The competition among boats was occasionally as fierce as the feeding frenzy of their prey. There are gripping accounts of an elegant, well-handled mackerel schooner jigging fish, only to have

Tarring a mackerel seine, Monhegan, 1930 (left to right: Captain Ford Davis, Fred Townsend, Raymond Orne).

another one round up on her stern, heave-to downwind, and steal the school. In one day in 1850 off Portland alone, three hundred mackerel vessels were counted jigging for mackerel to pickle in brine and ship in casks to Boston, New York, and a hundred other world ports. That was back in the days when Roman Catholic holy days and Fridays were meatless, and Catholics were impiously called "mackerel snappers."

The Rise of Island Mackerel Catchers

The Penobscot Bay islands were at the center of the Maine mackerel business. Beginning in 1850 and for the next four decades, North Haven fishermen built larger vessels that specialized almost exclusively in mackerel fishing. By 1879, mackerel was almost the sole industry of the island community, with 20 elegant mackerel schooners ranging from thirty to fifty tons and employing 145 fishermen. Next door, on Vinalhaven, the same number of vessels were registered, but their average tonnage was a good deal less, and these boats employed only 98 fishermen.

North Haven did enough business exporting mackerel to the Caribbean, according to one observer at the time, to maintain "several West Indian goods stores in 1860" that were located on the island. By the early 1870s, three-quarters of the mackerel landed by American schooners was taken along the coast of Maine from such fishing grounds as Seguin, Monhegan, Matinicus Rock, and Mount Desert Rock—all in the midcoast region—and from the Isles of Shoals to the west and Grand Manan to the east.

The perennial high-liner of the Maine mackerel fleet was not from North Haven, however; he was Herman Joyce, of nearby Swan's Island. He had been doing well with his mackerel schooners, but when steam winches were introduced into the fishery in 1877, he immediately commissioned a large sail- and steam-powered seiner capable of deploying the largest net in the fishery.

The mackerel fishery changed overnight; purse seines allowed fishermen to quadruple their catch. In 1877, just before the purse seine was adapted to the mackerel fishery, Joyce's vessel, the ALICE, generated fifteen hundred barrels of pickled mackerel worth $9,200 for the season. Just four years later the ALICE landed forty-nine hundred barrels worth $28,000.

Suddenly the catches were so huge that it was impossible to clean and pickle the fish before they spoiled. In 1831 the mackerel catch from the Gulf of Maine had been seven million pounds; in 1880, at the height of the most prolific concentration of mackerel ever recorded in the Gulf of Maine, 294 million pounds were landed from American and Nova Scotia waters.

This marvelous abundance ended in 1885, almost in a heartbeat. After 100 million pounds of mackerel were landed that year, the fishery fell into a calamitous decline in 1886 that lasted for 25 years. By 1898, there was not a single mackerel boat left in the Swan's Island fleet; there had been 34 boats just 15 years earlier.

It's difficult to get a complete picture of the decline of the mackerel fishery. Certainly after the Civil War and the end of slavery, trading routes shifted out of the South, where the profitable three-way exchange of fish for cotton and cotton for molasses had fueled an international mercantile trade. In addition, competition for speed and the specialization of the mackerel schooners left these fishermen exposed to any downturn in the market, because it was difficult to re-rig such vessels for other fisheries.

On North Haven the decline had an even more profound effect than on Swan's, because it coincided with the appearance of the first rusticators, who began buying up the working waterfront, especially around Northern Harbor, which would shortly become known as Pulpit Harbor. With the end of North Haven's very successful, but narrow, specialization in mackerel fishing came the end of a way of life for the islanders.

TUNA: THE MAGIC OF MONEY

As anyone who has been to a sushi bar or eaten sashimi knows, well-prepared fresh tuna is worth paying for, although it is hard to conceive of New Englanders ever spending the fifty-five dollars per pound that Japanese consumers pay at the retail level for this Epicurean experience. Nevertheless, the changes the Japanese market has wrought on the harpoon fleet in the Gulf of Maine in a few short years are truly amazing.

In 1972-73, the Japanese market discovered the excellent quality of the giant bluefins in the Gulf of Maine, and the price jumped from five cents to $1.20 per pound. The fishery rapidly expanded as fishermen took bluefins by traps, hand lines, harpoons, purse seines, long lines, and rod-and-reel. As a result, catches and tuna abundance have sharply declined. Maine landings reflect the trends. A maximum of four hundred ten thousand pounds were landed in 1963, early in the expansion of the fishery. Catches subsequently were less than three hundred thousand pounds; by 1988, only eighty-three thousand pounds were landed in Maine, a figure that has persisted for nearly a decade.

> *Aboard the* JESSE, *July 9, 1975, 4:00 a.m.*
>
> *Jim Salisbury spent all his spare time this past spring rigging the* JESSE *with a crow's nest and a bow pulpit and a pair of harpoons handcrafted from ash trees from his woodlot. Salisbury has got it in his mind to put an iron into a bluefin tuna.*
>
> *All spring long the commentary among the other fishermen simmered just below scorn. No one had ever, as far back as memory and therefore history went, harpooned a tuna from Pigeon Hill Harbor. Mostly they thought it was just like some educated fool to go wasting time and money way offshore on fish that weren't there instead of tending gear on the lobster grounds.*
>
> *The day breaks over an oily gray ocean swell thirty miles offshore as the* JESSE *rounds up under the farthest rocky outpost off the Maine coast—magnificent, lonely Mount Desert Rock. Jim scrambles aloft into the tuna*

tower and begins running hour-long transects away from the rock, scanning the surface where low sky meets rolling sea. After three to four hours of silent searching, he puts the helm over sharply.

Looking out in the direction of our new heading, Salisbury's mate, Al Richardson, and I are aware of the faint outlines of gray gulls darting and wheeling over the ocean surface. Jim quietly calls Al to the helm while he moves quickly down to the deck, where the bronze-tipped harpoon with its one hundred and fifty fathoms of line and attached buoy have been carefully rigged and stowed aft. Al slowly opens the throttle to run down on the area where the birds are hovering and dipping. He must try to get a sense of whether there are tuna beneath the gulls and, if so, their direction of travel, so he can maneuver the boat to come in behind the fish. Meanwhile Jim has moved into the bow pulpit with the long harpoon and stands leaning slightly forward, arms raised, silhouetted in the pose of a fisherman holding his most ancient and honored weapon.

The bluefin tuna comes to the Gulf of Maine with adaptations for speed and mobility unmatched in the marine world. It has evolved a means of regulating its body temperature by capturing the heat energy produced in its highly dense muscle and transporting the heat quickly through its body via tissue richly ribboned with blood vessels. Shaped like a large, hydrodynamic and acrobatic bullet with retractable fins, a bluefin tuna can reach speeds of forty knots and is capable of changing direction ninety degrees in any plane in almost an instant. Its appetite is insatiable; during its three- to four-month stay in the Gulf of Maine, it consumes 10 percent of its body weight per day in mackerel, herring, hake, bluefish, and squid.

Aboard the JESSE, SE of Mount Desert Rock, 11 a.m.

Al Richardson has closed with the flock of gulls. On the flat gray ocean surface we see only the slight ripple of a wake—the telltale sign that there are giant bluefin tuna six to eight feet below the surface. In the next few minutes we begin closing down on this slight ripple. Where there is one bluefin, there is likely to be a school of anywhere between fifteen and fifty individuals varying in size between three hundred and perhaps a thousand pounds. Jim and Al must concentrate on a single thought without talking; two minds, one vision. It is rare that a harpooner gets a second shot.

Jim is focusing on a single bluefin, pointing the harpoon at its wake while Al tries to follow the giant slalom course of the school, which is traveling at only a fraction of the speed of which they're capable. The fish nearest the surface are only a boat length or so away, and even I can see in the green-gray depths the flashing silver sheen of their immense sides. As likely as not, the individuals nearest the surface are in front of the main body of the school, which is running deeper. But I didn't know this until later.

Tuna may live twenty years. They travel in groups sorted by age and by size, following migratory patterns characteristic for each age group. Juvenile or "schoolie" tuna may weigh from five to seventy pounds; medium fish range from seventy to two hundred and seventy; and giant bluefins from two hundred and seventy pounds to one thousand or more.

All life seems to have its trade-offs; other fish have gill plates, which are fanned to provide a constant supply of oxygen, but bluefin tuna have given up these plates (which increase friction as the fish passes through the water), so they must keep moving or suffocate. While not feeding, the tuna swims ceaselessly, traveling a hundred to a hundred and fifty miles a day. A fifteen-year-old adult will have traveled through a million nautical miles of ocean, mostly on one side or the other of the North Atlantic. Some of the older fish have navigated the entire North and South Atlantic.

Aboard the Jesse, *11:10 a.m.*

In one graceful motion, Jim launches the harpoon. An instant later we know he's ironed a giant, because the three-eighths-inch line is disappearing overboard with a high-pitched hum as it uncoils like a shot spring. Jim scrambles aft to make sure the line doesn't foul. Soon all one hundred and fifty fathoms of line are out and the keg buoy is making a broken field pattern across the water's surface. Jim quickly begins rigging another harpoon in the event we intercept a second school, while Al heads us off to follow the orange fleck now being towed by the harpooned fish.

After three hours of combined efforts, most of the one hundred and fifty fathoms of line have been hauled back on deck and the darted bluefin is careening from port to starboard quarter in its last bursts of life. After another quarter of an hour of skill versus instinct and muscle versus muscle, the bluefin is gaffed alongside. Jim deftly reaches in and cuts the gill artery, an important consideration not only for landing the tuna but for the highly discriminating Japanese palate, which can tell not only a well-bled fish but

Salt flake yard at Vinalhaven fish plant, 1890.   FRANK CLAES COLLECTION

the fat content of its flesh. The iridescent sheen of this great creature along-side transfixes all of us in a moment of transcendent pride and humility. Six hundred pounds of the North Atlantic's evolutionary masterpiece is hauled aboard.

That evening Jim and Al iced down the tuna, and Jim drove up the peninsula at 3:30 a.m. to be in Portland at 7:00 a.m. when the Japanese buyers arrive. The day before—the opening day of the season—the price for giant bluefin stood at $1.10 a pound. Knowing that no one with tuna caught on the first day of the season can keep the fish fresh beyond the second day, the buyers offer Jim ten cents a pound this morning. Jim is numb with fatigue and doesn't argue much. He just backs his truck to the end of the wharf and, under the incredulous stares of the buyers, heaves the giant fish overboard, climbs back in the cab, and heads slowly back down east.

It should come as no surprise that the huge international rewards the international bluefin tuna market presents can create a lot of tension and controversy; money works its own magic whenever it's in play. Like every other contentious issue on the water, the proper balance between the twin imperatives of market opportunity and resource conservation is nearly impossible to find by consensus. But when any strategy depends on answering questions such as how many giant bluefin are actually out there in the Gulf of Maine, meaning someone has to come up with a credible and defensible number in such a high-stakes, high-visibility game, this arena is not for the faint of heart.

Dressing and washing cod for drying, 1890.

In Cod We Trust

Never could the Spaniard with all his mines of gold and silver pay his debts, his friends and army half so truly as the Hollanders still have done by this contemptible trade of fish. But this is their mine and the sea the source of those silvery streams of all their virtue.

—Captain John Smith, 1624

In New England, the Narragansett Indian word for cod translated as "the fish that comes a little before spring," a name that George Brown Goode writes "is suggestive in the extreme" in the introduction to his work on America's fisheries. Cod have been known since before recorded history to congregate in immense schools inshore in late winter to spawn. This habit created a winter fishery in New England that was the underpinning of the settlement of the area from the earliest days of the seventeenth century. Few people remember that the Pilgrims' first awful winter in Plymouth was saved only by a voyage to the fishing station at Damariscove Island off Boothbay Harbor on the midcoast, where they were resupplied with dried salt cod.

Unlike other groundfish species, cod migrate inshore to lay eggs toward the end of winter, massing in enormous numbers in well-defined locations south of the Isles of Shoals, off Richmond Island in Cape Elizabeth, off Damariscove Island near the mouth of the Sheepscot River, and off Vinalhaven and Matinicus in Penobscot Bay. All the bays of Maine, in fact, had cod spawning grounds, but the biggest ones were discovered earliest.

John Smith—who not only explored the coast of Maine in a small boat in 1614 but caught enough fish during his stay to turn a handsome profit at the conclusion of his voyage—was one of the early popularizers of the idea of a Maine winter fishery. He did not exaggerate when he wrote that the cod that had fattened themselves all summer long were more valuable when they agregated inshore prior to the spawning season: "Each hundred is as good as two or three hundred in the New-found-land . . . and you can have your fish to market before they have any." Islands such as the Isles of Shoals, Richmond, Damariscove, and Monhegan—all of which were handy to the winter cod grounds—became important outposts for this new fishery.

The Richmond Island Cod Fishery

History books tell us Gulf of Maine fish was different than Georges Bank fish. It has to do with what they fed on . . . They had to salt Georges fish heavy. Maine fish were superior. The reason we had fish here was that we used small boats.

—Willie Spear, Cousins Island

Jonathan Winter of Richmond Island, the agent for the influential Bristol merchant Robert Trelawney in the 1630s and 1640s, wrote to his employer that the best catches were landed in January and February: "If you propose to follow fishing here, you must expect to have your ship here by Christmas."

Richmond Island's winter fishing was done in small boats called "shallops," with crews of four. A fifth crew member stayed ashore to wash the salt out of the boat and dry the fish when the shallop returned from a two- or three-day trip to the cod grounds. The fish were "kenched" on board, which involved gutting them and stacking them so they would drain. Drying the cod, called "making fish," involved placing split fish on flakes inclined at an angle to keep the sun from parching them. At night they were covered with wooden boxes, and during storms they were mounded up. Making salt fish became a community enterprise during the heyday of the cod fishery.

The full-grown and fat cod that weighed between forty and sixty pounds were sold on the

Continent; smaller cod that were not good enough for the Spanish or Portuguese markets were sold to the Virginia Colony. Dried fish of inferior quality—they may have been salt-burned and spotted or simply not as full fleshed but still wholesome and sweet—were packed in casks and sent to the West Indies to be fed to plantation slaves. Other products from this fishing station included "core fish," or corned fish, which were salted in brine without being dried, and "traine," or cod liver oil. ("Dun" was yet another product, this one peculiar to the Isles of Shoals. Dun was pollock caught in summer and cured in the sun without much salt, then piled together and covered with marsh hay until they "ripened." Dun fish became a high-priced specialty product in the Mediterranean.)

Cod Mouths and Eggs

Henry Bigelow, in his monumental report "Fishes of the Gulf of Maine" (co-authored with William Schroeder), wrote: "It would be useless to give a catalog of species found in their stomachs. For a long period of time, before naturalists learned to use the hand dredge, a favorite place to search for rare invertebrates of deep water was at the fish dealers store from the stomachs of cod. From their stomachs, scores of shells new to science have been taken." According to Bigelow, one report mentioned great banks of shells found on the cod grounds off Grand Manan Island at the mouth of the Bay of Fundy, as well as in Ipswich Bay. These shells are "nested," the smaller inside the larger, sometimes six or seven in a set, having been consumed by cod and spit out after the soft parts were digested.

"They feed on crabs of all kinds, lobsters, sea anemones," Bigelow continued, "and have been seen at surface catching potato beetles and June bugs which have drifted out from shore." A hundred years ago, Captain Epes W. Merchant of Gloucester, one of the contributors to Goode's classic volumes on Maine's fisheries, tells of remarkable schools of codfish that frequented Massachusetts Bay between 1815 and 1830. Called the "shad" school, they were caught with alewives and shad that were then used for bait from early April to the middle of May. The fishermen were accustomed to getting these fish for bait as soon as they began to run. The cod seemed to be waiting for them.

Goode's colleague Edward Earll described a spawning school of cod that arrived in Ipswich Bay off Cape Ann in 1879. The school was discovered in January. "The news spread rapidly, and soon all the shore fleet were in the Bay, while vessels of sixty or seventy tons abandoned the other fisheries and fitted out for this locality. By the middle of February, 104 sail, with upwards of 600 men, were fishing within a radius of six or seven miles and 20,000 to 25,000 pounds were sometimes taken by the crew of a single schooner." Earll calculated that during four months of fishing on this school between the first of February and the last of May, an average of forty-five vessels would be fishing on any given day. With each carrying six dories with trawls (long lines with baited hooks that lay on the bottom) averaging 800 hooks, there were 216,000 baited hooks on the bottom day in and day out. "It is not surprising, therefore, that the catch reached 11,250,000 pounds on this little patch of ground."

Goode and his colleagues recorded the remarkable fecundity of mature female cod, which bear such prodigious quantities of eggs that it seems their numbers could never be depleted. A twenty-one-pound female contained 2.7 million eggs; a seventy-five-pound female bore 9.1 million eggs. In contrast the largest number of eggs found on a haddock was 1.84 million. The ovaries of a seventy-five-pound female cod weigh forty-five pounds, and the eggs when stripped filled nearly seven gallons.

THE RISE AND FALL OF GROUNDFISHING

Between 1770 and 1800, the population of Maine quintupled. On the eastern frontier suddenly there were more people pouring into the state and many more mouths to feed. Before the American Revolution, there were about sixty vessels employed in the fisheries from the District of Maine. Only a few of these went to the offshore banks such as Browns, Sable, or Roseway. Georges was considered too rough and dangerous for small craft. The vast majority fished the smaller banks closer to shore—Spot of Rocks, Saturday Night Ledge, Old Man's Pasture, Sou'sou'west, Kettle Bottom, Schoodic Ridges, and Clay Bank—from berths at the Isles of Shoals, Damariscove, Monhegan, North and South Fox islands, Swan's, Deer Isle, the Cranberries, Frenchboro, Mount Desert, and Beals Island.

The Isles of Shoals had probably the largest Gulf of Maine fishing station before the Revolution. Appledore, the biggest island in the Isles of Shoals group, with a population that fluctuated between three hundred and six hundred annually, cured three hundred thousand quintals (pronounced "kentals"; a quintal equaled one hundred and twelve pounds), mostly for the Spanish and West Indian markets. William Wood, the self-styled "Lord of the Isles," wrote, "He is a very bad fisher that cannot kill in one day with his hook and line one, two, or three hundred cods. And is it not a pretty sport to pull up two pense, six pense, twelve pense as fast as you can hale and wear a line?"

It is important to bear in mind the difference between the offshore fisheries and the so-called "shore fishery" or "boat fishery," which operated within thirty miles of the Maine coast and in which virtually every coastal and island village was involved. The intense focus on Maine and Massachusetts fleet activities in what we might think of as the nation's first "distant water fishing" has had an unintended consequence of obscuring the importance of inshore fishing grounds along Maine's coastline, especially to the communities that fronted this magnificent endowment.

The inshore cod fishery represented a kind of local breadbasket where boats, large and small, from small island towns went to fishing grounds in the Gulf of Maine or even to distant points in the western North Atlantic. In 1817, when Vinalhaven supported "fifteen sail of small schooners, the smaller fishing the shore," according to Edward Earll, "two or three of the larger were making voyages to the offshore banks." Deer Isle (Stonington) similarly reflected the division of effort between inshore and distant water fishing. In 1830, twelve large fishing vessels went to distant fishing grounds, whereas forty smaller boats fished "along the shore," according to the U.S. Fisheries Commission report. In 1840, the town could boast thirty large vessels and fifty smaller boats; twenty years later, in 1860, approximately the same number of boats participated in inshore and offshore fishing.

During the first hundred years of European settlement of the Maine coast and islands, a fisherman in a small vessel, with knowledge that was often handed down from father to son, could row to a given fishing ground and make a day's catch of cod. Bert Dyer recalled how tub trawling was done:

> Beautiful hand lining there, in the gully between Seal Island and the shoal. Christ, you'd go down there some days and load a boat with pollock. And big cod. Now you go down there, it's nothing. But, my God, in the spring of the year, you'd see sometimes fifteen, twenty boats right there hand lining, cod fishing. March, April—load right up. It's too bad! Christ, up inside there, in those tows, draggers would also get all kinds of flatfish and haddock.
>
> We all trawled. Tub trawls with eight hundred hooks to a tub, thirty-four inches apart on a gangion. In the summertime, when lobsters went to thirty cents, most of us would go haking—we had about fourteen boats then. We'd start middle of June and go through till October. We'd fish off the Ball and down to the Rock and what we called the Blue Ground and Skate Bank and the Bowdies. All that bottom west, sou'west of the Rock over to Monhegan. The Blue Ground—that was always a hard haul. I see why they call it that. You'd always part gear when the big tides was running.

For the first three centuries after the Maine islands were settled, primarily by fishermen, the prosaic method of hand lining for cod and other groundfish from small boats in inshore waters to make salt fish for the coastwise trade became a steady and arguably more lasting part of the local economy than the grand salt bankers that sailed to far more treacherous places in large boats for mercantile interests. Catches from small boats could range from several hundred to several thousand pounds per day, and good fishing meant perhaps an average of six hundred pounds. Between spring and fall, year in and year out, some fish could be caught for curing every day that the weather allowed small boats to set out. Worth only pennies per pound, even after it was cured, cod fished in inshore waters was not a way to get rich quick, but it was a living, tried and true.

> Willie Spear, Cousins Island:
>
> Our best fishing was off the end of Cape Elizabeth, Wood Island. History books tell us that there was the best fishing in North America. These fishermen there could catch the same fish all year round. Traditional spawning grounds. The bottom is conducive and they still return. Not in any numbers like before. But it's held up for four hundred years.

The early fishing enterprises of the islands, like those of small ports on the mainland, were characterized not just by their small size but also by the practice of fishing "on shares," whereby each crew member was paid on the basis of the value of a portion of the landings. This form of democratic "ownership" of the catch, which evolved in New England, was an important reflection of the political culture of the region and has survived as a continuing and nearly unique feature of many local fisheries, including lobstering, herring fishing, and groundfishing. Of course a few capitalists emerged, such as David Thurlow of Deer Isle, who sent four fishing vessels to sea in 1829, including the seventy-six-ton LYDIA. Captain Timothy Lane of Vinalhaven rose to prominence in the 1850s as a successful fleet owner and salt fish merchant. In 1851, Lane shipped $70,000 worth of dried cod to Boston, an enormous volume. But these enterprises were the exception rather than the rule.

By 1860, the democratic structure of the Maine fishing fleet, the skill of its crews, and the productivity of the local waters all contributed to the fact that Maine had more fishermen (4,607) than any other state in the nation; a great number of them were islanders. According to Maine coast fisheries historian Wayne O'Leary, the leading cod fishing region in Maine was almost invariably the Penobscot district. In 1860, Deer Isle (which included Stonington), where 45 percent of the population was completely dependent on fishing, had more fishermen than any other coastal village in Maine. In 1860, there were 11,375 mariners in the state of Maine—one-fifth of the working population.

Industrialization: "All sails set and the engine running wide open"

At the turn of the twentieth century, wooden fishing vessels were in eclipse, and the rise of steel shipbuilding at Bath and elsewhere presaged the end of business for scores of large and small shipyards building wooden boats. The development of mechanized fishing from steam-powered steel vessels also decreased the labor needed to supply the world with inexpensive protein from North Atlantic fisheries. At the turn of the century on Vinalhaven, for instance, two hundred fishermen in boats were needed to supply a hundred persons ashore processing the fish; shortly afterward, the new technology and economics of fishing reversed these numbers, so that many fewer fishermen were needed to supply a much larger number of fish-processing jobs ashore.

Historian Sidney Winslow reports that in 1903 "the Vinalhaven Fish Co. had the largest amount of business of any year up to that time, having handled between seven and eight million pounds. It had become the largest fish curing plant in the State of Maine and one of the largest in the country." The report of the commissioner of Sea and Shore Fisheries for the same year, however, complains that the "salt fishery has generally been most unprofitable and discouraging to owners and fishermen alike." In contrast, the commissioner writes: "The vessels which have been in the business of bringing in their fares fresh and preserved on ice, popularly known as 'shack' fishermen, have been successful and made good profits." Although less than in previous years, twelve million pounds of groundfish were landed in Penobscot Bay ports in 1903 by approximately four hundred fishermen.

The "otter trawl," which is a large net (originally sixty-seven feet across at its mouth, depending on the size of the boat) towed over the bottom and attached by cables to winches aboard a steam-powered fishing boat, played a key role in the industrialization of New England fishing. The otter trawl was first developed in England for North Sea fishing in 1905 and appeared in southern New England the following year. By 1912 or 1913, virtually no new fishing boat in Maine was launched without one.

The introduction of small gasoline-powered engines for inshore fishing boats represented another important technological change of the early twentieth century. According to historian Sidney Winslow, this engine was first tried in the Vinalhaven fleet of lobster sloops and was in general use by 1910. "Fishermen were wont to fool themselves with the remark, 'We'll use the engine only when there is no wind,'" observed Winslow. "But it was only a short period of time before we

Sonny Lehtinen at his huge herring "shut-off" near Southern Island, Tenant's Harbor, 1982.   JOHN LAITIN

saw them going to and from their work when there was a good breeze, with all sails set and the engine running wide open."

Engines dramatically increased the catch of individual fishermen by increasing their effective fishing range. The mechanization of groundfishing not only increased vessel size and range, but the newly powered boats could also be rigged with otter trawls, which would eventually become so effective that whole populations of cod, haddock, flounder, and other groundfish could and would be eliminated from many fishing grounds. Improvements in refrigeration and cold storage around the turn of the century also spelled the beginning of the end for the salt fish trade. Consumers preferred fresh fish over salt fish if given the choice, and the appearance of the railroad in midcoast Maine during the second decade of the twentieth century gave impetus to the emergence of the fresh fish market.

Bert Dyer:

In the 1930s, hake would go for two cents a pound. Clyde [Bickford], he had a fish factory in Vinalhaven, and he'd put them into fish cakes and fish hash. You know, they'd fillet them and then they had potatoes and mixed them in. We'd go get ten thousand pounds for two hundred dollars and we'd think we'd raised hell with 'em. Christ, the other day I see hake is up around eighty to ninety cents a pound.

You could count on it every year, just as regular as could be. I don't know if it will ever be the same. If the farmers and fishermen can't make a go of it, who the hell is going to feed us? We can't eat plastic eggs. Plastic fish. You can't make a fisherman overnight. That's for goddamn sure.

I hate to see it go to hell like this.

The Groundfish Industry "Takes Care of Itself," 1900–08

The commissioner's report for the Sea and Shore Fisheries of Maine in 1907–08 states with evident satisfaction, "It has not been necessary for the State to pass any protective laws in reference to these deep-sea fish. The industry has heretofore taken care of itself." The biennial report describes the appearance in Portland of "two large steamers which have operated for the past three years and have beaten the world's record catching groundfish. It was thought at first that this method of catching fish would be disastrous to the fishing grounds, but after ten years of continuous work in winter and summer on the grounds, getting the largest catches within the last three years, the question in the State is open for discussion."

The pressure behind the increase in fishing power, according to the commissioner, came from the processors. "Many dealers say the market really needs this fleet as they can depend upon their coming to market as often as every week no matter what the weather may be, but time will solve the problem probably better than any tribunal now in session," wrote the commissioner. Time indeed.

Harvesting the Spawning Grounds

In 1918, the commissioner of Sea and Shore Fisheries issued a plea during a time when, according to him, "the industry is in a flourishing condition" that the industry and legislature "not disregard the urgent need of intelligent restrictions . . . [for] the protection of cod in the spawning season." The commissioner wrote: "It is a well established fact that during the spring months large cod heavy with spawn seek the bays and rivers on the coast of Maine to spawn, at which time the gill net fishermen capture them in large numbers."

One of Casco Bay's groundfishermen, Willie Spear, described the shoreward surge:

Old-timers always said, "Everything has to come to the shore to spawn." Sometime around Easter Sunday, the cod used to show up. That was because Easter Sunday comes on the first Sunday after the first full moon after the Spring Equinox. So it's because of the moon that you start to see those fish. Where the water temperatures are right and the bottom is right, that's where you'd find them. Anytime from the first of March they begin to congregate. And you could follow them right up in. The eggs and milt would be less and less as the fish got closer to shore. The old-timers said that in the old days they'd work themselves up into Casco Bay . . . off here, the fish would run west and northwest up into shallow water. By June, off Cape Elizabeth, the eggs and the milt would become less and less as they moved back out of the bays.

In shoal water the tides run hard and the water is rough. These conditions tend to maximize fertilization rates among the large number of individuals assembling to spawn. In migrations from winter feeding grounds (in the deep basins of the Gulf of Maine) to shoreside spawning grounds, where the cod aggregate into bigger and bigger schools, the fish don't necessarily follow the bottom but swim in horizontal planes of uniform temperature and density.

The report of the Sea and Shore Fisheries Department for 1913–14 makes reference to "a special law prohibiting netting for codfish at the mouth of the Sheepscot River. The purpose of the law is to prevent the destruction of female cod, which school in large numbers going up the Sheepscot River to the spawning beds. For some unknown reasons this locality seems to be the only known point where large numbers of cod are collected at one time for this purpose."

Apparently, other inshore spawning grounds had not yet been discovered by fishermen. A few years later, however, the commissioner's report for 1915–16 suggests that this situation was beginning to change: "The industry promises to increase from year to year, as new grounds are being discovered all along the Maine coast."

The completion of the Maine Central Railroad in 1920, connecting Rockland and midcoast Maine to Boston and New York, greatly expanded the fresh fish market. Spawning cod had been avoided by the salt-cod fishermen because their flesh was inferior and harder to dry, in part because they were caught earlier in the season when the weather was less favorable. Rather suddenly after the advent of the railroad, the spawning runs of fish close to shore, far up the estuaries, and around the shores of islands, began to be targeted by groundfishermen, with predictable results. Perhaps the only surprising thing is how long it took for the individual spawning runs to be located and fished to commercial extinction.

Technological innovations brought newer, larger boats into the fishery, and by 1930 the commissioner's recommendation to the legislature was to exhort Maine's fishing industry to "get on the bandwagon" and emulate other states (he was primarily talking about Massachusetts and Rhode Island) where "the fisheries are caught in a new tide of vessel building, vessel modernization and replacement, plant construction and modernization and inspired merchandizing." In other words, gear up and go farther and harder offshore to find the concentrations of fish to supply shoreside plants.

Like an accomplished politician, the commissioner also noted that the "otter trawl, a blessing to the industry because of its efficiency, is a necessary form of harvesting, but under the present form of operation causes the waste of hundreds of thousands of pounds of small, unmarketable fish. We believe that the adoption of a regulation allowing no boats to use a mesh of less than four and three-quarters inches in otter trawling in Maine waters is worthy of consideration." (The first regulations on mesh size in Maine waters were not adopted until 1978, however; they specified a five-inch mesh size for otter trawl nets.)

Nevertheless, by the 1930s there were clear signs that the fleet had grown too large in relation to the capacity of the local stocks to sustain themselves. In 1934, Maine's commissioner of Sea and

Shore fisheries reported: "[It] is an established fact that most species of groundfish are growing scarcer in our bays, harbors and inlets."

THE TWO-HUNDRED-MILE LIMIT

On a clear day you can see two hundred miles out to sea. Well, not quite, but once Congress passed the Fisheries Conservation and Management Act in 1976, known as the Magnuson Act or the Two-Hundred-Mile-Limit Law, over the bitter protests of powerful West Coast fishing interests and the strenuous opposition of Secretary of State Henry Kissinger, the outlook for Maine fishermen seemed a lot brighter.

Twenty years earlier, when American attention was riveted on producing meat and potatoes from the plains of the West, huge foreign fleets moved into the New England fishing grounds. The valuable offshore banks were targeted by large, efficient, subsidized, and—most important—unregulated foreign fishing vessels. The Gulf of Maine haddock catch had averaged forty-eight million pounds annually between 1917 and 1961. By 1965, after foreign fleets began pulse fishing on stocks on Georges Bank and in the Gulf of Maine, landings had reached one hundred and fifty million pounds, the highest on record.

Shortly after the appearance of the foreign effort, however, the catches began to decline. Cod landings in Maine, which peaked at more than fifty million pounds in the mid- to late sixties, declined to a paltry thirteen million pounds by 1973. And the herring industry, already suffering from declining domestic demand, suffered year after year of poor catches. The 1970 catch of thirty-six million pounds of herring was the lowest since 1938. The voracious appetites of the offshore fleets, which could seine up whole age classes, were the obvious culprits. Between 1965 and 1975, three hundred mostly Eastern European vessels circled through the Gulf of Maine or perched on Georges Banks and fished up more than three hundred and ten million pounds of fish a year, almost twice the average catch of the previous half century. Factory ships six hundred feet long processed half a million pounds of fish per day, which the refrigerator ships loaded alongside and carried back to Eastern Europe.

With a suddenness that surprised many of those who follow national political events, Congress began to heed the warnings about the fate of these historic fishing grounds and the moribund state of New England's fishing fleet. The resulting Magnuson Fisheries Conservation and Management Act of 1976 extended America's exclusive economic zone in coastal waters from twelve to two hundred miles from shore. With passage of the law, a new era opened for American fishing, especially in New England.

Willie Spear, Cousins Island:

A friend of mine and I bought a beat-up dragger in 1977 and converted it for gillnetting and we groundfished for pollock. Our trial by fire was to start in the winter in a small boat. Fished ever since then. I don't ever regret going groundfishing. I had a chance to see the spring schools and the fall runs of fish. I will never get over seeing them so close to shore, the size and amount of them. That's what fishing was all about. To see the codfish and haddock. Experiences you can never, ever replace. I thought fishing was supposed to be like that. After that we had to keep putting more nets on. And the handwriting was on the wall. We filled this boat I don't know how many times with pollock in the fall. In November and December. One year we almost lost our boat with so many fish in it.

I knew other fishermen who geared up to take advantage of the two-hundred-mile limit. One of them was Jim Salisbury, a fisherman from Pigeon Hill near Petit Manan Point, whom I watched build a new boat.

A fifty-foot gillnetter ran aground on Heron Neck Ledge returning at night from three days of fishing off-shore in 1991. It was successfully refloated at high water.   S. HEDDERICG

Fishing with Computer Chips: Launching the JESSE, April 7, 1979

From an assortment of itinerant boatbuilders and Bar Harbor fishermen, Jim Salisbury assembled a crew to lay up the steel frames and hull plates of the JESSE, a sixty-foot stern dragger. No naval architect, no detailed plans, not even a boat shed to get out of the winter wind that bit like a driven nail to the bone. In early spring, when Jim's wife, Donna, broke the champagne bottle across JESSE's high bow and all the electronics were hooked up, Jim went groundfishing. After a decade of lobstering, Jim yearned to fish farther out, to comb the dark shadows of underwater pastures for a more raw, less certain kind of living than tending gear inshore would provide.

Shortly after the launching, I stood in the pilothouse with Jim as he showed me the phalanx of technology that would get him around and over the fishing banks. In addition to CB and VHF radios, Fathometer, and twenty-four-mile radar set that were all beginning to be standard features on fishing boats by then, Jim had installed a Loran C receiver, which monitors radio frequencies from shore towers to give boats precise triangulated readouts of their location. Accurate to within fifty feet, Loran technology meant that Jim could return to any fishing spot where he had previously had success with a precision that had been virtually impossible a few years earlier.

The screen from which I could not take my eyes was a new scanning sonar device. At the time few boats had them, because the early models were

very expensive, driven by a pricey color computer chip that has since become inexpensive and commonplace. As Jim fired up the scanner and punched some buttons, the split screen showed a view of both the midwater column—whatever slice of depth he chose—and the profile of the bottom underneath.

As we steamed out to test the scanner, the profile of the bottom changed, showing details of marine environments I'd only imagined before. Rocks and ledges and boulder fields, where expensive nets could be torn to pieces, were plainly visible. So were extensive flat expanses of bottom "plain," where long tows could be set up. From the density of the return signal, Jim could tell whether the bottom was mud, sand, gravel plain, or hard broken ledge. And from his knowledge of fish behavior, Jim knew what species he could expect to catch in each habitat. Even more amazing was the ability of the sonar scanner to "see" schools of fish. From the color monitor display an experienced captain could know with reasonable certainty what species he was looking at. By cross-referencing the sonar scanner with Loran C coordinates, he could find and return to even relatively small fishing grounds. It was like the children's story of the Chinaman who could swallow the sea and then roam the sea floor to scoop up its stranded denizens.

That day I had a vague premonition that fishing in the Gulf of Maine and out on Georges Banks would never be the same again. With the kind of technological sophistication that was at hand, there could simply be no place left for fish to hide. Everyone was impressed with the way Jim had harnessed a deep knowledge of fish ecology with the technological innovation, but we were all blind to the approaching calamity. I could sense the closing of the ocean frontier, but I couldn't see it. One should always listen to those inner voices.

The number of groundfishing boats in New England waters doubled from 650 in 1978 to 1,021 in 1984. By 1988, fishermen were spending 65 percent more days fishing than they were a decade earlier, but their catch was 25 percent smaller. In the mid-1990s, the federal government began buying back boats that it had earlier provided subsidized loans to help build.

The Tragedy of the Commons: Get Them Before Someone Else Does

By the late 1970s, with generous government-subsidized loans for bigger boats equipped with the latest technology, New England fishermen and sons of fishermen as well as those next door in Atlantic Canada who had passed their own two-hundred-mile law were eager to reclaim their rights to the rich fishing grounds within the Gulf of Maine and on Georges Bank. Boats that had rusted and rotted during the grim decade when subsidized foreign fishing fleets had driven the New England fleet to its knees were replaced with bright, new, larger, heavier, more powerful vessels that slid down the ways and went to sea.

Willie Spear:

We fished the way we always had. . . . Some of us tried to conserve, tow a five-and-a-quarter-inch cod end, but the philosophy was, if you left some fish behind, someone else was going to take them. You could be a conservationist, but the next guy was going to take them. You knew that you were taking more than were allowed to spawn. As fish became scarcer, they were farther from shore. We put on polyvalent doors shaped liked a jet wing so we could catch them. You could see as your effort went up, the catches went down.

But by 1984 the groundfish were disappearing.

After a few years of living under the two-hundred-mile limit, Maine fishermen were told by federal fisheries biologists that they, too, were capable of overfishing the resource. The traditional enmity between domestic fishermen and biologists, which had been buried while the biologists made their case against the foreign fleets, quickly resurfaced when cod quotas were set in 1978. The honeymoon had been brief. Many fishermen had made substantial investments in new gear and boats, and the New England fishery had experienced its first good years in decades. The groundfish quotas could hardly have been timed to be more painful and unpopular. While everyone argued, the resource slid inexorably downward.

THE COD END

I met Ted Ames somewhere along the Stonington waterfront in the 1980s. He was president of the Maine Gillnetters Association at the time, and I had listened to him at all kinds of public and private forums passionately urging the adoption of an increased mesh size in the cod ends of otter trawl nets in the Gulf of Maine. No one really gave him the time of day; fishermen in the western Gulf of Maine and southern New England said it would penalize them unfairly because of the nature of their fishery, in which smaller school fish predominate. And government scientists insisted that a six-inch mesh size wouldn't make any real difference in the spawning stock.

Ted Ames:

We were fishing on pretty local runs in various bays as well as right down the coast. We fished out each one as we came along. We ended up being a lot more mobile than the fish. Once everyone cleaned up local stock . . . the little guys had to get out of business and the big ones joined the parade to the next bay to do the same thing all over again. Eventually we ran out of new places to strip. We all did our share of it.

You could see that you were damaging the fishery, but I don't think that we as fishermen—and those before us, as far as that goes—really understood what a toll we were taking on the whole system. By the end of it we were fishing spawning areas, nursery areas. It didn't matter where—if there was a fish there, we caught it.

When Newfoundland's cod fishery was shut down in June 1996, Ames's warning took on new urgency. With the help of the Maine Gillnetters Association, the Island Institute brought a speaker from Newfoundland to Maine to tell us what had happened. Cabot Martin, who headed the Newfoundland Inshore Fishermen's Association, spoke with fishermen's groups along the coast of Maine, describing the sense of immense cultural despair that had gripped his island, "a black hole in the map of hope," comparing Newfoundlanders without cod to the Plains Indians without buffalo.

Soon thereafter the Island Institute began working with Ames to collect information on the inshore cod grounds of the bays of Maine, where cod had begun to disappear in the 1930s.

Ted Ames:

Nobody has ever recorded where the inshore spawning grounds for cod were. There were just a couple of historical references, one by Goode in 1880, the other by Walter Rich in the 1920s. Neither talked about spawning grounds or identified where they were. So I began to interview older fishermen to find out where they had found ripe or spawning cod inshore. Those of us who fished knew or knew people who knew where they were. A lot of people I talked to were seventy, eighty, or ninety years old. A great many of the spawning grounds have long since been wiped out. But I was able to document eleven hundred square miles of spawning area in the coastal waters of Maine.

For the past half century the problem between fishermen and scientists has persisted because of the inability of fisheries scientists to predict what will happen to fish populations if conservation measures are undertaken. Instead, scientists base their recommendations on the numbers of fish that can be caught, which they call "fishing mortality," whereas fishermen have always said that you cannot know how many fish can be caught because you can never count them convincingly enough to know how many fish there are in the sea from season to season, never mind year to year. Fisheries biologists are required by law to estimate stock size over the entirety of a species' range and are therefore mostly uninterested in the local variations and circumstances that are a fisherman's stock in trade. Until fisheries biologists and fishermen are able to find a common language based on an understanding of the ecological relationships among all the major species of fish and the unique environment in the Gulf of Maine, fisheries management plans seem doomed to fail.

Bert Dyer, Carvers Harbor:

Last summer we set six tubs of trawl. We went clear to Platts that time. Couldn't believe it. Should've gotten a boatload. Christ, we had, what, a hundred and fifty pounds of hake—two, three little codfish. I talked with a Vinalhaven boy and he goes out on a big boat out of Portland. He said they go on a ten, twelve-day trip, right 'round the clock, twenty-four hours a day. Great big net. He says sometimes after six hours they haul back and they have four hundred pounds in the net. Ten, twelve days at sea and they come in with only eighteen thousand pounds. Imagine that.

Why they used to come in, Christ, with a hundred thousand pounds. They're just draining them, that's all. It's too bad. I don't know what's going to take place. Honest to God.

FISHERMEN AND ISLANDERS

It's hard to know what motivates a man (and precious few women) to give up the relative comforts of terrestrial life, no matter how marginal, and venture out beyond the certainties of the known world, beyond the point where anyone is able to help you if you should need it, to float on the surface tension of the sea, to cast nets down for ancient kinds of life, to be a tiny speck of effort within the immense and lonely expanse of the ocean. All we know is that our earliest ancestors set out upon the ocean to pursue fish great and small before recorded civilizations first rose, before adventurers left records of their exploits in legend, and well before farmers turned forests and valleys into tamed landscapes.

Willie Spear:

Fishing has been good to me. . . . If you start out in your own boat as a kid, it's over with; you can't ever work for someone else. It's hard work, but it's better than working for someone else. You're the master of your own fate.

Most fishermen, it seems, couldn't live ashore even if they wanted to. Fishing is not so much a calling as a command. It appeals to those who are closer to their edges than their centers; it appeals to souls in flight, to the restless, rootless waywardness in our being, to those outlawed, to those whose view of life is confirmed again and again by the acute sensitivities called forth from places of gray convexity far offshore where nothing is solid, nothing is certain, where everything is floating, and the void of disaster and tragedy is near at hand. The Arctic tundra in its elemental winter white is perhaps the closest terrestrial equivalent to the pelagic fishermen's world.

Regardless of circumstance, fishermen and islanders, on a profound level, share a world view. Here are people drawn to the farthest edges of life. Islanders are inhabitants of an "ecotone," which ecologists define as the zone where two different habitats intersect or merge. These places are always richer in ecological terms, supporting a higher diversity of species than either of the two habitats support individually. Islands and their islanders circumscribe the narrow, shifting boundary between the terrestrial and marine ecosystems.

Fishermen patrol the ultimate ecotone, where solid footing is shrunk down to the hopelessly enclosed boundaries encompassed within the gunwales of a small vessel. If this familiar life fails to provide sustenance, or fails spiritually, as today it almost must, fishermen are cast ashore, like Jonah expelled from the belly of the whale. Those who fail to keep fishing are souls adrift, and often drown in what little hope may have driven them offshore in the first place.

9

The Gulf of Maine:
The System in the Sea

*A Vinalhaven lobsterman was asked by an incredulous yachtsman how he navigated in
the fog amid the rock-strewn ledges of the region. Had he memorized where they all are? "No,"
said the lobsterman, "I don't know where all the rocks are. I just know where they ain't."*

GETTING THE BIG PICTURE

The Gulf of Maine region, with its submerged banks, long and intricate coastline, large river
systems, islands, and estuaries, constitutes a globally significant marine ecosystem. In this "sea within
a sea," a vast pasture of plant and animal plankton blooms annually and is carried around the thirty-
six thousand square miles of the gulf on a unique counterclockwise gyre. This gyre underlies the
gulf's most fundamental processes and drives its marine productivity. For the first time ever, we are
beginning to see the system as a whole.

The Gulf of Maine's thirteen-thousand-mile coastline cradles an archipelago of more than six
thousand islands, which collectively serve as critical habitat for a wide variety of commercially
important marine species as well as marine mammals, seabirds, and other wildlife.

Ten large river systems, draining sixty-nine thousand square miles of forests, farmlands, and
cities, annually pour billions of gallons of sediments laden with nutrients and pollutants into two
dozen major estuarine embayments where virtually all of the region's islands are located. These
embayments stretch from Massachusetts Bay and Great Bay in the western Gulf of Maine to Casco,
Penobscot, Machias, Passamaquoddy, Chignecto, Minas, and Saint Mary's bays to the east. They are
stirred by some of the largest tides in the world.

Estuaries are generally considered to be among the most productive of the world's ecosystems,
and estuarine embayments that are partially enclosed and full of islands are even more so. These
areas are more productive and diverse, in fact, than either the open ocean or the freshwater systems
that enter them. It would be no exaggeration to say that in terms of their inherent biodiversity and
fundamental productivity, the island embayments that so completely characterize the Gulf of Maine
are its coral reefs and rain forests.

In four hundred years of our ancestors' stewardship, these treasure-houses of productivity and

*Opposite: South Sugarloaf Island, at the mouth of the Kennebec River, is a major estuarine area in the Gulf
of Maine where fresh- and salt-water currents converge.*
COURTESY MAINE DEPARTMENT OF INLAND FISHERIES AND WILDLIFE

diversity have been treated roughly, and the past fifty years have been the worst. We are just beginning to appreciate the extent of the damage done.

FATHER OF OCEANOGRAPHY: HENRY BRYANT BIGELOW

If we are beginning to see the big picture in the Gulf of Maine, it is because we have the benefit of pioneering visionaries such as Henry Bryant Bigelow, who almost single-handedly described the complex interconnections between the physical and biological oceanography of the gulf in the early decades of the twentieth century. From the deck of his fishing schooner and research vessel, GRAMPUS, and subsequently as founder of the Woods Hole Oceanographic Institution, Bigelow spent half a lifetime following current bottles around the Gulf of Maine, sampling the temperature and salinity of different water bodies, towing nets around this vast inland sea, and talking with fishermen, trying to understand how physical oceanographic conditions related to where fishermen caught different species of fish. The information that Bigelow gathered in our backyard, beginning a hundred years ago, on the plankton, fish, and hydrography of the gulf, is still generally referred to as the foundation of modern oceanography. You could say that a great deal is known about the Gulf of Maine, but at the same time you might wonder how we could have so badly mismanaged its resources.

THE GYRE

Henry Bigelow's current bottles slowly traced what is now called the Scotian Current, an offshoot of the Arctic-born Labrador Current, as it enters the eastern part of the Gulf of Maine where Browns Bank and the Scotian Shelf extend far offshore. At the inner edge of Browns, the Scotian Current merges with continental slope water that has surged through a narrow entrance into the Gulf of Maine known as Northeast Passage and then descends into the deep basins around Cape Sable and Saint Mary's Point, at the mouth of the gulf. Then the rotation of the earth begins deflecting the Scotian current, now combined with deep slope waters. All around this spinning gyre, tidal currents driven by the moon intersect these other deeper ocean currents, sometimes deflecting them, sometimes amplifying their effects. At the mouth of the Bay of Fundy, around Grand Manan Island, the current loops back to the west in a grand arc to become the Eastern Maine Coastal Current. At this very place, where the ground quickly shoals up, an underwater geyser of nitrogen-rich bottom water makes its vertical ascent to the surface. For fishermen, this is one of the sweetest and luckiest spots in the gulf.

> *June 6, 1982, Crossing the Gulf*
>
> *The steep and following sea lifts and drops SATORI skyward and seaward, skyward and seaward, in a rhythmic trance while a foamy spume knocks against her hull. The vessel's rude passage wakes noctiluca, green luminescence, from a tempestuous sleep. A thousand of these sea-lit fireflies are born in each instant.*
>
> *Somewhere in a shiny onyx sky a new moon hides. Unexpected streaks of meteor fire burn in silence now and again—tiny bursts of creation's glory. I think to myself, this is how the world began. Vision and night vision are delicate and disturbing when no other light intrudes. Large and Little Green islands lie somewhere to port and starboard like sleeping giants. The Southern Triangles, Southeast Breaker, and Collins Rock lie betwixt and between—half covered by the tide and half visible in the tired mind's eye. In this late-early hour, I strain to navigate safely past all this hazard, distrusting the course I have so foolishly laid.*

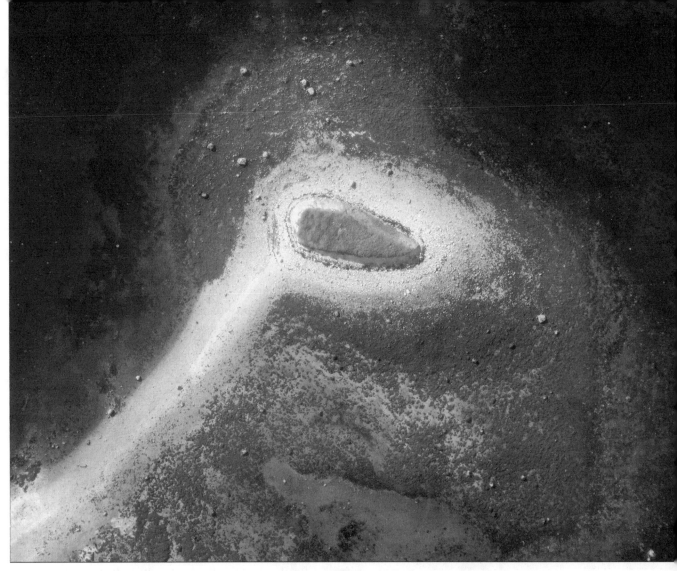

Lamp Island, at the boundary between Blue Hill and Jericho bays, is shaped by converging tidal currents that surge in and out of these deep embayments.

> ***Then, as if a wish were a kindred spirit, the northern sky off the port bow shines with an unearthly glow—a pale midnight dawn of green unlike any light I have ever seen. The aurora borealis, the northern lights off the top of the world, look at first tentative, unsure; then they are stunning, shining shafts of green like girders that hold apart the sea and sky. They burst in giant ionic curves along the outer edge of the sky and light a course through which we must pass. They provide enough light to transport body and soul, enough light to sail safely through these rocky channels.***

The Eastern Maine Coastal Current travels from Grand Manan along the mouth of every bay of Maine, all the way to the western edges of Penobscot Bay near Monhegan, spreading wealth on its southwesterly course. West of Penobscot Bay, the great force of the rivers of the mid-Maine coast—the Penobscot, the Kennebec and the Androscoggin, which collectively drain more than thirteen thousand square miles—combine to create the Western Maine Coastal Current, also flowing southwesterly. The coastal current of the western Gulf of Maine, though not as strong as the current in the eastern portion of the gulf, can nevertheless be detected all the way to Race Point on Cape Cod, where it is deflected back to the east by the northern escarpment of Georges Bank. Thus the Gulf of Maine is an immense gyre of rich coastal waters spinning slowly counterclockwise from Browns Bank, Nova Scotia, to Georges.

Brailing a herring pocket, Rockport Harbor. This picture hints at the legendary abundance of inshore waters.
C.T. BERRY

GREEN ISLAND, GREEN SEA

We tend to think of the oceans as an endless source of food that, if only we could harvest it more efficiently, could reduce deprivation in a protein-starved world with an ever-escalating population. But this is a myth, and a dangerous one. Biologically speaking, the oceans are deserts. With the exception of just a handful of places, the oceans support astonishingly little life per cubic volume of water. The Gulf of Maine, with Georges Bank and Browns Bank at its entrance, are important exceptions. And the islands in the Gulf of Maine are platforms from which patterns in the water can be distinguished; their shores are lenses through which marine biodiversity can be seen.

We gain the first hint of this productivity simply by staring down into the gulf's deep waters from any wharf or boat. In spring and summer, these waters are not the shades of blue most of us associate with the ocean but a dark emerald color—a reflection of the bloom of vast numbers of single-celled floating plants and animals called plankton. They are distributed around the vast basin of the gulf on internal currents.

Noctiluca, Hurricane Sound, June 8, 1977

Last night we put out from the granite wharf in a pulling boat—a cross between a whaleboat and a lifeboat—for a night of sail training up the bay. Almost as if by design, the clouds broke a bit as we cast off, and a fresh evening breeze blew up from the west—the fair-weather winds of the coast.

We held a course north up into the far reaches of Penobscot Bay. The winds played havoc with the remaining low clouds, which scudded overhead like flights of birds. Our watery furrow broke and followed us in a foamy wake hollowed out by the beam and flare of the hull. As the evening grew darker, island shadows crept closely in, and we hardened up on the wind. We began to notice in the wake, and in the splash of surf upon ledges, and then around our hand trailing in the water, an eerie green luminescence— noctiluca—issuing forth from the sea like a phosphorescent light. Like the ancient mariner, we beheld secrets on this moonless course as we navigated by smell and touch among the rocky shoals. The darker it grew late into the night, the brighter the play of light around us, haunting and weird, giving us over to morbid thoughts of committing our earthly souls there and then to the floating light not of our own making.

Understanding the biological richness in the Gulf of Maine is counterintuitive to most of us, because the relationship between productivity and temperature in water is almost diametrically opposed to what we know on land. By and large, the closer one gets to the equator, the more productive terrestrial ecosystems become. It's not hard to imagine that an acre of tropical rain forest produces more biomass (an ecologist's measure of productivity from the weight of all living things) than an acre of Arctic tundra. But in the water, the opposite holds: the closer one gets to the North and South poles, generally the more productive the marine systems become. This is partly because cold water is more physically capable than warm water of holding dissolved oxygen and carbon dioxide, the initial building blocks of all life, and partly because of the availability of nutrients—carbon, nitrogen, and phosphorus—from upwelling currents that converge and collide near the poles.

Most of the world's oceans have preciously small quantities of nitrogen and phosphorus. Whatever the supply of these nutrients in a marine ecosystem, they tend to grow scarce over time, because they are at the mercy of gravity. Diatoms, for example, with their silica cell walls, drift inevitably downward. Floating plants and animals feeding on them as they slowly filter down through the water column bring a portion of scarce resources back to the surface, but it is a losing battle. More and more diatoms eventually find their way to the bottom, where they enter the food chains of bottom-dwelling creatures, or benthos. Vast areas of the ocean are dark, abyssal depths where sunlight does not penetrate; in ecological terms these areas are lost in biological time and space. Because the Gulf of Maine has large areas of relatively shallow water, the banks and ledges— Browns, Grand Manan, Cashes, Jeffreys, Stellwagen, and the northern rim of Georges, just for starters—which are lit by the sun, are pulsing with photic energy while receiving the benefit of a constant rain of nutrients.

Nutrients lost from the ocean surface in the Gulf of Maine are replenished in one of two ways: imported in the two hundred and fifty billion gallons per year of river runoff or carried up from the depths by bottom currents that rise vertically to the surface where two currents collide or where a current hits a shoal or shelf and, like an air current, accelerates up its slope.

In the Gulf of Maine, there are a few large zones of upwelling and extensive areas of vertical mixing where bottom currents rise to the surface to enrich surface waters. The most ecologically important zone of upwelling in the Gulf of Maine is off Grand Manan Island at the eastern end of the gulf, where currents bubble to the surface and trend southwest in a thin band of enrichment that can be detected at least as far west as Matinicus Island at the outer edge of Penobscot Bay.

Grand Manan Upwelling, August 27, 1996

The course that we have charted for our passage to Grand Manan will take us within a few miles of Machias Seal Island, so we decide to dogleg past its famed shores. There might still be a few late-nesting seabirds in the vicinity. When we pass close to Machias Seal's outer shore, indeed the air and waters are so full of careening puffins and the larger, more stately razorbilled auks that the feel of oceanic delight is palpable. We round up under the lee of the lighthouse, where a Canadian flag snaps smartly in the southwesterly breeze, and pick up one of the mooring buoys.

We spread out our Canadian charts and are reminded that we are, in fact, still in U.S. waters, the flag overhead notwithstanding. While gulls swoop and dive for bait, three lobster boats spin in slow circles, their high "Novie" bows characteristic of those found in waters ruled by Fundy's powerful tides and immense fetch.

Outside of the little lee that swirls around our heavy mooring buoy, we

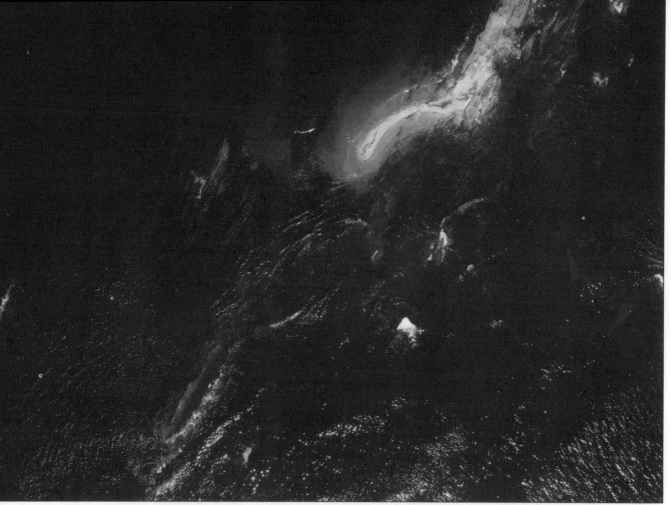

West end of West Brown Cow, Broad Sound, outer Casco Bay. Here westerly currents converge on deep water channels in and out of the bay, feeding plankton, larvae, fish, seabirds, and marine mammals.
COURTESY MAINE DEPARTMENT OF INLAND FISHERIES AND WILDLIFE

plainly see the region's famed tide rips. Standing waves mark the confluences of tides, surging back and forth into the basin of the Bay of Fundy, which intersect other, deeper currents of upwelling waters where nutrients are stirred into a rich broth. We are near the very spot where the upwelling arcs across the Fundy Channel, headed for the flank of the Maine coast. These rips are visible evidence of how the Gulf of Maine's productivity—including larvae from broodstock lobsters, herring, and cod—is spread southwesterly along the embayments of Maine.

Here, where porpoises patrol the edges of tide rips, is a timeless scene, the reverie heightened by the realization that the wellspring of marine production that seeds the bays of Maine begins under Grand Manan's cliffs and connects the Fundy and Maine coasts more intricately than we ever imagined.

GYRES WITHIN GYRES

The counterclockwise gyre in the Gulf of Maine, described by Henry Bigelow, is the region's most fundamental ecological feature, even though it is hard to see. It is most notable and noticeable along the Gulf's inner rim, where it constantly washes the outer shores of the Maine archipelago.

We are just beginning to comprehend some of the finer-scale features around the bays and islands of the gulf. Recent studies by University of Maine oceanographer Neal Pettigrew, collaborating with the Island Institute and NOAA's National Environmental Satellite Data Information Service, show that off Penobscot Bay the seaward edge of the coastal gyre encounters the submerged peaks and plateaus south of the bay—South Southwest Ground and Cashes Ledge—where part of the gyre is deflected toward the Northeast Peak of Georges to form the western edge of a smaller gyre encompassing the eastern Gulf of Maine. The circulation around Jordan Basin in the eastern Gulf of Maine sets up a gyre-within-a-gyre when part of it joins with water from the Scotian Shelf and the rest flows around the Northeast Peak of Georges Bank to set up a clockwise gyre over the center and edges of Georges Bank.

West of Penobscot Bay, the southerly trending rivers—such as the Kennebec, Androscoggin, Saco, and Piscataqua—pour off the land and curl southwesterly to add to the coastal gyre. In summer, their waters are warmer and so add to a stratified layer of warmth up the bays that mixes with deeper, colder waters that well up near the outer island edge of most of the bays of Maine, creating temperature, density, and salinity fronts that contribute to biological activity.

Seal Island Front, June 4, 1983

Situated astride the entrance of Maine's largest bay, Seal Island is near the center of a lucky spot in Maine's immense gulf. Seen from the high cliffs of Seal looking toward the farthest point of the horizon, the sea seems a featureless plain. But we watch for places where seabirds congregate over the water in long, thin ribbons of hovering flight. These places are where seawater currents collide. Known as fronts, they are the most ecologically productive features of the Gulf of Maine.

Just off Seal Island, near the underwater ridges of Haddock Nubble and Minerva Hub, is where the gyre intersects the deep bottom channels of Penobscot Bay. Here, where the turbulent waters come to the surface, the marine predators gather to feed: herring, mackerel, tuna, whales, and fishermen.

Currents, Temperature, and Circulation in Penobscot Bay

Henry Bigelow published his now-famous graphic showing the counterclockwise flow of currents around the perimeter of the Gulf of Maine in 1929, yet very little work has been done in the intervening seventy years to show how this regional feature interacts with the complex of islands, bays, and estuaries at the gulf's landward edge. In a complex embayment, perhaps this is not surprising. But such information is crucial to an understanding of how to manage and restore the gulf's legendary productivity.

Recent studies by Pettigrew and colleagues Deirdre Byrne and Andrew Thomas of the University of Maine and Chris Brehme of the Island Institute suggest how the Gulf of Maine gyre interacts with Penobscot Bay. By deploying buoys in east and west Penobscot bays to collect current, temperature, and salinity data at different depths, and by collecting high-resolution satellite imagery of sea surface temperatures correlated with currents, they have been able to develop a picture of circulation patterns during different seasons.

When outflow from the Penobscot River is high during the spring, a plume of cold, fresh water rides over the denser salt water and empties into the upper portions of east and west Penobscot bays, spreading out along both shores of Islesboro and freshening the upper surface waters by as much as five parts per thousand. This freshwater plume, which is confined to the top fifteen feet or so of the bay, extends farther south in west Penobscot Bay and is discernible as far south as Gilkey Harbor on Islesboro and Northport on the mainland. In the east bay, the fresh river water mixes thoroughly with salt water in the vicinity of Cape Rosier. In fact, the west bay salinity record from the moored buoy is consistently fresher than that from east bay buoy, and shows episodic freshening events detectable at a depth of forty-five feet as far south as Monroe Island off Owls Head, more than ten miles from the mouth of the river. Salinity records in east Penobscot Bay, on the other hand, show that mid-bay waters off the shores of North Haven and Vinalhaven are nearly full-strength seawater, with no discernible freshening effects from river flow.

Pettigrew, Byrne, and Brehme have independently found evidence of a gyre around the mid-bay islands of Vinalhaven and North Haven. This previously unknown feature appears to dominate the circulation in the outer bay and control the exchange between the Eastern Maine Coastal Current and Penobscot Bay. Pettigrew concludes that "should this interpretation withstand continued scrutiny, it would have a major impact on our understanding of nutrient and larval transports . . . and the entire bay's ecosystem."

We are just beginning to appreciate the dynamics of temperature fronts. Identifying the areas where these fronts develop has enormous consequences for fish and fisheries management, because the turbulent fronts, whether they are far up a bay or out near the deep basins, create areas where nutrients are more rapidly cycled and where fish and seabirds congregate to feed.

TIDES AND EDDIES

The tides of the Gulf of Maine are some of the most impressive and complex marine features on earth. Imagine the moon pulling a wave, really a gravitational bulge, westward across the entire North Atlantic. When the lunar wave spills into the Gulf of Maine, it sloshes around the broad, shallow rim of the gulf, rising west to east (high tide in Portland is fifteen minutes ahead of high tide in Eastport). When it reaches the Bay of Fundy, the depth and configuration of this unique basin sets up a harmonic resonance, so the wave is amplified. This basin is like a bathtub; when you slide back and forth, you can get the wave almost to jump out of the tub.

Tides measured from Casco Bay to Mount Desert Island range from eight feet on neap tides to more than thirteen feet on spring tides, when the moon and sun line up to exert greater gravitational pull on the bay's waters. But east of Schoodic Point, the tides range from eighteen to twenty-four feet around the islands of Cobscook Bay and an astonishing forty-eight feet in Minas Basin at the head of the Bay of Fundy.

Although every lobsterman, sailor, and small-boat handler knows only too well that the rising tide on the Maine coast generally floods northward and eastward within embayments, the situation is actually incredibly complex at the local level. Less has been written about local currents than any of the other significant ecological features around the islands, because the situations are so idiosyncratic and difficult to see. But the tremendous number of islands in the Gulf of Maine have important localized effects on tidal currents.

Wherever tide-driven currents surge up or down a north-south trending bay, at the edges, counter currents or back eddies develop trending the opposite direction, similar to what we see in rivers along their shores near rapids. Islands and odd-shaped necks or arms of a mainland shore can also divert currents by their mere physical shape, creating unusual current conditions that can often be seen on the surface. These counter-currents and eddies can bedevil cruising sailors, but have important ecological consequences in altering the directions where floating larvae or the river of nutrients trends or does not trend.

If there is a constriction between two islands or between an island and the mainland, local currents increase in velocity. Known as the Venturi effect, the funneling of fluids increases their velocity. For filter feeders in such areas, this means the dinner conveyor moves by more rapidly, carrying more feed, and creating regions of enhanced productivity. All of these factors within the island-studded embayments of the Gulf of Maine interact to create unique local conditions we are just beginning to see and understand.

GREEN LIGHT, GREEN WATER

Because light rays are more slanted when they strike the earth's surface at the higher latitudes in a place like the Gulf of Maine, they do not penetrate the water as deeply, and because light is restricted to the surface layers, the great concentrations of plants that fix the sun's energy into life are confined to the same regions. Where there are dense blooms of surface plant life—diatoms and dinoflagellates that collectively make up the floating phytoplankton—more of the light is absorbed near the surface. This is known as a positive-feedback loop. More light confined to the surface means more plants, and more plants at the surface absorb more of the light. This interplay between sunlight and plant life in the Gulf of Maine creates living green water.

Over most of the surface of the globe, the sea is blue—a reflection of the color of the sky. But in the rich waters of the Gulf of Maine it is a lively and murky green—the sign that the water is full of food. Only in winter in the Gulf of Maine is underwater visibility anything like that in the clear water of the tropics, where planktonic life is much less concentrated.

Long days at high latitudes can be too much of a good thing for surface-living planktonic animals—copepods, little shrimp called krill, and odd-looking larval forms of crabs, lobsters, squid, and emaciated shapes with bug eyes and big mouths that it is hard to believe will turn into fish. It is during the day that this collection of not-yet-fish, crabs, lobsters, and whatnot is most vulnerable to other species of marine animals with a temporary size advantage. During the free-floating stage that most marine animals must go through, great numbers fall prey to some distant marine relative. But

School of bluefin tuna lie at a fish packing plant in Southwest Harbor, handy to Mount Desert Rock, where tuna have been hunted for millenia.   COURTESY MAINE STATE MUSEUM

the delight of the marine world is that the tables soon are turned, and animals that were prey weeks ago become the predators of smaller members of the same species that had just pruned their ranks. It's as if half-grown rabbits, with a slight size advantage over baby foxes, could have the foxes for dinner.

Because of this eat-and-be-eaten arrangement of life in the water, most of the planktonic animals that feed on diatoms spend the daytime near the lower limits of light penetration and migrate upward to feed after the sun sets. Plankton-eating fish such as herring follow their prey up and down in the water column from night to day, but they are most easily caught at the surface when the sun goes down. Schooling herring or sardines at night disturb multitudes of luminescent animals and thus often reveal their presence to fishermen, who look for the play of eerie green lights on the nighttime water.

FOOD CHAINS: WATER VERSUS LAND

The Gulf of Maine has a more stable environment than that of the land. The seasonal temperature variations in the gulf are on the order of twenty to thirty degrees Fahrenheit, whereas those on land fluctuate five times as much. This causes all kinds of hardships for terrestrial life, but marine life in the Gulf of Maine just shifts slightly, horizontally or vertically, in the water column to find a more comfortable temperature and a supply of food.

For people accustomed to thinking in terrestrial terms, the cyclical nature of marine food supplies is at first hard to grasp. In a few places, such as the Gulf of Maine, all the ingredients are present for an incredibly rich assemblage of marine life. The total supply of food is vast, but it disappears temporarily as cycles come in and out of sync with one another. Consider the tiny, floating crustaceans called copepods, which make up a great portion of the Gulf of Maine's zooplankton. Copepods feed on blooms of phytoplankton and are in turn fed on by small fish. Some copepods can go through an entire life cycle—birth, reproduction, and death—in ten days. An individual female copepod lays fifty eggs, which can produce twelve hundred and fifty individuals ten days later, which produce sixty-two thousand and five hundred in the next fortnight, seven hundred eighty-one thousand and two hundred and fifty in the following, and so on. At the beginning of the cycle, there is perhaps one copepod for every decimeter (a four-inch cube) of seawater, but by the fourth generation there will be five hundred copepods per cubic inch. Soon they exceed the numbers of the phytoplankton upon which they feed, and they die off. If a school of fish finds them first, however, a great finned feast fattens the fish until the next meal presents itself; otherwise, they sink and feed the benthos instead.

Endless tides and currents bring food to the animals as well; the great majority of the creatures just float in opportune places and eat what comes along. Imagine land animals adapted to feeding on airborne particles of food strained out by some sort of terrestrial equivalent of gill rakers, so that they could just move about the landscape looking for wind currents, for floating pastures of plenty. The gaps between mountains or spots near the tops of high hills, where the wind accelerates up and over the landscape, would be places where current feeders could congregate and filter out the food that swept by endlessly. Now substitute water for air, and you get the picture.

Ocean animals have more food available to them than those on land, but they have less need of it, because their stable environment requires less energy to move about. Also, because they are cold-blooded, they have no internal temperature controls that require the burning of energy to generate heat or the evaporation of water to reduce it. They simply move around in oceanic space to occupy temperature and salinity zones rather than staying put and trying to overcome the biological demands of heat storage.

Because water is more dense than air, marine creatures have a harder time overcoming inertia than land dwellers do. No animal in the ocean can even begin to approach the speed at which birds fly or ungulates gallop. On the other hand, most marine animals have evolved to a mass that displaces about the same weight of water, so they can expend less energy moving about. Exceptions to this generalization are the marine mammals, which propel themselves by whiplike up-and-down movements of their flukes or tails, setting an oscillating wave over their skin, thus increasing laminar flow and reducing friction; and tuna, the torpedoes of the sea.

The important point is that temperature and feeding zones appear in predictable places and times in the Gulf of Maine, give or take some here and there, along temperature or tidal fronts and over particular bottoms where upwellings or specialized bottom habitats are located. They may not be persistent—they may break down at any given location during the tidal cycle, for example—but they reappear and reassemble themselves in a way that looks surprisingly like order. Just because processes are complex doesn't mean that simple patterns cannot be distinguished within them.

BANKS AND BASINS: THE GEOMORPHOLOGY OF THE GULF OF MAINE

The sea floor of the gulf descends to more than nine hundred feet in some places and rises to ten feet on Georges Shoal, one of the sand ridges that run northwest-southeast across Georges Bank. In general, the bottom of the Gulf of Maine is irregular and shallow, averaging only about thirty-five fathoms over its great breadth. Much of the gulf, therefore, is in the zone where light can penetrate.

The underwater topography of the rest of the East Coast is much simpler: a submerged coastal plain of varying width that slopes gradually away from the edge of the land to where the sea floor drops off sharply into the depths of the ocean.

The outer banks of the Gulf of Maine, on the other hand, are ramparts that serve as a barrier. Without them, the long tropical fingers of the Gulf Stream would invade the basin of the Gulf of Maine. The intrusion of the Gulf Stream might make swimming more inviting for humans, but it would also make fishing less productive, because its warmer, saltier waters, on the rare occasions that they find their way up and over the banks, have had disastrous effects on fish populations adapted to the strict temperature regimens of Gulf of Maine waters. Scattered inshore of the gulf's outer banks are innumerable smaller banks and ledges.

Fishermen and scientists have added richly to our picture of the gulf and its banks by filling in the details of the underwater topography of this vast marine region. Decades of new oceanographic data from underwater sonar profiles and submersible submarine expeditions have provided images of the gulf's canyons, cliffs, seamounts, and deep basins. These sources of information, combined with fishermen's knowledge and understanding of fish behavior, present an increasingly detailed ecological picture of the region.

Between the deep offshore basins of the Gulf of Maine, where groundfish such as cod and haddock overwinter, and the edge of the rim of the gulf is a submarine feature of great biological significance: a long, sinuous underwater ridge that runs eastward from Stellwagen Bank and Jeffreys Ledge all the way to the Bay of Fundy. Fisherman Willie Spear calls it the Fifty-Fathom Ridge:

> It's just like a wall, and the fish will be up against that wall when they first start to congregate to do their spring migration, I guess you could call it. There's cracks and fingers all along that fifty-fathom edge, you know, that go up into the shallow water—all the way from Jeffreys, and we used to follow them as far as Mount Desert. We would go as far south as the Isles of Shoals and find the cracks and fingers and fish them with gill nets. Just followed one ridge or plateau to the next. Fish like different types of feed, like shrimp and so on. But the cod had their mind set on the Fifty-Fathom Ridge, that's where they would eat. Each fish has its own bottom.

AMMEN ROCK

The most ancient rocks within the gulf are a series of huge, sharp undersea ridges—veritable Katahdins and Monadnocks—called "seamounts" that run from south of Georges Bank up through the central and western section of the gulf. These underwater scarps are of volcanic origin; they are associated with the formation of the Atlantic Ocean basin when the ancient supercontinent Pangaea broke up and the sea entered the seam between the drifting North Atlantic and European continents two hundred million years ago. The most prominent of these scarps are Parker Ridge and Cashes Ledge, Sigsbee Ridge, and Three Dory Ridge.

Fifty nautical miles south-southeast of Boothbay Harbor, a ten-mile-long series of underwater ridges rises abruptly from the bottom of the gulf six hundred feet beneath the surface. Cashes Ledge is one of the most commercially important fishing grounds in the interior of the Gulf of Maine and is heavily fished by gillnetters and otter trawlers. Midway along this north-south submarine ridge is a striking geological anomaly: Ammen Rock. It is an underwater pinnacle, a sea stack that rises to within four fathoms of the sea surface. The underwater topography is so rugged and the currents so unpredictable as they surge around Ammen that it is virtually impossible to set nets here. Ammen Rock is one place left, perhaps the only place, where clues to the original structure of the gulf reside relatively undisturbed; it is a tiny oasis where some of the original structure of the gulf can be viewed.

Videotapes of the environment surrounding Ammen Rock give an inkling of what concerns fisheries scientists. Here are schools of cod and haddock—some individuals weighing as much as thirty pounds—that are completely absent from the rest of the Gulf of Maine and Georges Bank. Here are still found giant halibut and dense underwater forests of kelps and sea anemones, which provide habitat and nursery areas for smaller fish. During a night dive, when a submersible research vessel's lights suddenly illuminate the darkness, swarms of shrimplike copepods are so thick that they make Maine's spring black flies look insignificant.

VISUALIZING THE BENTHOS

During the Pleistocene glaciation, nine million cubic miles of the sea were swallowed up in ice and then spit back into the ocean when the ice melted. The benthic, or bottom, environments of the edge of the gulf are largely the result of these geological events.

Sixteen thousand years ago, a continental ice shelf covered the entire northeastern part of North America. The ice sheet reached its farthest southward extension over a rocky plateau that would become Georges Bank. In the process of advancing and retreating, the ice sheet also scraped and scoured the rolling coastal lowlands that would become the bottom of the Gulf of Maine.

At the height of glaciation, approximately a third of the continent's entire supply of freshwater was tied up as ice, compared with 3 percent today. Then, in a relatively short period of time, all the ice melted, resulting in floods of what must have been biblical magnitude. The water pouring forth from the melting ice fields caused the sea level to rise hundreds of feet along the coast of Maine. As the sea rose, it surrounded thousands of hilltops, ridgelines, and mountains to create the islands and ledges that give places such as Penobscot Bay their most distinctive characteristic. But the ice age also created, just beneath the surface of the sea, an equally distinctive and intricate constellation of ledges, shoals, pinnacles, deltas, sand plains, and gravel ridges that figure significantly in the Gulf of Maine's marine biodiversity.

Seal Island, September 6, 1991, Edge of the Underwater River
We land the dinghy on the sloping boulder beach at Seal Island. When you land, you are at the toe of an eroded vertical bluff that the rising sea is

in the process of undercutting. If you look carefully, you can see distinct strata: layers of boulders, pebbles, sand, and silt. Thirteen thousand years ago, a vast sub-Arctic ice sheet covered the land and sea with a mile-high sheet of ice in which fully a third of the world's total freshwater supply was captured—ten times as much as today. Then it all melted, in the blink of a geological eye.

For several thousand years, water cascading off the retreating ice sheets in the north poured incalculable torrents into the sea and carried thousands of tons of sediments that had been scraped by the grinding ice. Boulders as large as Cadillacs were rolled along the channels of raging meltwater rivers not even present in Alaska today. This is the force of the water that shaped our coastal landscape.

Here at Seal's Western Bight, you stand at the edge of an eddy of a branch of the largest river artery in New England. The ancient glacial Penobscot pours out of the interior of the north and piles its churning cargo of sediments where it is forced to turn against Seal's obdurate ridge of granite. At Seal's mile-long ridgeline, the bottom of the Gulf of Maine rises steeply from a depth of more than three hundred feet to crest on the island's sixty-foot headlands. It was this two-mile-long, three-hundred-sixty-foot vertical escarpment that turned the powerful Penobscot and caught the deposit of boulders and cobbles you see today at the edge of Seal's grassy meadow. It is a powerful place, and it has been for as far back in geological history as we can see. It is, in this sense, a piece of the Pleistocene.

When you climb over the bluff and get on Seal's bare bones, you are struck by the regular architectonics of the island. Its granite ridgeline runs off to the northeast. Cutting across the ancient, weathered granite at regular right angles are narrow ribbons of younger black rocks that have pushed up through fault lines and fractures in Seal's underpinnings. Geologists call them dikes. They range in width from a foot or so to six to eight yards. The effect, especially on the seaward side of Seal, is that huge blocks of granite have been quarried off the escarpment, leaving smooth, vertical walls that would entice and challenge a seagoing Sherpa. The feel of this cliff is compelling and unsettling. The sheer foreground at which the sea heaves gives way to an immeasurable pelagic view. There is no middle ground here. Nothing but rock and sea and the surge piling from deep below and heaving up the cliff to sweep you up and off and out.

The variety of benthic habitats—coupled with the cold, nutrient-enriched waters, stirred continuously in a great circle and oxygenated by intense tidal activity, especially around islands—all factor into the biodiversity of the "sea within a sea."

In part these underwater banks and ledges are the result of glacial scouring, and in part they are the topographic remnants of the rolling coastal plain that was flooded by rising seas. The composition of the shelves and basins varies from hard rock to cobble, sand, gravel, clay, ooze, and shell fragments. Together they represent an incredible variety of habitats for the diverse marine forms that spend portions of their lives feeding over and around them. These benthic habitats play a variety of ecological roles. The biodiversity of cobble and gravel bottoms, for example, is high because so much of their interstitial space is covered with epifauna, little packages of bite-sized food. Many different species of fish congregate near and over such bottoms for spawning.

Some twenty-five species of marine mammals frequent our waters. Twice as many species of seabirds and wading birds feed on saltwater life. There are more than two hundred species of fish and, at last count, approximately four hundred species of floating invertebrates including zooplankton. But there are some sixteen hundred species of benthic organisms; this count is rising steadily as more and more of the sea bottom is explored.

Although our ability to explore the bottom is improving, until now it has relied on fairly primitive methods of sending down small instruments to bring back tiny samples to study. Picture yourself as a benthic ecologist from another planet visiting Earth, say New York City, which is covered by an impenetrable atmosphere. The only way to get a picture of what life is like below is to reach down and grab things and bring them back up—a piece of building or an occasional pedestrian or taxi. The resulting picture would be laughably incomplete. It's not until you can see the pattern of organization—the hustle and bustle on the street and the behavior of swarms of people—that you have any idea of what is really going on. Submarines used to be the only way to overcome these handicaps. Now the cutting edge of benthic exploration is the ROV, or remotely operated vehicle, deployed from the surface and equipped with high-intensity lights and good optical recording devices, that brings pictures, not just samples, to the surface.

UP THE ESTUARIES

Into the Gulf of Maine gyre pour massive volumes of nutrients from the large drainages of the Saint John, Penobscot, Kennebec, Androscoggin, Piscataqua, Merrimac, and a host of minor rivers. In their waters are prodigious amounts of sediments, to which adhere a variety of organic and inorganic nutrients. Suspended in this same water are industrial wastes from towns hundreds of miles from the sea. It is therefore important to see the Gulf of Maine not just as a thirty-five-thousand-square-mile partially enclosed sea, but as an even larger watershed draining an additional sixty-seven thousand square miles. The Penobscot River, for example, flows at an average rate of thirty-five thousand cubic feet per second. But for several thousand years as the continental glacier melted, the Penobscot must have flowed at rates several orders of magnitude greater. If a small stream has enough force to roll a grain of sand along its bottom, the raging Penobscot during glacial melting could roll not only large boulders and cobbles along its bottom, but also immense volumes of suspended sand, silt, and clay. Where these waters spilled into the bays of Maine, their loads began settling out, the heaviest first, then the next-heaviest, and so on, to create a mixture of underwater substrates, from cobble and sandy deltas strewn with boulders to extensive mud plains.

> ### Penobscot River Transect, October 21, 1994
>
> RAVEN *heads north past Stockton Springs to Sandy Point, where Penobscot Bay narrows again and the tide and the currents begin dancing in more complex syncopations. Massive sand deposits line the shores past which glacial rivers once roared. The chart shows a large expanse of gravel deposits left by the river after a rage of water. It is here, older fishermen say, on these gravel bottoms where river and bay waters mix, that cod used to come in large numbers to spawn. They are only fifty years gone, after being here for centuries we know of and millennia we don't.*
>
> *Just north of Fort Point, a headland that thrusts its jaw into the flow of the river and bay, where the water quickens, little patches of foam float mysteriously by like some unearthly flotilla of by-the-wind sailors. Although foam can also be the byproduct of natural biological processes, it is the first reminder that the Penobscot is also a major industrial artery.*

Larval shrimp.   COURTESY BIGELOW LABORATORY FOR OCEAN SCIENCES

Farther into the estuary, the channel narrows and deepens. At Gundalow Cove, the tidal current increases noticeably as the lunar surge from the bay streaming northward up the watershed collides head-on with the river that drains a massive watershed to the north. In the main channel of the river opposite Verona Island, the basaltic cliffs of Bucksport, once a great codfishing town, rise over the Penobscot. Here the tide against the green cans marks the fast water surging past and sucking them down into the current. The last few lobster-trap buoys mark the mean tidal edges of saline bottom water that is pushing the freshwater wedge upstream. An oil response barge is tied up at Champion International's groundwood mill at the narrows opposite Fort Knox, which looms over this strategic location.

Above Bucksport we glide over smooth backwaters past Prospect's and Frankfort's granite outcrops. Here the shores are lined with tawny marsh grasses. The salt marsh complex collectively contributes massive nutrient enrichment to these waters. We begin to see evidence of waterfowl: first in twos and threes and then in larger numbers as winged blurs start up out of the grasses and careen off to port and starboard. Behind the salt marshes are extensive stands of white pine set off by the splendidly colored mixed northern hardwoods. Because all of the original farms were sited on the high ground away from the river, few houses are visible.

THE MYSTERY OF RED TIDES

During the last two decades, extensive portions of the Gulf of Maine and its island shorelines have been regularly closed to shellfish harvesting due to the presence of a species of phytoplankton, *Alexandrium tamarense*, which can erupt in massive numbers. Such "blooms" are called red tide. Although harmless to the filter-feeding shellfish that ingest it, *Alexandrium* causes paralytic shellfish poisoning in people.

Maureen Kellar, a scientist who has studied the creature at the Bigelow Laboratory for Ocean Sciences at Boothbay Harbor, has been collaborating with the Island Institute, oceanographers at the School of Marine Science at Orono, and others throughout the gulf to understand the distribution of red tide. *Alexandrium* has a unique life cycle that alternates between mobile cells of its dinoflagellate stage and resting cysts that sink into the sediments for a necessary period of dormancy. A few years ago, a survey vessel on Georges Bank collected *Alexandrium tamarense* for the first time. In the past half century of intensive scientific surveys, *Alexandrium* had never before been collected or observed. Although red tides are a naturally occurring phenomenon in many oceans of the world, there is little doubt among scientists that the incidence of red tide is increasing. Many believe that this is related to increased nutrient loadings from human activities concentrated in the coastal fringe.

Yet for unknown reasons, Penobscot Bay and its surrounding islands are relatively free of the toxins associated with this organism, even though significant red tide closures affect nearby geographic regions both to the east and west of the bay. It appears that the infrequency of *Alexandrium* outbreaks may be related to coastal current patterns, which tend to create zones that are free of red tide. We know that at the southern edge of Penobscot Bay, a major coastal current, the Eastern Maine Coastal Current, turns offshore. This current may serve as the primary conduit and transport mechanism of *Alexandrium* cells to coastal waters of the Gulf of Maine from the Bay of Fundy, where major blooms occur each year.

Further to the west, satellite images of the Gulf of Maine show how the Kennebec and Androscoggin rivers, draining a vast watershed extending to northwestern Maine and New Hampshire, and whose banks are dotted with half a dozen large pulp and paper mills, and three times as many sewage treatment plants, may become prime contributors to red tide blooms. From space, during a spring freshet, the combined discharge of these two rivers looks like a huge outfall pipe emptying into the Gulf of Maine. Meanwhile in the southern part of the Gulf of Maine, red tide blooms have become increasingly more common where previously they were infrequent events.

Thus the engineer whose job it is to control the effluent of a sewage treatment plant or a paper mill in northern New Hampshire can affect the livelihood of a fisherman hundreds of miles away out to sea, even though their worlds are largely unknown to each other.

THE PRINCIPLE OF INTERCONNECTEDNESS

Today you cannot pick up a newspaper or magazine without reading about ecosystems, but does anyone really know what one looks like? Although nobody can say they've "seen" an ecosystem, which is, after all, an abstraction of the human mind, most of us have a vague sense of what one is. All of us remember the freshwater aquarium of yesterday's science class, where aquatic plants produced oxygen that was taken up by guppies and tadpoles, which, in turn, produced carbon dioxide that was taken up by the plants. Visualizing an ecosystem, particularly one as large as the Gulf of Maine, is a lot more difficult, although the principles of interconnectedness and of hierarchies in nature are the same.

Each species of creature, from the single-celled plankton to the giant whale, has its niche in this undersea world and plays a role in the grand ecological theater of the gulf. But how are all these creatures related?

The problems that confront us are symptomatic of our failure to think of the region as an interconnected whole, as an ecosystem. The principle of interconnectedness has application for the dozens of species of fish that move freely back and forth across the international boundary between Maine and Canada. The regulations governing fishing on one side of the border obviously cannot work without a common understanding of their status and some form of information sharing, if not joint management.

The transboundary stocks of cod, lobster, and herring migrate back and forth across the waters of the Gulf of Maine without the slightest recognition of the location of the Hague Line. The upwelling current that stirs feed into the water column to sustain schools of herring that Canadians catch is the same upwelling that sends larval lobsters into eastern Maine. It is abundantly clear that our maritime communities on either side of the invisible international boundary share gifts from the sea as certainly as island communities in the Gulf of Maine share a common fate. No official recognition of this obvious fact appears to have penetrated our political systems.

> ### *Seal Harbor, Grand Manan, August 28, 1996*
>
> RAVEN *steams into Seal Harbor, the southernmost harbor on Grand Manan's eastern shore. When we round up into the harbor behind the massive stone and concrete wharf, Peter Ralston and I find half a dozen purse seiners tied up at the end of the day. We are surprised by the hospitality of the local fishermen who pleasantly hail us and are willing to let us tie up alongside them, because they won't be fishing tomorrow or maybe because there's only one other cruising vessel in the harbor. The old traditions of maritime hospitality are badly worn in certain Maine harbors, now choked by seasonal passersby.*
>
> *In the mysterious manner of the invisible island grapevine, our friends Janice Harvey and her husband, David Coon, have been alerted to our arrival, and they appear at the wharf within minutes of our tying up. Janice and David are with the Conservation Council of New Brunswick. Janice grew up on Grand Manan, one of three children of the manager of the island's largest herring packing plant.*
>
> *We eat on one of the wharves that has been recently converted from an earlier life as a herring smokehouse. These picturesque smokehouses are fading fast on Grand Manan's shores, as they have in Eastport and Lubec. Janice Harvey says that the demand for smoked herring is primarily in Europe, and that the investment made in new and more efficient technology by Prince Edward Island firms has driven Grand Manan's hundred-year-old smokehouses to the end of their lives, the end of the century, the end of the line.*

THE INTERNATIONAL COMMONS

In 1989, when the governors of three American states and the premiers of two Canadian provinces created the Gulf of Maine Council on the Marine Environment, they produced a map of the region that outlined the boundaries of the shared international watershed. This simple map is one of the few representations of the region that does not impose the artificial political boundaries we have come to accept. Instead it presents one view of the ecosystem that we inhabit with people from different states and nationalities. But we also share this watershed with a large number of fish, birds, and other wildlife that migrate freely back and forth across boundaries. The laws that influence whether these creatures are hunted, hooked, or enjoyed on one side of a boundary or the other must reflect the basic reality of sharing an international commons.

It is increasingly clear, on both sides of the boundary between the United States and Canada, that the natural resources that have sustained human life for centuries around the gulf are preciously finite. In 1993, Canada suspended fishing for cod and other groundfish in the waters off its Atlantic provinces. In the United States in 1995, to protect depleted cod, haddock, and flounder stocks, federal regulators closed major areas of Georges Bank for the first time in history. For more than two centuries the United States has been one of the world's leading seafood exporting nations; but during the last decade we have been transformed into one of the world's largest seafood importers, partly as a result of declining wild supplies and partly as a result of our increasing appetite for the protein fish and shellfish provide.

AN ALTERED GULF

Spencer Apollonio is an intense man of owlish expression, with a passion for understanding how commercial fishing in the Gulf of Maine has altered its ecological structure. Apollonio served two terms as Maine's Commissioner of the Department of Marine Resources in the 1980s. In between his terms as commissioner, Apollonio served as the first executive director of the New England Fisheries Management Council, the unique effort to include fishermen in the regulation of American fisheries following the passage of the original Magnuson Fisheries Management and Conservation Act in 1976, popularly known as the Two-Hundred-Mile-Limit Law.

In the eighteenth century, according to Apollonio's crude estimates, New England fishermen eliminated about seven hundred and fifty thousand tons of biomass by harvesting the great whales that cycled in and out of the Gulf of Maine from their travels through the North Atlantic Ocean. In the nineteenth century, fishermen took out one hundred thousand tons of long-lived halibut along with perhaps a similar volume of "whale cod," the forty- to eighty-pound cod that came into shoal water to spawn. Then in the mid-twentieth century fishermen took out another hundred thousand

Zooplankton bloom entering the Gulf of Maine as a "white tide."

S. ACKLESON, BIGELOW LABORATORY FOR OCEAN SCIENCES

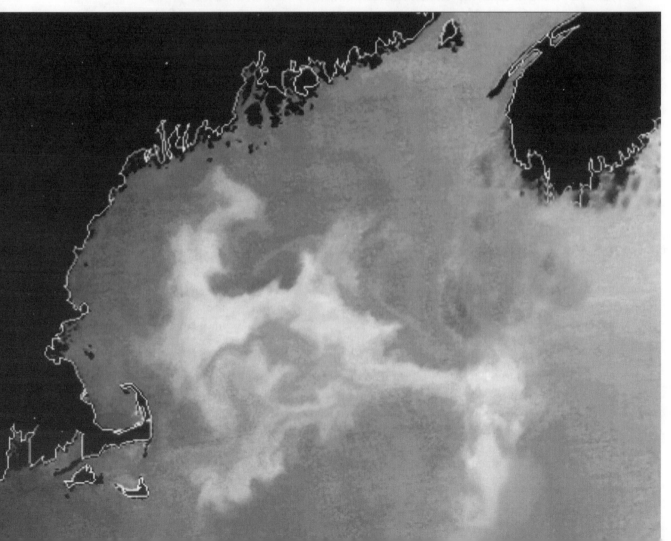

tons of ocean redfish from the basins of the Gulf of Maine. Recently we have eliminated an additional two hundred thousand tons of haddock, two hundred thousand tons of flounder, and two hundred thousand tons of cod. Is it any wonder that we are now down to harvesting the skates, rays, monkfish, and dogfish that until just a few years ago were considered "trash" fish? Is it any wonder that the system seems derailed?

What fishing has done is systematically target the oldest, biggest fish first, then the next biggest, and so on. But it hasn't always been this way. The types and sizes of fishhooks used in longlining and trawling a century and a half ago indicate that fishermen in the Gulf of Maine were once more selective for middle-sized fish; many old individuals were left to spawn while the younger ones (traveling along the bottom underneath the larger fish) were more likely to take the hooks.

The system hadn't completely crashed until recently because of what fisheries biologists call the "compensation mechanism." When mature females are taken out of a population at a high rate, the average reproductive age of the remaining females decreases. It's as if the "teenagers" in the population—the two- to three-year-olds in a heavily exploited population of cod or haddock, for instance—greatly increase their sexual activity. So the breeding stock gets younger and compensates up to a point. However, most young fish make lousy mothers—their eggs are smaller, less hardy, and altogether less likely to produce juvenile recruitment, much less new adults. So the number of larvae can be high and the juveniles few and far between, and before you know it, you're in big trouble.

WHY FISHERIES MANAGEMENT HAS FAILED

In the most simple terms, the science underlying virtually all state, federal, and provincial fisheries management throughout the Gulf of Maine is based on the premise that the only way anyone can manage fish populations is to regulate the harvest effort of fishermen. For practical purposes the marine environment is considered to be constant, so it doesn't particularly matter when, where, or how you fish; the only thing that matters is how many fish are killed.

Another fundamental, but flawed, assumption is that annual fish population numbers can be accurately estimated on a species-by-species basis from a combination of random larval surveys and landings data—that is, by estimating how many larvae are produced and how many adults are caught. Fisheries scientists use these numbers to calculate the spawning stock biomass—an estimate of a fish population's reproductive potential—and then determine the annual surplus of fish that can be harvested. This number is called the maximum sustainable yield. If the catch exceeds a certain level, overfishing will lead to population decline.

It sounds simple, clean, and mathematically elegant. In reality, it isn't. This approach easily leads to overfishing during poor reproductive years, and helps explain why marine fisheries can suffer apparently catastrophic declines or collapse, even in the face of predictions from government scientists that populations are stable or merely "declining" from overfishing. This approach also cannot predict particularly good years, when relatively small changes in larval survival lead to rapidly increased stocks in a short period of time.

No fishermen and few ecologists believe that the marine environment can reliably be treated as uniform. The assumption that "recruitment" (that is, the number of young fish following the larval phase when mortality rates decline steeply) in a given stock is closely related to larval abundance as determined by annual surveys has been questioned for decades. When there are millions, hundreds of millions, or billions of larvae, small changes in the marine environment can cause big changes in the number of young.

An additional problem with fish population surveys is that the sampling stations are chosen randomly from a geographic grid for the purposes of statistical analysis. An obvious limitation of these surveys is the inherent patchiness of the marine environment, where large populations, especially of high-level finfish predators and prey species such as herring, may be scattered in dense aggregations around such features as temperature fronts or areas of upwelling and yet be scarce elsewhere. The fact that the ocean environment is considered uniform for the purposes of a random sample design can lead to errors of plus or minus 100 percent—hardly a comfort to fishermen who are the community on whom stock assessment uncertainty falls the hardest.

Fisheries management strategies must explicitly take into account a fundamental fact of marine biology: namely, that among higher-level marine organisms fecundity increases (often exponentially) with age. A two-and-a-half-year-old female cod might produce several hundred thousand eggs, but a single gravid female cod weighing fifty pounds extrudes approximately seven million eggs over a period of months and months, long enough to outlast any temporary disturbance in the marine environment. Not only is the number of eggs exponentially higher than from younger fish, but older females produce much higher-quality eggs that have a significantly greater potential to be recruited into the population. When you're talking about hundreds of millions, not to mention hundreds of billions, of cod eggs, very small differences in survival rates translate into very large numbers of juveniles that join the population.

Quota management can never work for cod because the quotas can't be low enough (practically, for social reasons) to preserve the fewer older fish in the population that provide a critical reproductive hedge, year in and year out, due to their exceptional fecundity. All fish in the sea are not equal, not by a long shot.

A Preference for Quota Management

Concepts such as "maximum sustainable yield" and "spawning stock biomass" lead almost inexorably to management approaches based on the establishment of quotas. Ignoring the inherent uncertainties in the estimates, politicians and managers use quotas as a convenient and handy "scientific" tool for allocating the harvest among user groups.

Quotas, however, are an anathema to fishermen throughout New England and the Atlantic Maritimes, because these systems almost inevitably concentrate the harvest in the hands of larger, corporate enterprises. The owner-operator fishermen who inhabit the oldest fishing regions in the New World feel that they lose out. In fishing communities, fisheries science is not only not considered part of the solution, it is widely perceived to be the problem.

Problems with fisheries science and management are part of the reason that, in many different regions of the world, fisheries managers have failed to reverse the decline of fish stocks. This failure is especially apparent in complex marine environments such as the Gulf of Maine and Georges Bank, where habitat considerations are of overriding importance.

> *Whitehead Island, Grand Manan archipelago, August 29, 1996*
>   *On our last morning before turning back to the west, we decide to cross the twisting, tide-tortured channel from Seal Harbor to visit the small island community of Whitehead, about four miles to the east. All the other small islands around Grand Manan have depopulated, mostly during the present century. Kent Island has become a biological station, operated in summer by Bowdoin College. Nantucket, Ingalls, and the others are now abandoned. Only Whitehead survives as a year-round community of some two hundred souls, mostly dependent on fishing.*
>   *The day reveals a thickness of fog. Our course to Whitehead will need to dogleg through some treacherous narrows, but the tide is making, which*

gives us some margin of confidence, although we must also be mindful of the ferry running every other hour between Grand Manan and Whitehead. We cast off after breakfast and poke our way easterly. The entrance to White-head Harbor is confusing on the radar; we can see from the chart that a breakwater marks the harbor entrance, but the eerie green images on the radar screen are abstract and opaque. After an hour of peering into a sight-less murk, a huge bow looms up, luckily made fast to Whitehead's wharf, and soon we are alongside and glad of it.

The weir fishing has been good in recent years—"real good," says Brian Knight, a local man who befriends us on the pier and generously offers to take us on a tour of the island in his truck. The weirs here are all named, and one of them, known as the Mumps, caught a million dollars' worth of herring last year. In an era of unprecedented marine exploitation, it is com-forting to know that there are parts of the Gulf of Maine that are as provi-dential as ever.

In fact, Brian tells us, quite a few of his high-school classmates, sons of fishermen, went off to college but are now returning to Whitehead Island to take up fishing. After four to five years ashore as junior executives making $30,000 (Canadian) a year, they're just scraping by. Meanwhile Brian's got a house, a boat with a license, a share in a weir, and, to top it off, a new wife. From his bedroom at night, he says, he can sometimes hear the snuffled spouting of whales rolling in the surge of the giving and forgiving sea. Life, it seems, couldn't be better.

But there is a catch. Canada manages its fisheries strictly by a quota sys-tem, which has been bitterly resisted by the cussedly independent New England fishermen. In Canadian waters, every fishery is divided among a fixed number of fishermen set by the government, and a person must there-fore buy someone else's license to go fishing. Brian, for instance, bought his lobster license for $8,000 half a dozen years ago. His classmates returning to the island four to five years later will have to spend $30,000 to buy a license. College was not just a waste of time, Brian implies, but an expensive one at that. The large seiner tied up at the wharf next to RAVEN *has licenses worth upward of $400,000, which the captain will sell off for his retirement. This is good for the captain, and may be good for the fishery, but a community development model that creates a few wealthy fishermen and excludes nearly everyone else is not a compelling one.*

Canada's quota system did not prevent the collapse of the Newfoundland cod fishery or the Trinity Ledge herring stock in Nova Scotia, although it has met with some success in managing the herring purse-seine fleet. But setting up a system that lets the government, in effect, choose who will be the big winners and losers in fishing communities runs deeply against the egalitarian grain of New England's mostly small maritime waterfronts.

ECOSYSTEM MANAGEMENT FOR GULF OF MAINE FISHERIES

In 1996, after more than three years of legislative wrangling and partisan positioning, the Magnuson-Stevens Fisheries Conservation and Management Act, the law that governs how American fisheries are to be managed, was reauthorized by Congress. Also known as the Sustainable Fisheries Act, the law mandates three significant changes in the way the nation's fisheries are to be

managed. "By-catch" of non-target species must be reduced; essential fisheries habitat must be identified and protected in fisheries management plans; and, finally, a panel is directed to recommend to
Congress how best to "integrate ecosystem principles into future fisheries research and management."

This last section of the legislation was introduced by Senator Olympia Snowe, who in 1995
had just become the chairperson of the Senate's Subcommittee on Oceans and Fisheries, where the
nation's fisheries management policies are forged.

The members of the panel were drawn from a wide variety of backgrounds and included fishermen, scientists, managers, and environmentalists. I was among those appointed. According to the
panel's final report, for the past twenty years fisheries management plans "have been driven by narrow single species management models that take too much time to put together, and depend on
counting fish, which no one can actually do with any degree of confidence."

The panel's recommendations stress the difficulty of predicting the behavior of marine ecosystems, while emphasizing that these systems also have real limits that can result in irreversible
changes when these limits have been exceeded. Marine ecosystems have strong linkages, they change
with time, and their boundaries are open, meaning that energy, nutrients, and populations of plants
and animals usually move through marine systems more actively and incessantly than in many terrestrial ecosystems. Finally, biodiversity is important to the functioning of marine systems, although
we are in the infancy of our understanding of biodiversity's components

Following these principles, the panel endorsed changing the "burden of proof" for managers,
directing them to protect marine ecosystems rather than fisheries *per se*. This means, for practical
purposes, that in the future, marine fisheries will not be presumed to be open for harvest until the
effort is made to analyze how harvests will affect the rest of the ecosystem. The principle of "limited
predictability" in complex marine ecosystems, furthermore, argues that we should "purchase insur-
ance" against unforeseen adverse impacts. Adopting a precautionary approach to fisheries management could ensure that we will also maintain the health and sustainability of the ecosystem.

Perhaps the most notable recommendations of the panel lie in its efforts to incorporate an
understanding of human ecology in marine ecosystem management. Because humans have altered
most, if not all, marine ecosystems in the world's oceans, it will be critically important not just to
learn from past mistakes, but to increase participation, fairness, and equity among all those who
derive benefits from marine ecosystems.

The nation's policy should also explicitly recognize a larger group of stakeholders in the future
of fisheries management than has been recognized in the past, including those of us who crowd our
coastlines in increasing numbers each year.

COMMUNITY MANAGEMENT

The freedom to fish whenever and wherever and for whatever one wants cannot be sustained
in the face of the kind of powerful technology that is now integral to the fishing business. In many
different regions of the world, fisheries managers have generally failed to reverse the decline of fish
stocks subject to heavy fishing pressure.

The New England Fisheries Management Council has repeatedly demonstrated that it cannot
respond to changing conditions in the fishery in a timely enough manner to be effective at the scale
that management can work—the local scale. Japan, with the most intensively harvested and productive shorelines in the world, regulates its fisheries, shellfisheries, and seaweeds on a bay-by-bay basis,
with fishermen's agreements on appropriate boundaries and fishing techniques. The Japanese system,
which acts to protect heterogeneity in the environment, should be an important model.

Community-based closures and locally enforced limits on gear are being tested in the Maine lobster fishery, with its seven new management zones, each with its own elected council. These zones may empower lobstermen to take control of their own fishing and future.

We now know where many of the important spawning grounds are, and we need to concentrate our sampling surveys there to understand better how different specific areas contribute to the long-term productivity of the Gulf of Maine. A geographic picture of these areas already exists in the minds and diaries of most successful fishermen. These fishermen should be given the incentive to capture and record that data systematically and share it in localized management arenas. Because fishermen are already proficient at this, they can and should demand a well-deserved seat at the scientific table that has long been closed to them—and everyone else, for that matter, who was not a biological statistician.

Fishermen's knowledge, integrated with benthic maps made from side-scanning sonar and underwater video pictures, can be a piece of a geographically and ecologically based system of co-management. We will find that such a system for fisheries management will reverse the damage caused by decades of woefully inadequate communication between fishermen and scientists.

Real-time ocean temperature and color data downloaded from orbiting sensors, linked to moored buoys that can telemeter data ashore, will enable us to see and predict the effects of dynamic changes in the water and could become the basis for such a management system. The Island Institute, with funding from NOAA/NESDIS (National Environmental Satellite Data Information Service), is currently testing the practicality of such a system in Penobscot Bay.

Herring on racks at a smokehouse in Seal Harbor, Grand Manan, 1995.
PETER RALSTON

Willie Spear, Cousins Island:
You have to close areas to spawning, you got to let the fish spawn . . . close areas big enough to let fish go through to spawn. You can't have quotas, you can't tell fish to stay away from your net. You can close areas and keep boats out for a while. It's worth a try. Let's try it on a community level. It's do-able and it's enforceable. Anything is better than the federal level. It's got to be better than waiting twenty years. You've got to leave something for the next generation, that's why I'm doing it . . . for my kids. I think with the proper management it will come back. When, I don't know. It could happen again, it's so big. Those fish could come back if you leave them alone for a while . . .

Ted Ames, the fisherman from Vinalhaven and Stonington who worked with the Island Institute interviewing other fishermen on the location of cod and haddock spawning grounds, is restive about what he perceives to be the National Marine Fisheries Service's penchant for putting fishermen into regulatory boxes. But he believes that, among fishermen of the Gulf of Maine, a strong conservation ethic already exists waiting to be tapped, waiting for the appropriate forums for expression.

Ted Ames:

When the local stocks got wiped out, a lot of the people who strongly believed in conservation got out of the business. But many of the rest of us fishermen feel the same way, that you have to take care of the stock, although not many people are willing to say how and not many are sure how to do it. The ethic is there for those who want to make a living out of fishing . . . but for those who just want to get rich, that's always been a problem in every business. What we need is a set of ground rules that holds back the greedy ones just enough so that the whole system can work well, so that everybody can make a living, or at least those of us who are willing to try. The conservation ethic is really just a matter of practical common sense on how to stay in business. Because if you take care of the stock, it will take care of you.

CO-MANAGEMENT: LISTENING TO FISHERMEN

During the last few years, the State of Maine has launched a major initiative (most visible in the lobster fishery but also affecting the urchin, groundfish, and herring fisheries) to develop realistic, effective, localized co-management structures. "Co-management" means different things to different people, but most people agree that it involves integrating fishermen's localized knowledge into management decisions. Logically, such a process might begin with discussions of how specific habitats intersect with the life cycles of certain species. This approach means, among other things, that we must begin to identify pre-spawning aggregations, spawning grounds, and nursery grounds of the Gulf of Maine, mapping them accurately at least as far out as Fifty-Fathom Ledge.

In 1998, the State of Maine banned all commercial groundfishing in state waters for the months of April, May, and June for the next five years. The closure was a huge step forward, covering over 2,900 square miles of habitat off the coast of Maine. It is believed to be the largest fishing closure ever imposed by any state in the nation. The closure was ultimately based on Ted Ames's interviews with older fishermen to locate historic spawning grounds of once prolific stocks of cod and haddock, many of which had been fished out a half century earlier. Ames's data, carefully mapped and published in 1996, showed that over half of the total of 1,069 square miles of known spawning grounds for cod and haddock lie inside Maine's territorial waters.

This single map helped change the course of debate in Maine. It showed that an important part of the coastal stock once spawned inshore. Robin Alden, former commissioner of the Department of Marine Resources, who worked on developing the closures, noted that fishermen know where cod bunch up when they're spawning. "This is a chance to use the same strategy in reverse: protect those spawning areas during the spawning season and allow them to get re-established," said Alden.

TOWARD A SYSTEM OF MARINE RESERVES

No one knows whether the Gulf of Maine's legendary stocks of cod and haddock will come back on their own—just that they haven't. Many fishermen believe the absence of cod is directly related to the abundance of lobster, even though in many localized instances the cod had been gone for decades before lobsters began to increase in the late 1980s. But there may be a connection between increased lobster landings and additional conservation regulations that lobstermen imposed on themselves in recent decades: an increase in the minimum size of lobsters that can be landed, the V-notching of egg-bearing females, and the escape vent to prevent "ghost" fishing.

Still, it is arresting how little we know about the relationship of different stock complexes in the inshore waters of the Gulf of Maine and their connection to other parts of the marine ecosystem. After harvesting these species for four hundred years along this coast, isn't it about time we address some of the basic questions, such as what changes human activities are imposing on the marine environment, and what changes in the marine environment are occurring naturally?

Even to begin to approach such big questions, we need undisturbed "baseline" areas to separate out environmental "noise." We also need places—marine reserves—where big, old fish can hide. We need to restore the natural refuges that protected some fish before technological improvements eliminated all their hiding places.

The Gulf of Maine is a vastly different ecosystem than it was even a scant fifty years ago, not to mention a century or even two centuries ago when thousands of whales and huge schools of top-of-the-food-chain predators roamed it. We will never return the Gulf of Maine to its unexploited condition, and marine reserves are not about creating a "wilderness" in the sense we think of on land.

A strategy adopted in New Zealand, which has become an international leader in the designation of marine reserves, emphasizes a large number of smaller reserves (ten to one hundred acres) based on critical habitat, rather than large reserves.

Outside of the marine reserve boundaries under such a system, management could be less burdensome than it currently is. In such a geographically- and ecologically-based management system, fishermen outside of closed zones would compete with one another, perhaps with many fewer rules than currently exist.

Marine reserves may not be politically acceptable in the short run, but they are the only long-range strategy that will help us unravel the centuries-old debate over how nature affects the marine environment vs. how human activities are altering it. With $250 million in value in fisheries just along the Maine coast, and larger values in both Massachusetts and in the Bay of Fundy, not to mention all the billions of dollars of indirect value to coastal real estate and four hundred years of cultural values, wouldn't an additional investment in reserves make sense?

Malcolm Ledge, June 12, 1979

Walter Wotton, who grew up on and around Metinic and Dix islands, where his father lobster fished, backed down on the spring line to swing the bow of the RELIANCE *away from the granite pier, and nosed up through the ledges on the western side of Hurricane Sound. A stiffening sou'west breeze would come on in the early afternoon as the tide turned, he said, but we ought to get maybe three hours of fishing around high slack tide. Might get greasy, he added, so don't bring too much breakfast with you.*

He pointed to the spot on the chart more than an hour's steam out there, where it comes up steep against Malcolm Ledge and where the tide runs "wicked." There's good bottom at thirty to forty fathoms—sandy, gravelly—where, on a day like this, he says, without too much wind, you can always find cod, good big cod, when they're running.

We rounded up and Walter took his ranges off a headland of Seal Island and the twin light towers on Matinicus Rock, and cut the engine. He retrieved the hand lines he had made up with stout twine, rounded sinkers, and large hooks on long gangions, the way he learned to rig a line from his father. Walter had dug clams the day before, and it was easy to bait up. He

Walter Day, Vinalhaven, mending the herring nets after drying up the pocket.   GEORGE PUTZ

showed how to use the gunwales to feel the line running down and hitting the bottom and then how to take up a fathom or so off the bottom, where the bigger fish are anyway. And he showed how to keep the line moving in rhythmic jerks, letting the sinker thud at the end when your elbow comes down straight, and to keep free of the boat as it drifted in near slack water off toward the southwest.

It was like magic. He hadn't wetted his line for more than a few minutes when he had a fish on the hook, and then two more on the next heave of the line, until we, too, got the right timing, the right motion to set the hook. After the long haul back up, you saw a form take shape, the white of its belly catching the sun's glint. These fish were running four to five pounds. Walter hauled up a nice eight-pounder and one that would run about twelve pounds. He showed how to grab them with thumb and ring finger stuck right in the eye sockets so they hardly moved, then how to twist the hook out before putting them in one of the tubs and quickly rebaiting.

"This is good; we're definitely into some fish," said Walter. Every once in a while, after we'd drifted off this ground, Walter would fire up RELIANCE *and make a slow circle back to the marks, the range between Seal Island and Matinicus Rock, and we'd get back to business. It was like that for two and a half or three hours; one loses track easily when the fish are coming on like that. But Walter could peddle only so many pounds of these fat cod back*

ashore. Also a chop was beginning to build, and adjusting to the motion was harder.

We cleaned the fifty or so fish; Walter figured they weighed maybe three hundred pounds. Their heads were huge; the first third of their body length was almost all mouth and jaw. They need that length of mouth to grind up the shells that are the staple of their diet—the nearly endless supply of gastropods, large snails, moon snails, and big whelks that Walter showed us in their bellies, all finely ground up into a white paste.

"Large day," he said, looking up at the high blue dome overhead and the thin white line of shore back across the ocean.

AT THE TOP OF THE FOOD CHAIN

Bluefin tuna appear in the Gulf of Maine each summer as an interlude in a spectacular migration that includes most of the North Atlantic. The fish arrive in the Gulf of Maine by mid or late June after migrating from the Caribbean and the Straits of Florida, and they disappear from the Maine coast by late September. By far the greatest abundance of bluefin tuna are in the near shore waters where their favored food are concentrated. While in the coastal waters of the Gulf of Maine, tuna feed heavily, especially on schooling species like mackerel, herring, silver hake, and squid. They may also feed on crustaceans or occasionally on bottom fish species.

Starting in 1982, the international body that regulates the harvest of bluefin tuna (International Commission for the Conservation of Atlantic Tunas or ICCAT, generally known to all as "eye-cat") banned Japanese fishermen from the Gulf of Mexico, where their voracious boats had been long lining thousands of tons of spawning bluefin tuna, which, in combination with the increasing international fishing effort, had caused a precipitous decline in tuna stocks. Gradually as supplies diminished and quotas were tightened through conservation efforts (widely considered by scientists to be inadequate), the simple laws of supply and demand have required the Japanese to pay fabulous prices for a fish that on the U.S. market had previously been chiefly used for cat food.

Monhegan, January 9, 1990

Lexi Krause spins his elegant, thirty-eight-foot ARCO FELICE into Barstow's wharf in Port Clyde, loads a few bags of groceries and a couple of coils of lines, and is quickly underway for Monhegan on a mild winter's day. Lexi and his partner, Shermie (actually Sherman Stanley Jr., to distinguish him from his father, Sherman Stanley Sr.), during the course of a few months of fishing last year, harpooned and landed more giant bluefin than any other fishermen along the coast of Maine, and have thus earned themselves an enduring place among fishermen's most elite ranks in the Atlantic: the men who seek and slay tuna with harpoons.

Although modest about the last few years of his success with the harpoon, Lexi is proud that he started out in an era before the hallmarks of the bluefin fishery came to be its highly specialized technology and the astronomical prices the Japanese will pay for certain fish. To put a finer point on the arithmetic, the market has consistently paid a fisherman $30,000–$40,000 for a single fish. However, thousand-pound bluefins are rare, and the average price paid to fishermen might be closer to $15 per pound. . . . Still, you get the idea that honor aside, skill is richly rewarded.

There are two hundred and fifty harpoon boats between Cape Cod and Mount Desert that rig up for the tuna season, and another few thousand boats in the general commercial category (not to mention additional thousands of rod-and-reelers, handliners and other sport fishermen), but Lexi figures that roughly a dozen boats catch 90 percent of the tuna during the short, highly regulated season in the Gulf of Maine. The elite harpoon boats from a handful of Maine harbors form a culture all their own. With over seventy giant bluefin between Lexi's and his partner Shermie's teamwork, the pair had what you might call a good season.

The highline tuna boats move peripetically from port to port trying to figure where roaming schools of giant bluefin will surface during their legendary migration through the Gulf of Maine. During the season, the successful boats must try not only to disguise their whereabouts from each other, but also to stay closely in touch with their sales representatives, who are responsible for moving prime fish from any given wharf in specially designed wooden crates called "coffins," directly to the Tokyo tuna auctions. To accomplish these mutually exclusive tasks, the highline tunamen use multi-channel scanners, a variety of secret frequencies, cell phones, and elaborate codes to discuss where they're at and what they've seen or struck.

Monhegan, January 9, 1990

Lexi's and Shermie's harpoons are no longer fashioned from ash as they once were, but from a deft and secret combination of light and heavy metals —aluminum, lead, stainless steel, and bronze. To see one up close is to look at the ultimate sleek weapon of the sea, adapted from a design as old as fishing itself.

As the fire burns down in the fish house stove, the flames light up the evening's story telling as Lexi and Shermie recall one of the last days of the 1989 tuna season. All the other boats were chasing small groups of bluefin that were thrashing on the surface as they fed on mackerel. Lexi's and Shermie's spotter pilot was trying to coax them away from these tuna, which are difficult to get an iron into anyway, and toward another spot a half hour farther offshore. Over the radio he couldn't say why, but when they arrived at this new area, the sight was like nothing they'd ever seen before. "You could see four hundred or five hundred tuna on the surface, with maybe another thousand bluefin below," says Lexi. "It was just like Niagara Falls: the water was foaming." And then leaning back to cradle his harpoon in the crook of his arm, Lexi says dreamily, "You live for one or two days like that every summer."

The National Audubon Society entered the giant bluefin arena in 1990, after despairing that ICCAT, the regulatory body made up of twenty-three member nations responsible for managing tuna on both sides of the Atlantic, would ever effectively manage the population of this magnificent fish before it became commercially extinct. National Audubon's strategy, designed by Dr. Carl Safina, essentially aimed to go over the head of ICCAT to the international community to try to get the Atlantic bluefin tuna listed as an endangered species under CITES (Convention on International Trafficking of Endangered Species). This provision aimed directly at the heart of the Japanese market and if successful would make the export of giant bluefin from the Gulf of Maine or anywhere else as illegal as the ivory trade.

Fishermen throughout the Gulf of Maine insisted then and now that there are more giant bluefin tuna than the National Marine Fisheries Service (NMFS) says and that American fishermen

Tuna hunters Sherm Stanley and Lexi Krause of Monhegan Island have for two decades followed bluefin on their vast migration through the Gulf of Maine.   PETER RALSTON

have in the last decade already substantially reduced their harvests. Not until other fishermen on the far side of the Atlantic, off the coasts of Spain and Portugal and in the Mediterranean, reduce their harvests down to the level of ours should the U.S. fishermen cut back further. The politically well-connected fishermen forced a review of the science underlying NMFS' management plan for the bluefin by the National Research Council in 1994. When the National Research Council concluded that the bluefin in the Atlantic is indeed one stock not two, fishermen rejoiced along the entire Atlantic coast of the United States including in the Gulf of Maine, but as usual it is really difficult to tell who has won and lost here.

One thing is clear—there will be no respite for the mighty giants arcing into the inshore waters of the Gulf of Maine on their mysterious journeys through the watery three-fifths of our world.

10

Islands at the Ends of the Gulf

When people are marginal, by race, by culture or by geography, that marginality often creates a particular brilliance, because they are restless by virtue of their special discomfort.
—Anthony P. Maingot

DISPARATE VIEWS OF THE FUTURE

The inhabited islands of Maine stand out as examples of an idea at once simple and complex: the special nature of individual islands creates unique island cultures, each distinct and marching to a different drummer. Here the beat is not "bigger is better" but "small is beautiful"; here lifeways are built not around conveniences but around continuities. Islands in the Gulf of Maine are places where nature is not tamed but where human nature is tamed, places made singular by their special emboundedness within the isolating expanses of the sea. Maine island communities stand out as examples of cultures starkly different from those of the mainland, where our special American genius for the marketplace blurs so much cultural heterogeneity.

Sonny Sprague, whose family has been on Swan's Island "since forever," describes island culture this way:

> I don't believe an island is really an island unless it's a year-round community. If it isn't a year-round community, it's just a piece of real estate with some trees on it and some people that come in the summer. Even though they love the place, they don't know what it's really like.

To most Maine islanders, summer people have become an essential inconvenience, necessary because they pay a large percentage of the taxes in Maine's fifteen year-round island communities. As long as seasonal residents build on the back shore, stay out of the fishermen's way, and don't intrude into local island politics, everyone stays reasonably civil, even happy.

That different island communities reflect distinct human and natural histories seems a simple truism. But this is only part of the story. The Gulf of Maine's disparate islands also represent the many choices that island communities have consciously made and continue to make. Island schools are the best place to begin to ask about the future of the islands.

SMALL WONDERS

If Maine's island communities have a significance beyond the small numbers of people who inhabit them year-round, if they are to develop into more than seasonal enclaves served by a highly

---

Opposite: Sonny Sprague (right rear), General Manager of Island Aquaculture Co., Swan's Island, describing the cod and haddock restocking project, 1996.
PETER RALSTON

Small Schools Conference at Islesford (Little Cranberry Island), spring, 1995, with students from the Cranberries, Frenchboro, Monhegan, and Matinicus.   ISLAND INSTITUTE FILES

competent class of caretakers, the question of their future stares out most starkly from the windows of island schoolhouses. Of the fifteen year-round island communities in Maine, fourteen have schools; eight of these are one-room schoolhouses. No other island institution holds more inherent hope and conflict than the island school, where adversity and disadvantage are honed by competition and compensation and where the future is glimpsed and lived every day.

In a sense, the Maine islands' most valuable exports, especially in the twentieth century, have been their children. Since 1900, there have been precious few jobs on islands to which young people can return after getting an education. So the young have left in droves—a deep sadness of island life. If the question is whether this can change in the future, the answer lies in whether island life will become more diverse.

Sonny Sprague:

A lot of our children go away. I guess the ones that get the most education don't come back. I wish it were different than that. I wish everybody would go and get an education, and those that wanted to go, fine, but those that wanted to come back could. It wouldn't hurt for them to go and get an education under their hat—and then come home and be part of the community.

Chellie Pingree, a state senator who lives on North Haven and once worked in the island school, where her three children were educated, puts it this way:

There is nothing that comes close to an island school in terms of the value it can give our kids. I have a firsthand sense of how important it is to grow up in a safe and caring community where people are active in good ways and bad. They get just as mad at town meeting as anybody else, maybe even more so, but people get involved partly because they have such a stake in the community. You don't just pack up and take a job somewhere else. You don't give up when your dump is full. We have to worry about all those things and know that they're our future.

WINDWARD ISLANDS: MARTHA'S VINEYARD AND NANTUCKET

Islands everywhere are the object of dreams, the quintessential crossroads where the "more-is-better" imperative collides with the question of how much is too much. Maine islanders have tended to address this dilemma pragmatically; many of them believing in the reverse of the *Field of Dreams* dictum: if you don't build it, they won't come. This approach works its own special magic to keep things the way they are, sort of, and has been the preferred solution for island planning.

However besieged Maine islanders feel about summer tourism, it is evident that we experience nothing like the kinds of oppression routinely endured by our southern New England island neighbors. If you are taking the ferry to Martha's Vineyard, you cannot park anywhere near the Steamship Authority Wharf in Woods Hole but must ride a shuttle bus from a massive parking lot in the next town north, Cumberland. Chebeague Islanders in Casco Bay have been reduced to similar circumstances. Even Port Clyde, now called Park Clyde by grumpy Maine natives, which serves as a jumping-off point for hordes of Monhegan-bound tourists, seems spacious and easygoing by comparison.

During the height of the building boom of the mid- and late 1980s, one new house was completed each day on Martha's Vineyard. In August, Nantucket is the second-busiest airport in New England after Boston's Logan Airport. During the past four years there have been $2.5 billion dollars' worth of property transactions on Nantucket, which among other things increased the number of lawyers on the island from twenty to seventy-five. On Block Island, where the private ferry plans its timetable to accommodate tourists, a recent meeting with Rhode Island state officials to study the island's transportation problems had to be postponed because the ferry was too crowded with tourists for the officials to board.

Once you step ashore on Martha's Vineyard, the challenges begin to assault your senses. Edgartown, one of five towns wedged within the island's boundaries, supports thirty-one T-shirt shops downtown, and there is simply not room enough on the sidewalks for the mixture of day-trippers, harbor gawkers, and weekenders who repair to this island even before Memorial Day.

August weekends on the Vineyard have reached surreal proportions. Visitors routinely exceed the lemming-like level of one hundred thousand on an island only twice the size of Vinalhaven, where most of my year-round island neighbors feel oppressed by the six thousand visitors the island now hosts during the summer.

> ### Nantucket Island, November 1, 1993
> *With the tail of the season's first northeaster still dragging up the New England coast, I head to Nantucket aboard a little commuter airplane that butterflies its way through thirty-knot gusts of wind before settling down uncertainly onto Nantucket's runway. On the road into town, as we pass the new island high school, which cost a whopping $31 million, the taxi driver tells me with pride, "It has everything." "Even metal detectors?" asks a visitor from the city who is sharing the ride. "Oh, yes," the driver replies, thinking of the little machines people use to prospect for lost coins on Nantucket's*

beaches. But the visitor is referring to the heavy bars at school entrances between which students must pass to be checked for concealed weapons.

Although Nantucket is worlds away from big-city problems, I begin to encounter a pervasive sense of unease that is common to many Maine island natives and newcomers alike, an unease that is perhaps endemic to all resort communities. It is a sense that community members are not in control of their fate, a sense that the quality of island life is compromised by ever more plentiful visitors and the affluent owners of seasonal properties. Not to be in control of your fate is more painful to New England islanders perhaps than to any other citizen of the region, because island independence is still a cherished community ideal, no matter how tarnished it might be in reality.

In fact, this sense has drawn the Nantucket island community together to research the question of how to encourage a more sustainable year-round economy. Everyone knows that the tourist economy on Nantucket is flourishing, but the Nantucket Planning and Economic Development Commission wanted to collect baseline economic data to get a better picture of the year-round economy.

Jack Gardner, who filed the original legislation to create the Nantucket Planning Commission fifteen years ago, is from one of the founding families—the ten "proprietors" and an equal number of associates who purchased the island in 1659. Short, big-shouldered, square-jawed, with a neatly trimmed beard, he seems to have stepped right out of a Herman Melville novel. One senses in him the moral certainty of intensely local, intensely insular blood. He has been a selectman, a member of the planning board, Nantucket's road commissioner, and the hearing officer for traffic court. "We take in between $175,000 and $200,000 a year in fines," he tells me later with some satisfaction.

I want to get Jack's views of the different parts of Nantucket's economy, and together we drive through a bewildering knot of one-way streets that wind through downtown to the waterfront, where Jack points to a few fishing vessels, tied up waiting for the lashing northeast seas to settle. His gesture also takes in the well-maintained private wharf at the bottom of Main Street, where scores of famous whaling vessels and the ships that were at the Boston Tea Party once berthed.

"We lost our fishing industry in the 1940s and 1950s," Jack explained. "It was easier for the boats to steam into New Bedford to unload, and we just couldn't compete. Back then we could have bought Straight Wharf for a dollar, but it was pretty far gone, pretty well washed away. Then Beinecke came along and started redoing the waterfront. Private ownership can do a real good job."

You cannot talk about Nantucket today without talking about Walter Beinecke, the marketing genius and heir to the S & H Green Stamps fortune who reshaped Nantucket as one of the world's preeminent island destination resorts.

"Back in the 1960s, you could buy a house for $12,000 to $15,000," recalls Joe. "But Beinecke would come in and offer $30,000 to $35,000, fix it up as a historical house, and then turn it over for $100,000 to the right people—whoever the right people are . . . He sold to a different kind of people. He was often quoted as saying, 'I'd rather sell one steak than a hundred hot dogs.'"

And sell steak he did. In fact, you could say that Beinecke sold filet mignon in the restaurants, upscale shops, and stores that he systematically acquired and artfully restored in the brick and cobblestone village to re-create a seamless and compelling historic ambiance.

Beinecke was among the first New Englanders to appreciate the enormous market appeal of historic seaside architecture. He also had a deft sense of how to avoid some of the unfortunate downsides of tourism in resort communities.

"It used to be that business would come in, make their money and take it 'round Brant Point by Labor Day," Jack points out. "Beinecke put in all his leases that they couldn't close down before Columbus Day; then he extended it to November 1. Now our season goes through Christmas."

"Tourism is our business, no doubt," concludes Jack pragmatically, but you get the sense that he also has an islander's appreciation of how resources such as money need to be cycled and recycled through an island community year-round.

Despite the booming tourism industry, many islanders worry about Nantucket's intractable problems, such as the need for affordable housing and more reliable year-round employment, especially between January and April, the most difficult season in any New England island community. On Nantucket, a "starter" house costs about $275,000, down from more than $300,000 during the go-go years at the end of the 1980s but still prohibitively expensive for most island families. Even rental costs are a hardship, approximating the rates common in Boston. So islanders are reduced to the "Nantucket Shuffle," which they define as "holding down a couple of jobs, moving around a lot because you can't afford housing, and living a kind of hand-to-mouth existence."

FOUR THOUSAND ISLANDS OF SOLITUDE

The vast majority of islands in the Gulf of Maine, most of which are within the political boundaries of Maine, are uninhabited today. They are simply too rugged or too sparse to provide for the beast that walks upright, who is now only a temporary visitor.

Islands such as these inspire people, perhaps because they are a kind of archetypal landscape of the mind where it is possible to believe that life can be stripped down to its essential qualities, places where nature can be directly and personally experienced. Because islands are so completely and exactly defined by their watery margins, they are often exquisite vantage points from which to experience the rhythms and moods of the sea, to collect the gifts that are cast upon its shores from wherever, and to see and feel and hear the complex interactions between sea, shore, winds, and sounds that work their way toward the inner core of being.

Brimstone Island, August 28, 1975

Beyond the ragged southern fringe of Vinalhaven are half a dozen islands in a group, all treeless and burnished a tawny gold in the late-summer sun. The largest of these is Brimstone, named for its beautiful, peculiar bedrock, which pokes like dark bones from beneath its thin skin of heath. Brimstone's bedrock has been quarried into a billion tiny pieces by pounding sea and prying ice and piled onto a pair of steep cobble beaches on either side of the island where on a calm day you can land.

I ascend the high hill, cross to the outer shore, and start to climb down one of the cliffs toward a little beach. The outcrops get steeper, with only a narrow ledge for footing, and as I edge my way along, face to the cliff, hands reaching for a grip, I run out of ledge at a crevice that I cannot cross. I am about to turn back when I am startled to see a raven staring at me across the crevice at eye level about four feet away. For a minute or so, neither of us moves. Something is wrong; there is no nest in sight, so why is the bird motionless? As I start to ponder, it takes off, beating one wing furiously while trailing a useless broken wing behind. It careens downward like Icarus and lands a few hundred feet out from the base of the cliff, wild, dark feathers scattered in the sea. Within seconds, a gull cuts a tight circle in the air and shrieks above the raven, which is now trying to paddle away with its one good wing. In three more seconds the gull is joined by several others—large black-backs and gray herring gulls—which swoop and stall above their victim on steep downward glides.

The shrieks of the gulls, which soon number a dozen, are met by an eerie cry from the raven, which knows that the gulls mean to kill it. The raven is on its back facing its tormentors; it rises up out of the water, beak first, to parry the dives of the murderous circling gulls. Then two gulls work in tandem; as one swoops in toward the raven, which again arches itself up, the other hits it from the back, breaking its neck. The horror is over. Limp and dark, the raven looks like a spot of oil in the morning sunlight. Its fading blue-black sheen is for a few more moments the color of sea-worn brimstone. The gulls do not even eat it.

So long as I live, I will never forget the sound the crow made to drown out the shrieking cries of the gulls. But it was also without remorse, without any quality except the purest essence of wild defiance. I will carry this sound in my inner ear to the grave.

WORKING WATERFRONTS

The persistence of island communities in Maine in the face of an ever rising tide of cultural homogeneity is testament to another simple truth: the real and renewable wealth of the islands has been and is still found in the water. Without a healthy and productive Gulf of Maine, island communities would no doubt still exist, but it would be difficult to perceive their distinction. At the dawn of the information age, islands could easily become convenient places where writers, telecommuters, and Internet entrepreneurs would be able to out-compete native islanders for scarce resources such as housing, shore privileges, and education. Waterfronts might look better, more picked up, less chaotic than some of them do now, and there might be plenty of seasonal jobs, paying well enough to carry islanders through the long, hard winters. But such islands would be Potemkin villages.

It is almost too easy to predict how well-intentioned noise and lighting ordinances drafted under the banner of maintaining the public weal of peace and quiet would fare at town meeting, and you could bet your left nostril that bait barrels would be strictly regulated. It doesn't take much to tip a community balance.

Yacht Club Cruise, June 2, 1993

A representative of a renowned yacht club was dispatched to Maine to visit each of the harbors where the yacht club planned to moor to inquire about such necessities as ice, lobsters, and shoreside facilities. Burnt Coat Harbor on Swan's Island, a busy lobstering community off Mount Desert, was one of the harbors planned for the cruise, and the representative called ahead and arranged to meet the harbormaster at the fishermen's co-operative to discuss the logistics.

Her first mistake was to get car reservations on the ferry both going and coming, thereby taking up valuable space on the boat needed by islanders, even though the harbormaster had offered to meet her at the ferry and drive her the four miles across the island to Burnt Coat. Off-islanders, unaware of such subtleties, make these mistakes.

On the appointed day, the representative, swishly dressed in her city finest, drove off the ferry, drove across the island to the fishermen's co-op,

The real estate speculation frenzy of the late 1980s led to an ordinance in Portland protecting its working waterfront from incompatible development.   PETER RALSTON

and surveyed the almost archetypal scene. After all the arrangements had been agreed upon, she began effusing about the wonderfully elegant lobster-boats steaming in and out of the harbor, the beauty of the setting, how much she enjoyed being there, how much real estate might go for, and the like. "I just love it here," she exclaimed. "It's so different. Why, even the way you talk is different." "Ma'am," replied the harbormaster, a dignified retired lobsterman, "the only one who sounds different around here is you."

Fishing, boatbuilding, and a multitude of other activities around the rim of the gulf depend on shoreside access. Perhaps only 10 percent of Maine's "working waterfront" is located in protected harbors, and only 10 percent of a harbor has deepwater frontage for boats at all tides and has commercial access to town roads. Thus when fishermen in Bass Harbor, the last waterfront with a working fishing fleet on Mount Desert, were threatened with a large marina, the Island Institute got a call to see if there was anything we could do to help.

Bass Harbor, Mount Desert Island, August 11, 1991

RAVEN *passes under the long shadows cast by Cadillac's barren cliffs as we enter the harbor to attend a public meeting to discuss a proposal to construct an eighty-four-slip marina and "boatel" in Bass Harbor, the island's last working waterfront. The Town of Tremont, of which Bass Harbor is a part, has narrowly approved the marina. As fishing boats have been progressively displaced from Mount Desert's changing waterfronts at Bar*

Harbor, Seal Harbor, and Northeast Harbor, the viability of Bass Harbor's fleet of forty to fifty working vessels and the commercial enterprises that support them are threatened. The precarious balance between Bass Harbor's recreational and fishing vessels would be decisively tilted against fishing interests if such a proposal were approved.

Because all marinas are located over subtidal areas, which are public lands held in trust by the state, any private developer wanting exclusive use of this resource for private purposes must have a lease from the state Bureau of Public Lands as well as approval from the town. Fishermen who buy their bait and sell their catches at the C.H. Rich and Company, which abuts the proposed development, have asked the Island Institute to intervene on their behalf in the state proceedings, as have Bass Harbor's two commercial boat repair yards. The fishermen, along with other local citizens, have organized a meeting at the town hall and invited us to speak.

The discussion over the future of Bass Harbor's waterfront is testy and polarized; town officials who are present have an understandable interest in encouraging new uses for the abandoned sardine canning factory, where the proposed condominium and marina development would be situated. But the fishermen, backed by the harbor committee, develop a case with the help of the Island Institute, demonstrating the navigational conflicts that such a development would create in the limited harbor space.

Although the air is not cleared at the end of the August meeting, by fall the Bureau of Public Lands has ruled for the fishermen in a precedent-setting case, and by December the developer has withdrawn his court appeal. Bass Harbor's working waterfront is, for the moment, secure.

FISHING FOR THE FUTURE

The Maine islanders I know don't dream of a mythical nineteenth-century self-sufficiency; nor are they naive enough to believe that they are all captains of their own ship. Lobstermen no longer peddle their catch to their neighbors. Successful islanders, rather, are masterful at managing their interdependencies. Health-care delivery systems will never be better on islands than on the mainland; transportation costs per family will always be higher on the water than on the mainland. So how will islands manage?

The real answer comes from the island communities of the Gulf of Maine where people want to raise their children and where there is work that does not depend solely on bringing in more people during the summer for an "island experience."

Contrary to the impression left by reading big-city newspapers, the news is not all bad for Maine's working waterfronts, on the islands or the nearby mainland. In 1996, Maine seafood landings were a record $281 million. New fisheries and aquaculture landings have more than made up the shortfall in the traditional groundfish harvest. In 1995, there were record landings for lobsters ($100 million for the second year in a row), Atlantic salmon ($67 million, up 20 percent from the previous year), urchins ($41 million, down from the peak of a year earlier), and shrimp ($17 million— also a record).

Unlike Gloucester or New Bedford, whose fishing fleets depend almost exclusively on cod, haddock, flounder, and sea scallops, Maine has landings comprised of seventy-five different species, reflecting the inherent biodiversity of the marine environments of the Gulf of Maine. Many of those species were considered worthless just a few years ago; today they have gained footholds in the global market basket. Urchins and whelks come to mind, but who would have guessed that we would see glass eels selling for seven hundred dollars per pound, that eelpout and monkfish tails would find a ready market, or that sea cucumbers would become a commercial species?

The reasons for the increases are complex, but directly reflect the global markets whose buyers are knocking at the doors of the Gulf of Maine.

AQUACULTURE AT THE EDGE

No one seriously questions whether the marine resources of the Gulf of Maine are finite; they are, and we have reached or exceeded the limits of sustainable harvests for many species. Demands upon our shorelines for development and recreation, meanwhile, are increasing inexorably. The only real options that islanders have, as they seek to exercise more control over their own fates, are strategies for limiting development on land and capturing a greater portion of the sea's inherent productivity. They must find new species and new markets for creatures still abundant in the wild, or learn how to cultivate species under the controlled conditions of aquaculture.

If diversity is the biological key to protecting Maine's commercial fisheries and owner-operators are the cultural key to understanding the ownership system of these fisheries, you might think that these same two features characterize aquaculture. But such is not the case; more than 90 percent of the value of Maine's aquaculture landings comes from one species, Atlantic salmon, which, like an agricultural product from the Midwest, is raised in monocultures by increasingly large corporate enterprises. Only five or six other species are raised in commercial enterprises of any kind, reflecting how seldom we understand the basic biology of species well enough to raise them in farmed conditions. But this dearth of knowledge is beginning to change.

Swan's Island's Big Gamble

In 1992, Sonny Sprague, first selectman of Swan's Island, approached the Island Institute looking for backers to enable islanders to put together a company to acquire a bankrupt salmon farm that would otherwise have its assets auctioned off. Two successive owners had driven the farm to its knees; it was hemorrhaging cash and had suffered reverses from the effects of storms and lethally cold water on the farm's exposed site. Sprague was adamant and persuasive, insisting that the salmon farm had failed because its absentee owners didn't have good common sense and didn't listen to local advice. Besides, about thirty full-time and part time jobs were at stake, crucial to the economy of this island community of three hundred and fifty. By the spring of 1993, Sprague and the institute had raised a down payment and arranged state loan guarantees to start Island Aquaculture Company (IAC).

During the next few years the company slowly expanded, acquiring an additional lease site off another part of Swan's shoreline which satellite images show had warmer winter temperatures. Today the growth rate of the company's salmon compares favorably with other salmon farms, perhaps due to warmer summer water temperatures around Swan's than occur down east. Feed conversion rates have been very good, indicating the presence of a good deal of natural feed in the water column. These factors, along with sound on-site management, have enabled IAC's production costs per pound to be attractively low.

> ### Burnt Coat Harbor, January 28, 1994
> When Sonny Sprague came down the hill to Burnt Coat Harbor on Swan's Island the morning of January 28th, every boat left in the harbor was frozen fast in the ice. The thermometer, which had experienced record lows all around the state, hung at fourteen degrees below zero Fahrenheit at his house. Out at Hockamock Head, the harbor entrance, Sprague could just see

the tops of the masts of two lobster boats emerging out of the thick vapor that hung dense as fog over the water. The lobster boats were trying to keep enough of the ice broken up so that it might move on the tide. But Sonny was thinking of the condition of the hundred thousand pounds of salmon and trout that were still out in cages at Toothacher Cove. In a very real sense the fate of the farm that Sprague was trying to bring back from two previous failures was hanging in the balance. "It's always something," said Sprague philosophically. "You just have to put your head down and keep going."

The following day the crew returned to the harbor, which had been freed of ice as a new storm was beginning to build to full gale force. "The crew got down to the harbor at five thirty in the morning and crawled aboard the barge," said Sprague. "It was awful cold. One of them said, 'What a beautiful morning,' meanwhile I'm standing on the wharf shaking like a dog." The farm crew was able to get out to the pens in Toothacher Cove before the seas made the trip impossible, and determined that the fish in all the pens were still swimming. They reported, however, that the water temperature was still hanging dangerously close to what fish farmers call "super chill" conditions, when salt water dips below twenty-nine degrees Fahrenheit and ice crystals form in the blood of farmed fish, causing instant mortality. The storm from the south brought two days of a January thaw, before the mercury plummeted once again. But in those two days Sprague and his crew were able to complete the harvesting and processing of the remaining fifteen thousand pounds of trout from the pens.

Cleaning salmon at Bucks Harbor, Machias, 1996.   Peter Ralston

CORPORATE SALMON

During the past several years, the culture of Atlantic salmon among the islands of the bays of eastern Maine and on both sides of the Bay of Fundy has become a globally significant business. In eastern Maine the ultimate future of salmon aquaculture, the environmental impacts of which can be problematical, will be determined in island coves such as those at Cross Island.

Cross Island, August 23, 1996: King Salmon Is Getting Bigger

RAVEN rounds up into a cove at Cross Island. This thousand-acre wildlife refuge off Machias in eastern Washington County is managed by the U.S. Fish and Wildlife Service. Cross is also the site of the largest salmon farm on the Atlantic coast of the United States. In less than a decade, Maine's salmon industry has changed from a collection of start-up farms owned by individual entrepreneurs into multimillion-dollar, vertically integrated operations such as those at Cross Island, which now produce upwards of $60 million worth of fresh Atlantic salmon for U.S. markets.

Frank Gjerset, president of Atlantic Salmon-Maine, which owns the Cross Island operation, is also a forceful participant in the debate over whether and where large corporate farms will be able to expand westward from the island embayments of Washington County, where the industry has been centered during its first decade in Maine. The question is important, not just because the value of salmon "landings" from ocean net pen operations have quickly become Maine's second most valuable harvest ($67 million in 1995, up from $54 million in 1994), behind only lobsters, but also because Gjerset and others insist that the industry must get much bigger in order to compete with the scale of operations that characterize salmon farming internationally.

Amid Cross Island's expansive forests, cliffs, and wetlands, Atlantic Salmon's eighty salmon pens are tucked up inside Northwest Cove. The island supports, among other superlative wildlife assets, nesting eagles, osprey, and eiders along with the deer, moose, and occasional black bear that inhabit the lush boreal interior. The U.S. Fish and Wildlife Service and its sister agency, the National Marine Fisheries Service, which is in charge of fish and mammals such as seals, have been profoundly uneasy with the proximity of farmed salmon near eastern Maine rivers with runs of wild Atlantic salmon.

Peter Ralston and I meet Clayton Coffin, site manager of the Cross Island operation for the last seven years. Clayton gestures out over the five acres of salmon pens covering the water and reels off the dizzying figures that characterize this operation: a million fish under his care in eighty pens will be fed about eight tons of feed today by a few men, while a larger crew on a barge harvests forty thousand pounds of salmon. All this activity on the water is coordinated out of a two-story floating office building with sleeping quarters where the night watchman stays. The floating office serves as the physical hub of this ocean net pen site.

Coffin says that until recently the Cross Island salmon were all fed by hand, which he referred to as "hard, injury-prone work." But now the company's investment in automatic feeding technology has begun to pay off. Coffin points to the large feeding machine at one end of the barge into which a forklift has emptied a two-thousand-pound bag of salmon feed embla-

zoned with a corporate tag line, "feeding for profit." While the machine digests its load, we follow one of many black plastic pipes that snake out over the water to one of the pens. There a technician has pulled out a handheld computer that looks like a cell phone and punched in some instructions. Sounding like rain, the pellets rattle out through the pipes, propelled by a dose of air that blows a specified amount of feed to the pen.

At the edge of the pen where the plastic pipe terminates, a spreader showers the feed over the pen's circumference, sending the salmon into a feeding frenzy. Although it looks easy now, Coffin says that it has taken the company several years of fiddling with the feeder to get it to perform in all weather conditions. Knowing that feed costs are $17,000 per day, I am not surprised to cross paths with the company's chief financial officer, who is conducting his own tour describing the farm's prospects to a banker.

As a result of their skill in fine-tuning the system, the farm has been able to approach an astonishing goal, says Coffin proudly: a feed conversion ratio of 1:1. This means that one pound of feed is converted to one pound of salmon—a figure that would make even Frank Perdue's heart skip a beat.

CULTIVATING THE GARDEN IN THE SEA

Ed Myers calls himself a "wharfinger," the term for an owner or keeper of a wharf. At various times, however, in his nearly fifty-year career in the fish business, Ed Myers has bought, sold, and brokered to restaurants and customers halfway around the world virtually every type of seafood the Gulf of Maine has to offer. Most important, Ed Myers has been a purveyor of Maine lobsters, clams, and mussels.

Myers's wharf is a classic of understatement as it fingers delicately out on long, spindly spiles into Clark Cove not far from the mouth of the Damariscotta River. Squinting at the narrow, weather-beaten wharf he built forty years ago, Ed says, "We keep things too long here; oak pilings just won't last forty years." Then after a pause he adds, "Well, they will on top and bottom; it's just their middles that go." Nevertheless, from Ed's land on the cove two river lobstermen still maintain wharf privileges for their dinghies. In the deeper water off the spruce- and pine-lined cove, sixty strings of mussels are suspended on ropes in the water column; at the other end of the cove, oysters are being finished off.

Attired as usual in blue jeans, sea boots, white shirt, and bow tie, Myers is an unusual man on a coast where unusual men and women are commonplace. He came "from away" nearly fifty years ago with his wife, Julia, to raise four children around the edges of this green and giving cove. His cultivated blue mussels produced here at Clark Cove helped establish this underutilized species as a gourmet item in upscale restaurants throughout cities in the East. Listening to him talk about seafood is like attending simultaneous lectures in marine biology and gastronomy; you get the feeling that there is no species too humble to escape the attention of this tireless seafood advocate.

Take smelt, a freshwater-spawning relative of the sea herring. Smelt swim by Ed's wharf and capture his attention this morning because he knows they have recently finished their spawning run upriver and because his neighbors have been out on a smelting expedition. "The mother smelt is looking for 93 percent saltwater and 7 percent freshwater because this will make her eggs hatch, but the little smelt will still have the sense to go back to sea when they're born," says Myers. The freshwater carried down from the land and the heavier, denser saltwater from the ocean depths mix in Clark Cove to just the right degree, which perhaps no one understands as well as Ed Myers, who has watched their flows for half a century.

"Estuary" is the name that marine biologists give to water bodies where fresh- and saltwater mix. In some senses the entire Gulf of Maine operates as an estuary because of the influence of the massive flows of freshwater that drain its sixty-eight-thousand-square-mile basin. The rivers flowing into the gulf deliver an average of two hundred and fifty billion gallons of freshwater each year, although this flow may be tripled in an especially wet year. However, these year-to-year variations are dwarfed by seasonal variations; the flow during the spring runoff can be ten times as great as the flow in late summer. The Damariscotta River of itself is not a major contributor—it is dwarfed by the Saint John, Penobscot, Kennebec and Androscoggin drainages—but it nonetheless provides river-borne nutrients and lower salinity for the critical juvenile stages of commercially significant fish and shellfish. To look off Ed Myers's wharf into the rich green waters is to see estuarine productivity up close and personal, the way a wharfinger does nearly every day.

THE CULTIVATED MUSSEL

Ed Myers sensed an opportunity in a couple of statistics reported by a graduate student at the University of Maine's Darling Center in Walpole. The graduate student had learned how to tell the age of a mussel by a microscopic examination of patterns in the shell and discovered that the average age of a wild mussel harvested from the intertidal zone of Maine was well over eight years. A cultivated mussel could be grown in a little more than three years. Examining the shells of wild and cultivated mussels around the shores of Clark Cove convinced Ed to establish a mussel-raising opera-

Raising trout at Allen Island in Georges Harbor, 1988—one of the independent fish farms that wasn't big enough to survive.
PETER RALSTON

tion there. In 1973, it was the first commercial aquaculture business in the state. "We had mussels fifty feet apart, one on a rope in the cove, one in the intertidal along the shore," he says. "The cultivated shell was 40 percent of the weight of the wild shell, which means if you're weighing out a bushel of mussels you are going to get 25 to 35 percent more meat from the cultivated mussel, with half as much shell to dispose of."

This kind of frugal advantage was too great a temptation for Ed Myers to pass up. For the next twenty-odd years until he sold his business to a neighboring saltwater farmer, Ed Myers cultivated blue mussels and distributed them throughout New England and the East Coast. As with his previous lobster business, he also began studying the interaction between blue mussel biology and gastron-omy. "When the water temperature reaches ten degrees Celsius," Myers says, "the first full moon after that, the mussels will spawn. I'm convinced that mussel spawn is timed three weeks before the spring phytoplankton bloom, so the larvae will have plenty to eat. I don't know what the mussel thinks, but it's a wondrous system." Knowing when mussels spawn is important to Ed, because after they do, they are not nearly as sweet and meaty.

Corrie Roberts, cultivating blue mussels on ropes at Allen Island, 1996.
BOB COOMBS

Ed Myers never became the mussel industry's largest dealer, but he is indisputably the aquaculture industry's first and most visionary spokesman. "With a hundred thousand acres of ocean off here, we can produce mussels for the world," he says. And not just mussels, one might add, but also a broad array of other native species—oysters, clams, scallops, urchins, and seaweeds—if we can commit to a strategy of learning enough biology to understand how to nudge these species a little more toward human ends.

BIG AQUACULTURE

Shellfish farms among the islands and estuaries of the Gulf of Maine exist at the "small is beautiful" end of the aquaculture spectrum. A single oyster farmer can raise a million oysters on an acre of leased bottom with a half-time helper. At fifty cents an oyster, if your survival rate is reasonable—well, you do the math. Shellfish farms have other advantages: they take up less space than finfish farms, they basically depend upon the marine environment to provide the feed, and they aren't likely to overload the marine environment with feed byproducts.

Big-time salmon aquaculture, in contrast, faces enormous challenges. Just across the international border, for example, Canadian environmental officials for the past three years have been responding to a series of ecological crises that appear to be related to the density of farms in the restricted waters of Passamaquoddy Bay, once thought to be an optimal place to raise salmon. The region's huge tides, the conventional wisdom had always held, made environmental problems around the farms unlikely to occur. But an epidemic of sea lice (actually a small crab that attaches to the bodies of salmon in cages), followed by a series of serious pathogenic diseases and damaging allegations about the use and abuse of pesticides and antibiotics, have damaged not only Canadian salmon farms but the credibility of the government that jump-started them as well.

Nearby Cobscook Bay, the center of Maine's salmon industry, has not been immune. New research coordinated by The Nature Conservancy suggests that persistent circulating currents in Cobscook Bay could play a role in spreading disease, organic nutrient pollution, and pesticides or antibiotics used on a particular farm around the bay before it completely flushes. It seems doubtful that additional expansion of the salmon industry in Cobscook's waters is desirable. If the industry is to compete, it can only expand to the west, but not too far without colliding head-on into entrenched interests that have little intention of losing more bottom or more scenery.

Rearing Cod and Haddock

Sonny Sprague and his partners at Island Aquaculture Company became interested in diversifying into other finfish species. At the same time, at the request of fishermen's groups who volunteered to tax themselves, the legislature convened a Groundfish Hatchery Study Commission to examine the feasibility of a marine hatchery in Maine.

After issuing its report in January 1994, commission members formed an alliance to develop a marine hatchery. The alliance, of which the Island Institute is a member, concluded that the Island Aquaculture's Swan's Island facilities were suitable for operating a marine hatchery and began conducting small scale cod and haddock trials.

There is some precedent for such an undertaking. The National Marine Fisheries Service operated cod hatcheries in the region for a long period of time, including one in Gloucester and another in Boothbay Harbor between 1885 and 1940.

The alliance has proposed testing whether hatchery production could be used to increase the number of active spawning sites along the coast; if so, spawning success would be greatly enhanced. This in turn, would drastically reduce the recovery time of overfished stocks. The commission recommended that young cod and haddock be released in the vicinity of formerly productive spawning grounds and nursery areas in order to "jump start" them into renewed production.

Now Sprague with his Swan's Island labor force, and with the advice and technical support of others who have backed this project, has successfully produced cod and haddock fry and larger fish for enhancement studies and produced cod and haddock fingerlings for aquaculture growout operations. But perhaps most important, the group is developing the communication and cooperation between aquaculture and commercial fishing that would be required to ensure acceptance of aquaculture as an alternative employment opportunity.

Swan's Island July 23, 1997
Monica Cease, Island Aquaculture Company's microbiologist in charge of feeding the tiny cod growing in tanks in and around the building and

*wharf along the eastern side of Burnt Coat Harbor, hunches over her micro-
scope to check the condition of the zooplankton she's raising for cod feed.
"Fish are like babies," she says. "We wean them from one feed to the next,
and hopefully they'll reach the stage where they can be released into the wild."*

*In previous attempts it has been difficult to get newly hatched larvae to
feed because they come from extremely small eggs with small yolk supplies.
But up in Orono, in the basement of an old chicken feeding building, Dr.
Linda Kling, a nutritionist, has turned her attention to the diet larval cod
and haddock need and has had notable success. Cease credits Kling with helping to get the cod at the Swan's Island hatchery over the critical early life history stages. Now Cease says that "mortality among the ten thousand finger-
ling cod in the tanks is nearly zero."*

*The plan for these fish, once they are larger in the fall, is to split them
between aquaculture and stock enhancement projects. The fish to be raised in
a pilot aquaculture venture are being raised near Head Harbor on Campobello, in an unusual cooperative international effort. The remainder will go
to Rich Langton at Maine's Department of Marine Resources. The Island
Institute will help fund the placing of sonar tags on them, so they can be followed when they are released in the Sheepscot River estuary during 1998.*

THE MONHEGAN ISLAND CONSERVATION AREA

As the twenty-first century dawns, the Monhegan Island community is truly a microcosm, balanced between two competing philosophies. The choice the community makes will determine
whether it will persist as an isolated winter fishing village, or follow the fate of Criehaven, the last
island community to go locally "extinct" after its fishermen moved to the mainland.

Monhegan Island, January 14, 1997

*The winter grinds on in its ponderous way, with rosy bruised dawn
breaking like a shiner an eye-blink earlier each morn. The furious gales of
wind abate for a few days or a week before getting up on their hind legs
again and battering their way across windswept pastures. The winter of '98
on Monhegan Island is a particularly dark and troubled time, not from brutal weather or the price of lobster, but from the mounting pressures of fishermen from mainland towns who have mounted a campaign to fish inside
Monhegan's territorial waters. This deeply rooted conflict has flared and
simmered for at least a generation, but reached a flash point this winter in
the Maine Legislature. "The future of Monhegan is on the line," said Doug
Boynton, a Monhegan lobsterman. "Without our traditional fishing territory, Monhegan would just be a summer community." So be it, say the fishermen from Friendship, this is our ocean, too.*

*Nothing is simple or clear cut on the water, but the facts are these:
since 1907 when Monhegan lobstermen successfully petitioned the Maine
legislature for a restricted, six-month winter season beginning in January,
Monhegan lobstermen have fished a season harder on the body, but more
rewarding for occurring the half year when prices are about twice what they
are during the summer and fall when everyone else is fishing. Monhegan's
special territory and fishing season, the only one of its kind in all of New
England, has been further restricted since 1976, according to Boynton, by*

informal agreements among Monhegan's lobstermen to limit their numbers to twelve and the number of traps they fish to six hundred.

The 1907 legislation, in a single paragraph, defined a two-mile boundary around the island in which fishing was restricted to a six-month season. Although Monhegan's waters traditionally extended another six to eight miles farther offshore into federal waters, this seaward area was not at issue for most of this century because mainland boats were not big enough for offshore winter lobster fishing, leaving the island's seaward territorial limit undefined, but not undisputed nor undefended, by Monhegan's "law of the knife."

Two years ago, five hard-working Friendship fishermen moved lobster gear into this no-man's land to the south just outside Monhegan's two-mile limit, asserting their rights as licensed fishermen to set gear anywhere within state waters where they were not prohibited. They sparked a dangerous confrontation, temporarily defused by Marine Resources commissioner Robin Alden, who brokered a settlement that formalized the Monhegan Island Conservation Area in 1995. The 1995 legislation, among other provisions, closed the southern boundary at three miles, while permitting anyone to fish inside Monhegan's traditional territory who agreed to the restricted season and six-hundred-trap limit. When the five Friendship lobstermen applied for permits to fish inside the Monhegan Island Conservation Area, as was their undeniable right, all hell broke loose again.

The Monheganers went back to the legislature during the winter of 1998 to propose that a two-year apprenticeship program be required before new entrants would be allowed to fish inside Monhegan's waters. With this, the Friendship fishermen cried foul: after fishing for twenty-five or more years, the Friendship Five were not about to take two years off from being captains of their own fate to become mere sternmen on Monhegan boats. "Special rights," said the Friendship fishermen. "They want to be able to fish in federal waters during the summer and then go back into their own private lobster reserve in the winter. Unfair!" But they lost the argument when the legislature sided with Monhegan.

The bitterness of the confrontation between Monhegan and Friendship was much more than a local fight between two fishing communities; it was a confrontation between two different management philosophies, both of which have deep roots in Maine. Friendship represents the open access philosophy—the ocean is available for anyone to fish anywhere they can to maximize individual returns, under the government's rules (which fishermen have a well-deserved reputation for ingeniously evading). Monhegan represents the other end of the fisheries management spectrum where fishermen have evolved informal local rules that fishermen themselves enforce for their collective benefit.

Island Boundaries

We're back to the same questions with which we began this book: How should islands be defined? Where do they begin and end? And who has rights to use the areas around islands? Such questions have plagued island communities for most of this millennium, and will undoubtedly spill into the next.

Barry Bartmann, a professor at the Institute for Island Studies at the University of Prince Edward Island, has written an intriguing review of the question of island sovereignty and its relation to political boundaries. For the quarter-century following the end of World War II, he points out, only three islands were accorded nation status in the United Nations. But today there are some thirty island nations represented in the General Assembly. Since geological processes are not creating new islands (at least not at this rate), what happened?

The answers are varied and complex, and often associated with the peculiarities of an island's

Launching the Johnson Sea Link *submersible to collect data on lobster brood stock and density at Monhegan Island, October, 1997.*

Philip Conkling

history, but one factor had an influence above all others: the international acceptance of the two-hundred-mile limit as within the "exclusive economic zone" (EEZ) of a coastal state following 1976, when the U.S. Congress explicitly recognized this expanded jurisdiction. Suddenly it became possible for all sorts of places in the middle of oceans to assert control over a much expanded EEZ, and to the extent that fisheries, oil, or other resources sufficient for economic independence exist in this larger jurisdiction, islands everywhere gained independence, often from the remnants of decaying colonial empires.

There is an analogy in the Monhegan case: the Maine legislature has affirmed that the ability of islanders to protect their boundaries—not at two hundred miles, but perhaps two miles—is an essential economic underpinning to their independence and to their survival as year-round communities.

ISLANDS OF MEANING

> *When it comes to islands, what we all seek are people just like us, whoever we may be—and not very many of them! That is the instinctive, lusty power of islands. When our inner selves come to understand our parochial feelings, we tend to sublimate them into delusions of protectionism. Our dreams of islands are nearly always dreams of exclusions. We must beware of our island dreams, they could just happen.*
>
> —George Putz

"I truly believe," says Chellie Pingree, "that there is something about the culture of an island community that needs to protect itself from people and ideas from away. If there wasn't some resistance to change and to outsiders, you wouldn't be able to maintain the integrity of a culture that's existed for so long. And that's part of what we value. We need to be able to live in communities like this, but still have them accessible to teach us what they know.

"I think the islands are going to need real advocates," continues Pingree, "who make sure that they, along with a lot of other small rural communities, aren't just cut out of the economic pie, as we focus on bigger businesses, bigger communities, places where there's lots of money."

None of us, nor any island, is an island complete. It is our friends and friendships, both given and received, across oceans of different experiences, that rekindle our essential humanity. And when one among us falters through misfortune, sickness, or simply the luck of the draw, then a hand, an encouragement, a lifeline skillfully offered can sometimes make the difference between continuity and extinction.

A hundred years from now, just as today, surviving island cultures will give the region a distinction that no other place in America and few on the globe can replicate. And all their friends can and must do their small parts to help.

Epilogue

In the life of each of us there is a place remote and islanded, and given to endless regret or secret happiness.

—Sarah Orne Jewett

For as this appalling ocean surrounds the verdant land, so in the soul of man there lies one insular Tahiti, full of peace and joy, but encompassed by all the horrors of the half-known life.

—Herman Melville

From whatever indistinct point in biological time *Homo sapiens* became one of the earth's newest species, we have been radiating into all kinds of unlikely environments, from the frozen polar tundra to the blazing equatorial deserts, and even into the black void of space. But we occupy no habitat more densely or tenaciously than the shores of the earth's major bodies of water. In ecological terms we are, more than anything else, a littoral species.

In the western world, coastal island cultures grew up, flourished, and all but disappeared in historic times. The earliest Neolithic settlers in the British Isles evidently preferred the small Orkney and Shetland islands to the island continent of Great Britain. Tiny Saint Kilda Island, at the outer rim of the Hebrides, was an intact insular community whose economy for a millennium was based on harvesting of seabird oil, eggs, feathers, and meat. During the sixth and seventh centuries, the uninhabited islands off the coasts of Ireland and England were settled by Christian ascetics who chose these remote rocks on which to live the life of their resurrection. In Maine, the first half-dozen unsuccessful settlements were located on islands, and the first permanent settlement was successfully established on Damariscove Island in 1622. Through much of human history, it has been far more efficient to travel and trade by boat than overland.

The motives behind these island settlements have varied, but the ecological underpinnings for them have not. Islands are surrounded by productive littoral zones that shelter edible marine life nourished by nutrients washing off the land and circulated by tidal rhythms. The coastal marshes and intervales provided ideal livestock pasturage, from the shores of which small homemade fishing vessels were easily launched on expeditions to supplement the agricultural efforts.

In the early decades of the twentieth century, the entire coast of Maine fell on hard times because of a combination of overfishing, overcutting, poor soil management, the decline of merchant sail, the disappearance of markets for such products as salt cod and granite, and the withdrawal of government support for the offshore fisheries. Those island communities that depended most heavily on fishing and shipping fell into a decline more rapid and more serious than occurred in similar communities on the mainland, where shifts to other means of earning a living were possible. Along with this decline, an independent, thrifty, hardworking, self-reliant, and vigilant way of life largely

Opposite: Carver's Harbor, Vinalhaven.

Christopher Ayres

disappeared. If it were not for the remarkable resurgence of the lobster fishery, it is doubtful whether much of a fishing, boatbuilding, and maritime tradition would have persisted in Maine.

As with all tragedies, this decline has all too human a face. An island community that loses its economic identity when its fisheries disappear is almost literally adrift in an ocean of storms. As a culture is cut off from the roots that have sustained it, disillusionment and demoralization can be expressed in accelerated rates of alcoholism and drug abuse.

THE WEALTH IS IN THE WATER

From a climatic point of view, Maine is hardly hospitable. Depending on where you live within the vast reaches of this northern state, the challenges the weather presents dominate one's calculations of the art of the possible almost on a day-to-day basis. Cruel winters give way to long-delayed, cranky springs. And the sweet short months of summer too soon give way to fall gales and frosts.

But in the water, it's a whole 'nother story. The growing season begins by the end of February, when planktonic pastures ignite a vernal bloom that doesn't stop until December. That's a growing season of almost ten months—twice as long as on land, producing a vast and wondrous supply of cod, herring, and lobsters, which explorers knew well how to turn to their profit. Is it any wonder that these islands became the first outposts, or outports, in the northern part of the New World?

Today, much of the complex tapestry of the marine environment in our backyard has been ripped apart, or is at best tattered and frayed. We are not alone in this misery; according to the United Nations, 80 percent of the world's fish stocks are overfished or seriously depleted. Elsewhere in the world, in one marine ecosystem after another, fleets are now fishing on smaller and smaller fish that once fed larger fish. To our north, Newfoundland has experienced a crash of the once-legendary cod stocks off its shores, creating a cultural crisis Cabot Martin has likened to the effect of the extermination of the American buffalo on the culture of the Plains Indians.

And yet, miraculously, despite the increasing assaults on and insults to this marvelous "fish pond," as John Smith called the Gulf of Maine, the essential productive capacity of this great body of circulating waters that wash the shores of our world-renowned archipelago has not yet been destroyed. Wrenched and altered, yes, more out of ignorance than greed, but not yet distorted beyond recognition and repair. We owe this relative good fortune not to foresight, but to the essential biodiversity of the Gulf of Maine. There are so many species here, and so many with commercial value, that for ten generations, when one stock declined or collapsed, there was always another with a new market to be exploited. Who would have thought, even five years ago, that dogfish could be overfished? That a new fishery would develop for the homely monkfish or the sea cucumber? But this is the situation we face.

So we are warned, and rightly so, that our fates at this moment in time look bleak. But we are not doomed to follow in the wake of Newfoundland and the other vast stretches of oceans and islands that are now nearly barren of their once fabulous treasures. The tasks of restoring the native wealth of this region, so much of which lies below the high tide line, are immense and daunting. It can be said that we don't even know what we don't know. But our ignorance is no excuse to forestall the radical changes in fishing behavior, scientific process, and public participation—changes that will be required to turn the ebbing tide of opportunity for those who are part of Maine island cultures.

We bring real assets to the tasks of restoring the systems of the Gulf of Maine: vibrant island and fishing communities around the rim of the gulf, proud of their heritage and willing to play responsible roles in reclaiming the traditions that give them a distinct identity. Arrayed around the rim of the Gulf of Maine, in addition, are some of the world's greatest centers of knowledge of marine environments, from Woods Hole in Massachusetts and Bigelow Lab in Maine to the Hunts-

Traps in winter, Vinalhaven, 1985.

PETER RALSTON

man Marine Laboratory in New Brunswick and the Bedford Institute of Oceanography in Nova Scotia. Sadly, due to the peculiar economics and exigencies of scientific research, these institutions are full of world experts on the Antarctic Ocean or the Arabian Sea, who don't necessarily know much about the problems in their own backyards. The University of Maine's new School of Marine Sciences is a recent addition to this mix. The College of the Atlantic in Bar Harbor, though smaller than the others, has a particular expertise in understanding the roles of marine mammals. Collectively, the institutions of this region represent the highest density of intellectual resources for understanding the marine environment, anywhere in the world. And after four hundred years of exploiting the Gulf of Maine and its rich outer banks, it's about time we turned this intellectual fire-power on the problems back home. A lot of us would benefit.

Sources and Resources

Acheson, James M. *The Lobster Gangs of Maine.* Hanover: University Press, 1988. The best social anthropology research ever conducted in coastal Maine, describing informal systems of maintaining lobster boundaries in inshore waters.

Albion, R. G. *Forests and Seapower.* Cambridge, Massachusetts: Harvard University Press, 1926. Authoritative study of British interest in the settlement of Maine from the point of view of their drive to control the supply of masts of white pine from the coast and islands.

Albion, R. G., W. A. Baker, and B. W. Labaree. *New England and the Sea.* Mystic, Connecticut: Mystic Seaport Museum, Inc., 1972. A nicely written, informative history of New Englanders' involvement with the sea from the age of exploration to the beginning of the twentieth century.

Ames, Edward A., 1996. *Cod and Haddock Spawning Grounds in the Gulf of Maine.* Rockland, Maine: Island Institute. Based on interviews with two dozen retired fishermen, it lays out the case for protecting spawning grounds, including those inside state waters, which once supported local stocks.

Apollonio, Spencer. *The Gulf of Maine.* Rockland, Maine: Courier-Gazette, 1979. Highly informative, technical book on the physical and chemical oceanography of Maine waters written by Maine's former commissioner of marine resources.

Atkins, C. G. *Sixth Report of the Commission of Fisheries of the State of Maine.* Augusta, Maine, 1872. Useful for its line drawings of various types of fish weirs used at the time.

Audubon, Maria R. *Audubon and His Journals.* New York: Charles Scribner's Sons, 1897. Audubon's letters describing his voyages to Eastport, Maine, where he fitted out for his Labrador expedition.

Babcock, Charles. *Along the Shores from Boston to Mount Desert.* 1865. Pamphlet describing the coast of Maine from deckside, with a few descriptions of the islands.

Backus, Richard H., ed. *Georges Bank.* Cambridge, Massachusetts: MIT Press, 1987. A fabulous treasure trove on Georges Bank and the Gulf of Maine. The publication is in large format and rich in maps and scientific illustrations.

Baird, John C. "Some Ecological Aspects of the White-Tailed Deer on Isle au Haut, Maine." University of Maine, Orono, Maine: Master's Thesis, 1966. Documents how island deer use intertidal seaweeds.

Barbour, M. G. et al. *Coastal Ecology.* Berkeley: University of California Press, 1979. Basic ecological characteristics of coastal plant habitats.

Baxter, James P., ed. The Trelawney Papers, in Collections of Maine Historical Society, Second Series, Documentary, Vol. III. Portland, Maine, 1884. The letters of Jonathan Winter, giving the best early description of island living, including accounts of fishing, farming, and lumbering on Richmond Island and Casco Bay islands, 1632–45.

_____. George Cleeve of Casco. Portland, Maine, 1885. As is the rest of Baxter's work, this is a highly readable account of early Maine history that provides ecological details omitted in many accounts.

_____. Sir Ferdinando Gorges and His Province of Maine. Boston, 1890. Description of the Popham Colony on Georgetown Island and references to later settlements on Damariscove and Monhegan.

Opposite: Nubbins Islands are in an estuarine area near the mouths of the Medomak and Meduncook rivers, where fresh and saltier waters and diverse benthic habitats combine to create small gardens in the sea.
COURTESY MAINE DEPARTMENT OF INLAND FISHERIES AND WILDLIFE

_____. Christopher Levett of York. Portland, Maine, 1893. Levett's account of his voyage to the Maine coast is one of the best sources of ecological information on the pre-settlement forests. Nicely edited by Baxter.

Beacom, Seward E. *Pulpit Harbor: Two Hundred Years.* Rockport, Maine: Archimedes Press, 1985. Excellent local history of the first settlement of the "North Island," Northern Harbor, which was the center of the town during its first one hundred-fifty years.

Belknap, Jeremy. *History of New Hampshire, Vol. I*, 1784; *Vols. II* and *III*, later. One of the few contemporary accounts of the white pine masting industry conducted along the coasts of Maine and New Hampshire.

Bent, Arthur C. "Life Histories of North American Petrels and Pelicans and Their Allies." Washington, D.C.: Bulletin, Smithsonian Institution, 1922. Reprint. New York: Dover Press. Breeding information on Leach's storm-petrels on Maine islands.

_____. "Life Histories of North American Wildfowl," Part II. Washington, D.C.: Bulletin, Smithsonian Institution, 1925. Reprint. New York: Dover Press. Information on eiders and winter ducks.

_____. "Life Histories of North American Birds of Prey," Parts I and II. Washington, D.C.: Bulletin, Smithsonian Institution, 1937 and 1938. Reprint. New York: Dover Press. Accounts of the distribution of ospreys and eagles on Maine islands.

Beveridge, Norwood P. *The North Island: Early Times to Yesterday.* North Haven, Maine, 1976. Bicentennial history with informative descriptions of North Haven farming and shipbuilding.

Bigelow, Henry B. "Physical Oceanography in the Gulf of Maine." U.S. Bureau of Fisheries Bulletin, Vol. 40, Part 2, 1927. Companion piece to Bigelow's pioneering work, "Fishes of the Gulf of Maine," this volume lays out what Bigelow deduced of the gulf current and temperatures from two decades of research cruises.

Bigelow, Henry B., and William C. Schroeder. "Fishes of the Gulf of Maine." Fishery Bulletin No. 74. U.S. Fish and Wildlife Service. Washington, D.C.: Government Printing Office, 1953. Wonderfully descriptive species accounts of all the commercial and noncommercial fish found in Maine waters. Bigelow was probably the most famous and knowledgeable oceanographer of these waters; he was one of the few scientists who had the respect of both his colleagues and a great many fishermen because he was an excellent seaman.

Bishop, W. H. "Fish and Men in the Maine Islands." *Harper's New Monthly Magazine*, 1880. Reprint. Camden, Maine: Lillian Berliawsky Books.

Blunt, Edmund M. *The American Coastal Pilot, Containing Directions for the Principal Harbors, Capes and Headlands on the Coasts of North and South America.* 1800, with revised editions every few years. Navigational directions into several Maine harbors give detailed descriptions of the conditions of various islands; useful in reconstructing the composition of original island forests.

Bolton, Charles K. *The Real Founders of New England: The Stories of Their Life Along the Coast, 1602–1628.* Boston, 1929. Firsthand accounts of the techniques of mackereling, haking, longlining, salting, drying, lobstering, canning, et cetera, conducted on and around the Maine islands at the height of the fishing industry. Excellent drawings.

Bourque, Bruce. "Aboriginal Settlement and Subsistence on the Maine Coast." *Man in the Northeast.* No. 6, Fall 1973.

_____. "Fishing in the Gulf of Maine: A 5,000-Year History." *Blackberry Reader*, Gary Lawless, ed. Brunswick, Maine: Blackberry Press. Bourque's two articles give one of the most recent reviews of Indian use of the resources of the islands of Maine. Much of the information is based on artifacts excavated from North Haven. Bourque is an archaeologist at the Maine State Museum.

Bureau of Industrial and Labor Statistics of Maine. "The Granite Industry of Maine." 16th Annual Report. Augusta, Maine, 1902. Listing of all the major island and inland quarries and a summary of the major projects for which each supplied stone.

Burrage, Henry S., ed. *Early English and French Voyages, Chiefly from Hakluyt, 1534–1608.* New York, 1906. Annotated accounts of Rosier's relation of Waymouth's exploration of the Saint George Islands in Muscongus Bay. Also, Pring's discovery of the Fox Islands and the relation of the voyage to Sagadahoc (the account of the failure of the Popham Colony).

Byrne, Deirdre and Andrew Thomas. "Remote Sensing and Hydrographic Characterization of Penobscot Bay," Penobscot Bay Marine Research Collaborative, Year One Report. Rockland, Maine: Island Institute, 1997.

Cabot, Thomas D. *Avelinda, The Legacy of a Yankee Yachtsman.* Rockland, Maine: Island Institute, 1991. Reminiscences and elegant photography of the author's forty years cruising the islands of Maine.

Carleton, W. M. "Masts and the King's Navy." New England Quarterly, 12, (1939): 4–18.

Centennial Committee. *Brief Historical Sketch of the Town of Vinalhaven.* Rockland, Maine, 1900. One of the few early histories of Vinalhaven, mostly reconstructed from the town records, with a few important pieces of information.

Chadbourne, Ava H. *Maine Place Names and the Peopling of Its Towns.* Freeport, Maine: Bond Wheelwright Co., 1955. Town-by-town summaries of the dates of incorporation, with important facts about the establishment of island communities. Reissued in 1970 by counties.

Chapman, Carleton A. *Geology of Acadia National Park.* Greenwich, Connecticut: Chatham Press, 1970. Best single source of technical information on Maine coast geology, emphasizing the granite belt and written for a non-technical audience. Also includes self-guided tours of Mount Desert and Schoodic islands. Self-guided tours are the best way to teach yourself geology.

Clark, Charles E. *The Eastern Frontier, The Settlement of Northern New England, 1610–1763.* Hanover, New Hampshire: University Press of New England, 1983. A comprehensive and readable account of the settlements of Southern Maine prior to 1763.

Clifford, Harold. *The Boothbay Harbor Region 1906–1960.* Freeport, Maine: Bond Wheelwright Co., 1960. Some interesting details of the fishing industry at the beginning of 1900 and hard times in the industry.

Colby, A. H. *Colby's Atlas.* Portland, Maine, 1881. Shows the numbers of dwellings and commercial establishments on islands, particularly around Vinalhaven, Deer Isle, and Mount Desert.

Collins J. W. and Rathbun. "The Mackerel Fishery" Section V, Part II of "The Fisheries and Fishery Industries of the United States," ed. George Brown Goode. Washington, D.C.: Government Printing Office, 1887. Excellent description of the mackerel fishery, including the Gulf of Maine, at the height of the industry before the collapse.

Conkling, Philip W. *A Natural History Guide to the Coastal Islands of Maine.* Rockland, Maine: Hurricane Island Outward Bound School, 1979. Detailed island by island, contains descriptions of approximately two hundred islands used by the Outward Bound Programs.

——————. *Green Islands, Green Sea.* Rockland, Maine: Hurricane Island Outward Bound School, 1980. Guide to foraging on the islands of Maine. Good drawings by Kate Fitzgerald.

Conkling, Philip W., ed. *From Cape Cod to the Bay of Fundy, An Environmental Atlas of the Gulf of Maine.* Cambridge, Massachusetts: MIT Press, 1995. Includes one hundred-sixty illustrations, primarily using satellite images to show ecological features in the Gulf of Maine.

Cook, Melville B. *Records of Meduncook Plantation and Friendship, Maine, 1762–1899.* Rockland, Maine: Shore Village Historical Society, 1985. A comprehensive history of old Meduncook (Friendship, Maine) including its islands.

Cook, Sherwood. Interview with Jayne Lello. Tenants Harbor, Maine. March 1972 (typed transcript). Northeast Archives of Folklore and Oral History, Department of Anthropology, University of Maine at Orono.

Crowell, Kenneth L. "Experimental zoogeography: introductions of mice to small islands." *American Naturalist,* Vol. 107, No. 956, 1973. Describes Crowell's experiments with mice on Maine islands for the technical audience.

——————. "Downeast Mice." *Natural History*, October 1975. Same information for nontechnical readers.

Daughters of Liberty. *Historical Researches of Gouldsboro, Maine.* Bar Harbor, Maine, 1904. A few bits of information on Stave and Ironbound Islands in Frenchman Bay.

Davis, H. A. *An International Community on the St. Croix (1604–1930).* Orono, Maine: University of Maine, 1974. A good local history of this important area straddling the border between Maine and New Brunswick.

Davis, Ronald B. "Spruce-Fir Forests of the Coast of Maine." Ecological Monographs, Vol. 36, Spring 1966. Best technical introduction to the vascular flora of coastal spruce forests.

Day, Clarence A. *A History of Maine Agriculture 1604–1865.* Orono, Maine: University of Maine Study Series No. 68, 1954. Comprehensive account of farming methods from the earliest settlement to the Civil War, with a surprising amount of interesting ecological detail.

_____. *Farming in Maine 1860–1940.* Orono, Maine: University of Maine Study Series No. 78, 1963. Good description of island sheep farms.

Diamond Island Association. *Great Diamond Island.* Portland, Maine, 1972. Mostly late-nineteenth- and twentieth-century history of this Casco Bay island.

Dow, Robert L. "The Need for a Technological Revolution in the Methods of Catching Marine Fish and Shellfish." Marine Technology Society Journal, December 1979–January 1980. Useful summary of the recent history of commercial fishing in the Gulf of Maine, with some summaries of landings for the 1960s.

Drury, William H. Jr. *Chance and Change, Ecology for Conservationists.* Berkeley and Los Angeles: University of California Press, 1998. Excellent discussion of evolutionary biology with many examples of Drury's decades of Maine island research.

Drury, William H. "Rare Species." Biological Conservation, Vol. 6, pp. 162–68. Theoretical discussion of the importance of islands for maintaining sources of genetic diversity.

_____. "Population Changes in New England Seabirds." Bird Banding, Vol. 44, pp. 267–313, and Vol. 45, pp. 1–15, 1973–74. Definitive study of the breeding ecology of the major species of seabirds nesting on the New England coast, and an account of how their numbers fluctuate over time.

Duncan, Roger F. *Coastal Maine.* New York: W.W. Norton, 1992. The best single volume of Maine's maritime history from the colonial period though the present.

Earll, R. Edward. "The Herring Fishery and the Sardine Industry," Section V, Part VI of "The Fisheries and Fishery Industries of the United States," ed. George Brown Goode. Washington, D.C.: Government Printing Office, 1887. Important details of the structure of the herring industry and fishing practices, particulary centered around Eastport and Lubec.

Eastman, Joel W. *A History of Sears Island,* Searsport, Maine. Searsport Historical Society, 1976. Well-researched history of this north Penobscot Bay island, gleaned mostly from the Knox Papers. The study was financed by Central Maine Power Company, which proposed in recent years to build either a nuclear or a coal-fired power plant on this island.

Eaton, Cyrus L. *Annals of the Town of Warren, etc.* Hallowell, Maine, 1872. Good details of early shipbuilding along the upper reaches of the Saint George River.

_____. *History of Thomaston, Rockland and South Thomaston, Maine, from their first exploration, A.D. 1605.* Hallowell, Maine: Masters, Smith, 1865. Includes family genealogies.

Eckert, Allan W. *Great Auk.* Boston: Little, Brown, 1963. Story of the extinction of this giant seabird, told from the point of view of the auk with a great deal of ecological detail.

Eckstrom, Fannie Hardy. *Indian Place Names of the Penobscot Valley and Maine Coast.* Orono, Maine: University of Maine Study Series No. 55, 1941. Compendium of definitive information and carefully documented research on the meaning of Indian place names.

Eliot, Charles. *John Gilley, Maine Farmer and Fisherman.* Boston: Beacon Press, 1899. Admiring portrait of the paterfamilias of Baker Island by one of Mount Desert Island's early summer people, who was, incidentally, president of Harvard College.

Enk, John C. *A Family Island in Penobscot: The Story of Eagle Island.* Rockland, Maine: Courier-Gazette, 1953. Mostly the recollections of Capt. Erland Quinn of the four generations of Quinns who inhabited Eagle Island and the various occupations they pursued.

Fairburn, William A. *Merchant Sail.* 6 vols. Center Lovell, Maine: Fairburn Marine Educational Foundation, 1945. Unique work of everything anyone will ever want to know about the days of merchant sail. The section on Maine boats is as comprehensive as that of any work in print.

Farrow, John P. *History of Islesborough, Maine.* Bangor, Maine, 1893. Mostly genealogies of the early settlers, some of whom settled on the smaller surrounding islands. The written descriptions of original lots on the island give a surprisingly detailed look at the composition of the original forest.

_____. *The Romantic Story of David Robertson Among the Islands, Off and On the Coast of Maine.* Belfast, Maine, 1898. This story might not be as interesting if it hadn't been written by a historian. With great attention to detail, it describes the life of the original settler of Lime Island in Penobscot Bay.

Faulkner, A., and G.F. Faulkner, *The French at Pentagoet, 1635–1674, An Archaeological Portrait of the Acadian Frontier.* Maine Historic Preservation Commission, Augusta, ME, 1987. The complete archeological history and role played by the French at Castine in the thirty-one years covered.

Fillmore, Robert B. *Gems of the Ocean.* Privately published, 1914. Various facts about turn-of-the-century life on Matinicus and Ragged Islands and Matinicus Rock. Available from the Maine State Library.

Goldburg, Rebecca and Tracy Triplett. *Murky Waters: Environmental Effects of Aquaculture in the United States.* Washington, D.C.: Environmental Defense Fund, 1997. Includes case studies on New England and New Brunswick, Canada.

Goode, George Brown. "Fishery Industries of the United States." U.S. 47th Congress, 1st Session (1881–1882), Miscellaneous Documents, Vol. 7, Section II, 1882. Valuable source of information on American fishing near its height; compiled by regions.

Goode, George Brown and Joseph W. Collins. "The Cod, Haddock, and Hake Fisheries," Section V, Part II of "The Fisheries and Fishery Industries of the United States," ed. G. B. Goode. Washington, D.C.: Government Printing Office, 1887. The most comprehensive account of fishing, including port to port descriptions beginning from Eastport, Maine, to reveal in detail the fisheries prosecuted during the nineteenth century.

Goold, Nathan. *A History of Peaks Island and Its People.* Portland, Maine, 1897. Smattering of useful historical details.

Graham, Frank. *Gulls—A Social History.* New York: Random House, 1975. Complete history of the relationship of gulls and men from the mid–nineteenth century through the present. The majority of it focuses on Maine nesting islands. Also, lovely photography by Chris Ayres.

Grant, W. L. *Voyages of Samuel de Champlain, 1604–1618.* New York: Charles Scribner's Sons, 1907. Descriptions of Champlain's two voyages along the Maine coast, reconstructed and annotated from Champlain's detailed notebooks.

Greene, Francis B. *History of Boothbay, Southport and Boothbay Harbor, Maine, 1623–1905.* Portland, Maine, 1906. Standard and comprehensive history.

Greenleaf, Moses. *A Survey of the State of Maine (in Reference to its Geographical Features, Statistics and Political Economy).* Portland, Maine, 1829. Greenleaf was the man hired to survey the publicly owned islands after Maine became a state. Lots of original hard data.

Griffin, Carl R. III, and Alaric Faulkner. *Coming of Age on Damariscove Island, Maine.* Orono, Maine: The Northeast Folklore Society, 1981. A lovely little book that covers the history of this important Maine Island, based largely on the reminiscences of Alberta Poole Rowe.

Grindle, Roger. *Quarry and Kiln, The Story of Maine's Lime Industry.* Rockland, Maine: Courier-Gazette, 1971. Grindle, who grew up in Rockland, provides a look at the lime industry mostly gleaned through old newspaper accounts.

_____. *Tombstones and Paving Blocks, The History of the Maine Granite Industry.* Rockland, Maine: Courier-Gazette, 1972. Useful background information on the operations on Vinalhaven, Hurricane Island, Clark Island, and Dix Island.

Gross, A. O. "The Present Status of the Double-Crested Cormorant on the Coast of Maine." *Auk,* Vol. 62, pp. 513–97. Valuable historical review of the fortunes of the cormorant.

"The Present Status of the Great Black-Backed Gull on the Coast of Maine." *Auk*, Vol. 62, pp. 241–56. Describes the range extension of this Arctic species.

Gross, Clayton. *Island Chronicles: Accounts of Days Past in Deer Isle and Stonington.* Stonington, Maine: Penobscot Bay Press, 1977. Some interesting information on the fishing industry of Deer Isle at the start of the twentieth century, written by a resident.

Halle, Louis J. *The Storm Petrel and the Owl of Athena.* Princeton, New Jersey: Princeton University Press, 1970. Delightful series of essays about pelagic seabirds written by a gifted amateur naturalist.

Hallowell, Maine, 1865. Reprint. Courier-Gazette, Rockland, Maine, 1972. Good early history of the islands off these towns, with some interesting details on animal life.

Hayden, Anne. *Eelgrass and Fisheries in the Gulf of Maine.* Rockland, Maine: Island Institute, 1996. Sixteen pages. The relationship between eelgrass and fisheries.

Hill, A. F. "The Vegetation of the Penobscot Bay Region, Maine." Proceedings of the Portland Society of Natural History, Vol. 3, Part 3 (1923), pp. 305–438. Comprehensive and useful description of island vegetation in Penobscot Bay; written by a botanist of the old school (that is, someone who went out and identified plants in the field and arranged them according to habitat).

Hosmer, George L. *An Historical Sketch of the Town of Deer Isle, Maine; with Notices of Its Settlers and Early Inhabitants.* Boston, 1886. Definitive history of Deer Isle that contains a great deal of interesting detail about this island and the smaller ones in Merchant Row.

Island Institute. *Island Journal, Volumes 1–16.* A celebration of the islands and waters of the Gulf of Maine including art, science, politics, literature, and culture.

Jenney, Charles F. *The Fortunate Island of Monhegan, A Historical Monograph.* Proceedings of the American Antiquarian Society, Vol. 31. Summary of Monhegan's history compiled from secondary sources.

Jewett, Sarah Orne. *The Country of the Pointed Firs.* New York: Houghton Mifflin Co., 1910. Sketches of coastal life and the inhabitants of a small fishing village. Includes one or two island characters.

Johnson, Douglas W. *The New England Acadian Shoreline.* New York: Hafner, 1925. Classic study of the physiography of the New England coast that describes why regions look the way they do.

Johnston, John. *A History of Bristol and Bremen.* Albany, New York, 1873. Good descriptions of the various Indian tribes that influenced the early history of Maine.

Jones, Herbert G. *The Isles of Casco Bay in Fact and Fancy.* Portland, Maine, 1946. Mostly fancy.

Josselyn, John. *An Account of Two Voyages to New England.* William Veazie, ed. Boston, 1865. Excellent source of contemporary descriptions of everything from fishing and fishermen to black flies, Indians, lobsters, and wolves around his brother's plantation in Saco during the 1630s and 1640s.

——————————. *New England Rarities Discovered.* Edward Tuckerman, ed. Boston, 1865. Josselyn's second volume from his recollections of his stay in the New World is a source of descriptions of native grasses and wildflowers. His species accounts of New England wildlife, although entertaining, are sometimes fantastic and at other times misleading.

Joy, Barbara E. *Historical Notes on Mount Desert Island.* Bar Harbor, Maine, 1975. Compendium of historical facts that provide some interesting details not available in the standard histories of the area.

Katona, S. K., V. Rough, and D. T. Richardson. *A Field Guide to the Whales, Porpoises and Seals of the Gulf of Maine and Eastern Canada: Cape Cod to Newfoundland (3rd edition).* New York: Charles Scribner's Sons, 1983. Popular field guide covering the Gulf of Maine, from Cape Cod to Newfoundland, with complete species accounting and life cycle of each animal.

Kelley, J. T., D. F. Belknap, 1989. *Geomorphology and Sedimentary Framework of Penobscot Bay and Adjacent Inner Continental Shelf.* Maine Geological Survey, Report #89-3.

Kingsbury, John M. *The Rocky Shore.* Greenwich, Connecticut: Chatham Press, 1970. One of the best introductions available to the life found in the rocky intertidal zone, by the former director of the Isles of Shoals Marine Laboratory. Fine drawings by Marcia and Edward Norman allow it to be used as a field guide.

Kobbe, Gustow. "Heroism in the Lighthouse Service: A description of life on Matinicus Rock." *Century Magazine,* 1897. A few useful tidbits.

Kohl, J. G. *History of the Discovery of Maine.* Collections of the Maine Historical Society, Portland, Maine, 1869. Good introduction to the geography of the coast and the waters of the Gulf of Maine by an authoritative German geographer.

Korschgan, Carl E. *Coastal Waterbird Colonies: Maine.* U.S. Fish and Wildlife Service, Biological Services Program, 1979. Listing of the number and distribution of the various waterbirds that breed on the Maine coast. Also includes a useful summary of historical changes and a good bibliography.

Kress, Stephen W. "The History and Future of North Atlantic Seabird Populations." Unpublished pamphlet, available from the National Audubon Society.

Kurlansky, Mark. *Cod, A Biography of the Fish that Changed the World.* New York: Walker and Company, 1997. This epic story of the history of cod is a classic, ending with the tragic collapse of cod throughout the North Atlantic.

Lewis, J. R. *The Ecology of Rocky Shores.* London: Hodder and Stoughton, 1964. British text that gives the most comprehensive account of the dominant plant and animal communities of rocky shores.

Lockely, R. M. *Gray Seal, Common Seal.* New York: October House, 1968. Detailed species accounts of these two seals common to Maine waters. Written in informative, nontechnical language.

Long, Charles A. E. *Matinicus Isle, Its Story and Its People.* Salem, Massachusetts: Higginson Book Company, 1926. Re-issue of an important early history of this island community in outer Penobscot Bay.

Loomis, Alfred F. *Ranging the Maine Coast.* New York: Norton, 1939. Classic account by one of *Yachting* magazine's excellent writers. Lots of interesting historical information woven into the narrative of his voyages aboard the HOTSPUR.

Lunt, Vivian. *Frenchboro, Long Island Plantation, The First Hundred Years.* Penobscot, Maine: Penobscot Graphics, 1980. A delightful pictorial history of the island community from the late nineteenth century to the present.

MacGinitie, G. E., and Nettie MacGinitie. *Natural History of Marine Animals.* New York: McGraw-Hill, 1968. Husband-and-wife team who obviously spend their spare time together collecting creatures from California's rocky intertidal zone. This volume was most useful for its introductory chapters on marine food webs.

Maine DMR. 1976. *Maine Landings: 1955–1976.* U.S. Dept of Commerce, Washington, D.C. Fish landings compiled by the Maine Department of Marine Resources for a twenty-year period.

Manley, Sean, and Robert Manley. *Islands: Their Lives, Legends and Lore.* Philadelphia: Chilton, 1970. For hard-core island buffs.

Manville, Richard H. "The Vertebrate Fauna of Isle au Haut, Maine." *American Midland Naturalist,* Vol. 72, 1964. One of the few accurate accounts of mammalian species found on an offshore island of Maine.

Martin, Kenneth R., and Nathan R. Lipfert. *Lobstering and the Maine Coast.* Bath, Maine: Maine Maritime Museum, 1985. Excellent book on the history of lobstering on the Maine coast.

May, R. M. "Island Biogeography and the Design of Wildlife Preserves." *Nature,* Vol. 254, pp. 177–78 Interesting theoretical discussion that bears on the preservation issues confronting Maine islands.

McLane, Charles B., with Carol Evarts McLane. *Islands of the Mid-Maine Coast, Vol. II: Mount Desert to Machias Bay.* Falmouth, Maine: Kennebec River Press, 1989.

_____. *Islands of the Mid-Maine Coast, Vol. III: Muscongus Bay and Monhegan Island.* Gardiner, Maine: Tilbury House and Rockland, Maine: Island Institute, 1992

_____. *Islands of the Mid-Maine Coast, Vol. IV: Pemaquid Point to the Kennebec River.* Gardiner, Maine: Tilbury House, 1994.

_____. *Islands of the Mid-Maine Coast, Vol. I: Penobscot Bay.* (revised edition). Gardiner, Maine: Tilbury House and Rockland, Maine: Island Institute, 1997. McLane's four volumes of histories of approximately eight hundred islands is the most important scholarly contribution to the histories and family histories of the islanders who originally shaped their landscapes.

Mendall, H. L. "The Home-Life and Economic Status of the Double-Crested Cormorant, *Phalacrocorax auritus auritus.*" Orono, Maine: University of Maine Study Series (2nd Series) No. 38, 1936. Detailed history and biology of the cormorant.

_____. "Eider Ducks, Islands and People." *Maine Fish and Wildlife,* Vol. 18, 1976, No. 2, 4–7. Author's hypotheses on the disturbance to nesting eiders posed by human visitation to islands.

Merrill, John, and Suzanne Merrill, eds. *Squirrel Island, Maine, The First Hundred Years.* Freeport, Maine: Bond Wheelwright Co., 1973. Story of the island's summer colony.

Miller, S., 1995. Bibliography of Penobscot Bay Scientific Research. Island Institute. Comprehensive listing by subject, author, title of published research covering Penobscot Bay.

Monks, John P. *History of Roque Island, Maine.* Boston: The Colonial Society of Massachusetts, 1967. Good history of this unique island.

_____. "Final Report, Feeding Habits and Population Studies of Maine's Harbor and Gray Seals." Augusta, Maine: Department of Sea and Shore Fisheries, 1973. The only original research on the feeding habits of seals on the Maine coast.

Morison, Samuel E. *The Story of Mount Desert Island, Maine.* Boston: Little, Brown, 1960. A colorful and amusing history by one of Mount Desert's most respected summer residents.

_____. *The European Discovery of America: The Northern Voyages.* Boston: Little, Brown, 1971. What makes Morison such an excellent naval historian is that he has cruised much of the same area as the original explorers. Also, few other historians have such a graceful prose style.

_____. *Samuel de Champlain: Father of New France.* Boston: Little, Brown, 1972. Morison on Morison's favorite explorer. Includes a good description of Champlain's two expeditions along Maine's coast.

Morse, Ivan. *Friendship Long Island.* Middletown, New York: Whitlock Press, 1974. The recollections of one of the island's oldest residents, whose memory stretches back to before the turn of this century. A good oral history.

Norton, Arthur H. "Some Noteworthy Plants from the Islands and Coast of Maine." *Rhodora,* Vol. 15, No. 176, 1913. Norton was the backbone of the Portland Museum of Natural History for almost three decades and traveled extensively along the Maine coast visiting nesting islands and collecting plants.

O'Leary, Wayne M. *Maine Sea Fisheries: The Rise and Fall of a Native Industry, 1830–1890.* Boston: Northeastern University, 1996.

Palmer, Ralph S. "Maine Birds." *Bulletin of the Museum of Comparative Zoology.* Cambridge, Massachusetts: Harvard College, 1949. Palmer graciously acknowledges that this volume is "based largely on data gathered by Arthur Herbert Norton." It provides a unique look at the breeding colonies of the Maine islands with many notes on the condition of the vegetation.

Platt, David D., ed. *Penobscot: The Forest, River and Bay.* Rockland, Maine: Island Institute. 1996. 202 pages. Survey of history and ecology of towns of the Penobscot watershed, including river towns, island towns, and towns of the eastern and western bays.

Platt, David D., ed. *Rim of the Gulf, Restoring Estuaries in the Gulf of Maine.* Rockland, Maine: Island Institute, 1998. This book, with its maps, photographs, and narration, chronicles the estuaries of the Gulf of Maine. It highlights the need for action, research, and public education.

Porter, Eliot. *Summer Island.* Sierra Club. A lovely book about a Penobscot Bay island, written by the man who nearly invented color nature photography.

Raisz, Edwin J. "The Scenery of Mount Desert Island, Its Origin and Development." New York Academy of Sciences, Vol. 31, 1929. Good description of the glacial epoch and its effects in shaping landscapes.

Richardson, David T. "Final Report, Assessment of Harbor and Gray Seal Populations in Maine." Augusta, Maine: Department of Marine Resources, 1975. Solid research.

Rowe, William H. *Shipbuilding Days on Casco Bay.* Portland, Maine, 1946. Accounts of forest cutting for shipbuilding.

_____. *The Maritime History of Maine: Three Centuries of Shipbuilding and Seafaring.* Freeport, Maine: Bond Wheelwright Co., 1948. Sequel to the volume described above.

Russell, Howard S. *A Long Deep Furrow: Three Centuries of Farming in New England.* Hanover, New Hampshire: University Press of New England, 1976. One-of-a-kind book that is both an encyclopedic historical reference and a good treatment of the ecology of farming.

_____. *Indian New England Before the Mayflower.* Hanover, New Hampshire: University Press of New England, 1980. A useful reference for how Indian cultures affected the New England landscape.

St. Pierre, James A. "Maine's Coastal Islands: Recreation and Conservation." Augusta, Maine: Bureau of Parks and Recreation, 1978. Listing of the significant resources attached to Maine islands. Also a comprehensive bibliography.

Sauer, Carl O. *Northern Mists.* San Francisco: Turtle Island Foundation, 1968. One of the only serious histories of European exploration of the New World to research the question of whether early unrecorded fishing voyages visited the New England coast.

Schemnitz, Sanford D. "Marine Island-Mainland Movements of White-Tailed Deer." *Journal of Mammalogy,* Vol. 56, 1975. Documents the swimming abilities and migratory habits of white-tailed deer.

Simmons, M. H. "Report on Island Titles Along the Coast of Maine, under the Resolve of 1913, Chapter 180." *Report of the Maine Forest Commissioner.* Augusta, Maine, 1914. Listing of the islands that were found to be in the public domain in 1913.

Simpson, Dorothy. *The Maine Islands in Story and Legend.* Philadelphia: J.B. Lippincott, 1960. Research material compiled from the Maine Writers Research Club.

Small, H. W. *A History of Swan's Island, Maine.* Ellsworth, Maine, 1898. Thorough history of the island compiled by a resident and based on many firsthand recollections of the island's old people.

Smalley, Albert J. *St. George, Maine.* Typewritten manuscript. First-rate informative history of everything from the design of tidal sawmills to a description of the methods of quarrying granite. Available from the Maine State Library.

Smith, George Otis. "Description of the Penobscot Bay Quadrangle, Maine." Geologic Atlas Folio, 149. Washington, D.C.: Government Printing Office.

Smith, John (Capt.). *A Description of New England: or the Observations and Discoveries of Captain John Smith (Admiral of that Country) in the North of America in the Year of Our Lord 1614.* London, 1614. Smith's account of his voyage to the coast of Maine, which, together with Rosier's and Levett's accounts, gives us the best look at the condition of Maine's forest and fishing resources at that time.

Snow, Wilbert. *Collected Poems.* Middletown, Connecticut: Wesleyan University Press, 1963. Snow was born on Whitehead Island in the Muscle Ridge, where his father was part of the lifesaving-station crew. His poetry reflects a great deal of the flavor of Maine island living, from fishing to quarrying to hunting.

State Planning Office, Maine Coastal Program. *Sustaining Island Communities: The Story of the economy and life of Maine's year-round islands.* Rockland, Maine: Island Institute, 1997. Descriptions of what it takes for Maine's fifteen year-round island communities to sustain themselves.

Sterling, Robert T. *Lighthouses of the Maine Coast.* Brattleboro, Vermont: Stephen Greene Press, 1995. Dates of the construction (and often the automation) of every lighthouse on the Maine coast, with a short anecdote from the history of each light.

Stern, William L., ed. *Adaptive Aspects of Insular Evolution.* Bellingham, Washington: Washington State University Press, 1974. Theoretical discussion of the effect of isolation of small gene pools.

Tinbergen, Niko. *The Herring Gull's World. A Study of the Social Behavior of Birds.* New York: Harper and Row, 1960. Classic account of the behavior of this highly social bird by the man who helped define and later won the Nobel prize for ethnology.

Townsend, David W,. and Peter F. Larsen, eds. *The Gulf of Maine, NOAA Coastal Ocean Program Regional Synthesis Series Number 1.* Washington, D.C.: U.S. Department of Commerce, February 1992. An important collection of scientific papers.

Tyler, Harry. "Common Terns, Arctic Terns and Roseate Terns in Maine." Augusta, Maine: State Planning Office. One of a continuing series of pamphlets describing Maine's bird life and other unique natural features. All are written for a general audience and are good educational tools.

Varney, George J. *Gazetteer of the State of Maine.* Boston, 1882. Valuable source of odd pieces of historical data for island towns.

Vinalhaven Historical Society. *Images of America: Vinalhaven Island.* Dover, New Hampshire: Arcadia Publishing, 1997. Important archival photographs covering quarrys, early boat building, and fishing of this Penobscot Bay island.

Wallace, Gordon T., and Eugenia F. Braasch, eds. *Proceedings of the Gulf of Maine Ecosystem Dynamics, Scientific Symposium and Workshop.* RARGOM Report, 97-1. Hanover, New Hampshire: Regional Association for Research on the Gulf of Maine, 1997. Collection of two dozen scientific articles on fisheries, aquaculture, oceanography, and ecology in the Gulf of Maine.

Wasson, George S. *Sailing Days on the Penobscot: The Story of the River and the Bay in the Old Days.* New York: Norton, 1932. Description of the coasting world in the 1870s and 1880s with an interesting chapter on Isle au Haut.

Westbrook, Perry D. *Biography of an Island: The story of a Maine Island, Its People and Their Unique Way of Life.* Cranbury, New Jersey: Thomas Yoseloff Publisher, 1958. A fascinating picture of island communities during the 1950s.

Wheeler, George A., and Henry W. Wheeler. *History of Brunswick, Topsham and Harpswell.* Boston, 1878. Dates of early settlement for the islands on this side of Casco Bay.

Whipple, J. M. *A Geographical Review of the District of Maine.* Bangor, Maine, 1816. Interesting listing of the timber products that were commercially valuable at the time, with notes on their distribution.

Williamson, William D. *The History of the State of Maine 1602–1820.* 2 vols. Hallowell, Maine, 1832. Good coverage of the Indian Wars. Volume 1 has a section on the islands.

Winship, G. P. *Sailors' Narratives of Voyages Along the New England Coast 1524–1624.* New York, 1905. Descriptions and accounts of little-known voyages to Maine.

Winslow, Sidney L. *Fish Scales and Stone Chips.* Portland, Maine: Machigonne Press, 1952. Closest thing to a history of Vinalhaven, written by a man whose father was part of the quarry era.

Wise, David M. G. et al. *Coastal Ecology.* Berkeley: University of California Press, 1979. Basic ecological characteristics of coastal plant habitats.

Index

Abagadasset River, 56–57, 93
Abnaki, 59. *See also* Indians
Acadia (French), 63
Acadia National Park, 72, 121, 178
Accipters, 146
Acheson, Jim, 185, 194
Albatross, 135
Alcids, 148, 152–55. *See also* Auks
Alden, Robin, 38, 266, 289
Alewives, 21–22, 67, 75, 138, 139, 223; as bait, 230
Algae, 188, 207
Allen, John, 20
Allen Island, *19*, 20, 30, *62*, 113, 147–48; aquaculture at, *285*; forest, 93, 94–96, *112*; and George Waymouth, 61; Indian encampment, 132; moose on, 175–76; pulpwood cut, 103–05, *104*; sheep shearing, 111, 172
Ambergris, 161
American Coast Pilot, 94, 108, 116
American Ornithological Union, 151
America's Cup Race, 18
Ames, Ted, 239–240, 266
Amherst, Lord Jeffrey, 64
Ammen Rock, 254
Andre the Seal, 168–69
Andros, Sir John, 69
Androscoggin River, 56, *57*, 120; currents 245, 248; drainage, 256, 285; Indians, 59; pines along, 93; pollution, 258
Anemone Cave (Mt. Desert), 121
Anemones, sea, 207, 254
Anglers, 75, 84, 137–38
Anguilla Island, 78
Apollonio, Spencer, 260
Appalachians, 57
Appledore Island, 20, 51–52, 231
Aquaculture, 84–85, 190, 280–81, *285*, 287. *See also* Clam; Mussel; Oyster; Salmon; Trout
Arctic flowers, 75, 89
Argall, Samuel, 96
Arrowsic Island, *58*, 63
Artists and poets, 35
Ash trees, 94, 96, 100
Asticou, Chief, 59
Atlantic Maritimes (Canada), 259, 262–63
Atlantic Neptune, 26, 72, 74, 78, 108
Atlantic Salmon–Maine, Inc., 283–84
Audubon, John James, 134
Audubon societies, 143
Auk: great, 133, 152–53, 156; razor–billed, 66, 134, 247
Avery Rock Light, 24

Babbidge, Roscoe C., 28
Bacchus Island, 94

Bachman, Herman (Junior), 204–05, 209
Back River, 93
Bailey Island, 54, *55*
Baird, Spencer, 219, 221
Baker Island, 21, 94, 134
Bald eagle, North American, 56, 132, 134, 139, 144–46, 172; nest, 69, 179, 283; population, 66, 82
Bald Island, 129.
Ballast Island, *78*, 119
Balsam fir, 90, 91–92
Bandit camps, 69
Bank fisheries, 137–38, 231, 236; dragging, 237–38
Bare Island, *80*
Bar Harbor, 69, *70*, 72, 163, 280
Bar Island (Frenchman Bay), *71*
Barnacle, 186; zone, 188
Bartlett Island, 20, 69, *70*
Bartman, Barry, 289
Basket Island, 94
Basque whalers, 165
Bass, striped, 75
Bass Harbor, *70*, 190, 279–80
Bath, 98, 100, 124, 162, 232
Bathysphere, 206
Bats, 159
Bay of Fundy, basin, 250; boats, 247; cod grounds, 230; currents, 244, 248; Fifty–Fathom Ridge, 253; French settlements, 54; red tide, 258; salmon culture, 283; spawning grounds, 212, 219, 222; shipbuilding, 232; tides, 83, 247, 248, 250; water temperatures, 200
Beacom, Seaward, 26
Beal, Edwin, 77
Beals Island, 49, 75–78, *76*, *77*, 117, 122, 204; bank fishing, 231; clam hatchery, 190; lobster cannery, 191–92
Bean Island, 71
Bear, black, 174–75, 182, 283
Bear Island, 174
Beaver, 159, 179
Beckman, John, 195–97, 201
Bedford Institute of Oceanography (Canada), 186, 295
Beech trees, 94, 96, 101
Beinecke, Walter, 276–77
Belfast, 122, 169, 218–19
Benner Island, *19*, 20, 21–22
Benthic habitat, 198–99, 203, 247, 253–56; organisms in, 247, 256
Berries, 107
Bickford, Clyde, 234
Biddeford, 63
Biddeford Pool, 52, *53*
Bigelow, Harry Bryant, 213, 216, 230, 244, 249

Bigelow Laboratory for Ocean Sciences, 199, 257–58, 294–95
Big Garden Island, 118–19
Biodiversity, 243, 262; extinction of, 182; in gulf, 246, 254–55, 280–81, 294; protection of, 85
Biogeography, 67, 181–82
Birch trees, yellow, 94–96, 97
Bird populations, 19, 132, 137, 156–57
Bird's eye primrose, 89
Birds of prey, 144–45
Black Head, *50*, 76
Black Island (Casco Passage), *70*, 94, 108
Black Island (Mount Desert), 123
Blessing of the fleet, Monhegan, 35
Block Island (RI), 275
Blueberry barrens, 75; rakers of, 71
Bluefish, 212
Blue geese, 142
Blue Ground, 231–32
Blue Hill, 72
Blue Hill Bay, 69–*70*, 94, 206–07
Bluff Island, *53*
Boat building, 77–78, 126, 232, 279; on islands, 26, 28, 53, 68, 98–100. *See also* Shipbuilding
Boat engines, 193, 234
Boats: lifesaving, 81; steam–powered, 234 (*see also* Steamships); tour, 60; work, 77
Boats, fishing, 18, 27, 51, 65–67, 68; dories, 191; federal buy-back of, 238; harpoon, 269–70; shallops, 229. *See also* Draggers; Factory ships; Lobster fishing; Schooners; Shipbuilding; Sloops
Bois Bubert Island, 20, 72, *73*, 74, 93
Boom Quarry (Vinalhaven), 129
Boon Island Light, 24, *52*
Boothbay, 57, *58*, 59–60
Boothbay Harbor, 57, 60, 229, 287
Borque, Bruce, 19
Boston, Maine exports to, 99; cordwood, 55, 101; fish, 27, 193, 235; granite, 124, 126; hay, 107
Bowdies, the, 231
Bowdoin College, 262
Boynton, Doug, 288–89
Bradbury Island, *65*, 174, 177
Brandies Ledges, 143
Brehme, Chris, 249–50
Bremen Long Island, 20
Bridges, 54–55, 57, 67, 76, 159. *See also* Ice bridges
Brimstone Island, *65*, *119*, 121, 157, 277
British Admiralty, 26, 72, 93, 96–97, 100, 119
Brothers Islands, *78*, 79, 96, 117–18
Brown, J.O. and Son, *28*, *199*
Browney Island, *76*
Browns Bank, 87, 231, 244–47
Bucks Harbor, *80*
Burgess, Abby, 20–21
Burgess, Ernie, 56
Burnham and Morrill Co., 192
Burning islands, 107–09, 112–13
Burnt Coat Harbor (Swan's Island), 35, 278–79, 281–83
Burnt Coat Island, *70*, 72
Burnt Island (Muscongus Bay), *62*, 93, 113, 122
Burnt islands, 107

Bustins Island, 20
Butter Island, 20, *65*, 111–12
By–catch, fish, 204, *210*, 211, 264
Byrne, Deidre, 249, 250

Cabot, John, 91
Cabot, Tom, 30
Calderwood Neck (Vinalhaven), 64
Calf Island (Flanders Bay), *71*
Calf islands, 110
Camden, *65*, 71, 102
Campbello Island (Canada), *82*, 288
Canada, 81; fisheries management, 259, 262–63
Canada geese, 97, 142
Cape Cod, island formations, 185
Cape Cod Bay, 165, 167
Cape Corneille, 76
Cape Elizabeth, 52, *55*, 116, 171; cod grounds, 229, 232, 235
Capelin, 152
Cape Newagen, 92–93
Cape Rosier, *65*, 249
Cape Sable, 49, 108, 244
Cape Small, *55*
Cape Split, 72, *73*, 74–75, *76*
Carageenan, 188
Caretakers, 273–74
Caribou, 19, 175, 182. *See also* Reindeer
Carson, Rachel, 156–57, 187, 188
Cartier, Jaques, 133
Carver, Reuben, 99
Carvers Harbor (Vinalhaven), 67, 127, 191, *292*
Casco Bay, 54, *55*, 57, 243; Appalachian foothills in, 57; cod spawning grounds, 235; eagles, 144–45; lobster fishery, 200, 201; pollution, 31; tides, 250; urchin fishery, 208
Casco Bay Island (Canada), *82*
Casco Bay islands, 20, 54–56, *55*, 117; beaches on, 120; development of, 30–33; forests on, 94; and Indians, 59, 132; named Stave, 101; shipyards on, 99
Casco Passage, 68, 70, 94, 108
Cashels Ledge, 247, 248, 254
Castine, 65, 201
Cathance River, *57*
Cease, Monica, 288
Cedar Island, 92
Cedar trees, 100; Atlantic white, 92
Cetaceans, 160
Champion International, 103–05, 257
Champlain, Samuel de, 54, 72, 75–76, 94, 96, 108
Chance Island, *80*
Chandler Bay, *76*
Channel Islands (CA), 174
Chapman, Frank, 151
Chase, Mary Ellen, 97
Chebeague Island, 32, 56, 94, 101, 126; residents, 275. *See also* Great Chebeague
Chestnut tree, 94, 96
Chignecto Bay, 243
Chopps Point, 56, *57*
C.H. Rich and Company, 280
Christmas bird count, 143–44
Cirone, Jenny, 172

Clam, 105, 179; diggers, 54–55, 58, 71, 83, 133, 205; management, 189–90; hatchery, 190

Clapboard Island, *55*, 93

Clark Cove, 284, 286

Clark Island 20, 123, 124

Clay Bank, 231

Clear–cuts, forest, 90, 103, 106, 175. *See also* Lumbering; Shipbuilding; Farming

Cliff Island, 32, *55*

Cobble habitat, 190, 199–200

Cobblestone, *114*, 123

Cobscook Bay, 81–83, *82*, 250; aquaculture industry, 287

Cocowesco, Chief, 59

Cod, 19, 39, 51, 67, 161, 213; biology, 19, 229–32, 235, 248, 262; impact on lobsters, 203, 267; restocking project, 287–88; schools of, 211–12, 230, 235, 253–54; spawning grounds, 59, 239–40, 256; spawning stocks, 109, 266; stock collapse, 191, 234–36, 263; transboundary stocks, 259

Cod, processing of, 81, 223, 228–30, 232, 235

Cod ends, 239

Cod fishing, 59, 160, 213, 229, 231, 232, 237; closures, 203, 239, 259–60, 265–66; dragging, 203; gillnet, 260–61, 267–69; landings, 236; quotas, 239, 262

Coffin, Clayton, 283–84

Coffins, tuna, 207

Coggins Head, 83–84

Cogswell, Francis, 101

College of the Atlantic, 135–36, 147, 295

Collins, Joseph, 221

Columbine, 102

Communities, 17–23, 273; culture of, 291; disappearance of, 27–28; economics of, 293–94; and fishing, 26–28, 262; and politics, 42–43; and tourism, 274–77; and waterfronts, 278–81

Communities, year–round. *See* Chebeague; Cliff; Frenchboro (Long Island); Great Cranberry; Great Diamond; Isle au Haut; Islesboro; Islesford; Long (Casco Bay); Matinicus; Monhegan; North Haven; Peaks; Swan's; Vinalhaven

Compensation mechanism, 261

Conservation Council of New Brunswick, 259

Conservation Law Foundation, 32

Convention on International Trafficking of Endangered Species, 270–71

Convergent evolution, 152

Cook, Sherwood, 194–95

Coon, David, 259

Copepods, 211, 214, 251–52, 254

Coral reefs, 243

Corbett family, 21

Cordwood trade, 20, 55, 101–02

Cormorants, 136, 141, 148; double–crested, *137*–39, *138*; Indian use of, 132; nesting, 97

Corra Cressey, 63–64

Cousens, David, 204

Cousins Island, 54, *55*

Cow islands, 110

Cows Yard, 76

Coyote, 170, 172–73, 182

Crab, 67, 179, 186, 188, 251, 287

Cranberry Island (Muscongus Bay), 20

Cranberry Isles, 49, 69, *70*; cod fishery, 231; shipyard, 99. *See also* Great Cranberry; Little Cranberry

Crie, Robert "King," 180

Criehaven, *37*, *65*, *108*; community, 20, 30, 288; fishermen, 35, 147; rabbits, 180. *See also* Ragged Island

Cross Island, 20, *80*–81, 96, 113, 175, 283–84; sea cave, 122–*23*

Cross River, 93

Crotch Island, 29, 69, 99, 124–*25*, 175

Crotch Island Company, 124

Crowell, Ken, 181

Crows, 76, 113, 145

Crumple Island, *76*

Crustaceans, 211–12

Culture, island, 35, 195, 274, 291–94

Cumberland, 31

Cundy's Harbor, 191

Cunner, 139

Curlew, 148

Cushing Island (Casco Bay), 20, 32, 33, *44*, *55*, 63

Damarill, Humphry, 59

Damariscotta River, *58*, 284, 285

Damariscove Island, 20, 57, *58*, 293; cod fishery, 19, 59, 229, 231; and Indian Wars, 63; settlement, 59

Dams, 101

Darling Center, 285

Davis, Ford, *224*

Day, Clarence, 110

Day, Jason, 127, 219–20, 221–22

Day, Walter, *268*

DDT, 144, 145

Deer, 92, 171, 172, 176–78, 182; fallow, 159, 175; white–tailed, 19; in winter, 50

Deer Island (Canada), *82*

Deer Isle, 49, *68*, 110, 111, 117, 181; and America's Cup crew, 18; clam flats, 189; cod fishery, 231, 232; community, 67; lobster cannery, 191–92; quarry, 68; sawmill, 101; shipyard, 100

Dennys Bay, *82*

Dennys River, 84

Diamond Islands, 178. *See also* Great Diamond; Little Diamond; Hog islands

Diatoms, 211, 247, 251, 252

Dikes, 255

Dinesen, Isak, 131

Dinoflagellates, 251, 258

District of Maine, 59, 63, 100, 231

Dix Island, 20, 123, 124

DNA, 171

Dogfish, 67, 261, 294

Dolan, Mary Beth, 37

Dolls eyes, white and red, 89

Dolphins, 160, 161, 163

Double Head Shot Islands, 78

Double Shot Islands (Englishman Bay), *78*

Double Shot Islands (Machias Bay), *80*

Down east, 20, 71–72, 81, 177; clam flats, 190; fishermen, 205; fogs 87; granites, 122; heritage, 209; islands, 93, 96

Downeast Lobstermen's Association, 204–05

Draggers, 37, 99, 203–04, 231, 238

Drake, Sir Francis, 60

Drisk Island, *76*

Drury, Bill, 147

Duck, 19, 141; brant, 142; bufflehead, 143–44; goldeneye, 143–44; harlequin, 143, Labrador, 156; old squaw, 143–44; scaup, 143; scoter, 143; teal, 142; winter, 134, 142–43, 151

Duck, eider, 133–34, 139; common, 141–42; down, 134; eggs, 148; nests, 56

Duck Harbor, (Isle au Haut) 67, 133

Ducks, the (isles), 69. *See also* Great Duck, Little Duck

Ducktrap River, 133

Dugongs, 160

Duke of Devonshire, 60

Dulse, 67, 216

Dun fish, 230

Dunlin, 148

Dunn and Elliot Shipyard, 98

Dunn Island, *78*

Dutcher, William, 151

Dyer, Bert, 197, 198, 231–32, 234, 240

Dyer, Phil, 99–100

Dyer Island, 20, *73*

Dyer Neck, 74

Eagle Island (Penobscot Bay), 18, 20, *65*, 133; Light, 24; schoolhouse, *38*

Eagle Island (Saco Bay), *53*

Earll, Edward, 189, 192, 223, 230

East Boston Quarry (Vinalhaven), 124

Eastern Bay, 75–*76*

Eastern Egg Rock, *62*, 154–55

Eastern Island, *74*

Eastern Maine Coastal Current, 87, 244, 250, 258

Eastern River, 56–57

Eastport, 81–*82*, 84–85, 134, 250; herring catcher, *85*

East Quoddy Head (Canada), *82*

Eaton, Cyrus, 171, 175

Eaton family, 20

Eaton Island, *287*

Eckstorm, Fanny Hardy, 61

Ecology, 78, 181–82, 186; coastal, 18–19; differences among islands, 113; features, 250; fish, 211; human, 264; niche, 89, 152, 159, 182; range, 112; zones, 188

Ecosystem, 49–50, 112–13, 171; forest, 90, 91; gulf, 243; interconnectedness, 150, 258–59; management, 209, 258–60; marine, 264, 267, 294; productivity, 247; recovery, 183; world, 243

Ecotone, 241

Ecotourism, 170

Edgartown (Martha's Vineyard), 275

Eel, 144

Eelpout, 67, 281

Eggemoggin Reach, *68*

Egging, 58, 132–34, 149, 153

Egg Rock (Frenchman Bay), *71*

Egg Rock (Narraguagus Bay), *73*

Egg Rock (Western Bay), *76*

Egret, 139, 141; snowy, 141

Eliot, Charles, 133

Embargo Act, 81, 110

Embayments, 243

Employment, 29, 34, 99, 123–25, 151, 218–19

Endangered Species Act, 84, 165

England, 127, 171; and Indian Wars, 63; and otter trawl, 234; settlements of, 70. *See also* French and Indian Wars

Englishman Bay, 77–81, *78*

Equinoxes, 46, 235

Eskimo curlew, 156

Estuaries, Gulf of Maine, 243–44, 249, 256, 258, 285, 287

Etchemin Indians, 18–19, 59

Exclusive economic zone, 236, 291

Extinction, 32, 152–53, 178, 181–83

Factory ships, 236

Fairburn, William, 99–100

Falcon, 144, 146; peregrin, *145*, 146–48

Falls Island, 82–84

Falmouth, *55*, 61, 63

Farming, 66, 109–13; crop, 105–107; and eagles, 144–45; livestock, 105

Federal government, 31–32, 41, 76, 151, 190, 205, 238

Fellows Island, *78*

Fifield's General Store (Vinalhaven), *27*

Fifty–Fathom Ridge, 253, 266

Filter feeders, 163, 186, 257

First Chain Link Island, *158*

Fish: bait, 138; dried, 51, ecology, 211, 238; fecundity, 262; finder, 18, 238; flake yards, *83*, 92, 187, 229–230; hooks, 231–32, 261; mortality, 240, 261; processors, 232–36; schooling behavior of, 188, 211, 212; weirs, 19, 75

Fisheries, gulf, 229–31, 253–54, 260; new, 280–81; and over-fishing, 239; transboundary stocks, 259

Fisheries Conservation and Management Act, 236. *See also* under Magnuson

Fisheries conservation ethic, 36, 39, 266

Fisheries Industries of the United States, 218

"Fishes in the Gulf of Maine," 230

Fisheries management, 109, 185–86, 235–36, 240, 258–67; by communities, 188–90, 264–65

Fisherman Island (Boothbay), 20, 57, 96

Fisherman Island (Western Bay), *76*

Fishermen, 36, 63, 92, 194–97, 240–41; bank, 137; and islands, 51, 66, 240–41; post–Civil War, 27, 191; quasi–legal rights of, 185–90; territories of, 193–95, 209; wives of, 49

Fishhouse, 23–25, 28, 46, 137, *213*, 263; privileges, 36–37

Fishing business practices, 232

Fishing fleets, 27, 31–32, 49–50, 232, 236; domestic, and the Embargo Act, 81; foreign, 238–39; harpoon, 225; lobster, 35, 234; schooner, 59; and storms, 49–50. *See also* New England; North Atlantic

Fishing village, 209, 231, 288. *See also* Communities

Fjord, 116

Flanders Bay, *71*

Flat Island, *73*, *76*, 216

Flint Island, 72, *73*, 74, 121–32

Flounder, 19, 67, 213; elimination of, 234, 261; fishing closure, 259

Fog, 71; ecology of, 87–88

Fog Island (Merchant Row), 110

Food chain, 41, 186–88, 247, 252–53; and bears, 174; and energy conversion, 163; and fish, 211–212, 269

Fore River, 55

Fort McKinley (Great Diamond), 31

Foster Island, 20, *73*, 81

Fox, 26, 50, 182; gray, 174; red, 174, 179–80; silver, 174

Fox Islands, 26, 50, 99, 173, 231. *See also* North Haven; Vinalhaven

Fox Island Thorofare, 28, 67; moose ashore at, *176*

France, 63; settlements of, 69–70. *See also* French and Indian Wars

Franklin Island, 21

French and Indian Wars, 63, 65, 69. *See also* Indian Wars

Frenchboro (Long Island), 69, *70*; aquaculture, 34; cod fishery, 231; community, 22–23, 38–40, 67; seals, 169; students from, *274*

Frenchman Bay, *71*, 101

French sardines, 222

Friendship, lobstermen, 39, 123, 176; sloops, 21, 191

Friendship Long Island, 20

Friends of Casco Bay, 32

Frigate bird, 136–37

Fucus, 188

Fundy Channel, 84, 248

Fundy current, 72, 83, 247, 248. *See also* Gulf of Maine

Funk Island (Canada), 133, 152–53

Galamanders, 126

Gangions, 232

Gannets, 133, 136, 152

Gardner, Jack, 276–77

Gay Island, 20

Geese, 19, 97, 134, 141

Geomorphology, 117, 118; Gulf of Maine, 244, 246–47, 250, 253–54

Georges Bank, 23, 246–47; cod fishery, 229; currents, 245, 248; fisheries management, 203, 260, 262; and foreign fleets, 236; geomorphology, 253, 254; red tide, 258

Georges Islands (Muscongus Bay) *19*, 108

Georges Shoal, 253

Georgetown Island, *58*, 61, 63, 93

Ghost fishing, 201, 205, 267

Gilbert, Raleigh, 93–94

Gilkey Harbor, 249

Gilley, John, family of, 21, 134

Gillnet, 167, 253

Gillnetters, 166, 236–*37*, 254; impact on cod, 235

Gjerst, Frank, 283

Glacial meltwater, 115–16, 256

Glacial till, 121

Glaciation, 116, 200, 254

Glaciers, 69, 79, 115–16, 190

Gloucester (MA), 163, 204, 215, 280, 287

Gloucester dory, 191

Godwit, 148

Goode, George Brown, 218, 220–21, 230, 239

Goodridge, Harry, 168–69

Goose Island (Cobscook Bay), *82*

Goose Islands (Maquoit Bay), *55*

Gorges, Sir Ferdinando, 52, 109

Gosnold, Bartholomew, 51

Gosport (Hog Island), 52

Gossip, 23–24

Gott Islands (Blue Hill Bay), 20, 69, *70*, 74

Gould, Stephen Jay, 172

GOVERNOR CURTIS, 46

Grackle, 151

Grand Banks, 189

Grand Manan Island (Canada), 72, 259; currents at, 87, 245, 247–48; islands off, 134; spawning grounds, 222, 230; and whales, 163, 166

Granite, 67–69, 113, 122–23, 124; Maine, used for public buildings, 123, 124–25, 126; movement, 121; pluton, 64, 69, 76, 124; quarries, 23, 66, 67, 68, 123–27, 180; shipping, 102, 126; tailings, 178–79

Gravel habitat, 190; ridges, 254

Graveyard of the Atlantic, 50

Great Bay, 243

Great Chebeague Island, *55*. *See also* Chebeague Island

Great Cranberry Island, 178. *See also* Cranberry Isles

Great Diamond Island, 30–32, 33, 56, 105; Association, 31–32

Great Duck Island, 21, 69, *70*, 112, 151, 169

Great Gott Island, 69, *70*. *See also* Gott islands

Great South Beach (Roque Island), 79–80, 120

Great Spoon Island, 119, 149–51

Great Spruce Island (Englishman Bay), *78*

Great Wass Island, 20, 75, *76*, 122

Green islands, 96–97

Greenland sandwort, 89

Green's Island (Vinalhaven), 149

Gristmill, 26, 55

Groundfish, 213, 229, 232, 233, 253; elimination of, 234, 239; hatchery, 35; stock declines, 236

Groundfishing, 84–85, 203, 236–37; boats, 231, 238; by–catch, 211; closures, 235, 239, 259–60, 266; landings, 233; nets, 236, 239; New England, 232, 234; quotas, 239

Grouse, 50, 151, 179

Guillemot, 133, 134, 139, 152; red–footed, 89, 122

Gular sac, 136

Gulf of Maine, 243; biomass, 247, 260; charts, 72, 73; currents, 244–49, 252, 253; light penetration, 246, 247, 251–53; productivity, 186, 244, 247–250, 265; river systems, 243, 245, 247; temperatures, 248, 252–53; tidal fronts, 248, 250, 253 (*see also* Tides)

Gulf of Maine Council on the Marine Environment, 259

Gulf Stream, 28, 45, 253

Gull, 134, 139, 141–*49*, 151–52, 163; black–backed gulls, 142, 149–51, 155, 157, 278; great black–backed, 135, 148–51; herring, 134, 141–42, 148–53, *150*, 155, 278; nesting, 56, 97

Gundalow Cove, 257

Gunnel, 139

Gunning rocks, 143

Guptill, Billy, 127, 113

Gyres, 204, 244–45, 248–250

Haddock, 67, 204, 212, 213; elimination of, 234, 261; fishery, 203, 231, 236, 237, 254; fishing closure, 259–60, 266; restocking project, 287–88; spawning grounds, 266

Haddock Nubble, 248

Hadlock, Samuel, 81

Hague Line, 259

Hake, silver, 67, 212, 232, 234, 240, 269

Hakluyt, Richard, 174

Halibut, 254, 261

Halifax Island, *78*
Hall, Ebenezer, 107
Hall Quarry, 124
Hamilton Inlet islands (Canada), 153
Hancock County, 72
Handlining, 84, 231–32, 268–69, 270
Harbor Branch Oceanographic Institution, 206
Harbor gangs, 185, 194, 201–02
Harbor Island, *62*
Harbors, 46
Hardwood Island, *70*, 94
Hardwood trees and forests, 19, 93–96, 97, 101, 141
Hare, 50, 159, 174, 180. *See also* rabbit
Harlow, Captain Edward, 61
Harpoon, 18, 162, 169, 269–70
Harris, George, 84–85
Harris Point, 84
Harvey, Janice, 259
Hawks, 144; broad–winged, 146; coopers, 146; red–tailed, 146; sharp–skinned, 146
Hawthorne, Nathaniel, 52
Haymarket Square (Boston), 65, 107
Head Harbor (Isle au Haut), *68*
Head Harbor Island, 20, *76*, 96, 122, 192
Head Harbor Passage (Canada), *82*
Heath islands, 96–97, 147, 277
Hebrides, 133, 293
Hedgehogs, 159
Hemlock tree, 92, 93, 96, 100
Heron, 134, 141; great blue, 97, 139, *140*, 414, 145; green, 151
Heron Islands, 139
Heronry, 60, 145
Herring, 67, 152, 155; as bait, 215, 223; biology, 211–14, 252; grounds, 213–14, 216–18, 248; schools, 211–15, 222, 251, 259, 269; spawning, 214, 216, 219, 222; stocks, 213, 219, 259, 263
Herring fishery: catchers, *85*, 213, 217–22; Canadian management of, 219; fishing territory, 194; landings, 216, 218, 221; nets, 18, 213–*14*, *246*; purse seines, 84, 214–18, 220; weirs, 84–85, 194, *213*, 215, 263
Herring processing: smoked, 85, 215–16, *217*, 218–29, 259. *See also* Sardine canneries
Hickory tree, 94, 96
High Island, 123, 124
Highline, 61, 217–18, 223–24, 270
History of Deer Isle, 110
Hockamock Head (Swan's Island), 35
Hog Island: Bremen, 175; Flanders Bay, *71*; Holmes Bay, *80*; Isles of Shoals, 52; Muscongus Bay, *62*
Hog islands, 105–06
Holland, Samuel, 72
Holmes Bay, *80*
Horan Head, 83–84
Hosmer, George, 101, 110, 133
House Island, 92
Howard, Clarence, 18
Hummingbirds, 159
Hungry Island, 20
Hunt, Thomas, 61
Huntsman Marine Laboratory, 294–95
Hupper Island, 20, 99

Hurricane Island, 20, *48*, 113; and clams, 189–90; Granite Company, 127, 146; quarry, 123–24, 126–29
Hurricanes, 49–50, 113
Hurricane Sound, 127, 146, 246
Huxley, Thomas, 211

Ibis, glossy, 141
Ice bridges, 50, 171, 174, 177, 180
Ice industry, 57
Iceland, 152, 160
Incze, Lew, 199
Independent Seiners Association, 220
Indian Island (Canada), *82*
Indian names, geographic, 54, 56, 61, 81
Indian River, *76*
Indians, 51, 92, 94, 174, 175; canoes, 54, 57; law, 61; genocide of, 59, 61, 63; hunting and fishing, 54–59, 67, 106–107, 132–33, 159–161; legends, 66; settlements, 18–19, 56–59, 113; shell middens, 18–19, 152, 175; trade with settlers, 54, 109, 178; warfare, 61, 63 (*see also* French and Indian Wars)
Indian Wars, 63, 106
Industrial wastes, 256, 258
Ingall's Island (Canada), 262
Institute for Island Studies (Canada), 289
Interconnectedness, principle of, 258–59
International Commission for the Conservation of Atlantic Tunas (ICCAT), 269, 270–71
Intertidal environments, 175, 187–90, *188*, 216
Introduced species, 179–83
Ipswitch Bay, 230
Irish moss, 188
Ironbound Island, 20, 69, *71*
Island Aquaculture Company, Inc., 35, 281–83, 287–88
Island Institute, 29–30, 248, 266; and fisheries, 239, 264, 266, 287–88; and Flat Island, 216; and Frenchboro, 38–40; and Great Diamond Island, 30–32; gyre study, 249; and Long Island, 32–33; and Mt. Desert, 279–80; red tide study, 257–58; satellite project, 248, 265; and Swan's Island, 33–35, 281–83
Islands: boundaries, 72, 185–86, 187, 289–91; coastline, 79–80, 186; definition of, 185; gulf, 18–19, 243, 246, 248–49, 277, 280; names, 78–79, 118; number of, 51, 67, 115; and politics, 42–43; and tidal effects, 247–50, 255; uninhabited, 277. *See also* Communities
Isle au Haut, 64, *68*, 72, 117; beach, 120; community, 67; deer, 178; ducks, 143; harbor, 133; lobster cannery, 191–92; post office, *66*; sheep, 112; shipyards, 99; whales off, 166
Isle de Bacchus, 54
Isle des Perroques, 78
Islesboro, 49, *65*; cod fishery, 253; currents around, 249; fishing, 19; forest, 96; land lots, 106; lime stone, 102; 106; pack ice, 50; settlers, 65; shipbuilding, 97–98, 99; tanneries, 93
Isles des Ranges, 96
Islesford, 200, 201, 215, *274*. *See also* Little Cranberry
Isles of Shoals, 20, 51–52, 92; fisheries, 19, 229, 230, 231; whales around, 161
Japan: fisheries management, 264–65; fish import markets, 207, 269–71; whaling, 160
Jefferson, Thomas, 81
Jeffreys Ledge, 162, 247, 253

Jericho Bay, 67–68
Jewell Island, *55*, 63
Jewett, Sarah Orne, 17, 293
Johns Bay, 57, *58*
Johns Island, 69, 169
Jones, William, 101
Jonesport, *76*, 87, 124
Jordan Basin, 248
Jordan Island, 20, *71*
Jordans Delight Island, *73*, 89–90, 113
Josselyn, John: and birds, 139, 144; and herring, 215; and Indians, 54, 132; and mammals, 161, 171, 174–75, 178
Joyce, Herman, 224
Junk of Pork Island (Casco Bay), *55*
Junk o' pork islands, 65

Kellar, Maureen, 257–58
Kelp, 106, 177, 185, 188–89, 208–09; beds, 216; forests, 189, 193, 209, 254
Kennebec River, 56–*57*, *58*, 93, 115–16, 145; currents, 245, 248; drainage, 256, 285; Indians, 59; pollution, 258
Kent, Rockwell, 35
Kent Island, 262
Kettle Bottom, 231
Killicks, 120
Killick Stone Island, 120
Kimball Island, *68*, 112
King, Angus, 42, 84, 167, 204
Kissinger, Henry, 236
Kittiwakes, 152
Kling, Linda, 288
Knight, Brian, 263
Knotted wrack, 188
Knox Woolen Mill, 110
Kraus, Scott, 166
Krause, Lexi, 269–70, *271*
Kress, Steve, 154–55
Krill, 251

Labrador, 81, 134, 148, 152, 165; Current, 45, 244
Laighton family, 52
Lairey Narrows, 46
Lakemaw Island, *78*
Lamp Island, 245
Landers, John, 127
Landers, Tom, 127
Lane, Timothy, 232
Lane Island, 18, 47, 107
Langton, Rich, 288
Large Green Island, 96, 107, 132, 195
Lawrence, D. H., 223
Leach's storm–petrel, 113, 135–36, 179–80
Leadbetter Island, 20; and family, 124
Leather tanning, 93
Leek, wild, 140
Leonard, Ray, 29–30
Lehtinen, Sonny, *233*
Levett, Christopher, 53, 54–55, 58, 92–94, 98, 101
Libby Island, 21, 79, 81, 96
Libby Islands, *80*
Lichens, 87–88, 89, 90, *91*
Lifesaving station, 81

Lighthouse: keepers 20–21, 151, 153–154, 157; stations, 20, 60, 129
Lime: industry, 101–02, 119; limestone, *103*
Lime Island, *65*, 102, *103*
Lines Island, 56
Little Chebeague Island, 20
Little Cranberry Island, 81. *See also* Cranberry Isles
Little Deer Isle, 67, *68*
Little Diamond Island, 32, 105
Little Duck Island, 69, 151, 169
Little Green Island, 194–95
Littlejohn Island, 54
Little Kennebec Bay, *78*
Little Machias Bay, *80*
Little Manan Island, 72
Little River Island (Cutler), 15, 21
Little Spruce Island (Englishman Bay), 78
Lobster, American, 33, 37–39, 47, 67, 185–87; biology, 39, 198–201, 248, 251, 259; broodstock, 204–07, 248; canneries, 191–93; impact of cod on, 203, 209, 230, 267; impact of seals on, 203; inshore movement, 186; range, 205; transboundary stocks, 259
Lobster conservation laws, 192–94, 197, 201–203, 267; 289; and management zones, 39, 202, 204, 265
Lobster fishing, 35–38, 167, 209, 232, 294; bait, 223; boats, 77–78, 193, *199*, *202*, 234; by–catch, 204; grounds, 61, 195–98; harbor gangs, 194; harvests, 191, 192–94; impact on stocks, 39, 193, 200–01, 203–04, 206; landings, 197–98, 200–05, 203–05; shorts, 192, 201, 203; territories, 185–86, 193–95; traps, 193, *295*; wars, 197, 201, 288–89
Lobstermen, 61, 166–67, 185, 205
Lobstermen's National Protective Association, 193
Long Cove (Searsport), 42
Longfellow, Henry Wadsworth, 105, 106
Long Island (Blue Hill Bay), 69
Long Island (Casco Bay), 32–33, *55*, 56
Long Island (Cobscook Bay), *82*
Long Island (Frenchboro), *70*
Long Island (Muscongus Bay), 20, *62*
Longlining, 261
Look, Oscar, 74–75
Loran C, 237–38
Louds Island (Muscongus Bay), 20, 59, *62*
Lowell, James Russell, 52
Lower Goose Island, 55
Lubec, *82*, 84–85
Lumbering, 101–05, 109, 144
Lunt, April, 39
Lunt, Danny, 207
Lunt, Vivian, *38*
Lunt and Lunt Lobster Company, 38–39
Lunt Harbor (Frenchboro), 22–23, 39
Lurvey, Abraham, 223
Lyme Disease, 178

MacArthur, Robert, 181–82
Machias, 81
Machias Bay, 79, *80*, 81, 123, 243
Machiasport, *80*
Machias River, 81
Machias Seal Island, 247

Mackerel, 67, 211–13, 223, 248; fishery, 27, 191, 223, 224; jigging, 65, 223, 224; landings, 225; pickled, 66, 224–25; schools, 223, 269; schooners, 27, 223–25; seiners, 59, 65, 223, *224*, 225; stock collapse, 27, 191
Mack Point (Sears Island), 41–42
Mackworth Island, 54, 55, 59
MacMahan Island, 20
Magnuson, Birger, 198
Magnuson Fisheries Management and Conservation Act, 236, 260
Magnuson–Stevens Fisheries Management and Conservation Act, 263–264
Maine Bureau of Public Lands, 280
Maine Central Railroad, 235
Maine coast, length, 50
Maine Coastal Current, 87
Maine Department of Environmental Protection, 31, 50–51
Maine Department of Inland Fish and Wildlife, 175
Maine Department of Marine Resources, 38, 170, 201, 208, 260, 266, 288
Maine Gilnetters' Association, 239
Maine Historic Preservation Commission, 18
Maine Legislature: bird protection, 151; cod fishing regulations, 234–35; groundfish study committee, 287; island secession, 32–33; lobster conservation, 192–93, 197, 201–02, 288–89, 291; urchin fishing regulation, 208
Maine Lobstermen's Association, 204
Maingot, Anthony, 274
Malcolm Ledge, 267
Maliseet Indians, 59. *See also* Indians
Maloney, Earnest, 16, 21–22
Manatees, 160
Maquoit Bay, *55*
Marine Colloids, 188
Marine Mammal Protection Act, 76, 167, 170
Marine mammals, 67, 159–61, 163, 253, 255; and College of the Atlantic, 295; habitat of, 244. *See also* Marine Mammal Protection Act
Marine reserves, 267
Mark Island (Chandler Bay), *76*, *95*
Mark Island (Penobscot Bay), *65*, *140*–41
Marshall Island, 20, *68*, *70*, 174
Martha's Vineyard, 43, 275
Martin, Cabot, 239, 294
Martin, Gill, 21
Mason, George, 52
Massachusetts: Court of, 59, 107; fishing vessels, 37, 191; fishing practices, 203–04, 235
Massachusetts Bay, 230, 243
Massachusetts Bay Colony, 59, 69
Massachusetts Institute of Technology, 124
Matinicus Island, 35, *65*; cod spawning grounds, 229; fishing station, 19, 59; Harbor, *83*; herring spawning grounds, 222; and Indian Wars, 63; lightkeepers, 157; murder of farmer, 107; students from, *274*; whales off, 166
Matinicus Rock, *65*, 121; lightkeepers, 20–21, 151, 157; fishing grounds, 224; puffins and auks, 66, 153–54; seals, 169
Maximum sustainable yield, 261
McGee Island, 20
McGlathery Island, 88–89
McLane, Charles, 15, 20, 93

Medomack River, 61, *62*
Meduncook River, *62*
Melville, Herman, 293
Menhaden, 59, 106, 211. *See also* Pogies
Merchant, Espes W., 230
Merchant Island, 67
Merchant marine, 19–20, 81, 100,
Merchant Row, 67, *68*, 76, 123, 181
Merchant Sail, 99
Merlin falcon, 146
Merrimac River, 256
Merrymeeting Bay, 56–*57*, 93, 120
Metinic Island, 20, *65*, 113, *114*, 152; lobster fishing, 194–95
Micmac Indians, 59. *See also* Indians
Milliner industry, 139, 151–52, 154
Minas Basin, 250
Minas Bay, 243
Minerva Hub, 248
Mink, 178–79; sea, 178, 182
Mink Island, *80*
Mistake Island, 20, *76*
Mitchell, George, 40
Monhegan Island, 19, 50, *62*, 121, 291; cod fishery, 229, 231–32; current at, 245; deer, 178; farm, 105; fishing station, 19, 59; Harbor, *220*; hardwoods, 94; and Indian Wars, 63; lobster fishing, 35–38, 288–89; mackerel fishing grounds, 224; pack ice, 50; sheep, 112; students from, *274*; tour boat, 60
Monkfish, 261, 294; tails, 281
Monroe Island, 249
Montsweag Bay, 93
Moore, Ruth, 46
Moore Harbor (Isle au Haut), 120
Moosabec Reach, *76*, 77
Moose, 19, 175–76, 177, 182
Moosehead Lake, 56, 109
Moosehorn National Wildlife Refuge, 83
Morison, Samuel Eliot, 76, 79, 101
Morse Island, 20
Moshier Island, 55
Mosquito Island, *62*, 108
Moss, 88, 90; bed, *91*
Mountain lion, 182
Mount Desert Island, 63, *70*, *71*–72, 116–17, 121; and Chief Asticou, 59; cod fishery, 231; eagles, 145; forest, 101; granite quarry, 123–24; islands surrounding, 69; marina proposal, 279–80; tides, 250
Mount Desert Rock, 162–63, 166, 176, 224
Mouse, 50; deer and field; 181. *See also* Voles
Murres, 133, 134, 148, 152
Muscle Ridge, 64, *65*, 123, 171, 192–93; Channel, 122
Muscongus Bay, *62*, 93, 106, 108; islands, 61–64, 117; lobster grounds, 195; pack ice, 50; shipyard, 99
Mussel, blue (aquacultured), 185, 284, 285–86
Mussel, blue (wild), 106, 118, 179, 185
Musselers, 154, 155, 185, 205, *208*
Mustilids, 178
Myers, Ed, 284–86

Nantucket (MA), 43, 161, 275–77
Nantucket Island (Canada), 262

Nantucket Planning and Economic Development Commission, 276
Narragansett Indians, 229
Narraguagus Bay, 72–75, *73*, 145
Narraguagus River, *73*, 75
Nash Islands, *73*, *76*, 172
Naskeag Point, *68*, *70*
National Audubon Society, 151, 154, 270–71
National Environmental Satellite Distribution Information Service (NESDIS), 248, 265
National Marine Fisheries Service, 167, 170, 200–05, 266, 271, 283, 287
National Oceanographic and Atmospheric Administration (NOAA), 248, 265
National Research Council, 271
Nature Conservancy, The, 90, 157, 287
New Bedford (MA), 161, 204, 280
New England, 92, 133, 171; charts, 72; clams, 189; cod fishing, 229–32; fishermen, 232, 239, 260–63; fleets, 234, 236, 239; groundfishing, 238; groundfish stock declines, 239; islands, 275–77; mussel sales in, 286; riparian rights, 133; whaling towns, 161
New England Aquarium, 166, 168
New England Fisheries Management Council, 204, 260, 264, 265
Newfoundland (Canada), 91, 152–53, 153, 239; cod stock collapse, 263, 294
Newfoundland Inshore Fishermen's Association, 239
New Hampshire, 203, 258
New York, Maine exports to: birds and feathers, 151; fish, 27, 235; granite, 124, 126
New Zealand, 267
Nitrates, 112–13
Noctiluca, 246
No Man's Land, 149, 151, 179–80
Nordmore grate, 211
North Atlantic: fisheries, 232; fleet, 31, 33, 165, 231; puffins, 78–79; tuna, 227, 269; whaling, 165, 260
Northeaster, 46, 49, 147
Northeast Harbor (Mt. Desert), 69, *70*, 280
Northeast Passage, 244
Northeast Peak, 248
Northern Harbor, 26
North Haven Island, 26–28, *65*, 99, *199*, 231; Catholic church, 127; current at, 250; eagles, 146; fisheries, 201, 223–25; Indian settlement, 18–19; lobster cannery, 192; settlers, 64; sheep, 112; shipyards, 28, 99–100; tanneries, 93. *See also* Fox Islands
North Maine Woods, 56, 172, 175
Northwest Harbor (Deer Isle), 67
Norton, Arthur, 146, 151
Norton family, 21
Norton Island, 72, *76*
Norway, 160, 162
Nova Scotia (Canada), 50, 133, 263
Nova Scotia Current, 45, 87. *See also* Scotian Current
Novie bows, 247
Nut trees, 54

Oaks, Elisha, 191
Oak trees, 71, 93–94, 96, 105

Oarweed, 106
Offshore Sheep Services, 172
O'Hara Corporation, 223
Oil refinery, 82, 84
Oil spills, 41, 82
Old Harbor (Vinalhaven), 174
Old Man Island, *80*, 137, 142
Old man's beard, 88
Old Man's Pasture, 231
Old Soaker, *71*
O'Leary, Wayne, 215, 232
Olgilvie, Elisabeth, 30
Opechee Island, 20, 94, 169
Orne, Raymond, 224
Orr's Island, 54, *55*
Osgood, Alfred, 217, 223
Osgood, David, 217
Osgood, Justin, 217
Osprey, American, 75, 134, 145–46
Otter, sea, 50, 159, 160, 178
Otter Cliff, *71*, 121
Otter Island (Muscongus Bay), *62*
Otter islands, 178, 182
Otter ponds, 178
Otter trawlers, 254. *See also* Trawling
Otter trawl nets, 233, 235–36, 239, 240
Outer Heron Island, 60–61
Outward Bound School (Hurricane Island), 102, 129
Ovens, the, 121
Overfishing, 261, 293. *See also* Fisheries management
Owls, 133, 147, 151; great horned, 247–48; snowy, 147–48
Oysters (aquacultured), 284, 287

Pangea, 254
Paper mills, 103–04. *See also* Pulp and paper mills
Paradise Cove, 101
Paralytic shellfish poisoning, 257
Parker, Captain, 101
Parker Island, 93
Parker Ridge, 254
Parsons, Josiah, house, 28
Partridge, 179
Passamaquoddy Bay, 212, 243; herring spawning grounds, 218; landings, 225; mackerel fishery, 223, 224; salmon farms, 287; tides, 81
Passamaquoddy Indians, 59, 71. *See also* Indians
Passenger pigeon, 89
Paulino, Paul, 220
PCBs, 144
Peaks Island, 32, 33, *55*, 56, 101, 144
Peat bogs, 71
Pelagic birds, 135. *See also* Seabirds
Pemaquid, 61, 63, 70, 101; Point, *58*
Penobscot Bay, *65*; bedrock, 122; cod fishery, 232; currents, 245, 248–50, 256; eagles, 66; estuary, 256, 257; fish spawning grounds, 217, 218, 229; groundfish landings, 233; islands and ledges, 254; lobster grounds, 195; lobster harvests, 192; NOAA/NESDIS research in, 265; outflow from river, 249; pack ice, 50, 174; red tide, 258; sharks, 169; Stave islands, 101; tidal bridge, *258*; Turtle Head Fault, 140; urchin fishery, 208

Penobscot Bay islands, 64–67; duck hunting on, 133–34; forested, 101–02; moose on, 175; sheep on, 112–13; shipyards on, 99

Penobscot Indians, 59, 66, 107. *See also* Indians

Penobscot River, 90, 115–16, 255, 285; coastal current, 245; drainage, 256; eagles, 145–46; estuary, 256–57; forests, 94; lobster trade, 191; outflow, 249; paper mill, 103–04; and trappers, 56

Periwinkle, 18, 67; zone, 188

Pesticides, 287

Petit Manan Bar, 93, 116

Petit Manan Island, 72, *73*, 93, 116

Petit Manan Point, 72, *73*, 117

Petit Plaisants, 69–70

Petrels, 134, 135–36, 147, 163. *See also* Leaches storm–petrel

Pettigrew, Neal, 248, 249, 250

Philbrook, Elisha, 107

Phosphorescence, 212, 214, 246

Photosynthesis, 186

Phytoplankton, 251, 252, 257, 286; bloom, 286. *See also* Red tide

Pigeon Hill, 72–74, *73*

Pigeon Hill Bay, 72

Pine: Broad Arrow, 93; forests, 71; pumpkin, 93, 125; scotch, 98; white, 93, 96, 100, 257

Pingree, Chellie, 274–75, 291

Piper, William, 28

Pipe staves, 95

Pirates, 75, 79. *See also* Privateers

Piscataqua River, 52, 92, 248, 256

Pittston Company, 81–82, 84

Placentia Island, 69–*70*, 94

Plankton, 211, 246, 258; blooms, 243. *See also* Copepod

Plantations, 54, 105–06, 215

Pleasant Bay, 72–74, *73*

Pleistocene glaciation, 254–55

Plovers, 148

Plummer Island, *76*

Plymouth (MA), 229

Pogies, 67, 211, 223

Point of Maine, *80*

Polecat, 159, 178

Pollock, 67, 212, 230; gillnetting for, 235, 236–37

Pollution, 31, 41, 243, 287; clamflat, 190; from toxins, 144–45. *See also* Industrial wastes; Oil spills; Sewage treatment

Pond Cave Island, *78*

Pond Island (Casco Passage), 94

Pond Island (Narraguagus Bay), *73*

Popham, John, 61, 94

Popham Colony, 59, 98, 109

Popplestones, 119–20

Porcupine Islands, *71*

Porcupines, the, 69

Porpoise, 160, 161, 163, 169; skins, 58

Port Clyde, 218–19, 248, 275

Portland, 62, 100; forts, 56; groundfish steamers, 234; islands, 30–33, 55; lobster cannery, 191; mackerel fishing off, 224; shipyards, 126; tide, 250

Portland cement, 127

Portland City Council, 31

Potato blight, 111

Pottle family, 21

Preble Island, *71*

Predators, marine, 251–52, 262

Presumpscott River, 55

Pring, Martin, 51, 174

Privateers, 65, 79, 81

Privilege, The (Vinalhaven), 28–29, 99, 101

Prouts Neck, *53*

Puffin, Atlantic, 66, 134, 152–55, 247; nesting, 78–79, 133

Pulp and paper mills, 90, 258

Pulpit Harbor (North Haven), 26–28, 146

Pulpit Rock, 238

Pulpwood, 101, 103–05; cutters, 71

Purse seine, 215

Putz, George, 23–24, 25, 29, 143, 184

Quahoggers, 205

Quammen, David, 182

Quinn, Beulah, 24

Quinn family, 20

Quota management, 262, 263, 269

Rabbit, 50, 179–180, 182

Raccoons, 56, 79, 179, *180*, 182

Race Point (MA), 245

Rackliffe, Cyrus, *130*

Rader, Don, 104

Ragged Arse Island, 81, 96

Ragged Island, *65*, 96, 112. *See also* Criehaven

Railroads, 234, 235

Rain forests, 243

Ralston, Peter, 29–30, 31, 259, 283

Ram Island, *76*

Rasberries, 107

Ravens, 76, 145, 277–78

Rays, 261

Real estate development, 56, 60, 69; Frenchboro, 38–39; Great Diamond, 30–32; Jordans Delight, 89–90; Martha's Vineyard and Nantucket, 275–77; Merchant Row, 67; North Haven, 27–28; and seabirds, 90; Sears Island, 40–42; Sheep, 97; Swan's, 33–34; Vinalhaven, 28–29

Red Bay (Canada), 165

Red fish, 261

Red Paint People, 18

Red tide, 257–58

Reindeer, 59, 175. *See also* Caribou

Resident species, 50, 175; reintroduction of, 182

Resort islands, 92, 56

Resource Protection Area, 56

Revolutionary War, 63, 64–65, 81

Rhoades, John, 235

Rich, Mo, 190

Rich, Walter, 239

Richmond Island, 20, 52–*53*–54, 55, 171; and Edward Trelawney, 49; cod fishery, 59, 229–30; farms, 105, 106; fishing station, 19; pumpkin pine, 93

Riches Head (Frenchboro), 22–23

Roaring Bull Ledges, 143

Robbins family, 20

Roberts, Corrie, *286*

Roberts Harbor (Vinalhaven), 23
Rockland, *65*, 102, 129, 218–19, 222–23, 235; Breakwater Light, 129
Rockport, 168; Harbor, 153
Rockweed, 106; zone, 188
Roque Island, 20, 77–*78*, *79*–80, 94, 113; beach, 120; dam, 101
Roosevelt, Franklin Delano, 83
Roseroot stonecrop, 89
Roseway Bank, 231
Rosier, James, 87; and birds, 139; and Indians, 61, 132; and mammals, 159–60, 175, 178; and trees, 91, 93–94
Rowe, William, 101
Royal Navy, 93
Royal River, 55
Rusticators, 27–28, 43

Sable Bank, 231
Saco Bay, 52–54, *53*, 132, 141
Saco River, *53*, 248
Saddleback Island, *68*
Safina, Carl, 270–71
Sagamores, 59, 132
Saint Croix River, 54
Saint George, 171, 192, 193; River, 61, *62*
Saint John River, 115, 256, 285
Saint Kilda Island (Hebrides), 132–33, 294
Saint Margaret's Bay (Canada) 186
Saint Mary's Bay, 243
Saint Mary's Point, 244
Salisbury, Jim, 225–28, 237–38
Salmon, Atlantic (aquacultured), 40, 67, 84–85, 287; culture of, 283; disease among 287; farming 34–35, 170, 281–84; impact on wild salmon, 75, 84–85, 137–39; landings, 280–81, 283
Salmon, Atlantic (wild), 56, 67, 75, 84–85, 137–38
Salt fish trade, 234; flake yard, *227*
Salt Island, *80*
Salt marsh, 83, 110, 115, 142, *187*, 258; grass, 109
Salt stress, 87, 90
Samoset, Chief, 59
Sand beaches, 79, 81, 115–16, 120–21
Sand Island (Western Bay), *76*
Sandpipers, 148
Sand plains, 190, 254
Sands Cove, 23
Sandwort, Greenland, 89
Sardine canneries, 84–85, 215–16, 218–19, 222, 280
Sasanoa River, *58*, 93
Sassafras trees, 174
Satellite images, 200, 248, 258, 265
Saturday Night Ledge, 231
Saw mills, 55, 68, 99, 101, 105
Sawyer Island, 93
Scabby Islands, *80*, 81
Scallop, sea, 67, 185; blue, 190–191; draggers, 185, 190, 207
Scarborough Marsh, *53*
Schoodic Point, *71*, 250
Schoodic Ridges, 231
School of Marine Science. *See* University of Maine
Schools, 273–76; students, *274*

Schooners, 59, 65, 66, 68, 99, 126
Schroeder, William, 230
Scotian current, 87, 129, 244
Sculpin, 19, 139
Seabird, 90, 154, 177, 256; colonies, 107, 150; and fishermen, 143–44; habitat, 243; hunting of, 132–34, 146, 151, 153; and impact on lobsters, 203; nesting islands, 56, 66, 96–97, 179; nesting sites, 113, 157; protection, 107, 157; restoration, 154. *See also* Egging
Sea cave, 81, 121–22, *123*
Sea cucumber, 218, 294
Seal, 159–60, 167–70; fur, 58; gray, 169–70; harbor, 76, *166*–70, *168*; impact on lobsters, 203; northern harp, *169*; recolonization, 183; whelping and haulout grounds, 68–69
Seal Harbor (Grand Manan), 259
Seal Harbor (Mt. Desert), 69, 280
Sea lice, 287
SEA LINK, JOHNSON, 206–07, *290*
Seal Island, 90, 96, 143, 153, 164–65; boulder beach, 254–55; cave, 122; cliffs, 133; and College of the Atlantic, 135–36; fire, 109; fisheries, 213–14, 231; seabirds, 151
Seal Trap (Isle au Haut), 66, 67
Seamounts, 254
Sea rockett, 118–19
Sears Island, 40–*42*, 248
Searsport, 71
Sea swallows, 151. *See also* Terns
Seavey Island, 20
Seaward Neck, *82*
Seaweeds, 83, 106, 110, 146, 216; productivity of, 186–87; types, 188; *See also* Kelp; Rockweed
Sea wrack, 188
Sebascodegan Island, 55, 56
Secession, 32–33
Sedgewick, 67
Seguin Island, *58*, 224; Light Station, 60
Seine net, 16, 18, *220*, 223, *224*–25
Seiner, 59, 224, 263
Settlers, 19–20, 65–65, 67–70, 77–78, 293; and trade with Indians, 54, 109, 178
Sewage treatment, 31–32, 258
Shad, 230
Shag Rock, 38
Shark, great white, 169
Shark Island, 62
Shaving mill, 65
Shearwaters, 163
Sheep, 109–113, 144, 172, 173
Sheep Island, *173*
Sheep Island (Vinalhaven), 97
Sheepscot Bay, 57, *58*
Sheepscot Indians, 59, 61
Sheepscot River, *58*, 93, 229, 238; cod spawning grounds, 59; fishing closure, 235
Shellfish farms, 287
Shell midden, 18
Shipbuilding, 97–100, 109, 232–33. *See also* Boats; Schooners
Ship Island (Blue Hill Bay), *70*
Shipping routes, 19–20, 63–64
Shipstern Island, *73*, 74, 118, 179

Shitpokes, 97, 139
Shoppee Island, *78*
Shorebirds, 19, 148; hunters of, 154
Shrimp, northern, 67, *210*–211, *257*; brine, 188; landings, 280
Sierra Club, 40
Sigsbee Ridge, 254
Simpson, Dorothy, 30
Sirenians, 160
Skate Bank, 231
Skates, 67, 261
Skunk, 178. *See also* Polecat
Sleighs, 174
Sloops, 126, 193, 234
Small Point, 79
Smalls Cove (Deer Isle), 67
Smelt, 67, 75, 152, 284
Smith, Irving, 103–04
Smith, Captain John, 51, 92, 294; and farming, 105; and
    fisheries, 159–61, 229; and hawks, 146; and Indians, 57,
    61; and trees, 93–94
Smith, Kim, 27
Smutty Nose Rock, 138
Snails, 188
Snow, Wilbert, 115
Snowe, Olympia, 40, 264
Somes Sound, 59, *70*; fjord, 116
Songbirds, 155
*Song of the Dodo: Island Biography in an Age of Extinctions,
    The*, 182
Sou'sou'west Banks, 231
South Addison, *73*, 74–75
Southeast Harbor (Stonington), 173
Southport Island, 59, 63, 92
South Southwest Ground, 248
South Sugarloaf Island, *242*, 243
Southwest Harbor, 69, *70*
Spanish moss, 88
Sparrows, 70, 155–56
Spawning area closures, 259–60
Spear, Willie, 229, 232, 235–36, 238–40, 253, 265
Spiess, Arthur, 18–29
Spinney, Herbert, 144
Spoon Islands (Merchant Row), *68*
Spot of Rocks, 231
Sprague, Myron (Sonny), *272*–74; aquaculture, 34–35,
    281–83, 287; lobster fishery, 202
Spruce, 94, 96, 103; budworm, 156; burls, *86*, 87; forests, 19,
    63, 70, 90–91, 93, *95*, 155; red, 88, 90, 95; white, 90, 95
Spruce forest birds, 70–71, 76
Sprucehead Island, *65*
Squid, 251, 269
Squirrel Island, *58*, 96
Stags, 175
Stanley, Mark (Markey's Law), 34
Stanley, Sherman, Jr., 269–*71*
Starboard Island, *80*
Starfish, 185
Star Island, 20, 52
Stave Island, 20, *71*
Stave islands, 101
Steamships, 64, 97, 162, 232, 234

Steel Harbor Island, 76
Stellwagen Bank, 166, 247, 253
Steneck, Bob, 198–200, 205–07
Stevenson, Robert Louis, 45
Stimpson Island and family, 20
Stockman Island, 56
Stonecutters, 125–27
Stone Island, *80*, 81, 120
Stonington, 123, 173, 181, 218–19, 232
Straight Bay, 83–84
Stratton, John, 54
Stratton Island, 20, 52–*53*, 54, 141, 142, 151
St. Regis Paper Company, 90, 103
Sturgeon, short-nosed, 19, 56–57
Summer people, 43, 52, 56, 201, 273, 276
Super chill, 35, 282
Sustainable Fisheries Act, 264. *See also* under Magnuson
Sutton Island, 20, *70*
Swallows, 155–56
Swampscott dory, 191
Swan, James, 68
Swan Island (Merrymeeting Bay), 56, *57*
Swans, 134, 141
Swan's Island, 33–35, 40, 49, *70*, 117; aquaculture, 281–83,
    287–88; bears, 174; ferry landing, *34*; fisheries, 191,
    201–02, 224–25, 231; forest cut, 93; granite, 68, 123;
    hardwood forest, 94; settlers, 67–68; shipyards, 99; yachts
    at, 278–279
Swanton, Joel, 104
Sweepstakes route, 181
Swordfish, 18

Tamarack, 71, 75, 100
Tanneries, 93
Taunton Bay, *71*
Teel Island, *62*; and family, 20
Terns, 134, 147–49, 151–52, 155, 163
Thaxter, Celia, 52, 92
Thomas, Andrew, 249
Thomaston, 98–99, 102, 109, 171
Three Dory Ridge, 254
Thrushes, 155–56
Thurlow, David, 99, 232
Tidal currents, 77, 83. *See also* Gulf of Maine; Tides
Tidepools, 187–88
Tides, gulf, 83, 186, 243, 248, 250, 252
Tillson, Davis, 127
Toothacher Cove (Swan's Island), 34, 282
Tourism, 35–36, 51, 59–60, 275–77
Townsend, Fred, *224*
Trafton Island, *73*
Tragedy of the commons, 208, 238
Transportation, 275
Trap Day (Monhegan), 35–37
Trawling, 85, 261; surveys, 205; tub, 231—32
Treat Island, *82*
Trelawney, Edward, 49, 171
Trelawney, Robert, 53–54, 105, 171, 229
Trelawney Papers, 53
Trout (aquacultured): Donaldson, 84; steelhead, 34, 84–85,
    282–83, *285*

Tuna, Atlantic bluefin, 176, 212, 225, 228–29, 269–71; biology, 226–27; fishing, 225–228; migration, 227, 269; packing plant, 251; off Seal Island, 248
Turner Farm (North Haven), 18–19
Turnstone, 148
Turpentine, 93
Turtle Head Fault, 140
Turtle Island, *71*, 90, 113
Two Bush Island, 188
Two–hundred–mile limit, 236–39, 260, 291

Ulbrich, Konrad, 105
Underwood, William, 191
Uni, 207
United Nations Food and Agriculture Organization, 203, 291, 294
University of Maine, 191, 198, 248–49; School of Marine Science, 257–58, 295
Urchin, green, 67, 185, ***206***, 281; biology, 208; fishery, 37–38, 185–86, 205, 207–09; landings, 280; roe, 207
U.S. Congress, 236, 263–64, 291. *See also* Federal government
U.S. Environmental Protection Agency, 40, 42
U.S. Fish and Wildlife Service, 75, 84, 135–37, 172, 283–84
U.S. Fisheries Commission, 189, 192, 220–21, 223, 231

Vandrieul, Marquis de, 64
Vegetation, 49, 50, 91
Venturi effect, 250
Verrazano, Giovanni da, 64, 91
Vinalhaven Fish Company, 233
Vinalhaven Island, 23–29, 33, 64, ***65***, 117, ***292***; bird count, 143–44; boat building, 98–100; and cod, 189, 229, 231; current at, 250; eagles, 144; eider hunting, 133–34; fishing fleet, 232–33; flake yard, ***227***; foxes, 177; granite, 49, 123–24, 127–28, 143; lobster fishery, 191, 193, 195, 234; mackerel fishing, 224; mudflats, ***192***; rodents, 179–80; sawmill, 101; settlement, 67; sheep, 97; whaling, 162. *See also* Fox Islands
Vineyards, 54
Volcanics, 69, 117, 123, 254
Voles, 181; meadow, 148

Wading birds, 256
Waldoboro, 171
Wallace, Dana, 189
Wallace boatyard, 99
Walnut trees, 94, 96
Warblers, 70, 147; wood, 155–156
Washington County, 72, 83–84, 182, 283
Wass family, 21
Wasson, George, 126
Waterfowl, 57, 66, 133, 141–42
Watershed, gulf, 256, 258–59; management, 266–67
Waymouth, George, 61, 87, 93, 95, 159, 175
Weld, William, 204
West Brown Cow, 250
West Chopps, *57*
Western Bay, 75–77, *76*
Western Maine Coastal Current, 245
Western Way Island, 174
West Quoddy Head, ***82***, 85
Wetlands, 186

Whale cod, 260
Whale, 159–63, 258; baleen, 163–64; blue, 162; bowhead, 165; finback, 161, 163; humpback, 161–62, ***164***–65, 183; hunting, 161–62, 165, 260; minke, 161, 163; oil, 58, 160–62, 165; orca, 163; pilot, 161, ***162***, 163; right, northern, 161, 162, 165–67, 183; off Seal Island, 248; sei, 161, 163; sperm, 161; watching, 162–63
Wharfinger, 284
Wharves, 187, 204–05
Wheaton Island, 83
Wheeler, Richard, 153
Whelkers, 105
Whelks, 281
White, Patten, 204
White Head (Monhegan), 121
Whitehead Cliffs (Cushing Island), ***44***
Whitehead Island (Penobscot Bay), 21, ***64***, ***65***, 108
White Island (Grand Manan), 262–63
White Islands (Boothbay), 94
Whiting Bay, ***82***, 83
Whittier, John Greenleaf, 52
Wildflowers, 89, 140–41
Wild rice, 56
Willet, 148
WILLIAM SILSBY, 34
Wilson, E. O., 181–82
Winslow, Sidney, 232, 234
Winter, Jonathan, 53, 93, 105, 229
Winter Harbor (Frenchman Bay), *71*
Wiscasset, 71, 98, 161–62
Witherspoon, Edward, 28, 170
Witherspoon family, 20
Wolf, 67, 105, 159, 170–71, 174, 182; eastern timber, 171
Wolf fish, 67
Wood, William, 161, 231
Wooden Ball Island, 147
Woods, William 51
Woods Hole Oceanographic Institute, 244, 294–95
Wool, 20, 110
Working waterfronts, 27–28, 43, 60, 222–23, 278–80
Wotton, Walter, 267–69
Wreck Island, 20
Wyeth, Andrew, 30
Wyeth, Betsy, 29–30, 105
Wyeth, Jamie, 35
WYOMING, 64

Yarmouth, ***55***, 132
Yellowhead Island, ***80***
Yew, 91–92; trailing, 140
York Island, 172–73

Zooplankton, 166, 252, 256, ***260***